Harald Niederreiter
Austrian Academy of Sciences

Random Number Generation and Quasi-Monte Carlo Methods

SOCIETY FOR INDUSTRIAL AND APPLIED MATHEMATICS

PHILADELPHIA, PENNSYLVANIA   1992

Printed by Capital City Press, Montpelier, Vermont

Library of Congress Cataloging-in-Publication Data

Niederreiter, Harald, 1944 –
    Random number generation and quasi-Monte Carlo methods / Harald Niederreiter.
      p. cm. — (CBMS-NSF regional conference series in applied mathematics : 63)
   ISBN 0-89871-295-5
   1. Monte Carlo method—Congresses. 2. Random number generations—
—Congresses.   I. Title.   II. Series.
QA298.N54   1992
519.2'82--dc20

                          92-12567

Contents

Preface

The NSF-CBMS Regional Research Conference on Random Number Generation and Quasi-Monte Carlo Methods was held at the University of Alaska at Fairbanks from August 13–17, 1990. The present lecture notes are an expanded written record of a series of ten talks presented by the author as the principal speaker at that conference. It was the aim of this series of lectures to familiarize a selected group of researchers with important recent developments in the related areas of quasi-Monte Carlo methods and uniform pseudorandom number generation. Accordingly, the exposition concentrates on recent work in these areas and stresses the interplay between uniform pseudorandom numbers and quasi-Monte Carlo methods. To make these lecture notes more accessible to nonspecialists, some background material was added.

Quasi-Monte Carlo methods can be succinctly described as deterministic versions of Monte Carlo methods. Determinism enters in two ways, namely, by working with deterministic points rather than random samples and by the availability of deterministic error bounds instead of the probabilistic Monte Carlo error bounds. It could be argued that most practical implementations of Monte Carlo methods are, in fact, quasi-Monte Carlo methods since the purportedly random samples that are used in a Monte Carlo calculation are often generated in the computer by a deterministic algorithm. This is one good reason for a serious study of quasi-Monte Carlo methods, and another reason is provided by the fact that a quasi-Monte Carlo method with judiciously chosen deterministic points usually leads to a faster rate of convergence than a corresponding Monte Carlo method. The connections between quasi-Monte Carlo methods and uniform pseudorandom numbers arise in the theoretical analysis of various methods for the generation of uniform pseudorandom numbers.

The last five years have seen tremendous progress in the subject areas of these lecture notes. The field of quasi-Monte Carlo methods was enriched by the systematic development of the theory of lattice rules and of the theory of nets and (t, s)-sequences, and new and better low-discrepancy point sets and sequences were constructed. Important advances in the area of uniform pseudorandom number generation include the introduction and the analysis of nonlinear congruential methods and the much deeper understanding we have gained of shift-register pseudorandom numbers. Furthermore, a systematic study of methods for pseudorandom vector generation was initiated.

The main aim of these lecture notes is to give an account of the recent developments mentioned above. The material in Chapter 4 on nets and (t, s)-sequences and in Chapter 5 on lattice rules is of central importance, since many of the new advances in quasi-Monte Carlo methods, and even in uniform pseudorandom number generation, revolve around the concepts and results in these two chapters. Indeed, nets and lattices appear in so many different contexts that they must be viewed as basic structures. Another fundamental notion is that of discrepancy, for which the essential facts are presented in Chapters 2 and 3. The concept of dispersion plays a role in Chapter 6 on quasi-Monte Carlo methods for optimization. In our discussion of uniform pseudorandom number generation in Chapters 7, 8, and 9, we emphasize those algorithms for which a detailed theoretical analysis has been performed.

For some results, especially for classical ones, the proof has been omitted, but a reference is always provided. The notes to each chapter contain supplementary information and historical comments. The bibliography is not meant to be comprehensive, but lists only those references that are cited in the text. Since a detailed bibliography up to 1978 is available in [225], the present bibliography concentrates on the more recent literature.

The conference would not have occurred without the initiative and the enthusiasm of Professor John P. Lambert of the University of Alaska at Fairbanks, who originated the idea, did all the necessary paper work, and organized the conference in a perfect manner. Many thanks, Pat, for the generous hospitality you extended to all participants and for making sure that everybody survived the white-water rafting on the Nenana River. I also want to express my gratitude to NSF-CBMS for the financial support of the conference. The actual production of these lecture notes relied heavily on the word-processing skills of Rainer Göttfert and Irene Hösch. Special words of appreciation go to Rainer Göttfert for his dedicated help in proofreading the manuscript and to Dipl.-Ing. Leonid Dimitrov and Dipl.-Ing. Reinhard Thaller for expert technical advice. The cooperation of the SIAM staff is also noted gratefully. Last, but by no means least, I wish to thank Gerlinde for putting up with a husband who was somewhere between the real world and mathematical elysium during the last 15 months.

Vienna, August 1991   H. NIEDERREITER

CHAPTER 1

Monte Carlo Methods and Quasi-Monte Carlo Methods

In this chapter we set the stage for the more detailed discussion of quasi-Monte Carlo methods in later chapters. An appreciation of the merits of quasi-Monte Carlo methods is impossible without an at least rudimentary understanding of Monte Carlo methods. For this reason, and also to motivate the introduction of quasi-Monte Carlo methods, we include a brief exposition of the statistical Monte Carlo method. A numerical problem that lends itself to a straightforward and illustrative comparison of classical, Monte Carlo, and quasi-Monte Carlo methods is that of numerical integration. We will use this problem to describe the basic ideas behind Monte Carlo and quasi-Monte Carlo methods in §§1.2 and 1.3, respectively.

1.1. Introduction.

We consider the problem of numerical integration in dimension s. For $s = 1$ there are classical integration rules such as the trapezoidal rule and Simpson's rule, to mention only two of the most well-known ones. For concreteness, let us look at the trapezoidal rule for the unit interval $[0, 1]$. In this case, the trapezoidal rule yields the approximation

$$(1.1) \qquad \int_0^1 f(u)\,du \approx \sum_{n=0}^{m} w_n f\left(\frac{n}{m}\right),$$

where m is a positive integer and the weights w_n are given by $w_0 = w_m = 1/(2m)$ and $w_n = 1/m$ for $1 \le n \le m - 1$. The error involved in this approximation is $O(m^{-2})$, provided that f has a continuous second derivative on $[0, 1]$.

In the multidimensional case $s \ge 2$ with an interval as integration domain, the classical numerical integration methods use Cartesian products of one-dimensional integration rules. In such multidimensional integration rules, the node set is a Cartesian product of one-dimensional node sets, and the weights are appropriate products of weights from the one-dimensional rules. These multidimensional integration rules are obtained by viewing the s-dimensional integral as an iteration of one-dimensional integrals and by applying a one-dimensional integration rule in each iteration. To illustrate this procedure, we state the s-fold

Cartesian product of the trapezoidal rule (1.1), which is

$$(1.2) \qquad \int_{\bar{I}^s} f(\mathbf{u})\, d\mathbf{u} \approx \sum_{n_1=0}^{m} \cdots \sum_{n_s=0}^{m} w_{n_1} \cdots w_{n_s} f\left(\frac{n_1}{m}, \ldots, \frac{n_s}{m}\right),$$

where $\bar{I}^s = [0,1]^s$ is the closed s-dimensional unit cube and the w_n are as in (1.1). The total number of nodes in (1.2) is $N = (m+1)^s$. From the error bound for (1.1), it follows that the error in (1.2) is $O(m^{-2})$, provided that $\partial^2 f/\partial u_i^2$ is continuous on $\bar{I}^s$ for $1 \leq i \leq s$. To see that the error in (1.2) need not, in general, be smaller than the one-dimensional error, it suffices to apply (1.2) with a function f on $\bar{I}^s$ that depends only on one variable, in which case (1.2) reduces to (1.1). In terms of the number N of nodes, the error in (1.2) is $O(N^{-2/s})$. With increasing dimension s, the usefulness of the error bound $O(N^{-2/s})$ declines drastically. Specifically, to guarantee a prescribed level of accuracy, say an error that is in absolute value $\leq 10^{-2}$, we must use roughly 10^s nodes; hence the required number of nodes increases exponentially with s. This phenomenon is often called the "curse of dimensionality."

The phenomenon described above manifests itself in an analogous way for the Cartesian product of any one-dimensional integration rule. For an s-fold Cartesian product, the order of magnitude of the error bound, in terms of the total number of nodes, is the sth root of the order of magnitude of the one-dimensional integration rule.

A decisive step in overcoming the curse of dimensionality was the development of the *Monte Carlo method* in the 1940s. The Monte Carlo method is actually a very general tool, and its applications are by no means restricted to numerical integration (for this reason, the plural "Monte Carlo methods" is also used frequently). In simple and general terms, the Monte Carlo method may be described as a numerical method based on random sampling. It is therefore a method with a strong statistical and probabilistic flavor. We will discuss the Monte Carlo method for numerical integration in §1.2 and the Monte Carlo method for global optimization in §6.1. An important fact about the Monte Carlo method for numerical integration is that it promises integration errors for which the order of magnitude, in terms of the number of nodes, is independent of the dimension. This is obviously a big step forward compared to classical methods based on Cartesian products of one-dimensional integration rules. However, the stochastic nature of the Monte Carlo method causes some unpleasant side effects. These drawbacks of the Monte Carlo method will be discussed more fully in §1.2. Let us mention now that the Monte Carlo method yields no guaranteed error bound (this is why we used the phrase "it *promises* integration errors $\cdots$ " earlier on).

A crucial task in the application of any Monte Carlo method is the generation of appropriate random samples. The success of a Monte Carlo calculation often stands or falls with the "quality" of the random samples that are used, where, by "quality," we mean how well the random samples reflect true randomness. This intuitive notion will attain a more precise meaning in §1.2 and Chapter 7, where the statistical requirements on random samples will be made concrete.

Because of the decisive role played by random samples, the subject of *random number generation* has become an important spin-off of the study of Monte Carlo methods. With the present trend toward parallelized algorithms there is a surge of interest in *random vector generation* as well. In the computational practice of Monte Carlo methods, the required random numbers and random vectors are actually generated by the computer in a deterministic subroutine. In this case of deterministic generation, we speak of *pseudorandom numbers* and *pseudorandom vectors*. The development of the theory of pseudorandom numbers and pseudorandom vectors has accompanied the development of the Monte Carlo method. Specific algorithms for the generation of pseudorandom numbers were already proposed in the late 1940s. We refer to Chapters 7–10 for a detailed treatment of pseudorandom number generation and pseudorandom vector generation.

As mentioned above, the Monte Carlo method has some disadvantages, which are inherent in the stochastic character of the method. For concreteness, let us again return to our standard example of numerical integration. In this case, the Monte Carlo method yields only a probabilistic bound on the integration error. On the other hand, a detailed analysis (see Chapter 2) reveals that, in Monte Carlo integration, it is not so much the true randomness of the samples that is relevant, but rather that the samples should be spread in a uniform manner over the integration domain (in a sense that can be made precise). Moreover, the analysis shows that a deterministic error bound can be established if deterministic nodes are used. This leads to the idea of selecting deterministic nodes in such a way that the error bound is as small as possible. This idea succinctly expresses the fundamental principle of a *quasi-Monte Carlo method*. A quasi-Monte Carlo method can be described in simple terms as the deterministic version of a Monte Carlo method, in the sense that the random samples in the Monte Carlo method are replaced by well-chosen deterministic points. The main aim is to select deterministic points for which the deterministic error bound is smaller than the probabilistic Monte Carlo error bound. In the case of numerical integration, this aim can be achieved in a convincing manner. There are, in fact, various types of quasi-Monte Carlo methods, and so this term is also often used in the plural.

It turns out that the technical tools developed in the theory of quasi-Monte Carlo methods are very useful in the theoretical analysis of several important methods for pseudorandom number generation and pseudorandom vector generation. Consequently, the material in these lecture notes is arranged in such a way that the chapters on pseudorandom numbers and pseudorandom vectors are preceded by the discussion of quasi-Monte Carlo methods.

1.2. Monte Carlo methods.

In a Monte Carlo method, the quantity to be calculated is interpreted in a stochastic model and subsequently estimated by random sampling. In this section, we illustrate this method in the context of numerical integration. A further application to global optimization will be described in §6.1.

Consider the problem of approximately calculating the integral $\int_B f(\mathbf{u})\,d\mathbf{u}$

with an integration domain $B \subseteq \mathbb{R}^s$ satisfying $0 < \lambda_s(B) < \infty$, where λ_s henceforth denotes the s-dimensional Lebesgue measure. We turn B into a probability space with probability measure $d\mu = d\mathbf{u}/\lambda_s(B)$. Then, for $f \in L^1(\mu)$, we have

$$(1.3) \qquad \int_B f(\mathbf{u})\, d\mathbf{u} = \lambda_s(B) \int_B f\, d\mu = \lambda_s(B)E(f),$$

where $E(f)$ is the *expected value* of the random variable f. The problem of numerical integration is thus reduced to the problem of the approximate calculation of an expected value. For the latter purpose, we use a basic idea from statistics, namely, to estimate an expected value by a sample means. This idea can be developed in the general framework of an arbitrary probability space.

Let f be a random variable on an arbitrary probability space $(A, \mathcal{A}, \lambda)$. Then the *Monte Carlo estimate* for the expected value $E(f)$ is obtained by taking N independent λ-distributed random samples $a_1, \dots, a_N \in A$ and letting

$$(1.4) \qquad E(f) \approx \frac{1}{N} \sum_{n=1}^{N} f(a_n).$$

The strong law of large numbers guarantees that this procedure converges almost surely in the sense that

$$\lim_{N \to \infty} \frac{1}{N} \sum_{n=1}^{N} f(a_n) = E(f) \qquad \lambda^\infty\text{-a.e.,}$$

where λ^∞ is the product measure of denumerably many copies of λ. For the probabilistic error analysis of the estimate (1.4), we need the *variance*

$$\sigma^2(f) = \int_A (f - E(f))^2\, d\lambda,$$

which is finite whenever $f \in L^2(\lambda)$.

THEOREM 1.1. *If $f \in L^2(\lambda)$, then, for any $N \geq 1$, we have*

$$\int_A \cdots \int_A \left(\frac{1}{N} \sum_{n=1}^{N} f(a_n) - E(f) \right)^2 d\lambda(a_1) \cdots d\lambda(a_N) = \frac{\sigma^2(f)}{N}.$$

Proof. Write $g = f - E(f)$; then $\int_A g\, d\lambda = 0$ and

$$\frac{1}{N} \sum_{n=1}^{N} f(a_n) - E(f) = \frac{1}{N} \sum_{n=1}^{N} g(a_n).$$

Thus

$$\int_A \cdots \int_A \left(\frac{1}{N}\sum_{n=1}^{N} f(a_n) - E(f)\right)^2 d\lambda(a_1)\cdots d\lambda(a_N)$$

$$= \int_A \cdots \int_A \left(\frac{1}{N}\sum_{n=1}^{N} g(a_n)\right)^2 d\lambda(a_1)\cdots d\lambda(a_N)$$

$$= \frac{1}{N^2}\sum_{n=1}^{N}\int_A \cdots \int_A g(a_n)^2\, d\lambda(a_1)\cdots d\lambda(a_N)$$

$$+ \frac{2}{N^2}\sum_{1\le m<n\le N}\int_A \cdots \int_A g(a_m)g(a_n)\, d\lambda(a_1)\cdots d\lambda(a_N)$$

$$= \frac{1}{N}\int_A g^2\, d\lambda = \frac{\sigma^2(f)}{N}. \qquad \square$$

Theorem 1.1 may be interpreted to mean that the absolute value of the error in (1.4) is, on the average, $\sigma(f)N^{-1/2}$, where $\sigma(f) = \left(\sigma^2(f)\right)^{1/2}$ is the *standard deviation* of f. Further probabilistic information about the error is obtained from the central limit theorem, which states that, if $0 < \sigma(f) < \infty$, then

$$\lim_{N\to\infty}\mathrm{Prob}\left(\frac{c_1\sigma(f)}{\sqrt{N}} \le \frac{1}{N}\sum_{n=1}^{N} f(a_n) - E(f) \le \frac{c_2\sigma(f)}{\sqrt{N}}\right) = \frac{1}{\sqrt{2\pi}}\int_{c_1}^{c_2} e^{-t^2/2}\, dt$$

for any constants $c_1 < c_2$, where $\mathrm{Prob}(\cdot)$ is the λ^∞-measure of the set of all sequences $a_1, a_2, \ldots$ of elements of A that have the property indicated between the parentheses.

If we apply the statistical estimate (1.4) to the original problem of approximately calculating the integral $\int_B f(\mathbf{u})\, d\mathbf{u}$, then, in view of (1.3), we obtain the *Monte Carlo estimate*

$$(1.5) \qquad \int_B f(\mathbf{u})\, d\mathbf{u} \approx \frac{\lambda_s(B)}{N}\sum_{n=1}^{N} f(\mathbf{x}_n),$$

where $\mathbf{x}_1, \ldots, \mathbf{x}_N$ are N independent μ-distributed random samples from B. By the above analysis, the absolute value of the error in (1.5) is then, on the average, $\lambda_s(B)\sigma(f)N^{-1/2}$. On the basis of this fact, or on the basis of the central limit theorem, we can state that the Monte Carlo method for numerical integration yields a probabilistic error bound of the form $O(N^{-1/2})$ in terms of the number N of nodes. The remarkable feature here is that this order of magnitude does not depend on the dimension s. This should be compared with the error bound $O(N^{-2/s})$ for the classical s-dimensional integration rule discussed in §1.1. The Monte Carlo method for numerical integration is definitely preferable to the classical integration rule for dimensions $s \ge 5$.

There is a case in which the statistical estimate (1.5) is not useful for the computational practice, namely, when the integration domain B is so complicated that $\lambda_s(B)$ is difficult to calculate. In this case, we can take recourse to the following alternative Monte Carlo estimate. By applying, if necessary, a suitable change of variables, it suffices to consider the situation where B is contained in the unit cube $\bar{I}^s$. Then we can write

$$\int_B f(\mathbf{u}) \, d\mathbf{u} = \int_{\bar{I}^s} f(\mathbf{u}) c_B(\mathbf{u}) \, d\mathbf{u},$$

where c_B is the characteristic function of B. If the last integral is estimated according to (1.5), then we arrive at the *Monte Carlo estimate*

(1.6)
$$\int_B f(\mathbf{u}) \, d\mathbf{u} \approx \frac{1}{N} \sum_{\substack{n=1 \\ \mathbf{x}_n \in B}}^{N} f(\mathbf{x}_n),$$

where $\mathbf{x}_1, \ldots, \mathbf{x}_N$ are N independent random samples from the uniform distribution on $\bar{I}^s$. Since the estimate (1.6) is derived from (1.5), it follows that for (1.6) we also have a probabilistic error bound of the form $O(N^{-1/2})$.

The preceding description of the Monte Carlo method for numerical integration gives some idea as to what the basic elements of Monte Carlo methods are, in general. The first step invariably consists of the statistical modeling of the given numerical problem, usually in terms of suitable random variables. This step is obvious in the case of numerical integration, since an integral can readily be interpreted in terms of the expected value of a random variable (compare with (1.3)). Subsequently, the random variables occurring in the model must be analyzed with regard to their statistical properties, such as law of distribution, statistical dependence or independence, and so on. Another important step is the generation of random samples that reflect these statistical properties. It is advisable not to be satisfied with just one run of a Monte Carlo calculation, but to use as many runs as is feasible—each time with renewed sampling—to increase the reliability of the result from the statistical point of view. These procedural steps in a Monte Carlo method are typical of the larger area of *stochastic simulation* to which Monte Carlo methods belong. Stochastic simulation deals with the simulation of stochastic phenomena by special, but randomly selected, instances. The methods used in stochastic simulation are often called *simulation methods*. Monte Carlo methods are thus examples of simulation methods.

Monte Carlo methods are used in a wide range of applications. In addition to the applications to numerical integration and global optimization discussed in these lecture notes, there are applications of Monte Carlo methods to many other basic problems of numerical analysis, such as the solution of large systems of linear equations, the solution of partial differential equations and of integral equations. Natural applications arise in problems with a stochastic background, for instance, in computational statistics, stochastic optimization, and queueing theory. There is also a wealth of applications to real-world problems in areas such as computational physics, structural mechanics, reliability theory, systems analysis, and so on.

As we have explained above, the Monte Carlo method for numerical integration offers a way of overcoming the curse of dimensionality. However, it must be pointed out that the Monte Carlo method is not a panacea. On the contrary, it has several deficiencies that may hamper its usefulness. First, the Monte Carlo method for numerical integration provides only a probabilistic error bound. In other words, there is never any guarantee that the expected accuracy is achieved in a concrete calculation. This is certainly not a desirable state of affairs, and, for some applications—e.g., in sensitive areas where highly reliable results are needed—it is actually an untenable situation.

We also draw attention to the following fact: the probabilistic error bound $O(N^{-1/2})$ in the Monte Carlo method for numerical integration holds under a very weak regularity condition, namely, for any square-integrable integrand, but no benefit is derived from any additional regularity of the integrand. The numerical practice teaches a different lesson: more regular functions are "easier" to integrate numerically, in the sense that they lead to a faster convergence rate when increasing the number of nodes in suitably constructed integration rules. The fact that the Monte Carlo error bound does not reflect any additional regularity of the integrand must therefore be seen as another drawback of the method.

A fundamental difficulty of the Monte Carlo method for numerical integration stems from the requirement that the nodes be independent random samples. This immediately raises the question of how to generate independent random samples concretely. The practitioners avoid this question and use pseudorandom numbers instead of truly random samples. Since "random sample" is a statistical concept that only makes sense in the context of a whole ensemble of samples, there is actually no way to define this concept rigorously for an individual sample.

To summarize, the following points must be viewed as *deficiencies of the Monte Carlo method* for numerical integration:

(i) There are only probabilistic error bounds;

(ii) The regularity of the integrand is not reflected;

(iii) Generating random samples is difficult.

As we have seen in Theorem 1.1, the mean-square error of the Monte Carlo estimate is equal to $\sigma^2(f)/N$. To improve the efficiency of the Monte Carlo method for numerical integration, a number of techniques for *variance reduction*, i.e., for decreasing the variance factor $\sigma^2(f)$, have been developed. One such technique is called *stratified sampling* and proceeds as follows. Let f again be a random variable on the probability space $(A, \mathcal{A}, \lambda)$. Partition A into the sets $A_1, \ldots, A_k \in \mathcal{A}$ with $\lambda(A_j) > 0$ for $1 \le j \le k$. For each j with $1 \le j \le k$, choose N_j independent μ_j-distributed random samples $a_1^{(j)}, \ldots, a_{N_j}^{(j)} \in A_j$, where $\mu_j = \lambda(A_j)^{-1}\lambda$ is the probability measure on A_j induced by λ. Then use the estimate

$$E(f) = \sum_{j=1}^{k} \int_{A_j} f \, d\lambda = \sum_{j=1}^{k} \lambda(A_j) \int_{A_j} f \, d\mu_j \approx \sum_{j=1}^{k} \frac{\lambda(A_j)}{N_j} \sum_{n=1}^{N_j} f(a_n^{(j)}).$$

The mean-square error of this estimate can be calculated by the method in the proof of Theorem 1.1, and this yields, instead of $\sigma^2(f)/N$, the expression

$$\sum_{j=1}^{k} \frac{\lambda(A_j)}{N_j} \int_{A_j} \left(f - \frac{1}{\lambda(A_j)} \int_{A_j} f \, d\lambda \right)^2 d\lambda.$$

The numbers N_j must be chosen suitably so as to achieve a variance reduction. Let $N = \sum_{j=1}^{k} N_j$ be the total number of sample points. Then the following standard choice yields a variance reduction.

PROPOSITION 1.2. *If the numbers* $N_j = \lambda(A_j)N$, $1 \le j \le k$, *are integers, then*

$$\sum_{j=1}^{k} \frac{\lambda(A_j)}{N_j} \int_{A_j} \left(f - \frac{1}{\lambda(A_j)} \int_{A_j} f \, d\lambda \right)^2 d\lambda \le \frac{\sigma^2(f)}{N}.$$

Proof. With the special form of the N_j it suffices to show that

$$\sum_{j=1}^{k} \int_{A_j} \left(f - \frac{1}{\lambda(A_j)} \int_{A_j} f \, d\lambda \right)^2 d\lambda \le \int_{A} (f - E(f))^2 \, d\lambda.$$

By expanding the square on both sides, it is seen that this is equivalent to proving

$$E(f)^2 \le \sum_{j=1}^{k} \frac{1}{\lambda(A_j)} \left(\int_{A_j} f \, d\lambda \right)^2,$$

and the latter inequality is obtained from the Cauchy–Schwarz inequality by noting that

$$E(f)^2 = \left(\sum_{j=1}^{k} \int_{A_j} f \, d\lambda \right)^2 = \left(\sum_{j=1}^{k} \lambda(A_j)^{1/2} \frac{1}{\lambda(A_j)^{1/2}} \int_{A_j} f \, d\lambda \right)^2$$

$$\le \left(\sum_{j=1}^{k} \lambda(A_j) \right) \sum_{j=1}^{k} \frac{1}{\lambda(A_j)} \left(\int_{A_j} f \, d\lambda \right)^2 = \sum_{j=1}^{k} \frac{1}{\lambda(A_j)} \left(\int_{A_j} f \, d\lambda \right)^2. \qquad \square$$

Another technique for variance reduction is the method of *antithetic variates*. We explain this method in the simple case of an integral

$$E(f) = \int_{0}^{1} f(u) \, du.$$

We introduce the auxiliary function

(1.7) $g(u) = \frac{1}{2} \left(f(u) + f(1-u) \right)$ for $0 \le u \le 1$

and use the estimate

$$E(f) = E(g) \approx \frac{1}{N} \sum_{n=1}^{N} g(x_n) = \frac{1}{2N} \sum_{n=1}^{N} \left(f(x_n) + f(1-x_n) \right)$$

with N independent and uniformly distributed random samples $x_1, \ldots, x_N \in [0,1]$. According to Theorem 1.1, the mean-square error of this estimate is $\sigma^2(g)/N$. Since there are $2N$ function values of f involved in this estimate, the mean-square error $\sigma^2(g)/N$ should be compared with the quantity $\sigma^2(f)/(2N)$. The following result shows a case in which a variance reduction is achieved.

PROPOSITION 1.3. *If f is a continuous monotone function on $[0,1]$ and g is defined by (1.7), then*

$$\sigma^2(g) \leq \tfrac{1}{2}\sigma^2(f).$$

Proof. We have

$$\sigma^2(g) = \int_0^1 (g(u) - E(g))^2 \, du = \int_0^1 \left(\frac{1}{2}f(u) + \frac{1}{2}f(1-u) - E(f)\right)^2 du$$
$$= \frac{1}{2}\int_0^1 f^2(u)\, du + \frac{1}{2}\int_0^1 f(u)f(1-u)\, du - E(f)^2.$$

The desired inequality is therefore equivalent to

$$(1.8) \qquad \int_0^1 f(u)f(1-u)\, du \leq E(f)^2.$$

By replacing, if necessary, f by $-f$, we can assume that f is nondecreasing. Then the function

$$F(u) = \int_0^u f(1-t)\, dt - E(f)u$$

on $[0,1]$ has the nonincreasing derivative $F'(u) = f(1-u) - E(f)$. Since $F(0) = F(1) = 0$, it follows that $F(u) \geq 0$ for all $u \in [0,1]$. This implies that

$$\int_0^1 F(u)\, df(u) \geq 0.$$

Integration by parts yields

$$\int_0^1 f(u)\, dF(u) = \int_0^1 f(u)F'(u)\, du \leq 0.$$

By inserting the formula for $F'(u)$, we arrive at (1.8). $\quad\square$

1.3.   Quasi-Monte Carlo methods.

We recall that in Monte Carlo integration with N random nodes the absolute value of the error has the average order of magnitude $N^{-1/2}$. Clearly, there exist sets of N nodes for which the absolute value of the error is not larger than the average. If we could construct such sets of nodes explicitly, this would already be a useful methodological advance. The *quasi-Monte Carlo method* for numerical integration aims much higher, as it seeks to construct sets of nodes that perform significantly better than average. The integration rules for the quasi-Monte Carlo method are taken from the appropriate Monte Carlo estimate. For instance, for the normalized integration domain $\bar{I}^s$, we have the *quasi-Monte Carlo approximation*

$$(1.9) \qquad \int_{\bar{I}^s} f(\mathbf{u})\,d\mathbf{u} \approx \frac{1}{N}\sum_{n=1}^{N} f(\mathbf{x}_n),$$

which formally looks like the Monte Carlo estimate but is now used with deterministic nodes $\mathbf{x}_1,\dots,\mathbf{x}_N \in \bar{I}^s$. These nodes should be chosen judiciously so as to guarantee a small error in (1.9). In analogy with the more general Monte Carlo estimate (1.6), we have the *quasi-Monte Carlo approximation*

$$(1.10) \qquad \int_B f(\mathbf{u})\,d\mathbf{u} \approx \frac{1}{N}\sum_{\substack{n=1 \\ \mathbf{x}_n \in B}}^{N} f(\mathbf{x}_n),$$

where B is a subset of $\bar{I}^s$ and $\mathbf{x}_1,\dots,\mathbf{x}_N \in \bar{I}^s$ are deterministic points.

The error analysis for the approximations (1.9) and (1.10) will be performed in §2.2 and for a special situation in Chapter 5. Explicit constructions of sets of deterministic nodes guaranteeing small errors will be the subject of Chapters 3, 4, and 5. We do not wish to preview these results at length, but the following very concise summary may be given at this early stage. If we assume (1.9) to be the standard case, then the benchmark is the probabilistic Monte Carlo error bound $O(N^{-1/2})$. The quasi-Monte Carlo method yields a much better result, giving us the deterministic error bound $O\big(N^{-1}(\log N)^{s-1}\big)$ for suitably chosen sets of nodes and for integrands with a relatively low degree of regularity. In the special circumstances considered in Chapter 5, even smaller error bounds can be achieved for sufficiently regular integrands. The sets of nodes producing this high accuracy in (1.9) are obtained by effective constructions.

This brings us to a discussion of the *advantages of the quasi-Monte Carlo method* for numerical integration, which should be compared with the list of deficiencies of the Monte Carlo method in §1.2. The very nature of the quasi-Monte Carlo method, with its completely deterministic procedures, implies that we get deterministic—and thus guaranteed—error bounds. In principle, it is therefore always possible to determine in advance an integration rule that yields a prescribed level of accuracy. Moreover, with the same computational effort, i.e., with the same number of function evaluations (which are the costly operations in numerical integration), the quasi-Monte Carlo method achieves a significantly higher accuracy than the Monte Carlo method. Thus, on two crucial accounts— determinism and precision—the quasi-Monte Carlo method is superior to the Monte Carlo method. For a special type of quasi-Monte Carlo method, the lattice rules to be discussed in Chapter 5, we have the desirable property that a higher degree of regularity of the integrand leads to more precision in the integration rule. The one problem with the Monte Carlo method that attains almost philosophical dimensions, namely, the difficulty of generating truly random samples, evaporates when we consider a quasi-Monte Carlo method, since here we just implement ready-made constructions to obtain the required nodes.

There are quasi-Monte Carlo methods not only for numerical integration, but also for various other numerical problems. In fact, for many Monte Carlo methods, it is possible to develop corresponding quasi-Monte Carlo methods as their deterministic versions. Invariably, the basic idea is to replace the random samples in the Monte Carlo method by deterministic points that are well suited for the problem at hand. A further illustration of this principle will be provided in Chapter 6, where we discuss quasi-Monte Carlo methods for global optimization.

Quasi-Monte Carlo methods have first been proposed in the 1950s, and their theory has since developed vigorously. However, for a rather long time, these methods remained the province of specialists. The wider acceptance of quasi-Monte Carlo methods was pioneered in computational physics where large-scale Monte Carlo calculations are very common and where it was recognized that quasi-Monte Carlo methods can lead to significant gains in efficiency. The refinements of quasi-Monte Carlo methods and the expanding scope of their applications have recently made these methods known to larger segments of the scientific computing community.

Fairly obvious applications of quasi-Monte Carlo methods arise in problems of numerical analysis that can be reduced to numerical integration. An example is the numerical solution of integral equations for which quasi-Monte Carlo methods are discussed in the books of Korobov [160, Chap. 4] and Hua and Wang [145, Chap. 10] and in the more recent work of Sarkar and Prasad [301] and Tichy [349]. For applications to initial value and boundary value problems, we refer to Hua and Wang [145, Chap. 10] and Taschner [340]. Important applications of quasi-Monte Carlo methods to the numerical solution of difficult integro-differential equations such as the Boltzmann equation have been developed by Babovsky et al. [12], Lécot [181], [182], [184], and Motta et al. [214]. Applications to approximation theory can already be found in the books of Korobov [160, Chap. 4] and Hua and Wang [145, Chap. 9]. Quasi-Monte Carlo methods for the numerical solution of systems of equations are studied in Hlawka [140] and Taschner [341]. A survey of quasi-Monte Carlo methods in computational statistics is presented in Shaw [309]. Deák [52] reviews applications to stochastic optimization, and Adlakha [1] describes an application to stochastic algorithms. Drmota [69] and Drmota and Tichy [70] have developed applications of quasi-Monte Carlo methods to statistical measurement techniques. Quasi-Monte Carlo methods for the approximate calculation of vector-valued integrals are sketched in Trendafilov [354]. Some further applications of quasi-Monte Carlo methods and corresponding references are listed in Niederreiter [225, §2].

Notes.

The "official" history of the Monte Carlo method began in 1949 with the publication of a paper by Metropolis and Ulam [211], but at that time the method had already been used for several years in secret projects of the U. S. Defense Department. This rather fascinating chapter in the early history of the Monte Carlo method is outlined in Eckhardt [74] and Metropolis [210]. Several precursors are mentioned in Hammersley and Handscomb [130, Chap. 1]. The latter book is

the classic on Monte Carlo methods. More recent books on Monte Carlo methods and on the general area of simulation are Bratley, Fox, and Schrage [34],
Deák [53], Kalos and Whitlock [150], Morgan [213], Ripley [295], and Rubinstein [297]. For a general background on numerical integration, we refer to Davis
and Rabinowitz [51].

Expository accounts of quasi-Monte Carlo methods are given in the books of
Korobov [160], Hlawka, Firneis, and Zinterhof [141], and Hua and Wang [145].
A detailed survey of quasi-Monte Carlo methods with an extensive bibliography
is presented in the article of Niederreiter [225], and a recent update of this
survey can be found in Niederreiter [251]. A brief review of quasi-Monte Carlo
methods is contained in Lambert [168]. The first article in which the expression
"quasi-Monte Carlo method" appeared seems to have been a technical report of
Richtmyer [293] from 1951.

CHAPTER 2

Quasi-Monte Carlo Methods for Numerical Integration

According to §1.3, the basic idea of a quasi-Monte Carlo method is to replace random samples in a Monte Carlo method by well-chosen deterministic points. The criterion for the choice of deterministic points depends on the numerical problem at hand. For the important problem of numerical integration, the selection criterion is easy to find and leads to the concepts of *uniformly distributed sequence* and *discrepancy*. The discrepancy can be viewed as a quantitative measure for the deviation from uniform distribution. Various types of discrepancies and their basic properties will be discussed in §2.1. The important role of the discrepancy in quasi-Monte Carlo integration is documented in §2.2, where deterministic bounds for the integration error in terms of the discrepancy are presented.

2.1. Discrepancy.

For the following discussion, we normalize the integration domain to be $\bar{I}^s :=$ $[\,0,1\,]^s$, the closed s-dimensional unit cube. For an integrand f, we use the quasi-Monte Carlo approximation

$$(2.1) \qquad \int_{\bar{I}^s} f(\mathbf{u})\,d\mathbf{u} \approx \frac{1}{N} \sum_{n=1}^{N} f(\mathbf{x}_n)$$

with $\mathbf{x}_1, \ldots, \mathbf{x}_N \in \bar{I}^s$. In an idealized model, which we adopt for the moment, we replace the set of nodes $\mathbf{x}_1, \ldots, \mathbf{x}_N$ by an infinite sequence $\mathbf{x}_1, \mathbf{x}_2, \ldots$ of points in $\bar{I}^s$. A basic requirement for this sequence is that we obtain a convergent method from (2.1). Thus we want a sequence $\mathbf{x}_1, \mathbf{x}_2, \ldots$ for which

$$(2.2) \qquad \lim_{N \to \infty} \frac{1}{N} \sum_{n=1}^{N} f(\mathbf{x}_n) = \int_{\bar{I}^s} f(\mathbf{u})\,d\mathbf{u}$$

holds for a reasonable class of integrands, say, for all continuous f on $\bar{I}^s$. The resulting condition means that the sequence $\mathbf{x}_1, \mathbf{x}_2, \ldots$ should be *uniformly distributed* in $\bar{I}^s$, according to one of the standard definitions of this notion (compare with Kuipers and Niederreiter [163]). An equivalent definition states that

13

$\mathbf{x}_1, \mathbf{x}_2, \ldots$ is uniformly distributed in $\bar{I}^s$ if

(2.3)
$$\lim_{N \to \infty} \frac{1}{N} \sum_{n=1}^{N} c_J(\mathbf{x}_n) = \lambda_s(J)$$

for all subintervals J of $\bar{I}^s$, where c_J is the characteristic function of J and λ_s denotes the s-dimensional Lebesgue measure. It is well known that, if $\mathbf{x}_1, \mathbf{x}_2, \ldots$ is uniformly distributed in $\bar{I}^s$, then (2.2) holds even for all Riemann-integrable functions f on $\bar{I}^s$ (see [163]).

The above discussion suggests that the desirable nodes in (2.1) are those for which the empirical distribution is close to the uniform distribution on $\bar{I}^s$. In an intuitive language, the nodes $\mathbf{x}_1, \ldots, \mathbf{x}_N$ should be "evenly distributed" over $\bar{I}^s$. The various notions of discrepancy that we will consider are quantitative measures for the deviation from uniform distribution, or, in other words, for the irregularity of distribution. The significance of the discrepancy for quasi-Monte Carlo integration will become even more pronounced in §2.2, where bounds for the integration error in terms of the discrepancy are shown.

Let P be a point set consisting of $\mathbf{x}_1, \ldots, \mathbf{x}_N \in \bar{I}^s$. We will always interpret "point set" in the sense of the combinatorial notion of "multiset," i.e., a set in which the multiplicity of elements matters. In the theory of uniform distribution of sequences, the term "finite sequence" is often used instead of "point set," but we will restrict the usage of "sequence" to its proper meaning in analysis, namely, that of an infinite sequence. For an arbitrary subset B of $\bar{I}^s$, we define

$$A(B; P) = \sum_{n=1}^{N} c_B(\mathbf{x}_n),$$

where c_B is the characteristic function of B. Thus $A(B; P)$ is the counting function that indicates the number of n with $1 \leq n \leq N$ for which $\mathbf{x}_n \in B$. If $\mathcal{B}$ is a nonempty family of Lebesgue-measurable subsets of $\bar{I}^s$, then a general notion of discrepancy of the point set P is given by

(2.4)
$$D_N(\mathcal{B}; P) = \sup_{B \in \mathcal{B}} \left| \frac{A(B; P)}{N} - \lambda_s(B) \right|.$$

Note that $0 \leq D_N(\mathcal{B}; P) \leq 1$ always. By suitable specializations of the family $\mathcal{B}$, we obtain the two most important concepts of discrepancy. We put $I^s = [0, 1)^s$.

DEFINITION 2.1. The *star discrepancy* $D_N^*(P) = D_N^*(\mathbf{x}_1, \ldots, \mathbf{x}_N)$ of the point set P is defined by $D_N^*(P) = D_N(\mathcal{J}^*; P)$, where $\mathcal{J}^*$ is the family of all subintervals of I^s of the form $\prod_{i=1}^{s} [0, u_i)$.

DEFINITION 2.2. The *(extreme) discrepancy* $D_N(P) = D_N(\mathbf{x}_1, \ldots, \mathbf{x}_N)$ of the point set P is defined by $D_N(P) = D_N(\mathcal{J}; P)$, where $\mathcal{J}$ is the family of all subintervals of I^s of the form $\prod_{i=1}^{s} [u_i, v_i)$.

REMARK 2.3. If the points of P are in I^s, which happens in most cases of practical interest, then $D_N^*(P) = D_N(\mathcal{J}_c^*; P)$ and $D_N(P) = D_N(\mathcal{J}_c; P)$, where

$\mathcal{J}_c^*$ is the family of all subintervals of I^s of the form $\prod_{i=1}^s [0, u_i]$ and $\mathcal{J}_c$ is the family of all closed subintervals of I^s.

PROPOSITION 2.4. *For any P consisting of points in $\bar{I}^s$, we have*

$$D_N^*(P) \le D_N(P) \le 2^s D_N^*(P).$$

Proof. The first inequality is trivial. For $s = 1$, the second inequality is immediately obtained from

$$A([u, v); P) = A([0, v); P) - A([0, u); P), \quad \lambda_1([u, v)) = \lambda_1([0, v)) - \lambda_1([0, u)),$$

and for $s \ge 2$ it is obtained from analogous identities (compare with [163, p. 93] for the case where $s = 2$). $\square$

In the case where $s = 1$, simple explicit formulas for the discrepancies $D_N^*(P)$ and $D_N(P)$ can be given. The following lemma is useful for the proofs.

LEMMA 2.5. *If $x_1, \dots, x_N, y_1, \dots, y_N \in [0, 1]$ satisfy $|x_n - y_n| \le \varepsilon$ for $1 \le n \le N$, then*

$$|D_N^*(x_1, \dots, x_N) - D_N^*(y_1, \dots, y_N)| \le \varepsilon,$$

$$|D_N(x_1, \dots, x_N) - D_N(y_1, \dots, y_N)| \le 2\varepsilon.$$

Proof. Denote by P the point set consisting of $x_1, \dots, x_N$, and by Q the point set consisting of $y_1, \dots, y_N$. Consider any interval $J = [0, u) \subseteq [0, 1)$. Whenever $y_n \in J$, then $x_n \in J_1 := [0, u + \varepsilon) \cap [0, 1]$; hence

$$\frac{A(J; Q)}{N} - \lambda_1(J) \le \frac{A(J_1; P)}{N} - \lambda_1(J_1) + \varepsilon \le D_N^*(P) + \varepsilon.$$

Whenever $x_n \in J_2 := [0, u - \varepsilon)$, then $y_n \in J$; hence

$$\frac{A(J; Q)}{N} - \lambda_1(J) \ge \frac{A(J_2; P)}{N} - \lambda_1(J_2) - \varepsilon \ge -D_N^*(P) - \varepsilon.$$

Thus $D_N^*(Q) \le D_N^*(P) + \varepsilon$. By interchanging the roles of P and Q, we obtain $D_N^*(P) \le D_N^*(Q) + \varepsilon$, and so $|D_N^*(P) - D_N^*(Q)| \le \varepsilon$. The second part of the lemma is shown similarly. $\square$

For $s = 1$, we may arrange the points $x_1, \dots, x_N$ of a given point set in nondecreasing order. The formula in Theorem 2.6 is due to Niederreiter [217], and the one in Theorem 2.7 is a simplified version of a formula of de Clerck [55].

THEOREM 2.6. *If $0 \le x_1 \le x_2 \le \cdots \le x_N \le 1$, then*

$$D_N^*(x_1, \dots, x_N) = \frac{1}{2N} + \max_{1 \le n \le N} \left| x_n - \frac{2n - 1}{2N} \right|.$$

Proof. Since D_N^* is a continuous function of $x_1, \cdots, x_N$ (see Lemma 2.5), we can assume that $0 < x_1 < x_2 < \cdots < x_N < 1$. Put $x_0 = 0$ and $x_{N+1} = 1$. If P

is the point set consisting of $x_1, \dots, x_N$, then

$$D_N^*(P) = \max_{0 \le n \le N} \sup_{x_n < u \le x_{n+1}} \left| \frac{A([0, u); P)}{N} - u \right|$$

$$= \max_{0 \le n \le N} \sup_{x_n < u \le x_{n+1}} \left| \frac{n}{N} - u \right|$$

$$= \max_{0 \le n \le N} \max \left(\left| \frac{n}{N} - x_n \right|, \left| \frac{n}{N} - x_{n+1} \right| \right)$$

$$= \max_{1 \le n \le N} \max \left(\left| \frac{n}{N} - x_n \right|, \left| \frac{n-1}{N} - x_n \right| \right)$$

$$= \frac{1}{2N} + \max_{1 \le n \le N} \left| x_n - \frac{2n-1}{2N} \right|. \qquad \square$$

THEOREM 2.7. *If* $0 \le x_1 \le x_2 \le \cdots \le x_N \le 1$, *then*

$$D_N(x_1, \dots, x_N) = \frac{1}{N} + \max_{1 \le n \le N} \left(\frac{n}{N} - x_n \right) - \min_{1 \le n \le N} \left(\frac{n}{N} - x_n \right).$$

Proof. As in the proof of Theorem 2.6, we can assume that $x_0 := 0 < x_1 < x_2 < \cdots < x_N < 1 =: x_{N+1}$. If P is the point set consisting of $x_1, \dots, x_N$, then

$$D_N(P) = \max_{0 \le i \le j \le N} \sup_{\substack{x_i < u \le x_{i+1} \\ x_j < v \le x_{j+1} \\ u < v}} \left| \frac{A([u, v); P)}{N} - (v - u) \right|$$

$$= \max_{0 \le i \le j \le N} \sup_{\substack{x_i < u \le x_{i+1} \\ x_j < v \le x_{j+1} \\ u < v}} \left| \frac{j - i}{N} - (v - u) \right|$$

$$= \max_{0 \le i \le j \le N} \max \left(\left| \frac{j - i}{N} - (x_{j+1} - x_i) \right|, \left| \frac{j - i}{N} - (x_j - x_{i+1}) \right| \right).$$

Put $r_n = n/N - x_n$ for $0 \le n \le N + 1$; then

$$D_N(P) = \max_{0 \le i \le j \le N} \max \left(\left| r_{j+1} - r_i - \frac{1}{N} \right|, \left| r_j - r_{i+1} + \frac{1}{N} \right| \right)$$

$$= \max_{\substack{0 \le i \le N \\ 1 \le j \le N+1}} \left| \frac{1}{N} + r_i - r_j \right|.$$

If the last maximum is restricted to $1 \le i, j \le N$, then its value is clearly given by the expression for $D_N(P)$ in the theorem. Using

$$\max_{1 \le n \le N} r_n \ge r_N \ge 0, \qquad \min_{1 \le n \le N} r_n \le r_1 \le \frac{1}{N},$$

it is seen that in the last expression for $D_N(P)$ the terms in the maximum corresponding to either $i = 0$ or $j = N + 1$ are dominated by the expression for $D_N(P)$ in the theorem. $\square$

For a sequence S of elements of $\bar{I}^s$, we write $D_N(S)$ for the discrepancy and $D_N^*(S)$ for the star discrepancy of the first N terms of S. According to a classical result in the theory of uniform distribution of sequences (see [163]), the following properties are equivalent:

 (i) S is uniformly distributed in $\bar{I}^s$;
 (ii) $\lim_{N\to\infty} D_N(S) = 0$;
 (iii) $\lim_{N\to\infty} D_N^*(S) = 0$.

In this sense, the discrepancy and the star discrepancy can be viewed as quantifications of the definition of a uniformly distributed sequence in $\bar{I}^s$ given in (2.3).

For integration domains that are more general than $\bar{I}^s$, we need various other types of discrepancies. The following notion is the appropriate one for general convex integration domains (compare with Theorem 2.14).

DEFINITION 2.8. The *isotropic discrepancy* $J_N(P) = J_N(\mathbf{x}_1, \dots, \mathbf{x}_N)$ of the point set P is defined by $J_N(P) = D_N(\mathcal{C}; P)$, where $\mathcal{C}$ is the family of all convex subsets of $\bar{I}^s$.

We always have $D_N(P) \leq J_N(P) \leq 4s D_N(P)^{1/s}$, where the first inequality is trivial, and the second one follows from a result of Niederreiter and Wills [278]. By combining this with a criterion mentioned above, we see that a sequence S is uniformly distributed in $\bar{I}^s$ if and only if $\lim_{N\to\infty} J_N(S) = 0$, where $J_N(S)$ is the isotropic discrepancy of the first N terms of S.

There is a classification of all Jordan-measurable subsets of $\bar{I}^s$ (i.e., of all subsets of $\bar{I}^s$ for which the characteristic function is Riemann integrable) in terms of the complexity of their boundary. For $B \subseteq \bar{I}^s$ and $\varepsilon > 0$, define

$$B_\varepsilon = \{\mathbf{x} \in \bar{I}^s : d(\mathbf{x}, \mathbf{y}) < \varepsilon \text{ for some } \mathbf{y} \in B\},$$
$$B_{-\varepsilon} = \{\mathbf{x} \in \bar{I}^s : d(\mathbf{x}, \mathbf{y}) \geq \varepsilon \text{ for all } \mathbf{y} \in \bar{I}^s \smallsetminus B\},$$

where d is the standard Euclidean metric in $\mathbb{R}^s$. Let $b = b(\varepsilon)$ be a positive nondecreasing function defined for all $\varepsilon > 0$ and satisfying $\lim_{\varepsilon\to 0+} b(\varepsilon) = 0$. Then we let $\mathcal{M}_b$ be the family of all Lebesgue-measurable $B \subseteq \bar{I}^s$ for which

$$\lambda_s(B_\varepsilon \smallsetminus B) \leq b(\varepsilon) \quad \text{and} \quad \lambda_s(B \smallsetminus B_{-\varepsilon}) \leq b(\varepsilon) \qquad \text{for all } \varepsilon > 0.$$

Every $B \in \mathcal{M}_b$ is actually Jordan measurable, and, conversely, every Jordan-measurable subset of $\bar{I}^s$ belongs to $\mathcal{M}_b$ for a suitable function b (see Niederreiter [219, pp. 168–169]).

For a family $\mathcal{M}_b$, we now consider the discrepancy $D_N(\mathcal{M}_b; P)$ defined according to (2.4). Niederreiter and Wills [278] have given a bound for this discrepancy in terms of $D_N(P)$. If the function b satisfies $b(\varepsilon) \geq \varepsilon$ for all $\varepsilon > 0$, then the bound can be simplified to yield

$$D_N(\mathcal{M}_b; P) \leq 4b(2\sqrt{s} D_N(P)^{1/s}).$$

In many cases of interest, the function b will have the form $b(\varepsilon) = C\varepsilon$ for some constant $C > 0$, and then the bound in [278] reduces to

$$D_N(\mathcal{M}_b; P) \leq (4C\sqrt{s} + 2C + 1) D_N(P)^{1/s}.$$

Since every convex subset of $\bar{I}^s$ belongs to $\mathcal{M}_{b_0}$ with b_0 being the function $b_0(\varepsilon) = 2s\varepsilon$, we have

$$J_N(P) \leq D_N(\mathcal{M}_b; P)$$

whenever the function b satisfies $b(\varepsilon) \geq 2s\varepsilon$ for all $\varepsilon > 0$. If the sequence S is uniformly distributed in $\bar{I}^s$, then, for any function b, we have $\lim_{N \to \infty} D_N(\mathcal{M}_b; S) = 0$, where $D_N(\mathcal{M}_b; S)$ is the appropriate discrepancy of the first N terms of S. Under suitable conditions on the function b, e.g., if $b(\varepsilon) \geq 2s\varepsilon$ for all $\varepsilon > 0$, we also have the converse result; namely, $\lim_{N \to \infty} D_N(\mathcal{M}_b; S) = 0$ implies that S is uniformly distributed in $\bar{I}^s$.

2.2. Error bounds.

We discuss the most important error bounds for the quasi-Monte Carlo approximation (2.1) and analogous bounds for more general integration domains. All these bounds involve a suitable notion of discrepancy. We start with the one-dimensional case in which the proofs are quite easy. A classical result is the following inequality of Koksma [155].

THEOREM 2.9. *If f has bounded variation $V(f)$ on $[0,1]$, then, for any $x_1, \ldots, x_N \in [0,1]$, we have*

$$\left| \frac{1}{N} \sum_{n=1}^{N} f(x_n) - \int_0^1 f(u) \, du \right| \leq V(f) D_N^*(x_1, \ldots, x_N).$$

Proof. We can assume that $x_1 \leq x_2 \leq \cdots \leq x_N$. Put $x_0 = 0$ and $x_{N+1} = 1$. Using summation by parts and integration by parts, we obtain

$$\frac{1}{N} \sum_{n=1}^{N} f(x_n) - \int_0^1 f(u) \, du = -\sum_{n=0}^{N} \frac{n}{N} (f(x_{n+1}) - f(x_n)) + \int_0^1 u \, df(u)$$

$$= \sum_{n=0}^{N} \int_{x_n}^{x_{n+1}} \left(u - \frac{n}{N} \right) df(u).$$

For fixed n with $0 \leq n \leq N$, we have

$$\left| u - \frac{n}{N} \right| \leq D_N^*(x_1, \ldots, x_N) \quad \text{for } x_n \leq u \leq x_{n+1}$$

by Theorem 2.6, and the desired inequality follows immediately. □

In Theorem 2.12, below, we will prove a result that implies that Koksma's inequality is, in general, the best possible, even for C^∞ functions. We recall that, for a continuous function f on $[0,1]$, its *modulus of continuity* is defined by

$$\omega(f; t) = \sup_{\substack{u,v \in [0,1] \\ |u-v| \leq t}} |f(u) - f(v)| \quad \text{for } t \geq 0.$$

The following error bound for continuous integrands was established by Niederreiter [218].

THEOREM 2.10. *If f is continuous on $[0,1]$, then, for any $x_1, \ldots, x_N \in [0,1]$, we have*

$$\left| \frac{1}{N} \sum_{n=1}^{N} f(x_n) - \int_0^1 f(u) \, du \right| \le \omega\left(f; D_N^*(x_1, \ldots, x_N)\right).$$

Proof. We can again assume that $x_1 \le x_2 \le \cdots \le x_N$. By the mean-value theorem for integrals, we have

$$\int_0^1 f(u) \, du = \sum_{n=1}^{N} \int_{(n-1)/N}^{n/N} f(u) \, du = \frac{1}{N} \sum_{n=1}^{N} f(t_n)$$

with $(n-1)/N < t_n < n/N$. Therefore

$$\frac{1}{N} \sum_{n=1}^{N} f(x_n) - \int_0^1 f(u) \, du = \frac{1}{N} \sum_{n=1}^{N} \left(f(x_n) - f(t_n) \right).$$

Now $|x_n - t_n| \le D_N^*(x_1, \ldots, x_N)$ for $1 \le n \le N$ by Theorem 2.6, and the result follows. □

To extend Koksma's inequality to the multidimensional case, an appropriate concept of total variation for functions of several variables is needed. For a function f on $\bar{I}^s$ and a subinterval J of $\bar{I}^s$, let $\Delta(f; J)$ be an alternating sum of the values of f at the vertices of J (i.e., function values at adjacent vertices have opposite signs). The *variation of f on $\bar{I}^s$ in the sense of Vitali* is defined by

$$V^{(s)}(f) = \sup_{\mathcal{P}} \sum_{J \in \mathcal{P}} |\Delta(f; J)|,$$

where the supremum is extended over all partitions $\mathcal{P}$ of $\bar{I}^s$ into subintervals. The more convenient formula

(2.5)
$$V^{(s)}(f) = \int_0^1 \cdots \int_0^1 \left| \frac{\partial^s f}{\partial u_1 \cdots \partial u_s} \right| du_1 \cdots du_s$$

holds whenever the indicated partial derivative is continuous on $\bar{I}^s$. For $1 \le k \le s$ and $1 \le i_1 < i_2 < \cdots < i_k \le s$, let $V^{(k)}(f; i_1, \ldots, i_k)$ be the variation in the sense of Vitali of the restriction of f to the k-dimensional face $\{(u_1, \ldots, u_s) \in \bar{I}^s : u_j = 1 \text{ for } j \ne i_1, \ldots, i_k\}$. Then

$$V(f) = \sum_{k=1}^{s} \sum_{1 \le i_1 < i_2 < \cdots < i_k \le s} V^{(k)}(f; i_1, \ldots, i_k)$$

is called the *variation of f on $\bar{I}^s$ in the sense of Hardy and Krause*, and f is of bounded variation in this sense if $V(f)$ is finite. With this notion of variation, we have the following inequality of Hlawka [134], which is often called the *Koksma–Hlawka inequality*. We again put $I^s = [0,1)^s$.

THEOREM 2.11. *If f has bounded variation $V(f)$ on $\bar{I}^s$ in the sense of Hardy and Krause, then, for any $\mathbf{x}_1, \ldots, \mathbf{x}_N \in I^s$, we have*

$$\left| \frac{1}{N} \sum_{n=1}^{N} f(\mathbf{x}_n) - \int_{\bar{I}^s} f(\mathbf{u})\, d\mathbf{u} \right| \leq V(f) D_N^*(\mathbf{x}_1, \ldots, \mathbf{x}_N).$$

THEOREM 2.12. *For any $\mathbf{x}_1, \ldots, \mathbf{x}_N \in I^s$ and any $\varepsilon > 0$, there exists a function $f \in C^\infty(\bar{I}^s)$ with $V(f) = 1$ and*

$$\left| \frac{1}{N} \sum_{n=1}^{N} f(\mathbf{x}_n) - \int_{\bar{I}^s} f(\mathbf{u})\, d\mathbf{u} \right| > D_N^*(\mathbf{x}_1, \ldots, \mathbf{x}_N) - \varepsilon.$$

Proof. By the definition of $D_N^*(P) = D_N^*(\mathbf{x}_1, \ldots, \mathbf{x}_N)$, there exists an interval $J = \prod_{i=1}^{s} [0, v_i)$ with $0 < v_i \leq 1$ for $1 \leq i \leq s$ and

$$\left| \frac{A(J; P)}{N} - \lambda_s(J) \right| > D_N^*(P) - \frac{\varepsilon}{2}.$$

Furthermore, there exists an interval $K = \prod_{i=1}^{s} [0, t_i]$ with $0 \leq t_i < v_i$ and $v_i - t_i < \varepsilon/(2s)$ for $1 \leq i \leq s$ such that $J \smallsetminus K$ does not contain any point $\mathbf{x}_n$. For any given $0 \leq t < v \leq 1$, we can construct a nonincreasing function $f_{t,v} \in C^\infty([0,1])$ with $f_{t,v}(u) = 1$ for $0 \leq u \leq t$ and $f_{t,v}(u) = 0$ for $v \leq u \leq 1$. Then

$$f(\mathbf{u}) = f(u_1, \ldots, u_s) = \prod_{i=1}^{s} f_{t_i, v_i}(u_i)$$

is a function in $C^\infty(\bar{I}^s)$ with $0 \leq f(\mathbf{u}) \leq 1$ for all $\mathbf{u} \in \bar{I}^s$, $f(\mathbf{u}) = 1$ for $\mathbf{u} \in K$, and $f(\mathbf{u}) = 0$ for $\mathbf{u} \notin J$. From (2.5) we obtain $V^{(s)}(f) = 1$. Since $f(\mathbf{u}) = 0$ whenever one of the coordinates of $\mathbf{u}$ is 1, we have $V^{(k)}(f; i_1, \ldots, i_k) = 0$ whenever $1 \leq k < s$. Altogether, we obtain $V(f) = 1$. It is clear that

$$\frac{1}{N} \sum_{n=1}^{N} f(\mathbf{x}_n) = \frac{A(J; P)}{N}.$$

and that

$$\lambda_s(K) \leq \int_{\bar{I}^s} f(\mathbf{u})\, d\mathbf{u} \leq \lambda_s(J).$$

Since $\lambda_s(J) - \lambda_s(K) \leq \sum_{i=1}^{s} (v_i - t_i) < \varepsilon/2$, it follows that

$$\left| \frac{1}{N} \sum_{n=1}^{N} f(\mathbf{x}_n) - \int_{\bar{I}^s} f(\mathbf{u})\, d\mathbf{u} \right| > \left| \frac{A(J; P)}{N} - \lambda_s(J) \right| - \frac{\varepsilon}{2} > D_N^*(P) - \varepsilon. \qquad \square$$

There is also a multidimensional version of Theorem 2.10. For a continuous function f on $\bar{I}^s$, we define its *modulus of continuity* by

(2.6) $\omega(f; t) = \sup\limits_{\substack{\mathbf{u}, \mathbf{v} \in \bar{I}^s \\ \|\mathbf{u}-\mathbf{v}\| \leq t}} |f(\mathbf{u}) - f(\mathbf{v})|$ for $t \geq 0$,

where $\|\mathbf{u}\| = \max_{1 \leq i \leq s} |u_i|$ for $\mathbf{u} = (u_1, \ldots, u_s) \in \mathbb{R}^s$. The following bound is due to Proinov [288].

THEOREM 2.13. *If f is continuous on $\bar{I}^s$, then, for any $\mathbf{x}_1, \ldots, \mathbf{x}_N \in \bar{I}^s$, we have*

$$\left| \frac{1}{N} \sum_{n=1}^{N} f(\mathbf{x}_n) - \int_{\bar{I}^s} f(\mathbf{u}) \, d\mathbf{u} \right| \leq 4\omega(f; D_N^*(\mathbf{x}_1, \ldots, \mathbf{x}_N)^{1/s}).$$

The error bounds given already in this section all lead to the same conclusion, namely, that point sets with small star discrepancy guarantee small errors in quasi-Monte Carlo integration over $\bar{I}^s$. Constructions of such point sets will be discussed in detail in the following chapters.

We now consider more general bounded integration domains. By applying, if necessary, a translation and a contraction, we can assume that such an integration domain B is contained in $\bar{I}^s$. We have already seen in (1.10) what the quasi-Monte Carlo approximation looks like in this case. For convex integration domains, the following error bound in terms of the isotropic discrepancy was proved by Zaremba [364].

THEOREM 2.14. *If $B \subseteq \bar{I}^s$ is convex and f has bounded variation $V(f)$ on $\bar{I}^s$ in the sense of Hardy and Krause, then, for any point set P consisting of $\mathbf{x}_1, \ldots, \mathbf{x}_N \in I^s$, we have*

$$\left| \frac{1}{N} \sum_{\substack{n=1 \\ \mathbf{x}_n \in B}}^{N} f(\mathbf{x}_n) - \int_B f(\mathbf{u}) \, d\mathbf{u} \right| \leq (V(f) + |f(1, \ldots, 1)|) J_N(P).$$

The most general situation that we consider is where B belongs to a family $\mathcal{M}_b$ of Jordan-measurable sets introduced in §2.1. The following theorem is an improvement by de Clerck [54] on a result of Niederreiter [219].

THEOREM 2.15. *If $B \in \mathcal{M}_b$ and f has bounded variation $V(f)$ on $\bar{I}^s$ in the sense of Hardy and Krause, then, for any point set P consisting of $\mathbf{x}_1, \ldots, \mathbf{x}_N \in I^s$, we have*

$$\left| \frac{1}{N} \sum_{\substack{n=1 \\ \mathbf{x}_n \in B}}^{N} f(\mathbf{x}_n) - \int_B f(\mathbf{u}) \, d\mathbf{u} \right| \leq (V(f) + |f(1, \ldots, 1)|) D_N(\mathcal{M}_b; P).$$

The term $|f(1, \ldots, 1)|$ is needed in the inequalities in Theorems 2.14 and 2.15 because without this term the bounds would fail to hold even for constant functions f.

Notes.

The notion of discrepancy was first studied in its own right by Bergström [24], but the applications to numerical analysis became apparent only after the later work of Koksma [155]. The use of the isotropic discrepancy was suggested by Hlawka [136]. The discrepancies $D_N(\mathcal{M}_b; P)$ were introduced by Niederreiter [219]. If, instead of the maximum deviation between the empirical distribution and the uniform distribution, we consider the mean-square deviation, then the L^2 discrepancy is obtained, and, more generally, an L^p discrepancy may be defined for $1 \leq p < \infty$. Discrepancies for point sets with nonequal weights and for nonuniform distributions have also been studied. See Niederreiter [225] for a survey of various notions of discrepancy and Niederreiter and Tichy [274], Niederreiter, Tichy, and Turnwald [277], Proinov [283], [285], [289], and Tichy [348] for more recent literature.

Apart from various types of discrepancy, there are other quantities measuring the irregularity of distribution of point sets, for instance, the *nonuniformity* due to Sobol' [322] (see also Niederreiter [225, §2]) and the *diaphony* introduced by Zinterhof [369] (see also Zinterhof and Stegbuchner [371]).

Multidimensional analogues of Theorems 2.6 and 2.7 are not easy to obtain. Partial results are given in Niederreiter [217] and de Clerck [55], [56]. For two-dimensional point sets with no repeated coordinates, de Clerck [56] established an explicit formula for the star discrepancy. The problem of calculating the isotropic discrepancy was considered by Niederreiter [217] and Zaremba [367]. An example of Zaremba [362] shows that the exponent $1/s$ in the inequality $J_N(P) \leq 4s D_N(P)^{1/s}$ is the best possible.

A proof of Theorem 2.11 different from that of Hlawka [134] can be found in Kuipers and Niederreiter [163, Chap. 2]. Theorem 2.12 is due to Niederreiter [234]. Versions of Theorem 2.13 with 4 replaced by larger constants were proved by Hlawka [137] and Shi [310], [311]; according to Proinov [288], the constant 4 cannot, in general, be replaced by a constant < 1. The paper of Hlawka [137] also contains an error bound for arbitrary Riemann-integrable functions; for the case where $s = 1$, see also Proinov [284]. A survey of further error bounds can be found in Niederreiter [225, §2]. A number of more recent papers have dealt with error bounds for integration rules with general weights in terms of an appropriate discrepancy; see Niederreiter and Tichy [274], Proinov [283], [284], [286], [287], [288], [289], and Totkov [353]. A variant of Koksma's inequality was shown by Horbowicz [142]. Integration rules involving values of derivatives of the integrand have also been considered, and error bounds in terms of suitable discrepancies were established; see Proinov [286], [287], [289], Proinov and Kirov [290], and Stegbuchner [334].

Since it is often difficult to obtain the exact value of the variation $V(f)$, a discretization scheme for the approximate calculation of $V(f)$ described in Niederreiter [237] can be useful in practice. Upper bounds for $V(f)$ are presented in Blümlinger and Tichy [29], Hua and Wang [145, Chap. 5], and Tichy [349].

The notion of discrepancy plays a central role in the theory of quasi-Monte Carlo methods and is also important for the theoretical analysis of pseudorandom numbers, as will become apparent in later chapters. Various types of discrepancy have also found useful applications in a wide range of other areas, such as the combinatorial theory of irregularities of partitions (Beck [18], Sós [332]), geometry (Laczkovich [164], Linhart [194]), statistics (Gyires [120], [121]), approximation theory (Proinov [286], [287]), stochastic algorithms (Lapeyre, Pagès, and Sab [170]), and cryptology (Niederreiter and Schnorr [270]).

CHAPTER 3

Low-Discrepancy Point Sets and Sequences

The error analysis for quasi-Monte Carlo integration in §2.2 has demonstrated that small errors are guaranteed if point sets with small star or extreme discrepancy are used. This is true not only for the normalized integration domain $\bar{I}^s$, but also for integration domains contained in $\bar{I}^s$, since the discrepancies occurring in the inequalities in Theorems 2.14 and 2.15 can be bounded in terms of the extreme discrepancy by results in §2.1. A point set P consisting of N elements of $\bar{I}^s$ is informally called a *low-discrepancy point set* if $D_N^*(P)$ or $D_N(P)$ is small. In the computational practice of quasi-Monte Carlo integration, it is often convenient to be able to change the value of N without losing the previously calculated function values. For this purpose, it is recommended to work with a sequence of nodes and then to take its first N terms whenever a value of N has been selected. In this way, N can be increased while all data from the earlier computation can still be used. The desirable notion in this connection is that of a *low-discrepancy sequence*, which is informally defined as a sequence S of elements of $\bar{I}^s$ for which $D_N^*(S)$ or $D_N(S)$ is small for all $N \geq 1$.

In this chapter, we initiate the study of low-discrepancy point sets and sequences (some authors speak of *quasirandom points* and *quasirandom sequences*, respectively). Further information on this topic can also be found in later chapters. In §3.1 we review some classical constructions of low-discrepancy point sets and sequences. Several general principles for obtaining upper and lower bounds for the discrepancy are presented in §3.2.

3.1. Classical constructions.

In the one-dimensional case, it is easy to determine the minimum of the star discrepancy $D_N^*(x_1, \ldots, x_N)$ and of the discrepancy $D_N(x_1, \ldots, x_N)$ if N is fixed. In fact, it follows from Theorem 2.6 that we always have

$$D_N^*(x_1, \ldots, x_N) \geq \frac{1}{2N},$$

and equality holds if $x_n = (2n-1)/(2N)$ for $1 \leq n \leq N$. The quasi-Monte Carlo approximation

$$\int_0^1 f(u)\, du \approx \frac{1}{N} \sum_{n=1}^N f\left(\frac{2n-1}{2N}\right)$$

with these nodes is a classical integration rule, namely, the N-panel midpoint rule for the interval $[0,1]$. Similarly, Theorem 2.7 shows that we always have

$$D_N(x_1,\ldots,x_N) \geq \frac{1}{N}$$

and that equality holds if $x_n = (2n-1)/(2N)$ for $1 \leq n \leq N$.

While $D_N(P) = O(N^{-1})$ is possible for N-element point sets P from $[0,1]$, there is no sequence S of elements of $[0,1]$ for which $D_N(S) = O(N^{-1})$ for all $N \geq 1$. On the contrary, we have the phenomenon of *irregularities of distribution*, according to which the discrepancy $D_N(S)$ is infinitely often of a larger order of magnitude. Concretely, we have a result of Schmidt [303], which says that there exists an absolute constant $c > 0$ such that, for any sequence S of elements of $[0,1]$, we have

$$D_N(S) \geq cN^{-1} \log N \qquad \text{for infinitely many } N.$$

Currently, the best value of c is $c = 0.12$ (see Béjian [22]). In view of Proposition 2.4, we obtain that, for any sequence S of elements of $[0,1]$, we have

$$D_N^*(S) \geq (0.06)N^{-1} \log N \qquad \text{for infinitely many } N.$$

Thus, for low-discrepancy sequences in the one-dimensional case, we cannot expect anything better than $D_N^*(S) = O(N^{-1} \log N)$ for all $N \geq 2$. This order of magnitude can indeed be achieved by several constructions. Although quasi-Monte Carlo methods are not so important in the one-dimensional case (classical integration rules are to be preferred for dimension $s = 1$), we discuss two constructions of one-dimensional low-discrepancy sequences, since these constructions form the basis for the extension to the multidimensional case.

For an integer $b \geq 2$, we put $Z_b = \{0,1,\ldots,b-1\}$; i.e., Z_b is the least residue system mod b. Every integer $n \geq 0$ has a unique digit expansion

$$(3.1) \qquad\qquad n = \sum_{j=0}^{\infty} a_j(n)b^j$$

in base b, where $a_j(n) \in Z_b$ for all $j \geq 0$ and $a_j(n) = 0$ for all sufficiently large j; i.e., the sum in (3.1) is actually finite.

DEFINITION 3.1. For an integer $b \geq 2$, the *radical-inverse function* ϕ_b in base b is defined by

$$\phi_b(n) = \sum_{j=0}^{\infty} a_j(n)b^{-j-1} \qquad \text{for all integers } n \geq 0,$$

where n is given by its digit expansion (3.1) in base b.

Thus $\phi_b(n)$ is obtained from n by a symmetric reflection of the expansion (3.1) in the "decimal point." Note that $\phi_b(n) \in I := [0,1)$ for all $n \geq 0$. In the construction of many low-discrepancy sequences, we find it convenient to index the terms by $n = 0, 1, \ldots$. In particular, in our constructions of one-dimensional low-discrepancy sequences S, we denote the terms by $x_0, x_1, \ldots$. Accordingly, we then write

$$D_N(S) = D_N(x_0, x_1, \ldots, x_{N-1})$$

for the discrepancy of the first N terms of S, and similarly for the star discrepancy.

DEFINITION 3.2. For an integer $b \geq 2$, the *van der Corput sequence in base* b is the sequence $x_0, x_1, \ldots$ with $x_n = \phi_b(n)$ for all $n \geq 0$.

If S_b is the van der Corput sequence in base b, then $D_N^*(S_b) = O(N^{-1} \log N)$ for all $N \geq 2$ with an implied constant depending only on b. This follows from a more general result shown in Theorem 3.6 below. Faure [94] established the following more precise asymptotic result:

$$\varlimsup_{N \to \infty} \frac{N D_N^*(S_b)}{\log N} = \varlimsup_{N \to \infty} \frac{N D_N(S_b)}{\log N} = \begin{cases} \dfrac{b^2}{4(b+1) \log b} & \text{for even } b, \\[3ex] \dfrac{b-1}{4 \log b} & \text{for odd } b. \end{cases}$$

Consequently, S_3 is asymptotically the best van der Corput sequence. The case where $b = 2$ is of historical interest, since S_2 is the sequence that was originally introduced by van der Corput [356]. In this case, Béjian and Faure [23] proved that

$$N D_N^*(S_2) = N D_N(S_2) \leq \frac{\log N}{\log 8} + 1 \quad \text{for all } N \geq 1$$

and

$$\varlimsup_{N \to \infty} \left(N D_N(S_2) - \frac{\log N}{\log 8} \right) = \frac{4}{9} + \frac{\log 3}{\log 8}.$$

Further improvements in terms of the asymptotic behavior of the discrepancy are obtained by considering a *generalized van der Corput sequence in base* b, which is defined by

$$x_n = \sum_{j=0}^{\infty} \sigma\left(a_j(n)\right) b^{-j-1} \quad \text{for all } n \geq 0,$$

where n is given by (3.1) and σ is a permutation of Z_b. This sequence can also be generated recursively by

$$x_0 = \frac{\sigma(0)}{b-1}, \quad x_{bn+r} = \frac{1}{b}(x_n + \sigma(r)) \quad \text{for } n \geq 0 \text{ and } 0 \leq r \leq b - 1.$$

Currently, the best choice of parameters is that found by Faure [100], who used $b = 36$ and a specific permutation σ of Z_{36} and showed that the resulting generalized van der Corput sequence S satisfies

$$\varlimsup_{N \to \infty} \frac{N D_N(S)}{\log N} = \frac{23}{35 \log 6} = 0.366 \ldots .$$

At this time, this is the sequence that yields the smallest value of the limit superior on the left-hand side for any known sequence of elements of $[0,1]$. For the star discrepancy, the current "record holder" is a generalized van der Corput sequence S^* in base 12 constructed by Faure [94], which satisfies

$$\overline{\lim_{N\to\infty}} \frac{ND_N^*(S^*)}{\log N} = \frac{1919}{3454\log 12} = 0.223\ldots .$$

Another class of one-dimensional low-discrepancy sequences is obtained by considering the multiples of suitable irrational numbers modulo 1. For $u \in \mathbb{R}$ let $\{u\} = u - \lfloor u \rfloor$ be the *fractional part* of u. Note that $\{u\} \in I$ always. For an irrational number z, let $S(z)$ be the sequence $x_0, x_1, \ldots$ with

$$x_n = \{nz\} \quad \text{for all } n \geq 0.$$

Let

$$z = [a_0; a_1, a_2, \ldots]$$

be the continued fraction expansion of z, with partial quotients $a_0, a_1, \ldots \in \mathbb{Z}$ and $a_i \geq 1$ for $i \geq 1$ (compare with Appendix B for a background on continued fractions). The denominators of the convergents to z are denoted by $q_0, q_1, \ldots$.

THEOREM 3.3. *Let z be irrational and $N \geq 1$. Then N can be represented in the form*

$$N = \sum_{i=0}^{l(N)} c_i q_i,$$

where $l(N)$ is the unique nonnegative integer with $q_{l(N)} \leq N < q_{l(N)+1}$ and where the c_i are integers with $0 \leq c_i \leq a_{i+1}$ for $0 \leq i \leq l(N)$. Furthermore, we have

$$D_N(S(z)) < \frac{1}{N} \sum_{\substack{i=0 \\ c_i \neq 0}}^{l(N)} (c_i + 1) \leq \frac{1}{N} \sum_{i=1}^{l(N)+1} a_i.$$

Proof. Since $1 = q_0 \leq q_1 < q_2 < \cdots$, the existence and uniqueness of $l(N)$ is guaranteed. Now we can write $N = c_{l(N)} q_{l(N)} + r$ with integers $c_{l(N)} \geq 1$ and $0 \leq r < q_{l(N)}$. If we had $c_{l(N)} > a_{l(N)+1}$, then

$$N \geq c_{l(N)} q_{l(N)} \geq a_{l(N)+1} q_{l(N)} + q_{l(N)} \geq q_{l(N)+1},$$

a contradiction. Thus $c_{l(N)} \leq a_{l(N)+1}$. If $r > 0$, then we apply this procedure to r instead of N, and, continuing in this manner, we arrive at the desired representation for N.

Given this representation, we decompose the point set $S_N(z)$ consisting of the first N terms of $S(z)$ into blocks of consecutive terms, namely, c_i blocks of length q_i for $0 \leq i \leq l(N)$. Consider such a block of length q_i for fixed i; it is a point set P_i consisting of the fractional parts $\{nz\}$, $n = n_i, n_i+1, \ldots, n_i+q_i-1$, for some integer $n_i \geq 0$. Let p_i/q_i be the ith convergent to z. Then, from the theory of continued fractions,

$$z = \frac{p_i}{q_i} + \frac{\delta_i}{q_i q_{i+1}} \quad \text{with } |\delta_i| < 1.$$

Thus, if $n = n_i + j$, $j \in Z_{q_i}$, as above, then we obtain

$$\{nz\} = \left\{ \frac{jp_i}{q_i} + n_i z + \frac{j\delta_i}{q_i q_{i+1}} \right\}.$$

Since $\gcd(p_i, q_i) = 1$, the fractional parts $\{jp_i/q_i + n_i z\}$, $j \in Z_{q_i}$, form a point set Q_i of q_i equidistant points in I with distance $1/q_i$, and these points have discrepancy $1/q_i$ by Theorem 2.7. Because

$$\left| \frac{j\delta_i}{q_i q_{i+1}} \right| < \frac{1}{q_{i+1}} \quad \text{for } j \in Z_{q_i},$$

the point set P_i is obtained by displacing modulo 1 the elements of Q_i in one direction (which depends only on the sign of δ_i) by distances $< 1/q_{i+1}$. Therefore

$$D_{q_i}(P_i) < \frac{1}{q_i} + \frac{1}{q_{i+1}}.$$

From the triangle inequality for discrepancies (see [163, p. 115]) and the way in which we decomposed $S_N(z)$, it follows that

$$ND_N(S(z)) < \sum_{i=0}^{l(N)} c_i \left(1 + \frac{q_i}{q_{i+1}} \right) \leq \sum_{\substack{i=0 \\ c_i \neq 0}}^{l(N)} \left(c_i + \frac{a_{i+1} q_i}{q_{i+1}} \right) \leq \sum_{\substack{i=0 \\ c_i \neq 0}}^{l(N)} (c_i + 1),$$

which is the first bound for $D_N(S(z))$ in the theorem. The second bound is deduced from two properties of the coefficients c_i obtained by the algorithm at the beginning of the proof, namely, that $c_0 < q_1 = a_1$ and that $c_i = a_{i+1}$ implies $c_{i-1} = 0$. To prove the second property, we note that, if $q_i \leq N < q_{i+1}$ and $c_i = a_{i+1}$, then $N - c_i q_i = N - a_{i+1} q_i < q_{i+1} - a_{i+1} q_i = q_{i-1}$. $\square$

COROLLARY 3.4. *If the irrational z is such that $\sum_{i=1}^{m} a_i = O(m)$, then $D_N(S(z)) = O(N^{-1} \log N)$ for all $N \geq 2$.*

Proof. Theorem 3.3 and the hypothesis imply $D_N(S(z)) = O(N^{-1}(l(N) + 1))$. Induction shows that $q_i \geq \alpha^{i-1}$ for all $i \geq 0$, where $\alpha = (1 + \sqrt{5})/2$. Thus $N \geq q_{l(N)} \geq \alpha^{l(N)-1}$, and the desired bound follows. $\square$

Theorem 3.3 and Corollary 3.4 show that $S(z)$ is a low-discrepancy sequence if the partial quotients a_i, $i \geq 1$, in the continued fraction expansion of z are small. The following is a particularly interesting special case.

COROLLARY 3.5. *If the irrational z is such that there exists a positive integer K with $a_i \leq K$ for all $i \geq 1$, then*

$$D_N(S(z)) < G(K)N^{-1} \log(N+1) \quad \text{for all } N \geq 1,$$

where $G(K) = 2/\log 2$ for $K = 1, 2, 3$ and $G(K) = (K+1)/\log(K+1)$ for $K \geq 4$.

Proof. In view of Theorem 3.3, it suffices to show that

$$(3.2) \qquad s(N) := \sum_{\substack{i=0 \\ c_i \neq 0}}^{l(N)} (c_i + 1) \leq G(K) \log(N+1) \qquad \text{for all } N \geq 1.$$

Here $s(N)$ is well defined if we use the coefficients c_i produced by the algorithm at the beginning of the proof of Theorem 3.3. We establish (3.2) by induction on the value of $l(N)$. If $q_0 < q_1$, then the least possible value of $l(N)$ is zero, and a corresponding N satisfies $1 \leq N < q_1 \leq K$. If $q_0 = q_1 = 1$, then the least possible value of $l(N)$ is 1, and a corresponding N satisfies $1 \leq N \leq q_2 - 1 \leq K$. Since $s(N) = N + 1$ for these N, it suffices to show, for the first step in the induction, that

$$(3.3) \qquad\qquad N + 1 \leq G(K) \log(N+1) \qquad \text{for } 1 \leq N \leq K.$$

This follows readily from the definition of $G(K)$, however. Now consider an arbitrary l with $q_l > 1$ and a corresponding N with $l(N) = l$, hence with $q_l \leq N < q_{l+1}$. We write $N = c_l q_l + r$ with $0 \leq r < q_l$. Then $s(N) = c_l + 1 + s(r)$, and the induction hypothesis yields

$$s(N) \leq c_l + 1 + G(K) \log(r+1),$$

which also holds for $r = 0$. Now $N + 1 = c_l q_l + r + 1 \geq (c_l + 1)(r + 1)$ and $1 \leq c_l \leq a_{l+1} \leq K$. Thus, by (3.3),

$$s(N) \leq G(K) \log(c_l + 1) + G(K) \log(r+1) \leq G(K) \log(N+1),$$

and (3.2) is shown. $\square$

The sequences $S(z)$ have an obvious analogue in the multidimensional case $s \geq 2$. We first define the *fractional part* of $\mathbf{u} = (u_1, \dots, u_s) \in \mathbb{R}^s$ by

$$\{\mathbf{u}\} = (\{u_1\}, \dots, \{u_s\}) \in I^s = [0,1)^s.$$

Now let $\mathbf{z} = (z_1, \dots, z_s) \in \mathbb{R}^s$ be such that $1, z_1, \dots, z_s$ are linearly independent over the rationals, and let $S(\mathbf{z})$ be the sequence $\mathbf{x}_0, \mathbf{x}_1, \dots$ with

$$\mathbf{x}_n = \{n\mathbf{z}\} \qquad \text{for all } n \geq 0.$$

Then, by a classical result [163, p. 48], the sequence $S(\mathbf{z})$ is uniformly distributed in $\bar{I}^s$. For the discrepancy of $S(\mathbf{z})$, there is a probabilistic result of Schmidt [302] to the effect that, for every $\varepsilon > 0$, we have $D_N(S(\mathbf{z})) = O\big(N^{-1}(1 + \log N)^{s+1+\varepsilon}\big)$ for λ_s-almost all $\mathbf{z} \in \mathbb{R}^s$. For $s \geq 2$, no individual $\mathbf{z} \in \mathbb{R}^s$ with $D_N(S(\mathbf{z})) = O\big(N^{-1}(1 + \log N)^{s+1}\big)$ is known. If the coordinates of $\mathbf{z} \in \mathbb{R}^s$ are algebraic numbers satisfying the linear independence condition stated above, then $D_N(S(\mathbf{z})) = O(N^{-1+\varepsilon})$ for every $\varepsilon > 0$ by a result of Niederreiter [218]. Point sets that can be viewed as discrete versions of the sequences $S(\mathbf{z})$ will be discussed in §5.1.

A more satisfactory way of producing low-discrepancy sequences in any dimension is obtained by extending the notion of a van der Corput sequence introduced in Definition 3.2. This leads to the family of *Halton sequences*. For a given dimension $s \geq 1$, let $b_1, \ldots, b_s$ be integers ≥ 2. Then, using the radical-inverse functions ϕ_b in Definition 3.1, we define the *Halton sequence in the bases* $b_1, \ldots, b_s$ as the sequence $\mathbf{x}_0, \mathbf{x}_1, \ldots$ with

$$\mathbf{x}_n = (\phi_{b_1}(n), \ldots, \phi_{b_s}(n)) \in I^s \quad \text{for all } n \geq 0.$$

For $s = 1$ this definition reduces to that of a van der Corput sequence.

THEOREM 3.6. *If S is the Halton sequence in the pairwise relatively prime bases $b_1, \ldots, b_s$, then*

$$D_N^*(S) < \frac{s}{N} + \frac{1}{N} \prod_{i=1}^{s} \left(\frac{b_i - 1}{2 \log b_i} \log N + \frac{b_i + 1}{2} \right) \quad \text{for all } N \geq 1.$$

Proof. Fix $N \geq 1$ and write $D(J) = A(J; S_N) - N\lambda_s(J)$ for an interval $J \subseteq I^s$, where S_N is the point set consisting of the first N terms of the Halton sequence. For $1 \leq i \leq s$ and an integer $e \geq 0$, let $\mathcal{E}_i(e)$ be the family of all intervals $[0, ab_i^{-e})$ with $a \in \mathbb{Z}$, $0 < a \leq b_i^e$, and let $\mathcal{F}_i(e)$ be the family of all intervals $[cb_i^{-f}, (c+1)b_i^{-f})$ with $c, f \in \mathbb{Z}$ satisfying $0 \leq f \leq e$ and $0 \leq c < b_i^f$. For integers $e_1, \ldots, e_s \geq 0$, let $\mathcal{E}(e_1, \ldots, e_s)$ be the family of all intervals $E = \prod_{i=1}^{s} E_i$ with $E_i \in \mathcal{E}_i(e_i) \cup \mathcal{F}_i(e_i)$ for $1 \leq i \leq s$. We claim that

(3.4)

$$|D(E)| \leq \prod_{\substack{i=1 \\ E_i \notin \mathcal{F}_i(e_i)}}^{s} \left(\frac{1}{2}(b_i - 1)e_i + 1 \right) \quad \text{for all } E = \prod_{i=1}^{s} E_i \in \mathcal{E}(e_1, \ldots, e_s),$$

where an empty product is meant to be 1. We prove (3.4) by induction on the number k of indices i for which $E_i \notin \mathcal{F}_i(e_i)$.

First, let $k = 0$, i.e., $E = \prod_{i=1}^{s}[c_i b_i^{-f_i}, (c_i + 1)b_i^{-f_i})$ with $c_i, f_i \in \mathbb{Z}$, $0 \leq f_i \leq e_i$, $0 \leq c_i < b_i^{f_i}$ for $1 \leq i \leq s$. Note that

$$\mathbf{x}_n = (\phi_{b_1}(n), \ldots, \phi_{b_s}(n)) \in E$$

if and only if, for $1 \leq i \leq s$, the first f_i digits (in base b_i) of $\phi_{b_i}(n)$ after the "decimal point" have certain prescribed values. Equivalently, for $1 \leq i \leq s$, the f_i least significant digits of n in base b_i must have certain prescribed values, or in other words, n must lie in a prescribed residue class mod $b_i^{f_i}$. Since $b_1, \ldots, b_s$ are pairwise relatively prime, it follows from the Chinese remainder theorem that the last condition is equivalent to n lying in a prescribed residue class mod $m = b_1^{f_1} \cdots b_s^{f_s}$. Consequently, among any m consecutive terms of S, exactly one of them lies in E. This implies that $|D(E)| \leq 1$.

Now suppose that for some $k \geq 1$ the claim has been established for $k - 1$, and consider $E = \prod_{i=1}^{s} E_i \in \mathcal{E}(e_1, \ldots, e_s)$, where we assume without loss of generality that $E_i \notin \mathcal{F}_i(e_i)$ for $1 \le i \le k$ and $E_i \in \mathcal{F}_i(e_i)$ for $k+1 \le i \le s$. Then $E_1 = [0, ab_1^{-e_1})$ for some $a \in \mathbb{Z}$, $0 < a < b_1^{e_1}$. Let

$$ab_1^{-e_1} = \sum_{j=1}^{e_1} d_j b_1^{-j}$$

be the digit expansion in base b_1. Then E_1 can be written as the disjoint union of d_1 intervals in $\mathcal{F}_1(e_1)$ of length b_1^{-1}, of d_2 intervals in $\mathcal{F}_1(e_1)$ of length b_1^{-2}, and so on. Thus

$$E_1 = \bigcup_{r=1}^{d} F_r$$

with pairwise disjoint $F_r \in \mathcal{F}_1(e_1)$ for $1 \le r \le d := \sum_{j=1}^{e_1} d_j$, and so E is the disjoint union

$$E = \bigcup_{r=1}^{d} (F_r \times E_2 \times \cdots \times E_s).$$

It follows that

$$(3.5) \quad |D(E)| \le \sum_{r=1}^{d} |D(F_r \times E_2 \times \cdots \times E_s)| \le d \prod_{i=2}^{k} \left(\frac{1}{2}(b_i - 1)e_i + 1 \right),$$

where in the second inequality we applied the induction hypothesis. With $G = [ab_1^{-e_1}, 1)$, we have $E_1 = [0, 1) \setminus G$; thus

$$|D(E)| \le |D([0,1) \times E_2 \times \cdots \times E_s)| + |D(G \times E_2 \times \cdots \times E_s)|$$

$$\le \prod_{i=2}^{k} \left(\frac{1}{2}(b_i - 1)e_i + 1 \right) + |D(G \times E_2 \times \cdots \times E_s)|.$$

Now G can be written as the disjoint union of $(b_1 - 1)e_1 - d + 1$ intervals in $\mathcal{F}_1(e_1)$; hence

$$|D(E)| \le ((b_1 - 1)e_1 - d + 2) \prod_{i=2}^{k} \left(\frac{1}{2}(b_i - 1)e_i + 1 \right).$$

Adding this inequality to (3.5) and dividing by 2, we get (3.4) for the value k.

Now let $J = \prod_{i=1}^{s} [0, u_i) \subseteq I^s$ be arbitrary. For $1 \le i \le s$, let e_i be the least integer with $b_i^{e_i} \ge N$ and let a_i be the least integer with $a_i b_i^{-e_i} \ge u_i$. Put $E = \prod_{i=1}^{s} [0, a_i b_i^{-e_i})$. Since the ith coordinates of all points of S_N are rationals with denominator $b_i^{e_i}$, we have $A(J; S_N) = A(E; S_N)$. Furthermore, we have $E \in \mathcal{E}(e_1, \dots, e_s)$, and so

$$|D(J)| \le N (\lambda_s(E) - \lambda_s(J)) + |D(E)|$$

$$\le N \sum_{i=1}^{s} b_i^{-e_i} + |D(E)| \le s + |D(E)|$$

$$\le s + \prod_{i=1}^{s} \left(\frac{1}{2}(b_i - 1)e_i + 1 \right)$$

by (3.4). To finish the proof, note that $e_i < 1 + (\log N)/(\log b_i)$ for $1 \leq i \leq s$. $\square$

For a dimension $s \geq 2$ and for integers $N \geq 1$ and $b_1, \ldots, b_{s-1} \geq 2$, the *N-element Hammersley point set in the bases* $b_1, \ldots, b_{s-1}$ is given by

$$\mathbf{x}_n = \left(\frac{n}{N}, \phi_{b_1}(n), \ldots, \phi_{b_{s-1}}(n) \right) \in I^s \quad \text{for } n = 0, 1, \ldots, N-1.$$

A bound for the star discrepancy of this point set is obtained from the following general principle.

LEMMA 3.7. *For $s \geq 2$, let S be an arbitrary sequence of points* $\mathbf{x}_0, \mathbf{x}_1, \ldots$ *in I^{s-1}. For $N \geq 1$, let P be the point set consisting of $(n/N, \mathbf{x}_n) \in I^s$ for $n = 0, 1, \ldots, N-1$. Then*

$$N D_N^*(P) \leq \max_{1 \leq M \leq N} M D_M^*(S) + 1.$$

Proof. For an arbitrary $J = \prod_{i=1}^{s}[0, u_i) \subseteq I^s$, we have $(n/N, \mathbf{x}_n) \in J$ if and only if $\mathbf{x}_n \in J' := \prod_{i=2}^{s}[0, u_i)$ and $n < Nu_1$. If M is the largest integer $< Nu_1 + 1$, then $A(J; P) = A(J'; S_M)$, where S_M is the point set consisting of the first M terms of S. Therefore

$$|A(J; P) - N\lambda_s(J)| \leq |A(J'; S_M) - M\lambda_{s-1}(J')| + |M\lambda_{s-1}(J') - N\lambda_s(J)|$$
$$\leq M D_M^*(S) + |M\lambda_{s-1}(J') - N\lambda_s(J)|.$$

Now $Nu_1 \leq M < Nu_1 + 1$; thus

$$0 \leq M\lambda_{s-1}(J') - N\lambda_s(J) \leq (Nu_1 + 1)\prod_{i=2}^{s} u_i - N\prod_{i=1}^{s} u_i \leq 1,$$

and the desired result follows. $\square$

THEOREM 3.8. *If P is the N-element Hammersley point set in the pairwise relatively prime bases $b_1, \ldots, b_{s-1}$, then*

$$D_N^*(P) < \frac{s}{N} + \frac{1}{N}\prod_{i=1}^{s-1} \left(\frac{b_i - 1}{2\log b_i}\log N + \frac{b_i + 1}{2} \right).$$

Proof. For the proof, use Theorem 3.6 and Lemma 3.7. $\square$

It follows from Theorem 3.6 that, if S is the Halton sequence in the pairwise relatively prime bases $b_1, \ldots, b_s$, then

$$D_N^*(S) \leq A(b_1, \ldots, b_s)N^{-1}(\log N)^s + O\big(N^{-1}(\log N)^{s-1}\big) \quad \text{for all } N \geq 2,$$

where the coefficient of the leading term is given by

$$A(b_1, \ldots, b_s) = \prod_{i=1}^{s} \frac{b_i - 1}{2\log b_i}.$$

The minimum value of this coefficient is obtained by letting $b_1, \ldots, b_s$ be the first s primes $p_1 = 2$, $p_2 = 3, \ldots, p_s$. In this case,

$$(3.6) \quad D_N^*(S) \leq A_s N^{-1}(\log N)^s + O\big(N^{-1}(\log N)^{s-1}\big) \quad \text{for all } N \geq 2,$$

where $A_s = A(p_1, \ldots, p_s)$. In a similar vein, to minimize the bound in Theorem 3.8, we choose $b_1, \ldots, b_{s-1}$ to be the first $s-1$ primes $p_1, \ldots, p_{s-1}$, and then we obtain

$$(3.7) \quad D_N^*(P) \leq A_{s-1} N^{-1}(\log N)^{s-1} + O\big(N^{-1}(\log N)^{s-2}\big)$$

for the corresponding N-element Hammersley point set P with $N \geq 2$. The discrepancy bounds for Hammersley point sets and Halton sequences serve as benchmarks for further constructions of low-discrepancy point sets and sequences. In fact, it has become customary to speak of low-discrepancy point sets and sequences only in the case where their (star) discrepancy is $O\big(N^{-1}(\log N)^s\big)$ in dimension s, with $N \geq 2$ being the number of points considered.

We emphasize that, in view of Theorem 2.11 and the discrepancy bounds above, the use of Hammersley point sets and Halton sequences in quasi-Monte Carlo integration leads to a dramatic improvement on the Monte Carlo error bound $O(N^{-1/2})$, at least as far as the order of magnitude is concerned. Concretely, if the integrand is of bounded variation on $\bar{I}^s$ in the sense of Hardy and Krause, then the quasi-Monte Carlo error bound is $O\big(N^{-1}(\log N)^{s-1}\big)$ for an N-element Hammersley point set in pairwise relatively prime bases, and $O\big(N^{-1}(\log N)^s\big)$ for the first N terms of a Halton sequence in pairwise relatively prime bases, where $N \geq 2$. Further advances in the construction of low-discrepancy point sets and sequences (see Chapter 4) yield corresponding improvements in quasi-Monte Carlo methods for numerical integration.

It is widely believed that, in the s-dimensional case, the star discrepancy of *any* N-element point set P satisfies

$$(3.8) \quad D_N^*(P) \geq B_s N^{-1}(\log N)^{s-1},$$

where the constant $B_s > 0$ depends only on s. This would mean that the star discrepancy of an N-element Hammersley point set in pairwise relatively prime bases attains the least possible order of magnitude. As mentioned previously in this section, (3.8) is obvious in the case where $s = 1$. For $s = 2$, (3.8) was established by Schmidt [303], but (3.8) is still open for $s \geq 3$. The best general result in this direction is due to Roth [296], who showed that, for any N-element point set P in dimension s, we have

$$D_N^*(P) \geq B_s N^{-1}(\log N)^{(s-1)/2}.$$

For $s = 3$, a slight improvement was recently obtained by Beck [19], namely, that

$$D_N^*(P) \geq B_3 N^{-1}(\log N)(\log\log N)^c \quad \text{for } N \geq 3,$$

where $c > 0$ is an absolute constant.

If (3.8) holds, then, with the help of Lemma 3.7, we would easily obtain that any s-dimensional sequence S satisfies

$$(3.9) \qquad D_N^*(S) \geq B_s' N^{-1}(\log N)^s \qquad \text{for infinitely many } N,$$

where the constant $B_s' > 0$ depends only on s. This would mean that the star discrepancy of a Halton sequence in pairwise relatively prime bases attains the least possible order of magnitude. By a result of Schmidt [303], mentioned previously in this section, (3.9) holds for $s = 1$, but this is the only case in which (3.9) is known. The results of Roth [296] and Beck [19], stated above, have analogues for sequences. For arbitrary s and any s-dimensional sequence S, we have

$$D_N^*(S) \geq B_s' N^{-1}(\log N)^{s/2} \qquad \text{for infinitely many } N,$$

while any two-dimensional sequence S satisfies

$$D_N^*(S) \geq B_2' N^{-1}(\log N)(\log \log N)^{c'} \qquad \text{for infinitely many } N,$$

where $c' > 0$ is an absolute constant. These results on irregularities of distribution are quite difficult to prove. Expository accounts of this topic are given in the books of Beck and Chen [20] and Kuipers and Niederreiter [163].

3.2. General discrepancy bounds.

Because of the finite-precision arithmetic of computers, all point sets and sequences of practical interest consist only of points with rational coordinates. For this case, there are several important principles for obtaining upper and lower discrepancy bounds.

For an integer $M \geq 2$, let $C(M) = (-M/2, M/2] \cap \mathbb{Z}$ and $C^*(M) = C(M) \smallsetminus \{0\}$. Furthermore, let $C_s(M)$ be the Cartesian product of s copies of $C(M)$ and $C_s^*(M) = C_s(M) \smallsetminus \{\mathbf{0}\}$. Put

$$r(h, M) = \begin{cases} M \sin \frac{\pi |h|}{M} & \text{for } h \in C^*(M), \\ 1 & \text{for } h = 0. \end{cases}$$

For $\mathbf{h} = (h_1, \dots, h_s) \in C_s(M)$, put

$$r(\mathbf{h}, M) = \prod_{i=1}^{s} r(h_i, M).$$

We write $e(u) = e^{2\pi\sqrt{-1}u}$ for $u \in \mathbb{R}$ and $\mathbf{x} \cdot \mathbf{y}$ for the standard inner product of $\mathbf{x}, \mathbf{y} \in \mathbb{R}^s$.

LEMMA 3.9. *Let $t_i, u_i \in [0, 1]$ for $1 \leq i \leq s$ and let $v \in [0, 1]$ be such that $|t_i - u_i| \leq v$ for $1 \leq i \leq s$. Then*

$$\left| \prod_{i=1}^{s} t_i - \prod_{i=1}^{s} u_i \right| \leq 1 - (1 - v)^s.$$

Proof. We proceed by induction on s, with the case $s = 1$ being trivial. If the inequality is shown for some $s \geq 1$ and we assume without loss of generality that $t_{s+1} \geq u_{s+1}$, then

$$\left| \prod_{i=1}^{s+1} t_i - \prod_{i=1}^{s+1} u_i \right| \leq (t_{s+1} - u_{s+1}) \prod_{i=1}^{s} t_i + u_{s+1} \left| \prod_{i=1}^{s} t_i - \prod_{i=1}^{s} u_i \right|$$

$$\leq t_{s+1} - u_{s+1} + u_{s+1} \left(1 - (1-v)^s \right)$$

$$= t_{s+1} \left(1 - (1-v)^s \right) + (t_{s+1} - u_{s+1}) (1-v)^s$$

$$\leq 1 - (1-v)^s + v(1-v)^s = 1 - (1-v)^{s+1}. \qquad \square$$

THEOREM 3.10. *For an integer $M \geq 2$ and $\mathbf{y}_0, \dots, \mathbf{y}_{N-1} \in \mathbb{Z}^s$, let P be the point set consisting of the fractional parts $\{M^{-1}\mathbf{y}_0\}, \dots, \{M^{-1}\mathbf{y}_{N-1}\}$. Then*

$$D_N(P) \leq 1 - \left(1 - \frac{1}{M}\right)^s + \sum_{\mathbf{h} \in C_s^*(M)} \frac{1}{r(\mathbf{h}, M)} \left| \frac{1}{N} \sum_{n=0}^{N-1} e\left(\frac{1}{M} \mathbf{h} \cdot \mathbf{y}_n \right) \right|.$$

Proof. For $\mathbf{k} = (k_1, \dots, k_s) \in \mathbb{Z}^s$, let $A(\mathbf{k})$ be the number of n with $0 \leq n \leq N - 1$ and $\mathbf{y}_n \equiv \mathbf{k} \bmod M$, where a congruence between vectors is meant componentwise. Then

$$A(\mathbf{k}) = \sum_{n=0}^{N-1} \frac{1}{M^s} \sum_{\mathbf{h} \in C_s(M)} e\left(\frac{1}{M} \mathbf{h} \cdot (\mathbf{y}_n - \mathbf{k}) \right),$$

since the inner sum has the value M^s if $\mathbf{y}_n \equiv \mathbf{k} \bmod M$ and the value zero otherwise. Therefore

$$(3.10) \qquad A(\mathbf{k}) - \frac{N}{M^s} = \frac{1}{M^s} \sum_{\mathbf{h} \in C_s^*(M)} e\left(-\frac{1}{M} \mathbf{h} \cdot \mathbf{k} \right) \sum_{n=0}^{N-1} e\left(\frac{1}{M} \mathbf{h} \cdot \mathbf{y}_n \right).$$

Now let $J = \prod_{i=1}^{s} [u_i, v_i)$ be a subinterval of I^s. For each i, $1 \leq i \leq s$, we choose the largest closed subinterval of $[u_i, v_i)$ of the form $[a_i/M, b_i/M]$ with integers $a_i \leq b_i$, which we again denote by $[a_i/M, b_i/M]$. The case where for some i no such subinterval of $[u_i, v_i)$ exists can be easily dealt with, since we then have $A(J; P) = 0$ and $v_i - u_i < 1/M$; hence

$$(3.11) \qquad \left| \frac{A(J; P)}{N} - \lambda_s(J) \right| = \lambda_s(J) < \frac{1}{M} \leq 1 - \left(1 - \frac{1}{M}\right)^s.$$

In the remaining case, the integers a_i, b_i, $1 \leq i \leq s$, are well defined, and we obtain, by (3.10),

$$\frac{A(J;P)}{N} - \lambda_s(J) = \sum_{\substack{\mathbf{k} \\ a_i \le k_i \le b_i}} \left(\frac{A(\mathbf{k})}{N} - \frac{1}{M^s} \right) + \frac{1}{M^s} \prod_{i=1}^{s} (b_i - a_i + 1) - \lambda_s(J)$$

$$= \frac{1}{M^s} \sum_{\mathbf{h} \in C_s^*(M)} \left(\sum_{\substack{\mathbf{k} \\ a_i \le k_i \le b_i}} e\left(-\frac{1}{M} \mathbf{h} \cdot \mathbf{k} \right) \right) \left(\frac{1}{N} \sum_{n=0}^{N-1} e\left(\frac{1}{M} \mathbf{h} \cdot \mathbf{y}_n \right) \right)$$

$$+ \frac{1}{M^s} \prod_{i=1}^{s} (b_i - a_i + 1) - \lambda_s(J).$$

Now

$$\left| \frac{b_i - a_i + 1}{M} - (v_i - u_i) \right| < \frac{1}{M} \qquad \text{for } 1 \le i \le s,$$

and so an application of Lemma 3.9 yields

$$(3.12) \quad \left| \frac{A(J;P)}{N} - \lambda_s(J) \right| < 1 - \left(1 - \frac{1}{M} \right)^s$$

$$+ \frac{1}{M^s} \sum_{\mathbf{h} \in C_s^*(M)} \left| \sum_{\substack{\mathbf{k} \\ a_i \le k_i \le b_i}} e\left(\frac{1}{M} \mathbf{h} \cdot \mathbf{k} \right) \right| \left| \frac{1}{N} \sum_{n=0}^{N-1} e\left(\frac{1}{M} \mathbf{h} \cdot \mathbf{y}_n \right) \right|.$$

For fixed $\mathbf{h} = (h_1, \dots, h_s) \in C_s^*(M)$, we have

$$\left| \sum_{\substack{\mathbf{k} \\ a_i \le k_i \le b_i}} e\left(\frac{1}{M} \mathbf{h} \cdot \mathbf{k} \right) \right| = \left| \sum_{\substack{\mathbf{k} \\ 0 \le k_i \le b_i - a_i}} e\left(\frac{1}{M} \mathbf{h} \cdot \mathbf{k} \right) \right| = \prod_{i=1}^{s} \left| \sum_{k_i=0}^{b_i-a_i} e\left(\frac{1}{M} h_i k_i \right) \right|.$$

If $h_i = 0$, then

$$\left| \sum_{k_i=0}^{b_i-a_i} e\left(\frac{1}{M} h_i k_i \right) \right| = b_i - a_i + 1 \le M = \frac{M}{r(h_i, M)},$$

whereas, for $h_i \in C^*(M)$, we have

$$\left| \sum_{k_i=0}^{b_i-a_i} e\left(\frac{1}{M} h_i k_i \right) \right| = \left| \frac{e\left(h_i(b_i - a_i + 1)/M \right) - 1}{e(h_i/M) - 1} \right| = \left| \frac{\sin\left(\pi h_i (b_i - a_i + 1)/M \right)}{\sin(\pi h_i/M)} \right|$$

$$\le \frac{1}{\sin(\pi |h_i|/M)} = \frac{M}{r(h_i, M)}.$$

Therefore

$$\left| \sum_{\substack{\mathbf{k} \\ a_i \le k_i \le b_i}} e\left(\frac{1}{M} \mathbf{h} \cdot \mathbf{k} \right) \right| \le \prod_{i=1}^{s} \frac{M}{r(h_i, M)} = \frac{M^s}{r(\mathbf{h}, M)}.$$

We use this in (3.12) and obtain a bound for the left-hand side, which is valid for all J because of (3.11). $\square$

COROLLARY 3.11. *Let P be as in Theorem 3.10 and suppose that the real number B is such that*

$$\left| \sum_{n=0}^{N-1} e\left(\frac{1}{M} \mathbf{h} \cdot \mathbf{y}_n \right) \right| \le B \quad \text{for all } \mathbf{h} \in C_s^*(M).$$

Then

$$D_N(P) \le 1 - \left(1 - \frac{1}{M} \right)^s + \frac{B}{N} \left(\frac{4}{\pi^2} \log M + 1.72 \right)^s.$$

Proof. From (3.12) we obtain

$$\left| \frac{A(J;P)}{N} - \lambda_s(J) \right| < 1 - \left(1 - \frac{1}{M} \right)^s + \frac{B}{M^s N} \sum_{\mathbf{h} \in C_s^*(M)} \left| \sum_{\substack{\mathbf{k} \\ a_i \le k_i \le b_i}} e\left(\frac{1}{M} \mathbf{h} \cdot \mathbf{k} \right) \right|.$$

From the proof of Theorem 3.10, we obtain

$$\sum_{\mathbf{h} \in C_s^*(M)} \left| \sum_{\substack{\mathbf{k} \\ a_i \le k_i \le b_i}} e\left(\frac{1}{M} \mathbf{h} \cdot \mathbf{k} \right) \right| < \sum_{\mathbf{h} \in C_s(M)} \prod_{i=1}^{s} \left| \sum_{k_i=0}^{b_i - a_i} e\left(\frac{1}{M} h_i k_i \right) \right|$$

$$= \prod_{i=1}^{s} \left(\sum_{h \in C(M)} \left| \sum_{k_i=0}^{b_i - a_i} e\left(\frac{1}{M} h k_i \right) \right| \right)$$

$$\le \prod_{i=1}^{s} \left(M + \sum_{h=1}^{M-1} \left| \frac{\sin(\pi h(b_i - a_i + 1)/M)}{\sin(\pi h/M)} \right| \right).$$

By an inequality of Cochrane [42], we have

(3.13) $$\sum_{h=1}^{M-1} \left| \frac{\sin(\pi h j/M)}{\sin(\pi h/M)} \right| < \frac{4}{\pi^2} M \log M + (0.41)M + 0.61$$

for any integer j, and this yields

$$\left| \frac{A(J;P)}{N} - \lambda_s(J) \right| < 1 - \left(1 - \frac{1}{M} \right)^s + \frac{B}{N} \left(\frac{4}{\pi^2} \log M + 1.41 + \frac{0.61}{M} \right)^s.$$

In view of (3.11), this holds for all J, so that the desired bound for $D_N(P)$ follows. $\square$

We now consider point sets for which all coordinates of all points have a finite digit expansion in a fixed base $b \ge 2$. Let

(3.14) $$\mathbf{w}_n = (w_n^{(1)}, \ldots, w_n^{(s)}) \in I^s \quad \text{for } n = 0, 1, \ldots, N-1,$$

where, for an integer $m \ge 1$, we have

$$w_n^{(i)} = \sum_{j=1}^{m} w_{n,j}^{(i)} b^{-j} \quad \text{for } 0 \le n \le N-1, \ 1 \le i \le s,$$

with $w_{n,j}^{(i)} \in Z_b$ for $0 \le n \le N-1$, $1 \le i \le s$, $1 \le j \le m$. For simplicity, we write $w_{nj}^{(i)}$ instead of $w_{n,j}^{(i)}$, and a similar convention applies in the rest of this section. For $(h_1, \dots, h_m) \in C_m(b)$, define

$$(3.15) \quad d(h_1, \dots, h_m) = \begin{cases} \text{largest } d \text{ with } h_d \ne 0 & \text{if } (h_1, \dots, h_m) \ne \mathbf{0}, \\ 0 & \text{if } (h_1, \dots, h_m) = \mathbf{0}. \end{cases}$$

For $b = 2$, put

$$(3.16) \qquad\qquad Q_b(h_1, \dots, h_m) = 2^{-d(h_1, \dots, h_m)}.$$

For $b > 2$, put

$$(3.17) \quad Q_b(h_1, \dots, h_m) = \begin{cases} b^{-d} \left(\csc \frac{\pi}{b} |h_d| + \sigma(d, m) \right) & \text{if } (h_1, \dots, h_m) \ne \mathbf{0}, \\ 1 & \text{if } (h_1, \dots, h_m) = \mathbf{0}, \end{cases}$$

where $d = d(h_1, \dots, h_m)$ and where $\sigma(d, m) = 1$ for $d < m$ and $\sigma(m, m) = 0$. Let $C(b)^{s \times m}$ be the set of all $s \times m$ matrices with entries in $C(b)$. For $H = (h_{ij}) \in C(b)^{s \times m}$, we define

$$(3.18) \qquad\qquad W_b(H) = \prod_{i=1}^{s} Q_b(h_{i1}, \dots, h_{im}).$$

THEOREM 3.12. *If P is the point set (3.14), then*

$$D_N^*(P) \le 1 - (1 - b^{-m})^s + \sum_{H \ne 0} W_b(H) \left| \frac{1}{N} \sum_{n=0}^{N-1} e\left(\frac{1}{b} \sum_{i=1}^{s} \sum_{j=1}^{m} h_{ij} w_{nj}^{(i)} \right) \right|,$$

where the outer sum is over all nonzero matrices $H = (h_{ij}) \in C(b)^{s \times m}$.

Proof. Let $J = \prod_{i=1}^{s} [0, t_i] \subseteq I^s$. Then

$$(3.19) \qquad\qquad A(J; P) = \sum_{n=0}^{N-1} c(t_1, w_n^{(1)}) \cdots c(t_s, w_n^{(s)}),$$

where $c(t, \cdot)$ is the characteristic function of the interval $[0, t]$. For $1 \le i \le s$, let

$$t_i = \sum_{r=1}^{\infty} t_{ir} b^{-r}$$

be the digit expansion of t_i in base b, where all $t_{ir} \in Z_b$, and, for each i, we have $t_{ir} < b - 1$ for infinitely many r. Put

$$(3.20) \qquad\qquad u_{ir} = \begin{cases} t_{ir} & \text{for } 1 \le r < m, \\ t_{ir} + 1 & \text{for } r = m. \end{cases}$$

For $v, w \in Z_b$ let $\delta(v, w) = 1$ if $v = w$ and $\delta(v, w) = 0$ if $v \neq w$. Then

$$c(t_i, w_n^{(i)}) = \sum_{r=1}^{m} \delta(u_{i1}, w_{n1}^{(i)}) \cdots \delta(u_{i,r-1}, w_{n,r-1}^{(i)}) \sum_{v=0}^{u_{ir}-1} \delta(v, w_{nr}^{(i)}),$$

where we henceforth use the standard convention that empty sums have the value zero and empty products have the value 1. Now

$$\delta(v, w) = \frac{1}{b} \sum_{h \in C(b)} e\left(\frac{h}{b}(w - v)\right),$$

and so

$$c(t_i, w_n^{(i)}) = \sum_{r=1}^{m} b^{-r} \sum_{h_1, \ldots, h_r \in C(b)} e\left(\frac{1}{b} \sum_{j=1}^{r} h_j w_{nj}^{(i)} - \frac{1}{b} \sum_{j=1}^{r-1} h_j u_{ij}\right) \sum_{v=0}^{u_{ir}-1} e\left(-\frac{1}{b} h_r v\right)$$

$$= \sum_{r=1}^{m} b^{-r} \sum_{h_1, \ldots, h_r \in C(b)} e\left(\frac{1}{b} \sum_{j=1}^{r} h_j(w_{nj}^{(i)} - u_{ij})\right) T(h_r, u_{ir})$$

with

$$T(h, L) = \sum_{v=1}^{L} e\left(\frac{hv}{b}\right) \quad \text{for } L \geq 0.$$

Substitution in (3.19) yields

$$A(J; P) = \sum_{n=0}^{N-1} \sum_{r_1, \ldots, r_s=1}^{m} b^{-r_1 - \cdots - r_s} \sum_{\substack{h_{ij} \in C(b) \\ 1 \leq j \leq r_i, 1 \leq i \leq s}} e\left(\frac{1}{b} \sum_{i=1}^{s} \sum_{j=1}^{r_i} h_{ij}(w_{nj}^{(i)} - u_{ij})\right)$$

$$\cdot T(h_{1r_1}, u_{1r_1}) \cdots T(h_{sr_s}, u_{sr_s}).$$

In the innermost sum, we split off the term corresponding to the choice $h_{ij} = 0$ for $1 \leq j \leq r_i$, $1 \leq i \leq s$. Also using $T(0, L) = L$ and putting

$$u_i = \sum_{r=1}^{m} u_{ir} b^{-r} \quad \text{for } 1 \leq i \leq s,$$

we obtain

$$A(J; P) = N \prod_{i=1}^{s} u_i + \sum_{r_1,\dots,r_s=1}^{m} b^{-r_1-\dots-r_s} \sum_{\substack{H \neq 0 \\ h_{ij}=0 \text{ for } j>r_i}} e\left(-\frac{1}{b}\sum_{i=1}^{s}\sum_{j=1}^{m} h_{ij}u_{ij}\right)$$

$$\cdot T(h_{1r_1}, u_{1r_1}) \cdots T(h_{sr_s}, u_{sr_s}) \sum_{n=0}^{N-1} e\left(\frac{1}{b}\sum_{i=1}^{s}\sum_{j=1}^{m} h_{ij}w_{nj}^{(i)}\right)$$

$$= \sum_{H \neq 0} e\left(-\frac{1}{b}\sum_{i=1}^{s}\sum_{j=1}^{m} h_{ij}u_{ij}\right)\left(\sum_{n=0}^{N-1} e\left(\frac{1}{b}\sum_{i=1}^{s}\sum_{j=1}^{m} h_{ij}w_{nj}^{(i)}\right)\right)$$

$$\cdot \sum_{r_1=a(\mathbf{h}_1)}^{m} \cdots \sum_{r_s=a(\mathbf{h}_s)}^{m} b^{-r_1-\dots-r_s} T(h_{1r_1}, u_{1r_1}) \cdots T(h_{sr_s}, u_{sr_s}),$$

where $\mathbf{h}_i = (h_{i1}, \dots, h_{im})$, $a(\mathbf{h}_i) = d(h_{i1}, \dots, h_{im})$ for $\mathbf{h}_i \neq 0$, and $a(0) = 1$. By (3.20) we have $|t_i - u_i| \leq b^{-m}$ for $1 \leq i \leq s$, and so an application of Lemma 3.9 yields

$$\left|\frac{A(J; P)}{N} - \lambda_s(J)\right| \leq 1 - (1 - b^{-m})^s$$

$$+ \sum_{H \neq 0} \left|\frac{1}{N}\sum_{n=0}^{N-1} e\left(\frac{1}{b}\sum_{i=1}^{s}\sum_{j=1}^{m} h_{ij}w_{nj}^{(i)}\right)\right| \prod_{i=1}^{s}|V(\mathbf{h}_i, u_i)|$$

with

$$V(\mathbf{h}_i, u_i) = \sum_{r=a(\mathbf{h}_i)}^{m} b^{-r} T(h_{ir}, u_{ir}).$$

To complete the proof, it thus suffices to show, in view of Remark 2.3 and (3.18), that

$$(3.21) \qquad |V(\mathbf{h}_i, u_i)| \leq Q_b(h_{i1}, \dots, h_{im}).$$

If $\mathbf{h}_i = 0$, then

$$|V(\mathbf{h}_i, u_i)| = \left|\sum_{r=1}^{m} b^{-r} T(0, u_{ir})\right| = \left|\sum_{r=1}^{m} b^{-r} u_{ir}\right| = u_i \leq 1,$$

and (3.21) is shown. If $\mathbf{h}_i \neq 0$ and $b = 2$, then put $d = a(\mathbf{h}_i) = d(h_{i1}, \dots, h_{im})$ and note that $T(1, L)$ attains only the values 0 or -1. Together with (3.15), this yields

$$V(\mathbf{h}_i, u_i) = 2^{-d} T(1, u_{id}) + \sum_{r=d+1}^{m} 2^{-r} u_{ir},$$

and so $|V(\mathbf{h}_i, u_i)| \leq 2^{-d}$, which proves (3.21) in view of (3.16). If $\mathbf{h}_i \neq \mathbf{0}$ and $b > 2$, then, again putting $d = a(\mathbf{h}_i) = d(h_{i1}, \ldots, h_{im})$, we obtain

$$|V(\mathbf{h}_i, u_i)| = \left| b^{-d} T(h_{id}, u_{id}) + \sum_{r=d+1}^{m} b^{-r} u_{ir} \right|$$

$$\leq b^{-d} |T(h_{id}, u_{id})| + b^{-d} \sigma(d, m).$$

For $h \in C^*(b)$, we have

$$|T(h, L)| = \left| \frac{e(hL/b) - 1}{e(h/b) - 1} \right| \leq \frac{2}{|e(h/b) - 1|} = \csc \frac{\pi|h|}{b};$$

thus (3.21) follows because of (3.17). $\square$

LEMMA 3.13. *Let $s \geq 1$ and $m \geq 1$ be integers. Then for $b > 2$ we have*

$$\sum_H W_b(H) = \left(\frac{m}{b} \sum_{h \in C^*(b)} \csc \frac{\pi|h|}{b} + m - \frac{m-1}{b} \right)^s$$

$$< \left(\frac{2}{\pi} m \log b + \frac{7}{5} m - \frac{m-1}{b} \right)^s,$$

where the first sum is extended over all matrices $H \in C(b)^{s \times m}$. In the case where $b = 2$, we have

$$\sum_H W_b(H) = \left(\frac{m}{2} + 1 \right)^s.$$

Proof. From (3.18) we obtain, for any b,

$$\sum_H W_b(H) = \sum_{H=(h_{ij})} \prod_{i=1}^{s} Q_b(h_{i1}, \ldots, h_{im})$$

$$= \left(\sum_{h_1, \ldots, h_m \in C(b)} Q_b(h_1, \ldots, h_m) \right)^s.$$

To evaluate the last sum, we split it up according to the value of $d(h_1, \ldots, h_m)$ for $(h_1, \ldots, h_m) \in C_m(b)$. For $1 \leq d \leq m$, there are b^{d-1} elements $(h_1, \ldots, h_m)$ of $C_m(b)$ with $d(h_1, \ldots, h_m) = d$ and a fixed nonzero value of h_d. Thus by (3.17) we obtain, for $b > 2$,

$$\sum_{h_1, \ldots, h_m \in C(b)} Q_b(h_1, \ldots, h_m) = 1 + \sum_{d=1}^{m} b^{d-1} b^{-d} \sum_{h \in C^*(b)} \left(\csc \frac{\pi|h|}{b} + \sigma(d, m) \right)$$

$$= 1 + \frac{m}{b} \sum_{h \in C^*(b)} \csc \frac{\pi|h|}{b} + \frac{b-1}{b} \sum_{d=1}^{m} \sigma(d, m)$$

$$= \frac{m}{b} \sum_{h \in C^*(b)} \csc \frac{\pi|h|}{b} + m - \frac{m-1}{b}.$$

By [222, p. 574], we have

$$(3.22) \qquad \sum_{h \in C^*(b)} \csc \frac{\pi |h|}{b} < \frac{2}{\pi} b \log b + \frac{2}{5} b \qquad \text{for any } b \ge 2,$$

and, by combining these results, we obtain the first part of the lemma. In the case where $b = 2$, we use (3.16) to obtain

$$\sum_{h_1, \ldots, h_m \in C(b)} Q_b(h_1, \ldots, h_m) = 1 + \sum_{d=1}^{m} 2^{d-1} 2^{-d} = \frac{m}{2} + 1,$$

and the second part of the lemma follows. $\square$

We now consider some general principles of obtaining lower bounds for the discrepancy. The following is an elementary lower bound for the discrepancy of point sets comprising only points with rational coordinates.

THEOREM 3.14. *Let $M \ge 2$ be an integer and let P be an s-dimensional point set with the property that all coordinates of all points are rational numbers in $[0, 1)$ with denominator M. Then*

$$D_N^*(P) \ge 1 - \left(1 - \frac{1}{M}\right)^s.$$

Proof. All points of P lie in the interval $J = [0, 1 - M^{-1}]^s \subseteq I^s$. Thus, by Remark 2.3, we obtain

$$D_N^*(P) \ge \left| \frac{A(J; P)}{N} - \lambda_s(J) \right| = 1 - \left(1 - \frac{1}{M}\right)^s. \qquad \square$$

REMARK 3.15. For an integer $M \ge 2$, consider the point set P consisting of the $N = M^s$ points $(n_1/M, \ldots, n_s/M) \in I^s$, where $n_1, \ldots, n_s$ run independently through Z_M. Then

$$D_N(P) \ge D_N^*(P) \ge 1 - \left(1 - \frac{1}{M}\right)^s$$

by Theorem 3.14. On the other hand, if the points of P are denoted by $M^{-1} \mathbf{y}_n$, $0 \le n \le N - 1$, then, for any $\mathbf{h} = (h_1, \ldots, h_s) \in C_s^*(M)$, we have

$$\sum_{n=0}^{N-1} e\left(\frac{1}{M} \mathbf{h} \cdot \mathbf{y}_n\right) = \sum_{n_1=0}^{M-1} \cdots \sum_{n_s=0}^{M-1} e\left(\frac{1}{M} \sum_{i=1}^{s} h_i n_i\right)$$

$$= \prod_{i=1}^{s} \left(\sum_{n=0}^{M-1} e\left(\frac{h_i n}{M}\right)\right) = 0,$$

and so Theorem 3.10 implies that $D_N(P) \leq 1 - (1 - M^{-1})^s$. Therefore

$$D_N(P) = D_N^*(P) = 1 - \left(1 - \frac{1}{M}\right)^s.$$

This shows, in particular, that the term $1 - (1 - M^{-1})^s$ in Theorems 3.10 and 3.14 is, in general, the best possible. The expression $1 - (1 - M^{-1})^s$ may be viewed as the *discretization error*, since it arises from the specific discreteness property of the point sets in Theorem 3.14. Note that in first approximation the discretization error is s/M for large M.

It is often easier to obtain formulas or lower bounds for cosine or exponential sums than for discrepancies. The following results can then be used to derive lower bounds for discrepancies. For $\mathbf{h} = (h_1, \dots, h_s) \in \mathbb{Z}^s$, we write

$$r(\mathbf{h}) = \prod_{i=1}^{s} \max(1, |h_i|).$$

Note that Theorem 3.16 and Corollary 3.17 can be viewed as special versions of Theorem 2.11.

THEOREM 3.16. *For arbitrary $\mathbf{t}_0, \mathbf{t}_1, \dots, \mathbf{t}_{N-1} \in \mathbb{R}^s$ let P be the point set consisting of the fractional parts $\{\mathbf{t}_0\}, \{\mathbf{t}_1\}, \dots, \{\mathbf{t}_{N-1}\}$. Then, for any nonzero $\mathbf{h} \in \mathbb{Z}^s$ and any real θ, we have*

$$\left| \frac{1}{N} \sum_{n=0}^{N-1} \cos 2\pi(\mathbf{h} \cdot \mathbf{t}_n - \theta) \right| \leq \frac{2}{\pi}((\pi + 1)^m - 1)r(\mathbf{h})D_N(P),$$

where m is the number of nonzero coordinates of $\mathbf{h}$.

Proof. We first consider the case where $\mathbf{h} = (h_1, \dots, h_s)$ with $|h_i| = 1$ for $1 \leq i \leq s$. Then the function $f(u_1, \dots, u_s) = f(\mathbf{u}) = \cos 2\pi(\mathbf{h} \cdot \mathbf{u} - \theta)$ satisfies

$$f(u_1, \dots, u_{k-1}, u_k + \tfrac{1}{2}, u_{k+1}, \dots, u_s) = -f(u_1, \dots, u_{k-1}, u_k, u_{k+1}, \dots, u_s)$$

for each k with $1 \leq k \leq s$ and all $u_1, \dots, u_{k-1}, u_{k+1}, \dots, u_s \in [0, 1]$, $u_k \in [0, \tfrac{1}{2}]$. Thus we can apply [234, Lemma 5.3]. With suitable $\theta_i \in \mathbb{R}$, this yields

$$\left| \frac{1}{N} \sum_{n=0}^{N-1} \cos 2\pi(\mathbf{h} \cdot \mathbf{t}_n - \theta) \right|$$

$$\leq D_N(P) \sum_{j=1}^{s} \binom{s}{j} (2\pi)^j \int_0^{1/2} \cdots \int_0^{1/2} \left| \cos 2\pi \left(\sum_{i=1}^{j} h_i u_i - \theta_i \right) \right| du_1 \cdots du_j.$$

Now

$$\int_0^{1/2} \cdots \int_0^{1/2} \left| \cos 2\pi \left(\sum_{i=1}^{j} h_i u_i - \theta_i \right) \right| du_1 \cdots du_j = \frac{1}{2^{j-1}\pi},$$

and we arrive at the inequality of the theorem in the case under consideration.

Next, we treat the case where $\mathbf{h} = (h_1, \ldots, h_s)$ with all $h_i \neq 0$. Let $\mathbf{t}_n = (t_n^{(1)}, \ldots, t_n^{(s)})$ and put $\mathbf{w}_n = (|h_1|t_n^{(1)}, \ldots, |h_s|t_n^{(s)})$ for $0 \leq n \leq N - 1$. Then $\mathbf{h} \cdot \mathbf{t}_n = \mathbf{l} \cdot \mathbf{w}_n$, where all coordinates of $\mathbf{l}$ have absolute value 1. According to what we have already established,

$$\left| \frac{1}{N} \sum_{n=0}^{N-1} \cos 2\pi (\mathbf{h} \cdot \mathbf{t}_n - \theta) \right| = \left| \frac{1}{N} \sum_{n=0}^{N-1} \cos 2\pi (\mathbf{l} \cdot \mathbf{w}_n - \theta) \right|$$

$$\leq \frac{2}{\pi} ((\pi + 1)^s - 1) D_N(\{\mathbf{w}_0\}, \ldots, \{\mathbf{w}_{N-1}\}).$$

To bound the last discrepancy, we note that, for a positive integer h and $t \in \mathbb{R}$, we have $\{ht\} \in [u, v) \subseteq [0, 1)$ if and only if $\{t\}$ belongs to one of the h intervals $[(q + u)/h, (q + v)/h)$, $q = 0, 1, \ldots, h - 1$. Using this property, we obtain

$$D_N(\{\mathbf{w}_0\}, \ldots, \{\mathbf{w}_{N-1}\}) \leq |h_1 \cdots h_s| D_N(P) = r(\mathbf{h}) D_N(P),$$

and this again yields the inequality of the theorem.

Finally, we consider an arbitrary $\mathbf{h} = (h_1, \ldots, h_s) \neq \mathbf{0}$. We can assume without loss of generality that $h_i \neq 0$ for $1 \leq i \leq m$ and $h_i = 0$ for $m+1 \leq i \leq s$. Let $\mathbf{h}' = (h_1, \ldots, h_m)$, and if $\mathbf{t}_n = (t_n^{(1)}, \ldots, t_n^{(s)})$, we put $\mathbf{t}'_n = (t_n^{(1)}, \ldots, t_n^{(m)})$ for $0 \leq n \leq N - 1$. According to what we have already established, we obtain

$$\left| \frac{1}{N} \sum_{n=0}^{N-1} \cos 2\pi (\mathbf{h} \cdot \mathbf{t}_n - \theta) \right| = \left| \frac{1}{N} \sum_{n=0}^{N-1} \cos 2\pi (\mathbf{h}' \cdot \mathbf{t}'_n - \theta) \right|$$

$$\leq \frac{2}{\pi} ((\pi + 1)^m - 1) r(\mathbf{h}') D_N(\{\mathbf{t}'_0\}, \ldots, \{\mathbf{t}'_{N-1}\}).$$

Now $r(\mathbf{h}') = r(\mathbf{h})$, and, from the definition of the discrepancy, we see that

$$D_N(\{\mathbf{t}'_0\}, \ldots, \{\mathbf{t}'_{N-1}\}) \leq D_N(P).$$

Thus we have proved the theorem in the general case. $\square$

COROLLARY 3.17. *For arbitrary* $\mathbf{t}_0, \mathbf{t}_1, \ldots, \mathbf{t}_{N-1} \in \mathbb{R}^s$, *let* P *be the point set consisting of the fractional parts* $\{\mathbf{t}_0\}, \{\mathbf{t}_1\}, \ldots, \{\mathbf{t}_{N-1}\}$. *Then, for any nonzero* $\mathbf{h} \in \mathbb{Z}^s$, *we have*

$$\left| \frac{1}{N} \sum_{n=0}^{N-1} e(\mathbf{h} \cdot \mathbf{t}_n) \right| \leq \frac{2}{\pi} ((\pi + 1)^m - 1) r(\mathbf{h}) D_N(P),$$

where m *is the number of nonzero coordinates of* $\mathbf{h}$.

Proof. We write

$$\sum_{n=0}^{N-1} e(\mathbf{h} \cdot \mathbf{t}_n) = e(\theta) \left| \sum_{n=0}^{N-1} e(\mathbf{h} \cdot \mathbf{t}_n) \right|$$

with some real θ, a representation that is possible for any complex number. Then

$$\left|\sum_{n=0}^{N-1} e(\mathbf{h} \cdot \mathbf{t}_n)\right| = \sum_{n=0}^{N-1} e(\mathbf{h} \cdot \mathbf{t}_n - \theta),$$

and, taking real parts, we obtain

$$\left|\sum_{n=0}^{N-1} e(\mathbf{h} \cdot \mathbf{t}_n)\right| = \sum_{n=0}^{N-1} \cos 2\pi(\mathbf{h} \cdot \mathbf{t}_n - \theta).$$

The desired bound now follows from Theorem 3.16. $\square$

Notes.

For the van der Corput sequence S_2 in base 2, a quick proof of $D_N(S_2) = O(N^{-1}\log(N + 1))$ can be found in [163, p. 127]. Haber [122] showed that $ND_N^*(S_2) \le (\log N)/(\log 8) + O(1)$ and that the constant $1/(\log 8)$ is the best possible. The van der Corput sequence in base b can be obtained by iteration of an ergodic transformation on $[0,1)$, as was demonstrated by Lambert [165]; see also Lapeyre and Pagès [169]. This fact was used by Lambert [166] for analogous constructions in dimensions $s = 2, 3, 4$. Further work on the (star) discrepancy of generalized van der Corput sequences was carried out by Béjian [21], Faure [94], [96], [97], [99], [100], and Thomas [347]. The study of the discrepancy of the sequences $S(z)$ with irrational z is a classical area of number theory; see [163, p. 128] for work prior to 1974. More recent papers on this topic are Dupain [72], Dupain and Sós [73], Ramshaw [291], Schoißengeier [305], [306], [307], and Sós [331]. In particular, Schoißengeier [305] has shown the converse of Corollary 3.4; i.e., if $D_N(S(z)) = O(N^{-1}\log N)$ for all $N \ge 2$, then necessarily $\sum_{i=1}^m a_i = O(m)$.

Distribution properties of the multidimensional sequences $S(\mathbf{z})$ were recently studied by Larcher [172], [176], [178] and Liardet [191]; see [163, p. 129] for references to earlier work. The sequences $S(\mathbf{z})$ play an important role in a quasi-Monte Carlo method for the numerical integration of periodic functions, which is based on the theory of diophantine approximations (see [225, §5]).

Halton sequences were introduced in Halton [125], and Hammersley point sets in Hammersley [129]. Discrepancy bounds of the orders of magnitude in Theorems 3.6 and 3.8, respectively, were established in Halton [125], and the implied constants were first improved by Meijer [209] and then by Faure [93]. The bounds in Theorems 3.6 and 3.8 are essentially those of the latter paper, but we have used a somewhat different method of proof. The principle in Lemma 3.7 is attributed to Roth [296]; for a converse of this principle, see [163, p. 106, Ex. 2.2]. The paper of Roth [296] already contains the construction of two-dimensional Hammersley point sets in the base 2. For this case, and for the number N of elements being a power of 2, an exact formula for the star discrepancy was established by Halton and Zaremba [128]. More generally, an exact formula for the star discrepancy of two-dimensional N-element Hammersley point sets in an arbitrary base b, with N being a power of b, was given by de Clerck [55], [56]. Computer implementations of Halton sequences and Hammersley point sets are described in Fox [107], Halton and Smith [127], and Lécot [183]. Generalized Halton sequences, which are the obvious analogues of generalized van der Corput sequences, were first considered by Braaten and Weller [32], and further results on these sequences can be found in Hellekalek [132]. For generalized Hammersley point sets in the two-dimensional case, see Faure [98]. Other variants of Hammersley point sets are discussed in [225, pp. 977–978].

Theorem 3.10 is due to Niederreiter [224]. Theorem 3.12 is a special case of a result of Niederreiter [241] in which the points (3.14) may be such that in each coordinate the digit expansions can have a different length and a different base. A somewhat weaker form of Theorem 3.12 was already stated in Niederreiter [229], and the one-dimensional case was proved in Niederreiter [232]. A discrepancy formula that is more general than that in Remark 3.15 was established in Niederreiter [241]; note that the discrepancy formula in Remark 3.15 can also be derived by elementary counting arguments. Theorem 3.16 was shown in Niederreiter [234], and, for Corollary 3.17, see Niederreiter [255]. In the one-dimensional case, the problem of obtaining a result like Corollary 3.17 with optimal constants was studied by Horbowicz and Niederreiter [143] and Niederreiter and Horbowicz [265].

Low-discrepancy point sets and sequences and irregularities of distribution have also been considered for domains other than intervals. A useful survey can be found in Beck and Chen [20]. The case of spheres has received special attention; see Hlawka [138] and Lubotzky, Phillips, and Sarnak [195], [196] for important work on this case, and Tichy [351] for applications. A detailed study of various other special domains was recently carried out by Hlawka [139].

CHAPTER 4

Nets and (t,s)-Sequences

We have seen in §3.1 that, for an s-dimensional Halton sequence in pairwise relatively prime bases, we have $D_N^*(S) = O(N^{-1}(\log N)^s)$ for all $N \geq 2$. By optimizing the choice of bases, we arrived at the discrepancy bound (3.6). Let us now take a closer look at the coefficient A_s of the leading term in this bound. We have $A_s = A(p_1, \ldots, p_s)$, where $p_1, \ldots, p_s$ are the first s primes. By the formula for $A(p_1, \ldots, p_s)$ and by the prime number theorem, we obtain

$$\lim_{s \to \infty} \frac{\log A_s}{s \log s} = 1.$$

Thus A_s increases superexponentially as $s \to \infty$. Similarly, for Hammersley point sets with an optimal choice of bases, we have the discrepancy bound (3.7), where the coefficient of the leading term again increases superexponentially as $s \to \infty$. This fast growth of A_s (compare also with Table 4.4) makes the bounds (3.6) and (3.7) practically useless for all but very small dimensions s. For most applications, we need point sets and sequences satisfying discrepancy bounds with much smaller implied constants. Constructions of such point sets and sequences will be described in this chapter.

In §4.1 we define point sets and sequences with a very regular distribution behavior. These will be called (t, m, s)-nets and (t, s)-sequences, respectively. On the basis of the strong properties enjoyed by these nets and (t, s)-sequences, we can derive very good discrepancy bounds. The definitions of (t, m, s)-nets and (t, s)-sequences have a certain combinatorial flavor, and some concrete connections with classical combinatorial problems are explored in §4.2. General principles for the construction of nets and (t, s)-sequences are presented in §4.3. These principles are used in §§4.4 and 4.5 for the construction of special families of nets and (t, s)-sequences, respectively. By optimizing the parameters in the construction of (t, s)-sequences in §4.5, we obtain sequences for any dimension $s \geq 2$, which asymptotically have the smallest discrepancy that is currently known.

4.1. Definitions and discrepancy bounds.

To motivate the following definitions, we focus on the following special property of the van der Corput sequence $x_0, x_1, \ldots$ in an arbitrary base $b \geq 2$ (this sequence was introduced in Definition 3.2). For fixed integers $k \geq 0$ and $m \geq 1$, consider the b^m points x_n with $kb^m \leq n < (k+1)b^m$. We claim that every b-adic interval $[ab^{-m}, (a+1)b^{-m})$, where $a \in \mathbb{Z}$ and $0 \leq a < b^m$, contains exactly one point x_n with $kb^m \leq n < (k+1)b^m$. To prove this, note that, for $kb^m \leq n < (k+1)b^m$, the m least significant digits in the digit expansion of n in base b can range freely, whereas the remaining leading digits are fixed; for $x_n = \phi_b(n)$ this means that its m leading digits after the "decimal point" can range freely, whereas the remaining digits are fixed; so each b-adic interval of length b^{-m} contains exactly one of these x_n.

For the subsequent definitions, we fix the dimension $s \geq 1$ and an integer $b \geq 2$. A subinterval E of I^s of the form

$$E = \prod_{i=1}^{s} [a_i b^{-d_i}, (a_i + 1)b^{-d_i})$$

with $a_i, d_i \in \mathbb{Z}$, $d_i \geq 0$, $0 \leq a_i < b^{d_i}$ for $1 \leq i \leq s$ is called an *elementary interval in base b*.

DEFINITION 4.1. Let $0 \leq t \leq m$ be integers. A (t, m, s)-net in base b is a point set P of b^m points in I^s such that $A(E; P) = b^t$ for every elementary interval E in base b with $\lambda_s(E) = b^{t-m}$.

DEFINITION 4.2. Let $t \geq 0$ be an integer. A sequence $\mathbf{x}_0, \mathbf{x}_1, \ldots$ of points in I^s is a (t, s)-sequence in base b if, for all integers $k \geq 0$ and $m > t$, the point set consisting of the $\mathbf{x}_n$ with $kb^m \leq n < (k+1)b^m$ is a (t, m, s)-net in base b.

In this language, the van der Corput sequence in base b is a $(0, 1)$-sequence in base b. Definitions 4.1 and 4.2 were introduced by Sobol' [323] in the case where $b = 2$; the general definitions were first given by Niederreiter [244].

REMARK 4.3. If P is a (t, m, s)-net in base b, then $A(E; P) = b^m \lambda_s(E)$ for every elementary interval E in base b with $\lambda_s(E) = b^{t-m}$. More generally, it follows that, if E is an elementary interval in base b with $\lambda_s(E) \geq b^{t-m}$, or a disjoint union of such intervals, then $A(E; P) = b^m \lambda_s(E)$ (observe that such sets E can be written as disjoint unions of elementary intervals in base b with λ_s-measure b^{t-m}). This implies that any (t, m, s)-net in base b is also a (u, m, s)-net in base b for integers $t \leq u \leq m$ and that any (t, s)-sequence in base b is also a (u, s)-sequence in base b for integers $u \geq t$. Therefore it is clear that smaller values of t mean stronger regularity properties.

We now establish upper bounds for the star discrepancy of nets. These results are due to Niederreiter [244]. We use a standard convention for binomial coefficients, namely, that $\binom{r}{i} = 0$ for $i > r$ or $i < 0$.

LEMMA 4.4. Let P be a (t, m, s)-net in base b, let E be an elementary interval in base b with $\lambda_s(E) = b^{-u}$, where $0 \leq u \leq m - t$, and let T be an affine transformation from E onto I^s. Then the points of P that belong to E are transformed by T into a $(t, m - u, s)$-net in base b.

Proof. It follows from Remark 4.3 that $A(E; P) = b^{m-u}$. If the points of P belonging to E are transformed by T, we obtain a point set P' of b^{m-u} points in I^s. To prove that P' is a $(t, m-u, s)$-net in base b, we take an elementary interval E' in base b with $\lambda_s(E') = b^{t-m+u}$ and note that for $\mathbf{x} \in E$ we have $T(\mathbf{x}) \in E'$ if and only if $\mathbf{x} \in T^{-1}(E')$. Now $T^{-1}(E')$ is an elementary interval in base b with $\lambda_s(T^{-1}(E')) = b^{t-m}$; hence $A(T^{-1}(E'); P) = b^t$, and so $A(E'; P') = b^t$. $\square$

THEOREM 4.5. *The star discrepancy of a (t, m, s)-net P in base $b \geq 3$ satisfies*

$$(4.1) \qquad ND_N^*(P) \leq b^t \sum_{i=0}^{s-1} \binom{s-1}{i} \binom{m-t}{i} \left\lfloor \frac{b}{2} \right\rfloor^i.$$

Proof. Write $D(J; P) = A(J; P) - N\lambda_s(J)$ for an interval $J \subseteq I^s$, where N is the number of points of P, and let $\Delta_b(t, m, s)$ denote the right-hand side of (4.1). We fix $t \geq 0$ and proceed by double induction on $s \geq 1$ and $m \geq t$. First, let $s = 1$ and consider an arbitrary $m \geq t$. If an interval $J = [0, u)$, $0 < u \leq 1$, is given, we split it up into the disjoint intervals $J_h = [hb^{t-m}, (h+1)b^{t-m})$, $h = 0, 1, \ldots, k-1$, and $J_k = [kb^{t-m}, u)$, where $k = \lfloor ub^{m-t} \rfloor$. For a $(t, m, 1)$-net P in base b, we have $D(J_h; P) = 0$ for $0 \leq h < k$; hence $D(J; P) = D(J_k; P)$. Now $0 \leq A(J_k; P) \leq b^t$ and $0 \leq b^m \lambda_1(J_k) \leq b^t$; thus $|D(J; P)| \leq b^t$. It follows that $ND_N^*(P) \leq b^t = \Delta_b(t, m, 1)$, and so (4.1) is shown for $s = 1$.

Now let $s \geq 2$ be given and suppose that (4.1) has been shown for the dimension $s - 1$ and all $m \geq t$. We verify (4.1) for the dimension s by induction on $m \geq t$. If $m = t$, then it is trivial that $ND_N^*(P) \leq N = b^t = \Delta_b(t, t, s)$.

Suppose that (4.1) has been established for some $m \geq t$ and consider a $(t, m+1, s)$-net P in base b. We must show

$$(4.2) \qquad |D(J; P)| \leq \Delta_b(t, m+1, s)$$

for every interval $J = \prod_{i=1}^s [0, u_i) \subseteq I^s$. We distinguish cases depending on the value of u_s. If $u_s = 1$, then we apply to P the projection $T : I^s \to I^{s-1}$ defined by

$$(4.3) \qquad T(v_1, \ldots, v_s) = (v_1, \ldots, v_{s-1}) \qquad \text{for } (v_1, \ldots, v_s) \in I^s.$$

This transforms P into a $(t, m+1, s-1)$-net P_1 in base b. Also $D(J; P) = D(T(J); P_1)$, and so by induction hypothesis

$$(4.4) \qquad |D(J; P)| \leq \Delta_b(t, m+1, s-1).$$

Hence (4.2) follows from the obvious inequality

$$\Delta_b(t, m+1, s-1) \leq \Delta_b(t, m+1, s).$$

If $u_s < 1$, then we introduce the integer $l = \lfloor bu_s \rfloor$ satisfying $0 \leq l \leq b-1$. Next, we consider the case where $0 \leq l \leq \lfloor b/2 \rfloor$. We split up J into the disjoint intervals

$$J_h = \prod_{i=1}^{s-1} [0, u_i) \times \left[\frac{h}{b}, \frac{h+1}{b}\right) \qquad \text{for } h = 0, 1, \dots, l-1,$$

$$J_l = \prod_{i=1}^{s-1} [0, u_i) \times \left[\frac{l}{b}, u_s\right).$$

Then

(4.5) $$D(J; P) = \sum_{h=0}^{l} D(J_h; P).$$

Put $E_l = [0, 1)^{s-1} \times [l/b, (l+1)/b)$ and let T_l be an affine transformation from E_l onto I^s. By Lemma 4.4, T_l transforms the points of P that belong to E_l into a (t, m, s)-net P_2 in base b. Also, $D(J_l; P) = D(T_l(J_l); P_2)$, and so, by induction hypothesis,

(4.6) $$|D(J_l; P)| \leq \Delta_b(t, m, s).$$

For $0 \leq h < l$, the projection $T : I^s \to I^{s-1}$ from (4.3) transforms the points of P that belong to $E_h = [0, 1)^{s-1} \times [h/b, (h+1)/b)$ into a $(t, m, s-1)$-net $P_3^{(h)}$ in base b. Also, $D(J_h; P) = D(T(J_h); P_3^{(h)})$, and so, by induction hypothesis,

(4.7) $$|D(J_h; P)| \leq \Delta_b(t, m, s-1) \qquad \text{for } 0 \leq h < l.$$

Combining (4.5), (4.6), and (4.7), we obtain

(4.8) $$|D(J; P)| \leq \Delta_b(t, m, s) + \lfloor b/2 \rfloor \Delta_b(t, m, s-1).$$

Therefore

$$|D(J; P)| \leq b^t \sum_{i=0}^{s-1} \binom{s-1}{i} \binom{m-t}{i} \left\lfloor \frac{b}{2} \right\rfloor^i + b^t \sum_{i=0}^{s-1} \binom{s-2}{i-1} \binom{m-t}{i-1} \left\lfloor \frac{b}{2} \right\rfloor^i$$

$$\leq b^t \sum_{i=0}^{s-1} \binom{s-1}{i} \binom{m-t}{i} \left\lfloor \frac{b}{2} \right\rfloor^i + b^t \sum_{i=0}^{s-1} \binom{s-1}{i} \binom{m-t}{i-1} \left\lfloor \frac{b}{2} \right\rfloor^i$$

$$= b^t \sum_{i=0}^{s-1} \binom{s-1}{i} \binom{m+1-t}{i} \left\lfloor \frac{b}{2} \right\rfloor^i = \Delta_b(t, m+1, s),$$

and so (4.2) is established.

Finally, we consider the case where $\lfloor b/2 \rfloor + 1 \leq l \leq b - 1$. We view J as the set-theoretic difference of the intervals $L = \prod_{i=1}^{s-1} [0, u_i) \times [0, 1)$ and $M = \prod_{i=1}^{s-1} [0, u_i) \times [u_s, 1)$, and we split up M into the disjoint intervals

$$M_l = \prod_{i=1}^{s-1} [0, u_i) \times \left[u_s, \frac{l+1}{b}\right),$$

$$M_h = \prod_{i=1}^{s-1} [0, u_i) \times \left[\frac{h}{b}, \frac{h+1}{b}\right) \qquad \text{for } h = l+1, l+2, \dots, b-1.$$

Then we have

$$(4.9) \qquad D(J;P) = D(L;P) - \sum_{h=l}^{b-1} D(M_h;P).$$

By (4.4) we obtain

$$|D(L;P)| \le \Delta_b(t, m+1, s-1).$$

The interval M_l is treated like the interval J_l in (4.6); hence

$$|D(M_l;P)| \le \Delta_b(t, m, s),$$

and, for $l < h \le b-1$, we obtain, as in (4.7),

$$|D(M_h;P)| \le \Delta_b(t, m, s-1).$$

Altogether, we obtain, from (4.9),

(4.10)

$$|D(J;P)| \le \Delta_b(t, m+1, s-1) + \Delta_b(t, m, s) + \left(b - \left\lfloor \frac{b}{2} \right\rfloor - 2\right)\Delta_b(t, m, s-1).$$

Therefore

$$|D(J;P)| \le b^t \sum_{i=0}^{s-2} \binom{s-2}{i}\binom{m+1-t}{i}\left\lfloor\frac{b}{2}\right\rfloor^i + b^t \sum_{i=0}^{s-1} \binom{s-1}{i}\binom{m-t}{i}\left\lfloor\frac{b}{2}\right\rfloor^i$$

$$+ \left(\left\lfloor\frac{b}{2}\right\rfloor - 1\right)b^t \sum_{i=0}^{s-2} \binom{s-2}{i}\binom{m-t}{i}\left\lfloor\frac{b}{2}\right\rfloor^i$$

$$= b^t \sum_{i=0}^{s-1} \binom{s-2}{i}\binom{m-t}{i-1}\left\lfloor\frac{b}{2}\right\rfloor^i + b^t \sum_{i=0}^{s-1} \binom{s-2}{i-1}\binom{m-t}{i-1}\left\lfloor\frac{b}{2}\right\rfloor^i$$

$$+ b^t \sum_{i=0}^{s-1} \binom{s-1}{i}\binom{m-t}{i}\left\lfloor\frac{b}{2}\right\rfloor^i$$

$$= b^t \sum_{i=0}^{s-1} \binom{s-1}{i}\binom{m+1-t}{i}\left\lfloor\frac{b}{2}\right\rfloor^i = \Delta_b(t, m+1, s),$$

and so we again have (4.2). $\square$

THEOREM 4.6. *The star discrepancy of a (t, m, s)-net P in an even base b satisfies*

(4.11)

$$ND_N^*(P) \le b^t \sum_{i=0}^{s-1} \binom{m-t}{i}\left(\frac{b}{2}\right)^i + \left(\frac{b}{2} - 1\right)b^t \sum_{i=0}^{s-2} \binom{m-t+i+1}{i}\left(\frac{b}{2}\right)^i.$$

Proof. Denote the right-hand side of (4.11) by $b^t E(m, s)$, where we suppress the dependence of $E(m, s)$ on b and t for simplicity. If we follow the proof of Theorem 4.5, then it is clear that it suffices to verify the analogue of (4.2). In view of (4.8) and (4.10), this amounts to proving the inequalities

$$(4.12) \qquad E(m, s) + \frac{b}{2} E(m, s - 1) \leq E(m + 1, s),$$

$$(4.13) \quad E(m + 1, s - 1) + E(m, s) + \left(\frac{b}{2} - 2 \right) E(m, s - 1) \leq E(m + 1, s)$$

for $s \geq 2$ and $m \geq t$. Now

$$E(m, s) + \frac{b}{2} E(m, s - 1) \leq \sum_{i=0}^{s-1} \binom{m - t}{i} \left(\frac{b}{2} \right)^i + \sum_{i=0}^{s-1} \binom{m - t}{i - 1} \left(\frac{b}{2} \right)^i$$

$$+ \left(\frac{b}{2} - 1 \right) \sum_{i=0}^{s-2} \binom{m - t + i + 1}{i} \left(\frac{b}{2} \right)^i + \left(\frac{b}{2} - 1 \right) \sum_{i=0}^{s-2} \binom{m - t + i + 1}{i - 1} \left(\frac{b}{2} \right)^i$$

$$= \sum_{i=0}^{s-1} \binom{m + 1 - t}{i} \left(\frac{b}{2} \right)^i + \left(\frac{b}{2} - 1 \right) \sum_{i=0}^{s-2} \binom{m - t + i + 2}{i} \left(\frac{b}{2} \right)^i = E(m + 1, s),$$

and so (4.12) is established. Note that the case corresponding to (4.13) in the proof of Theorem 4.5, namely, $\lfloor b/2 \rfloor + 1 \leq l \leq b - 1$, does not occur for $b = 2$; henceforth we can assume $b \geq 4$. We write

$$(4.14) \qquad E(m, s) = F(m, s) + \left(\frac{b}{2} - 1 \right) G(m, s)$$

with

$$F(m, s) = \sum_{i=0}^{s-1} \binom{m - t}{i} \left(\frac{b}{2} \right)^i, \qquad G(m, s) = \sum_{i=0}^{s-2} \binom{m - t + i + 1}{i} \left(\frac{b}{2} \right)^i.$$

Now

$$F(m + 1, s - 1) + F(m, s) + \left(\frac{b}{2} - 2 \right) F(m, s - 1)$$

$$= \sum_{i=0}^{s-1} \binom{m + 1 - t}{i} \left(\frac{b}{2} \right)^i + \sum_{i=0}^{s-2} \left(\binom{m + 1 - t}{i} - 2 \binom{m - t}{i} \right) \left(\frac{b}{2} \right)^i$$

$$= F(m + 1, s) + \sum_{i=0}^{s-2} \left(\binom{m - t}{i - 1} - \binom{m - t}{i} \right) \left(\frac{b}{2} \right)^i.$$

Furthermore,

$$G(m+1, s-1) + G(m, s) + \left(\frac{b}{2} - 2\right) G(m, s-1)$$

$$= G(m+1, s) - \binom{m-t+s}{s-2}\left(\frac{b}{2}\right)^{s-2} + \binom{m-t+s-1}{s-2}\left(\frac{b}{2}\right)^{s-2}$$

$$+ \sum_{i=0}^{s-2}\binom{m-t+i}{i-1}\left(\frac{b}{2}\right)^{i} - \sum_{i=0}^{s-3}\binom{m-t+i+1}{i}\left(\frac{b}{2}\right)^{i}$$

$$= G(m+1, s) - \binom{m-t+s-2}{s-4}\left(\frac{b}{2}\right)^{s-2} - \sum_{i=0}^{s-3}\binom{m-t+i}{i}\left(\frac{b}{2}\right)^{i}.$$

Because of (4.14), this yields

$$E(m+1, s-1) + E(m, s) + \left(\frac{b}{2} - 2\right) E(m, s-1) = E(m+1, s)$$

$$+ \sum_{i=0}^{s-2}\left(\binom{m-t}{i-1} - \binom{m-t}{i}\right)\left(\frac{b}{2}\right)^{i} - \binom{m-t+s-2}{s-4}\left(\frac{b}{2} - 1\right)\left(\frac{b}{2}\right)^{s-2}$$

$$- \left(\frac{b}{2} - 1\right) \sum_{i=0}^{s-3}\binom{m-t+i}{i}\left(\frac{b}{2}\right)^{i}.$$

To prove (4.13), it remains to show that

(4.15)
$$\sum_{i=0}^{s-2}\left(\binom{m-t}{i-1} - \binom{m-t}{i}\right)\left(\frac{b}{2}\right)^{i} \le \binom{m-t+s-2}{s-4}\left(\frac{b}{2} - 1\right)\left(\frac{b}{2}\right)^{s-2}$$

$$+ \left(\frac{b}{2} - 1\right) \sum_{i=0}^{s-3}\binom{m-t+i}{i}\left(\frac{b}{2}\right)^{i}.$$

For $s = 2$ and $s = 3$, this is a simple verification. For $s \ge 4$, we prove that, for $0 \le i \le s - 2$, the coefficient of $(b/2)^i$ on the left-hand side does not exceed the corresponding coefficient on the right-hand side of (4.15). This is trivial for $i = 0$. For $1 \le i \le s - 3$, we have

$$\binom{m-t}{i-1} - \binom{m-t}{i} \le \binom{m-t}{i-1} \le \binom{m-t+i-1}{i-1} \le \binom{m-t+i}{i}$$

$$\le \left(\frac{b}{2} - 1\right)\binom{m-t+i}{i}.$$

For $i = s - 2$, we must prove that

$$\binom{m-t}{s-3} - \binom{m-t}{s-2} \le \binom{m-t+s-2}{s-4}\left(\frac{b}{2} - 1\right).$$

This is trivial for $m = t$, and, for $m \geq t + 1$, we obtain

$$\binom{m-t}{s-3} - \binom{m-t}{s-2} = \binom{m-t-1}{s-4} - \binom{m-t-1}{s-2} \leq \binom{m-t-1}{s-4}$$

$$\leq \binom{m-t+s-2}{s-4}\left(\frac{b}{2}-1\right),$$

so that (4.15) is shown in all cases. $\quad\square$

If the bounds in (4.1) and (4.11) are expressed in terms of powers of $m - t$ with $m > t$, then they can be written in the form

$$ND_N^*(P) \leq \frac{b^t}{(s-1)!}\left\lfloor\frac{b}{2}\right\rfloor^{s-1}(m-t)^{s-1} + O\big(b^t(m-t)^{s-2}\big),$$

where the implied constant depends only on b and s. In terms of the number $N = b^m$ of points in a (t, m, s)-net in base b, this says that for $m > 0$ we have

$$ND_N^*(P) \leq \frac{b^t}{(s-1)!}\left(\frac{\lfloor b/2 \rfloor}{\log b}\right)^{s-1}(\log N)^{s-1} + O\big(b^t(\log N)^{s-2}\big)$$

with an implied constant depending only on b and s.

In the cases where $s = 2, 3, 4$, there is a different method of proof, which yields results that are sometimes better than Theorems 4.5 and 4.6. We illustrate this method in the case where $s = 2$, and we only state the resulting discrepancy bounds for $s = 3, 4$ (see Niederreiter [244] for the complete proofs in the latter cases).

THEOREM 4.7. *For $s = 2$, the star discrepancy of a (t, m, s)-net P in base b satisfies*

$$ND_N^*(P) \leq \left\lfloor\frac{b-1}{2}(m-t) + \frac{3}{2}\right\rfloor b^t.$$

Proof. Write $D(J; P) = A(J; P) - b^m \lambda_2(J)$ for an interval $J \subseteq I^2$. Now let $J = [0, u) \times [0, v) \subseteq I^2$. Write $u = \sum_{j=1}^{\infty} u_j b^{-j}$ with $u_j \in Z_b$ for all $j \geq 1$, and put $r = m - t$ and $d = \sum_{j=1}^{r} u_j$. Then $[0, \sum_{j=1}^{r} u_j b^{-j})$ can be represented as the disjoint union of u_1 elementary intervals in base b of length b^{-1}, of u_2 elementary intervals in base b of length b^{-2}, and so on, hence of d one-dimensional elementary intervals $E_1, \ldots, E_d$ in base b. With $F = [\sum_{j=1}^{r} u_j b^{-j}, u)$, we then obtain

$$(4.16) \qquad |D(J; P)| \leq \sum_{h=1}^{d} |D(E_h \times [0, v); P)| + |D(F \times [0, v); P)|.$$

Now let K be an arbitrary two-dimensional interval that is contained in some two-dimensional elementary interval in base b of area b^{-r}. Then $0 \leq A(K; P) \leq b^t$ and $0 \leq b^m \lambda_2(K) \leq b^t$; thus

$$(4.17) \qquad\qquad\qquad |D(K; P)| \leq b^t.$$

Next, we claim that, for any one-dimensional elementary interval E in base b, we have

$$(4.18) \qquad |D(E \times [0, v); P)| \leq b^t.$$

If $\lambda_1(E) \leq b^{-r}$, then (4.18) follows from (4.17). Otherwise, we have $\lambda_1(E) = b^{-a}$ for some $a \in \mathbb{Z}$ with $0 \leq a < r$. In this case, we split up $[0, v)$ into one-dimensional elementary intervals in base b of length b^{a-r} and a remaining interval F_1 of length $< b^{a-r}$. From Remark 4.3, it follows that $D(E \times [0, v); P) = D(E \times F_1; P)$. However, $E \times F_1$ is contained in a two-dimensional elementary interval in base b of area b^{-r}, and so (4.18) is implied by (4.17).

Note that $F \times [0, v)$ is contained in a two-dimensional elementary interval in base b of area b^{-r}. Thus it follows from (4.16), (4.17), and (4.18) that

$$(4.19) \qquad |D(J; P)| \leq (d+1)b^t.$$

Now consider $L = [u, 1) \times [0, v)$. By treating the interval $[u, 1)$ in the same way as $[0, u)$ at the beginning of the proof, we see that $[u, 1)$ can be represented as the disjoint union of $(b-1)r - d$ one-dimensional elementary intervals in base b and an interval that is contained in a one-dimensional elementary interval in base b of length b^{-r}. Hence, by the argument leading to (4.19), we obtain

$$|D(L; P)| \leq ((b-1)r - d + 1)b^t.$$

Furthermore,

$$D(J; P) = D([0, 1) \times [0, v); P) - D(L; P),$$

and, together with (4.18), this yields

$$(4.20) \qquad |D(J; P)| \leq ((b-1)r - d + 2)b^t.$$

It follows that $|D(J; P)|$ is bounded by the minimum of the right-hand sides of (4.19) and (4.20). Maximizing over $0 \leq d \leq (b-1)r$, we obtain the result of the theorem. $\square$

THEOREM 4.8. *For $s = 3$, the star discrepancy of a (t, m, s)-net P in base b satisfies*

$$ND_N^*(P) \leq \left\lfloor \left(\frac{b-1}{2}\right)^2 (m-t)^2 + \frac{b-1}{2}(m-t) + \frac{9}{4} \right\rfloor b^t.$$

THEOREM 4.9. *For $s = 4$, the star discrepancy of a (t, m, s)-net P in base b satisfies*

$$ND_N^*(P) \leq \left\lfloor \left(\frac{b-1}{2}\right)^3 (m-t)^3 + \frac{3}{8}(b-1)^2(m-t)^2 + \frac{3}{8}(b-1)(m-t) + \frac{15}{4} \right\rfloor b^t.$$

We combine these discrepancy bounds in such a way that, in the asymptotic form, the coefficient of the leading term is as small as possible. This yields the following result.

THEOREM 4.10. *The star discrepancy of a* (t, m, s)-*net* P *in base* b *with* $m > 0$ *satisfies*

$$ND_N^*(P) \leq B(s, b)b^t(\log N)^{s-1} + O\Big(b^t(\log N)^{s-2}\Big),$$

where the implied constant depends only on b *and* s. *Here*

$$B(s, b) = \left(\frac{b-1}{2\log b}\right)^{s-1}$$

if either $s = 2$ *or* $b = 2$, $s = 3, 4$; *otherwise*

$$B(s, b) = \frac{1}{(s-1)!}\left(\frac{\lfloor b/2 \rfloor}{\log b}\right)^{s-1}.$$

The fact that these upper bounds for the star discrepancy of nets are increasing functions of t is in accordance with an earlier observation on the values of t in Remark 4.3. We now consider the problem of bounding the star discrepancy of (t, s)-sequences. In the following general lemma, we let $\Delta_b(t, m, s)$ be a number for which $ND_N^*(P) \leq \Delta_b(t, m, s)$ holds for any (t, m, s)-net P in base b.

LEMMA 4.11. *For the star discrepancy* $D_N^*(S)$ *of the first* N *terms of a* (t, s)-*sequence* S *in base* b, *we have*

$$ND_N^*(S) \leq \frac{b-1}{2}\sum_{m=t}^{k}\Delta_b(t, m, s) + \frac{1}{2}\Delta_b(t, k+1, s) + \frac{1}{2}\max(b^t, \Delta_b(t, r, s))$$

for $N \geq b^t$, *where* k *is the largest integer with* $b^k \leq N$, *where* b^r *is the largest power of* b *dividing* N, *and where we set* $\Delta_b(t, r, s) = 0$ *if* $r < t$.

Proof. Let $\mathbf{x}_0, \mathbf{x}_1, \ldots$ be a (t, s)-sequence in base b. For $N \geq b^t$ let

$$N = \sum_{m=0}^{k} a_m b^m$$

be the digit expansion of N in base b, so that all $a_m \in Z_b$, $a_k \neq 0$, and $k \geq t$. We split up the point set $\mathbf{x}_0, \mathbf{x}_1, \ldots, \mathbf{x}_{N-1}$ into the point sets P_m, $0 \leq m \leq k$, defined as follows: Let P_k consist of the $\mathbf{x}_n$ with $0 \leq n < a_k b^k$, and, for $0 \leq m \leq k-1$, let P_m consist of the $\mathbf{x}_n$ with $\sum_{h=m+1}^{k} a_h b^h \leq n < \sum_{h=m}^{k} a_h b^h$. The P_m with $a_m \neq 0$ are nonempty, and, by the definition of a (t, s)-sequence in base b, they can be split up into a_m (t, m, s)-nets in base b provided that $m \geq t$. Therefore

(4.21) $$ND_N^*(S) \leq \sum_{m=t}^{k} a_m \Delta_b(t, m, s) + \sum_{m=0}^{t-1} a_m b^m.$$

Now we apply the same method to the point set consisting of the $\mathbf{x}_n$ with $N \leq n < b^{k+1}$. This point set has

$$b^{k+1} - N = \sum_{m=0}^{k} c_m b^m$$

points, where the right-hand side is the digit expansion in base b. Also, using the fact that the point set consisting of the $\mathbf{x}_n$ with $0 \leq n < b^{k+1}$ forms a $(t, k+1, s)$-net in base b, we obtain

$$(4.22) \qquad ND_N^*(S) \leq \Delta_b(t, k+1, s) + \sum_{m=t}^{k} c_m \Delta_b(t, m, s) + \sum_{m=0}^{t-1} c_m b^m.$$

Adding (4.21) and (4.22) and dividing by 2, see that

$$(4.23) \qquad ND_N^*(S) \leq \frac{1}{2} \sum_{m=t}^{k} (a_m + c_m) \Delta_b(t, m, s) + \frac{1}{2} \Delta_b(t, k+1, s)$$

$$+ \frac{1}{2} \sum_{m=0}^{t-1} (a_m + c_m) b^m.$$

From the definition of r, it follows that $a_m = c_m = 0$ for $0 \leq m < r$, $a_r + c_r = b$, and $a_m + c_m = b - 1$ for $r < m \leq k$. If $r \leq t - 1$, then (4.23) yields

$$ND_N^*(S) \leq \frac{b-1}{2} \sum_{m=t}^{k} \Delta_b(t, m, s) + \frac{1}{2} \Delta_b(t, k+1, s)$$

$$+ \frac{1}{2} \left(b^{r+1} + \sum_{m=r+1}^{t-1} (b-1) b^m \right)$$

$$= \frac{b-1}{2} \sum_{m=t}^{k} \Delta_b(t, m, s) + \frac{1}{2} \Delta_b(t, k+1, s) + \frac{1}{2} b^t,$$

which is the result of the lemma. If $r \geq t$, then (4.23) yields

$$ND_N^*(S) \leq \frac{b}{2} \Delta_b(t, r, s) + \frac{b-1}{2} \sum_{m=r+1}^{k} \Delta_b(t, m, s) + \frac{1}{2} \Delta_b(t, k+1, s)$$

$$\leq \frac{b-1}{2} \sum_{m=t}^{k} \Delta_b(t, m, s) + \frac{1}{2} \Delta_b(t, r, s) + \frac{1}{2} \Delta_b(t, k+1, s),$$

and the result of the lemma follows. $\square$

THEOREM 4.12. *The star discrepancy $D_N^*(S)$ of the first N terms of a (t, s)-sequence S in base $b \geq 3$ satisfies*

$$ND_N^*(S) \leq \frac{b-1}{2} b^t \sum_{i=1}^{s} \binom{s-1}{i-1} \binom{k+1-t}{i} \left\lfloor \frac{b}{2} \right\rfloor^{i-1}$$

$$+ \frac{1}{2} b^t \sum_{i=0}^{s-1} \binom{s-1}{i} \left(\binom{k+1-t}{i} + \binom{k-t}{i} \right) \left\lfloor \frac{b}{2} \right\rfloor^{i}$$

for $N \geq b^t$, where k is the largest integer with $b^k \leq N$.

Proof. By Theorem 4.5, we can use Lemma 4.11 with

$$\Delta_b(t, m, s) = b^t \sum_{i=0}^{s-1} \binom{s-1}{i} \binom{m-t}{i} \left\lfloor \frac{b}{2} \right\rfloor^i.$$

For $N \geq b^t$, we have $k \geq t$, and it is clear that the integer r in Lemma 4.11 satisfies $r \leq k$. We then obtain

$$ND_N^*(S) \leq \frac{b-1}{2} b^t \sum_{i=0}^{s-1} \binom{s-1}{i} \left\lfloor \frac{b}{2} \right\rfloor^i \sum_{m=0}^{k-t} \binom{m}{i} + \frac{1}{2} \Delta_b(t, k+1, s) + \frac{1}{2} \Delta_b(t, k, s).$$

An easy induction on M yields

(4.24) $$\sum_{m=0}^{M} \binom{m}{i} = \binom{M+1}{i+1} \qquad \text{for all } M \geq 0 \text{ and } i \geq 0,$$

and this implies the desired result. $\square$

THEOREM 4.13. *The star discrepancy $D_N^*(S)$ of the first N terms of a (t, s)-sequence S in an even base b satisfies*

$$ND_N^*(S) \leq (b-1) b^{t-1} \sum_{i=1}^{s} \binom{k+1-t}{i} \left(\frac{b}{2}\right)^i$$

$$+ \binom{b-1}{2} b^{t-1} \sum_{i=1}^{s-1} \binom{k+i+1-t}{i} \left(\frac{b}{2}\right)^i$$

$$+ \frac{1}{2} b^t \sum_{i=0}^{s-1} \left(\binom{k+1-t}{i} + \binom{k-t}{i} \right) \left(\frac{b}{2}\right)^i$$

$$+ \frac{b-2}{4} b^t \sum_{i=0}^{s-2} \left(\binom{k+i+2-t}{i} + \binom{k+i+1-t}{i} \right) \left(\frac{b}{2}\right)^i$$

for $N \geq b^t$, where k is the largest integer with $b^k \leq N$.

Proof. By Theorem 4.6, we can use Lemma 4.11 with

$$\Delta_b(t, m, s) = b^t \sum_{i=0}^{s-1} \binom{m-t}{i} \left(\frac{b}{2}\right)^i + \left(\frac{b}{2} - 1\right) b^t \sum_{i=0}^{s-2} \binom{m-t+i+1}{i} \left(\frac{b}{2}\right)^i.$$

Proceeding as in the proof of Theorem 4.12, we obtain

$$ND_N^*(S) \leq \frac{b-1}{2} b^t \sum_{i=0}^{s-1} \left(\frac{b}{2}\right)^i \sum_{m=0}^{k-t} \binom{m}{i} + \frac{1}{2} \binom{b-1}{2} b^t \sum_{i=0}^{s-2} \left(\frac{b}{2}\right)^i \sum_{m=0}^{k-t} \binom{m+i+1}{i}$$

$$+ \frac{1}{2} \Delta_b(t, k+1, s) + \frac{1}{2} \Delta_b(t, k, s).$$

for $N \geq b^t$. By (4.24) we have

$$\sum_{m=0}^{k-t} \binom{m}{i} = \binom{k+1-t}{i+1}$$

and

$$\sum_{m=0}^{k-t} \binom{m+i+1}{i} = \sum_{m=i+1}^{k+i+1-t} \binom{m}{i} < \sum_{m=0}^{k+i+1-t} \binom{m}{i} = \binom{k+i+2-t}{i+1},$$

and this implies the desired result. □

If the bounds in Theorems 4.12 and 4.13 are expressed in terms of powers of $k - t$ with $k > t$, then they can be written in the form

$$ND_N^*(S) \leq \frac{1}{s!} b^t \frac{b-1}{2} \left\lfloor \frac{b}{2} \right\rfloor^{s-1} (k-t)^s + O\big(b^t(k-t)^{s-1}\big),$$

where the implied constant depends only on b and s. Since $k \leq (\log N)/\log b$, this yields

$$ND_N^*(S) \leq \frac{1}{s!} b^t \frac{b-1}{2\lfloor b/2 \rfloor} \left(\frac{\lfloor b/2 \rfloor}{\log b} \right)^s (\log N)^s + O\big(b^t(\log N)^{s-1}\big) \qquad \text{for } N \geq 2,$$

with an implied constant depending only on b and s.

In the cases where $s = 2, 3, 4$, we obtain the following additional bounds by using Theorems 4.7, 4.8, and 4.9, together with Lemma 4.11 (see Niederreiter [244] for details).

THEOREM 4.14. *For $s = 2$, the star discrepancy $D_N^*(S)$ of the first N terms of a (t, s)-sequence S in base b satisfies*

$$ND_N^*(S) \leq \tfrac{1}{8}(b-1)^2 b^t (k-t)^2 + \tfrac{1}{8}(b-1)(b+9)b^t(k-t) + \tfrac{3}{4}(b+1)b^t$$

for $N \geq b^t$, where k is the largest integer with $b^k \leq N$.

THEOREM 4.15. *For $s = 3$, the star discrepancy $D_N^*(S)$ of the first N terms of a (t, s)-sequence S in base b satisfies*

$$ND_N^*(S) \leq \tfrac{1}{24}(b-1)^3 b^t (k-t)^3 + \tfrac{1}{16}(b-1)^2(b+5)b^t(k-t)^2$$
$$+ \tfrac{1}{48}(b-1)(b^2 + 16b + 61)b^t(k-t) + \tfrac{1}{8}(b^2 + 4b + 13)b^t$$

for $N \geq b^t$, where k is the largest integer with $b^k \leq N$.

THEOREM 4.16. *For $s = 4$, the star discrepancy $D_N^*(S)$ of the first N terms of a (t, s)-sequence S in base b satisfies*

$$ND_N^*(S) \leq \tfrac{1}{64}(b-1)^4 b^t (k-t)^4 + \tfrac{1}{32}(b-1)^3(b+5)b^t(k-t)^3$$
$$+ \tfrac{1}{64}(b-1)^2(b^2 + 16b + 13)b^t(k-t)^2$$
$$+ \tfrac{1}{32}(b-1)(7b^2 + b + 64)b^t(k-t) + \tfrac{1}{16}(b^3 + 8b + 51)b^t$$

for $N \geq b^t$, where k is the largest integer with $b^k \leq N$.

We combine these discrepancy bounds for (t, s)-sequences in such a way that, in the asymptotic form, the coefficient of the leading term is as small as possible. This leads to the following theorem.

THEOREM 4.17. *The star discrepancy $D_N^*(S)$ of the first N terms of a (t, s)-sequence S in base b satisfies*

$$ND_N^*(S) \leq C(s, b)b^t (\log N)^s + O\big(b^t (\log N)^{s-1}\big) \qquad \textit{for } N \geq 2,$$

where the implied constant depends only on b and s. Here

$$C(s, b) = \frac{1}{s}\left(\frac{b-1}{2\log b}\right)^s$$

if either $s = 2$ or $b = 2$, $s = 3, 4$; otherwise

$$C(s, b) = \frac{1}{s!} \cdot \frac{b-1}{2\lfloor b/2\rfloor}\left(\frac{\lfloor b/2\rfloor}{\log b}\right)^s.$$

4.2.   Combinatorial connections.

The definitions and results in §4.1 show that the (t, m, s)-nets and (t, s)-sequences with the most regular distribution behavior are those with $t = 0$. The main results of this section demonstrate that, except in trivial cases, $(0, m, s)$-nets in a given base b can only exist if s does not exceed a certain function of b, and a similar condition on s must hold so that a $(0, s)$-sequence in base b can exist. The principal tool is a connection between nets and the combinatorial theory of orthogonal latin squares.

In the cases where $m = 0, 1$, it is trivial to construct a $(0, m, s)$-net in base b for any $s \geq 1$ and $b \geq 2$. For $m = 0$ take one arbitrary point from I^s, and for $m = 1$ take the point set consisting of $(n/b, \ldots, n/b) \in I^s$, $n = 0, 1, \ldots, b-1$. Thus we can henceforth assume that $m \geq 2$.

We recall the following standard concepts from combinatorics (compare with Hall [124, Chap. 13]). For an integer $b \geq 2$, two b^2-tuples $\mathbf{e} = (e(0), e(1), \ldots, e(b^2 - 1))$ and $\mathbf{f} = (f(0), f(1), \ldots, f(b^2 - 1))$ with entries from the same set of cardinality b are called *orthogonal* if the b^2 ordered pairs $(e(h), f(h))$, $h = 0, 1, \ldots, b^2 - 1$, are all distinct. The b^2-tuples $\mathbf{e}_1, \ldots, \mathbf{e}_s$ with entries from the same set of cardinality b are called *mutually orthogonal* if $\mathbf{e}_i$ and $\mathbf{e}_j$ are orthogonal for all $1 \leq i < j \leq s$. Equivalently, the entries of a b^2-tuple may be arranged in a prescribed manner in a square array with b rows and b columns, and, with such an identification of b^2-tuples and $b \times b$ arrays, we speak of *orthogonal squares* of order b and *mutually orthogonal squares* of order b. A $b \times b$ array is called a *latin square* of order b if each row and each column is a permutation of the same set of cardinality b. If $M(b)$ is the maximum cardinality of a set of mutually orthogonal latin squares of order b, then we have $M(b) \leq b - 1$ for all $b \geq 2$ (see [59, p. 158], [299, p. 80]).

THEOREM 4.18. *There exists a $(0, 2, s)$-net in base b if and only if there exist $s - 2$ mutually orthogonal latin squares of order b.*

Proof. For $s = 1$, both conditions are trivially satisfied, so we assume that $s \geq 2$. Let $\mathbf{x}_n = (x_n^{(1)}, \dots, x_n^{(s)}) \in I^s$, $n = 0, 1, \dots, b^2 - 1$, be the points of a $(0, 2, s)$-net in base b. For $1 \leq i \leq s$, we define a b^2-tuple $\mathbf{e}_i = (e_i(0), e_i(1), \dots, e_i(b^2 - 1))$ with entries in Z_b by setting

$$e_i(n) = \lfloor b x_n^{(i)} \rfloor \quad \text{for } 0 \leq n \leq b^2 - 1.$$

We will prove that $\mathbf{e}_1, \dots, \mathbf{e}_s$ are mutually orthogonal. If $1 \leq i < j \leq s$ are given, then $\mathbf{e}_i$ and $\mathbf{e}_j$ will be shown to be orthogonal once we prove that, for any $c, d \in Z_b$, we have $(e_i(h), e_j(h)) = (c, d)$ for some h. Now $E = \prod_{r=1}^{s} E_r$ with $E_i = [c/b, (c+1)/b)$, $E_j = [d/b, (d+1)/b)$, and $E_r = [0, 1)$ for $r \neq i, j$ is an elementary interval in base b with $\lambda_s(E) = b^{-2}$; hence it contains a point $\mathbf{x}_h$. From $\mathbf{x}_h \in E$, it follows that $e_i(h) = c$ and $e_j(h) = d$. By [124, pp. 222–223] there exist s mutually orthogonal b^2-tuples if and only if there exist $s - 2$ mutually orthogonal latin squares of order b.

Conversely, if there exist $s - 2$ mutually orthogonal latin squares of order b, then there exist s mutually orthogonal b^2-tuples $\mathbf{e}_i = (e_i(0), e_i(1), \dots, e_i(b^2 - 1))$, $1 \leq i \leq s$, with entries in Z_b. If we fix i, then from the orthogonality of $\mathbf{e}_i$ with one of the other $\mathbf{e}_j$, $j \neq i$, it follows that each $v \in Z_b$ occurs exactly b times as an entry of $\mathbf{e}_i$. Thus there exists a map $\psi_i : Z_{b^2} \to Z_b$ with the property that, for each $v \in Z_b$, the restriction of ψ_i to the set $\{n \in Z_{b^2} : e_i(n) = v\}$ is a bijection. For $n \in Z_{b^2}$, we define

$$x_n^{(i)} = e_i(n) b^{-1} + \psi_i(n) b^{-2} \quad \text{for } 1 \leq i \leq s,$$
$$\mathbf{x}_n = (x_n^{(1)}, \dots, x_n^{(s)}) \in I^s.$$

We will show that the point set P consisting of the $\mathbf{x}_n$, $n = 0, 1, \dots, b^2 - 1$, is a $(0, 2, s)$-net in base b. If $E = \prod_{r=1}^{s} E_r$ is an elementary interval in base b with $\lambda_s(E) = b^{-2}$, then we have $E_r \neq [0, 1)$ for only one or for only two subscripts r. If $E_r \neq [0, 1)$ for only one subscript, say for $r = i$, then $E_i = [e/b^2, (e+1)/b^2)$ for some $e \in Z_{b^2}$ and $E_r = [0, 1)$ if $r \neq i$. Thus $\mathbf{x}_n \in E$ if and only if $e_i(n) b + \psi_i(n) = e$. If we write $e = vb + w$ with $v, w \in Z_b$, then $\mathbf{x}_n \in E$ if and only if $e_i(n) = v$ and $\psi_i(n) = w$. From the definition of ψ_i it follows that there is exactly one $n \in Z_{b^2}$ satisfying these conditions, hence $A(E; P) = 1$. If $E_r \neq [0, 1)$ for two subscripts, say for $r = i$ and $r = j$ with $1 \leq i < j \leq s$, then with suitable $c, d \in Z_b$ we have $E_i = [c/b, (c+1)/b)$, $E_j = [d/b, (d+1)/b)$, and $E_r = [0, 1)$ if $r \neq i, j$. Thus $\mathbf{x}_n \in E$ if and only if $e_i(n) = c$ and $e_j(n) = d$. Since $\mathbf{e}_i$ and $\mathbf{e}_j$ are orthogonal, we have $(e_i(n), e_j(n)) = (c, d)$ for exactly one $n \in Z_{b^2}$, hence $A(E; P) = 1$. $\square$

REMARK 4.19. Since the existence of $b - 1$ mutually orthogonal latin squares of order b is equivalent to the existence of a finite projective plane of order b (see [124, pp. 209–210]), it follows from Theorem 4.18 that there exists a finite projective plane of order b if and only if there exists a $(0, 2, b+1)$-net in base b. Thus the most celebrated problem in finite geometry is equivalent to a problem on the existence of certain nets.

THEOREM 4.20. *For* $m \geq 2$, *a* $(0, m, s)$-*net in base* b *can only exist if* $s \leq M(b) + 2$.

Proof. If there exists a $(0, m, s)$-net in base b for some $m \geq 2$, then, by Lemma 4.4, there exists a $(0, 2, s)$-net in base b. From Theorem 4.18, it follows that there exist $s - 2$ mutually orthogonal latin squares of order b; therefore $s - 2 \leq M(b)$. $\square$

COROLLARY 4.21. *For* $m \geq 2$, *a* $(0, m, s)$-*net in base* b *can only exist if* $s \leq b + 1$.

Proof. This follows from Theorem 4.20 and the inequality $M(b) \leq b - 1$. $\square$

Analogous necessary conditions hold for the existence of $(0, s)$-sequences in base b. The link with the above results is established by the following lemma.

LEMMA 4.22. *If there exists a* (t, s)-*sequence in base* b, *then, for every* $m \geq t$, *there exists a* $(t, m, s + 1)$-*net in base* b.

Proof. Let $\mathbf{x}_0, \mathbf{x}_1, \ldots$ be a (t, s)-sequence in base b. We will prove that, for fixed $m \geq t$, the point set P consisting of $(nb^{-m}, \mathbf{x}_n) \in I^{s+1}$, $n = 0, 1, \ldots, b^m - 1$, is a $(t, m, s + 1)$-net in base b. Let

$$E = \prod_{i=1}^{s+1} [a_i b^{-d_i}, (a_i + 1)b^{-d_i})$$

be an $(s + 1)$-dimensional elementary interval in base b with $\lambda_{s+1}(E) = b^{t-m}$; hence $\sum_{i=1}^{s+1} d_i = m - t$. We have $(nb^{-m}, \mathbf{x}_n) \in E$ if and only if $a_1 b^{m-d_1} \leq n < (a_1 + 1)b^{m-d_1}$ and

$$\mathbf{x}_n \in E' := \prod_{i=2}^{s+1} [a_i b^{-d_i}, (a_i + 1)b^{-d_i}).$$

Since $m - d_1 \geq t$ and the $\mathbf{x}_n$ form a (t, s)-sequence in base b, the point set P' consisting of the $\mathbf{x}_n$ with $a_1 b^{m-d_1} \leq n < (a_1 + 1)b^{m-d_1}$ is a $(t, m - d_1, s)$-net in base b. Now E' is an s-dimensional elementary interval in base b with $\lambda_s(E') = b^{t-m+d_1}$; hence $A(E'; P') = b^t$, and so $A(E; P) = b^t$. $\square$

THEOREM 4.23. *A* $(0, s)$-*sequence in base* b *can only exist if* $s \leq M(b) + 1$.

Proof. This follows from Theorem 4.20 and Lemma 4.22. $\square$

COROLLARY 4.24. *A* $(0, s)$-*sequence in base* b *can only exist if* $s \leq b$.

Proof. This follows from Theorem 4.23 and the inequality $M(b) \leq b - 1$. $\square$

DEFINITION 4.25. *For given integers* $b \geq 2$ *and* $s \geq 1$, *let* $t_b(s)$ *be the least value of* t *for which there exists a* (t, s)-*sequence in base* b.

Theorem 4.23 shows that $t_b(s) \geq 1$ for $s \geq M(b) + 2$. Note that $M(b) = b - 1$ for every prime power b, since $b - 1$ mutually orthogonal latin squares of order b can be constructed by using the existence of a finite field with b elements (see [192, Thm. 9.83]). For $b = 6$, we have $M(b) = 1$ by the negative solution of Euler's officer problem (see [299, pp. 84–85]).

4.3. General construction principles.

We now present general principles for the construction of nets and (t, s)-sequences in an arbitrary base. The special constructions of nets and (t, s)-sequences to be discussed in §§4.4 and 4.5, respectively, will be based on these principles.

First, we introduce a general principle for the construction of (t, m, s)-nets in base b. Let the integers $m \geq 1$, $s \geq 1$, and $b \geq 2$ be given. As before, we write $Z_b = \{0, 1, \dots, b-1\}$. We choose the following:

(N1) A commutative ring R with identity and $\mathrm{card}(R) = b$;

(N2) Bijections $\psi_r : Z_b \to R$ for $0 \leq r \leq m-1$;

(N3) Bijections $\eta_{ij} : R \to Z_b$ for $1 \leq i \leq s$ and $1 \leq j \leq m$;

(N4) Elements $c_{jr}^{(i)} \in R$ for $1 \leq i \leq s$, $1 \leq j \leq m$, and $0 \leq r \leq m-1$.

For $n = 0, 1, \dots, b^m - 1$, let

$$n = \sum_{r=0}^{m-1} a_r(n) b^r \quad \text{with all } a_r(n) \in Z_b$$

be the digit expansion of n in base b. We put

$$x_n^{(i)} = \sum_{j=1}^{m} y_{nj}^{(i)} b^{-j} \quad \text{for } 0 \leq n < b^m \text{ and } 1 \leq i \leq s,$$

with

$$y_{nj}^{(i)} = \eta_{ij}\left(\sum_{r=0}^{m-1} c_{jr}^{(i)} \psi_r(a_r(n)) \right) \in Z_b \quad \text{for } 0 \leq n < b^m, \ 1 \leq i \leq s, \ 1 \leq j \leq m,$$

and define the point set

(4.25) $\qquad \mathbf{x}_n = (x_n^{(1)}, \dots, x_n^{(s)}) \in I^s \quad \text{for } n = 0, 1, \dots, b^m - 1.$

THEOREM 4.26. *Suppose that the integer t with $0 \leq t \leq m$ satisfies the following property: For any integers $d_1, \cdots, d_s \geq 0$ with $\sum_{i=1}^{s} d_i = m - t$ and any $f_j^{(i)} \in R$, $1 \leq j \leq d_i$, $1 \leq i \leq s$, the system of $m - t$ linear equations*

$$\sum_{r=0}^{m-1} c_{jr}^{(i)} z_r = f_j^{(i)} \quad \text{for } 1 \leq j \leq d_i, \ 1 \leq i \leq s,$$

in the unknowns $z_0, \dots, z_{m-1}$ over R has exactly b^t solutions. Then the point set (4.25) is a (t, m, s)-net in base b.

Proof. Let

$$E = \prod_{i=1}^{s} [a_i b^{-d_i}, (a_i + 1) b^{-d_i})$$

be an elementary interval in base b with $\lambda_s(E) = b^{t-m}$; hence $\sum_{i=1}^{s} d_i = m - t$. For $1 \leq i \leq s$, let

$$a_i = \sum_{j=1}^{d_i} a_{ij} b^{d_i - j}$$

be the digit expansion in base b, where all $a_{ij} \in Z_b$. For the points $\mathbf{x}_n$ of the point set P in (4.25), we have $\mathbf{x}_n \in E$ if and only if

$$\sum_{j=1}^{m} y_{nj}^{(i)} b^{-j} \in \left[\sum_{j=1}^{d_i} a_{ij} b^{-j}, \sum_{j=1}^{d_i} a_{ij} b^{-j} + b^{-d_i} \right) \qquad \text{for } 1 \leq i \leq s.$$

This is equivalent to

$$y_{nj}^{(i)} = a_{ij} \qquad \text{for } 1 \leq j \leq d_i, \ 1 \leq i \leq s,$$

which is, in turn, equivalent to

$$\sum_{r=0}^{m-1} c_{jr}^{(i)} \psi_r(a_r(n)) = \eta_{ij}^{-1}(a_{ij}) \qquad \text{for } 1 \leq j \leq d_i, \ 1 \leq i \leq s,$$

where η_{ij}^{-1} denotes the inverse map of η_{ij}. By hypothesis, this system of linear equations in the unknowns $\psi_r(a_r(n))$, $0 \leq r \leq m - 1$, over R has exactly b^t solutions. Each solution corresponds to a unique m-tuple $(a_0(n), \dots, a_{m-1}(n))$, and each such m-tuple corresponds to a unique integer n with $0 \leq n < b^m$. Therefore $A(E; P) = b^t$. $\square$

We frequently consider the special case where b is a prime power. In this case, we write q instead of b, and we can take for the ring R the finite field F_q with q elements. We collect the elements $c_{jr}^{(i)} \in F_q$ in (N4) into a system of vectors

$$(4.26) \qquad \mathbf{c}_j^{(i)} = (c_{j0}^{(i)}, \dots, c_{j,m-1}^{(i)}) \in F_q^m \qquad \text{for } 1 \leq i \leq s, \ 1 \leq j \leq m,$$

and we introduce the following general notion.

DEFINITION 4.27. For a system $C = \{\mathbf{c}_j^{(i)} \in V : 1 \leq i \leq s, 1 \leq j \leq m\}$ of vectors in a finite-dimensional vector space V, let $\rho(C)$ be the largest integer d such that any system $\{\mathbf{c}_j^{(i)} : 1 \leq j \leq d_i, 1 \leq i \leq s\}$ with $0 \leq d_i \leq m$ for $1 \leq i \leq s$ and $\sum_{i=1}^{s} d_i = d$ is linearly independent in V (here the empty system is viewed as linearly independent).

It is clear that we always have $0 \leq \rho(C) \leq \dim(V)$. If we specialize C to be as in (4.26), which is the only case of interest in this chapter, then V is the vector space F_q^m over F_q, and so $0 \leq \rho(C) \leq m$. The significance of the number $\rho(C)$ is apparent from the following result.

THEOREM 4.28. *If q is a prime power, $R = F_q$, and the system C of vectors is given by (4.26), then the point set (4.25) is a (t, m, s)-net in base q with $t = m - \rho(C)$.*

Proof. It suffices to check the condition in Theorem 4.26 for $t = m - \rho(C)$. Consider integers $d_1, \ldots, d_s \geq 0$ with $\sum_{i=1}^{s} d_i = \rho(C)$. Then, by Definition 4.27, the vectors $\mathbf{c}_j^{(i)}$, $1 \leq j \leq d_i$, $1 \leq i \leq s$, are linearly independent over F_q. Thus the coefficient matrix of the system of $\rho(C)$ linear equations in Theorem 4.26 has rank $\rho(C)$, and so the system always has exactly $q^{m-\rho(C)} = q^t$ solutions. □

The principle in Theorem 4.28 can be extended to an arbitrary base $b \geq 2$ by using the following procedure. We can write b as a product of prime powers, say $b = \prod_{v=1}^{h} q_v$. Let R be the ring direct product $R = \prod_{v=1}^{h} F_{q_v}$ of the finite fields F_{q_v}, $1 \leq v \leq h$. Then the ring R satisfies the properties in (N1). Note that all operations in R are performed coordinatewise. The elements $c_{jr}^{(i)}$ in (N4) are of the form

$$(4.27) \qquad c_{jr}^{(i)} = (c_{jr1}^{(i)}, \ldots, c_{jrh}^{(i)}) \in R,$$

where $c_{jrv}^{(i)} \in F_{q_v}$. For fixed v, let C_v be the system of vectors

$$(4.28) \qquad \mathbf{c}_{jv}^{(i)} = (c_{j0v}^{(i)}, \ldots, c_{j,m-1,v}^{(i)}) \in F_{q_v}^m \qquad \text{for } 1 \leq i \leq s,\ 1 \leq j \leq m.$$

THEOREM 4.29. *If* $b = \prod_{v=1}^{h} q_v$ *is a product of prime powers* q_v, *if* $R = \prod_{v=1}^{h} F_{q_v}$, *and if the* $c_{jr}^{(i)} \in R$ *are given by* (4.27), *then the point set* (4.25) *is a* (t, m, s)-*net in base* b *with*

$$t = m - \min_{1 \leq v \leq h} \rho(C_v),$$

where the system C_v *of vectors is given by* (4.28).

Proof. We check the condition in Theorem 4.26 for $t = m - \min_{1 \leq v \leq h} \rho(C_v)$. For integers $d_1, \ldots, d_s \geq 0$ with $\sum_{i=1}^{s} d_i = m - t$ and elements

$$f_j^{(i)} = (f_{j1}^{(i)}, \ldots, f_{jh}^{(i)}) \in R \qquad \text{for } 1 \leq j \leq d_i,\ 1 \leq i \leq s,$$

consider the system

$$(4.29) \qquad \sum_{r=0}^{m-1} c_{jr}^{(i)} z_r = f_j^{(i)} \qquad \text{for } 1 \leq j \leq d_i,\ 1 \leq i \leq s,$$

in the unknowns $z_0, \ldots, z_{m-1}$ over R. Because of the direct product structure of R, this is equivalent to considering, for $1 \leq v \leq h$, the system of $m - t$ equations

$$(4.30) \qquad \sum_{r=0}^{m-1} c_{jrv}^{(i)} z_{rv} = f_{jv}^{(i)} \in F_{q_v} \qquad \text{for } 1 \leq j \leq d_i,\ 1 \leq i \leq s,$$

in the m unknowns $z_{0v}, \ldots, z_{m-1,v}$ over F_{q_v}. From $\rho(C_v) \geq m-t$, we obtain that the coefficient matrix of the system (4.30) has rank $m - t$ for each v. Thus the system (4.30) has exactly q_v^t solutions for each v. Consequently, the system (4.29) has exactly $\prod_{v=1}^{h} q_v^t = b^t$ solutions. □

The values of t obtained from Theorems 4.28 and 4.29 can be used in the general discrepancy bound for (t, m, s)-nets in Theorem 4.10. For simplicity, we state the resulting bound only for a prime power base q. In this case, the point set P in (4.25) satisfies

$$(4.31) \qquad D_N^*(P) \leq B(s, q) q^{-\rho(C)} (\log N)^{s-1} + O\left(q^{-\rho(C)} (\log N)^{s-2}\right),$$

where the implied constant depends only on q and s. We now show that there is also a lower bound for $D_N^*(P)$ in terms of $\rho(C)$.

THEOREM 4.30. *If q is a prime power and $R = F_q$, then, for the point set P in (4.25), we have*

$$D_N^*(P) \geq \left(\frac{1}{3} - \frac{1}{3q}\right) q^{-\rho(C)}.$$

If, in addition, the bijections η_{ij} are such that $\eta_{ij}(0) = 0$ for $1 \leq i \leq s$ and $1 \leq j \leq m$, then

$$D_N^*(P) \geq \left(\frac{1}{2} - \frac{1}{2q}\right) q^{-\rho(C)}.$$

Proof. By construction, we have

$$(4.32) \quad \sum_{r=0}^{m-1} c_{jr}^{(i)} \psi_r(a_r(n)) = \eta_{ij}^{-1}(y_{nj}^{(i)})$$

$$\text{for } 0 \leq n < q^m, \; 1 \leq i \leq s, \; 1 \leq j \leq m.$$

If $s = 1$ and $\rho(C) = m$, then the lower bounds for $D_N^*(P)$ follow from Theorem 2.6. Otherwise, the definition of $\rho(C)$ implies the existence of integers $d_1, \ldots, d_s$ with $0 \leq d_i \leq m$ for $1 \leq i \leq s$ and $\sum_{i=1}^{s} d_i = \rho(C) + 1$ such that the system $\{c_j^{(i)} \in F_q^m : 1 \leq j \leq d_i, \; 1 \leq i \leq s\}$ is linearly dependent over F_q. If w with $1 \leq w \leq s$ is the largest index for which $d_w \neq 0$, then there exist elements $h_j^{(i)} \in F_q$, $1 \leq j \leq d_i$, $1 \leq i \leq w$, not all zero such that

$$\sum_{i=1}^{w} \sum_{j=1}^{d_i} h_j^{(i)} c_j^{(i)} = 0 \in F_q^m.$$

We have $h_{d_w}^{(w)} \neq 0$ by the definition of $\rho(C)$. By comparing components, we obtain

$$\sum_{i=1}^{w} \sum_{j=1}^{d_i} h_j^{(i)} c_{jr}^{(i)} = 0 \qquad \text{for } 0 \leq r \leq m - 1.$$

Together with (4.32), this yields

$$(4.33) \qquad \sum_{i=1}^{w}\sum_{j=1}^{d_i} h_j^{(i)} \eta_{ij}^{-1}(y_{nj}^{(i)}) = \sum_{i=1}^{w}\sum_{j=1}^{d_i} h_j^{(i)} \sum_{r=0}^{m-1} c_{jr}^{(i)} \psi_r(a_r(n))$$

$$= \sum_{r=0}^{m-1} \psi_r(a_r(n)) \sum_{i=1}^{w}\sum_{j=1}^{d_i} h_j^{(i)} c_{jr}^{(i)} = 0$$

$$\text{for } 0 \le n < q^m.$$

Since $h_{d_w}^{(w)} \ne 0$, there exists a unique $c \in F_q$ with

$$(4.34) \qquad \sum_{i=1}^{w-1}\sum_{j=1}^{d_i} h_j^{(i)} \eta_{ij}^{-1}(0) + \sum_{j=1}^{d_w-1} h_j^{(w)} \eta_{wj}^{-1}(0) + h_{d_w}^{(w)} c = 0.$$

Put $a = \eta_{wd_w}(c) \in Z_q$. Define the intervals

$$J_i = [0, q^{-d_i}) \quad \text{for } 1 \le i < w,$$

$$J_w = \begin{cases} [(a+1)q^{-d_w}, q^{1-d_w}) & \text{if } a < (q-1)/3, \\ [0, aq^{-d_w}) & \text{if } a \ge (q-1)/3. \end{cases}$$

The subinterval J of I^s is then defined by

$$J = \prod_{i=1}^{w} J_i \times I^{s-w}.$$

We claim that $A(J;P) = 0$. Suppose, on the contrary, that $\mathbf{x}_n \in J$ for some n with $0 \le n < q^m$. Then $x_n^{(i)} \in J_i$ for $1 \le i \le w$. For $1 \le i < w$, it follows from the definition of J_i that $y_{nj}^{(i)} = 0$ for $1 \le j < d_i$. For $i = w$, it follows from the definition of J_w that $y_{nj}^{(w)} = 0$ for $1 \le j < d_w$ and $y_{nd_w}^{(w)} \ne a$. Thus (4.33) implies that

$$\sum_{i=1}^{w-1}\sum_{j=1}^{d_i} h_j^{(i)} \eta_{ij}^{-1}(0) + \sum_{j=1}^{d_w-1} h_j^{(w)} \eta_{wj}^{-1}(0) + h_{d_w}^{(w)} \eta_{wd_w}^{-1}(y_{nd_w}^{(w)}) = 0.$$

In view of (4.34), this yields $\eta_{wd_w}^{-1}(y_{nd_w}^{(w)}) = c$; hence $y_{nd_w}^{(w)} = \eta_{wd_w}(c) = a$, a contradiction. Thus the claim is shown.

Now we consider two cases, as in the definition of J_w. In the first case, let $a < (q-1)/3$. Define subintervals I_1 and I_2 of I^s by

$$I_1 = \prod_{i=1}^{w-1} J_i \times [0, q^{1-d_w}) \times I^{s-w},$$

$$I_2 = \prod_{i=1}^{w-1} J_i \times [0, (a+1)q^{-d_w}) \times I^{s-w}.$$

Then I_1 is the disjoint union of J and I_2. Since $A(J; P) = 0$, we obtain

$$\lambda_s(J) = \left|\frac{A(J; P)}{N} - \lambda_s(J)\right| \le \left|\frac{A(I_1; P)}{N} - \lambda_s(I_1)\right| + \left|\frac{A(I_2; P)}{N} - \lambda_s(I_2)\right| \le 2D_N^*(P).$$

Using $\sum_{i=1}^{w} d_i = \rho(C) + 1$, we see that

$$D_N^*(P) \ge \frac{1}{2}\lambda_s(J) = \frac{1}{2}(q - a - 1)q^{-d_1 - \cdots - d_w} = \frac{q - a - 1}{2q}q^{-\rho(C)} > \frac{q - 1}{3q}q^{-\rho(C)}.$$

In the second case, let $a \ge (q - 1)/3$. Then, from $A(J; P) = 0$, we obtain

$$D_N^*(P) \ge \left|\frac{A(J; P)}{N} - \lambda_s(J)\right| = \lambda_s(J) = aq^{-d_1 - \cdots - d_w} \ge \frac{q - 1}{3q}q^{-\rho(C)}.$$

Thus in both cases we have the first inequality in the theorem.

If, in addition, we have $\eta_{ij}(0) = 0$ for $1 \le i \le s$ and $1 \le j \le m$, then from (4.34) we get $c = 0$; hence $a = 0$. Thus, from the first case above, we obtain

$$D_N^*(P) \ge \frac{q - a - 1}{2q}q^{-\rho(C)} = \frac{q - 1}{2q}q^{-\rho(C)},$$

which is the second inequality in the theorem. $\square$

REMARK 4.31. Since the proof of Theorem 4.30 is based on the construction of an interval J containing none of the points $\mathbf{x}_n$ in (4.25), it follows that the lower bounds in Theorem 4.30 also hold for any point set consisting of the $\mathbf{x}_n$ with n running through an arbitrary nonempty subset of $\{0, 1, \ldots, q^m - 1\}$.

If q is a prime, then F_q and Z_q can be identified. There is also a canonical way of identifying elements of F_q and $C(q)$. Let $C = \{\mathbf{c}_j^{(i)} \in F_q^m : 1 \le i \le s, 1 \le j \le m\}$ be the system of vectors in (4.26). Using the quantities $W_q(H)$ defined in (3.18), we set

$$(4.35) \qquad\qquad R_q(C) = \sum_H W_q(H).$$

Here the sum runs over all nonzero $H = (h_{ij}) \in C(q)^{s \times m}$ with

$$\sum_{i=1}^{s} \sum_{j=1}^{m} h_{ij}\mathbf{c}_j^{(i)} = \mathbf{0} \in F_q^m,$$

where the h_{ij} are viewed as elements of F_q.

LEMMA 4.32. *If q is a prime, $R = F_q$, and every η_{ij} is the identity map, then the star discrepancy of the point set P in (4.25) satisfies*

$$D_N^*(P) \le 1 - \left(1 - \frac{1}{N}\right)^s + R_q(C) \le \frac{s}{N} + R_q(C).$$

Proof. By the assumption on the η_{ij}, we have

$$y_{nj}^{(i)} = \sum_{r=0}^{m-1} c_{jr}^{(i)} \psi_r(a_r(n)) \quad \text{for } 0 \le n < q^m,\ 1 \le i \le s,\ 1 \le j \le m.$$

An application of Theorem 3.12 yields

(4.36)

$$D_N^*(P) \le 1 - \left(1 - \frac{1}{N}\right)^s + \sum_{H \ne 0} W_q(H) \left| \frac{1}{N} \sum_{n=0}^{N-1} e\left(\frac{1}{q} \sum_{i=1}^{s} \sum_{j=1}^{m} h_{ij} y_{nj}^{(i)}\right) \right|,$$

where the outer sum is over all nonzero $H = (h_{ij}) \in C(q)^{s \times m}$. For fixed H, we have

$$\sum_{n=0}^{N-1} e\left(\frac{1}{q} \sum_{i=1}^{s} \sum_{j=1}^{m} h_{ij} y_{nj}^{(i)}\right) = \sum_{b_0,\dots,b_{m-1} \in Z_q} e\left(\frac{1}{q} \sum_{i=1}^{s} \sum_{j=1}^{m} h_{ij} \sum_{r=0}^{m-1} c_{jr}^{(i)} b_r\right)$$

$$= \sum_{b_0,\dots,b_{m-1} \in Z_q} e\left(\frac{1}{q} \sum_{r=0}^{m-1} b_r \sum_{i=1}^{s} \sum_{j=1}^{m} h_{ij} c_{jr}^{(i)}\right)$$

$$= \prod_{r=0}^{m-1} \left(\sum_{b=0}^{q-1} e\left(\frac{b}{q} \sum_{i=1}^{s} \sum_{j=1}^{m} h_{ij} c_{jr}^{(i)}\right)\right).$$

The last expression is equal to $q^m = N$ if

$$\sum_{i=1}^{s} \sum_{j=1}^{m} h_{ij} c_{jr}^{(i)} = 0 \in F_q \quad \text{for } 0 \le r \le m-1,$$

and equal to zero otherwise, where the h_{ij} are viewed as elements of F_q. The lemma now follows from (4.36) and the definition of $R_q(C)$ in (4.35). $\square$

On the basis of Lemma 4.32, we can show that the construction of the point sets (4.25) yields on the average a low-discrepancy point set.

THEOREM 4.33. *For a prime q and for integers $m \ge 1$ and $s \ge 1$, let*

$$M_q(m,s) = \frac{1}{\text{card}(\mathcal{C})} \sum_{C \in \mathcal{C}} R_q(C)$$

be the mean value of $R_q(C)$ extended over the set $\mathcal{C}$ of all choices for a system $C = \{\mathbf{c}_j^{(i)} \in F_q^m : 1 \le i \le s,\ 1 \le j \le m\}$. Then, with $N = q^m$, we have

$$M_q(m,s) = \frac{1}{N}\left(\frac{\log N}{\log 4} + 1\right)^s - \frac{1}{N} \quad \text{if } q = 2,$$

$$M_q(m,s) = \frac{1}{N}\left(\frac{m}{q} \sum_{h \in C^*(q)} \csc \frac{\pi|h|}{q} + m - \frac{m-1}{q}\right)^s - \frac{1}{N}$$

$$< \frac{1}{N}\left(\left(\frac{2}{\pi} + \frac{7}{5\log q} - \frac{1}{q \log q}\right)\log N + \frac{1}{q}\right)^s - \frac{1}{N} \quad \text{if } q > 2.$$

Proof. Inserting the definition of $R_q(C)$ into the expression for $M_q(m,s)$ and interchanging the order of summation, we obtain

$$M_q(m,s) = \frac{1}{\text{card}(\mathcal{C})} \sum_{H \neq 0} W_q(H) \sum_C 1,$$

where the outer sum is over all nonzero $H = (h_{ij}) \in C(q)^{s \times m}$ and the inner sum is over all $C = (\mathbf{c}_j^{(i)}) \in \mathcal{C}$ for which

$$(4.37) \qquad \sum_{i=1}^{s} \sum_{j=1}^{m} h_{ij} \mathbf{c}_j^{(i)} = \mathbf{0} \in F_q^m.$$

For a fixed nonzero $H \in C(q)^{s \times m}$, the inner sum in the last expression for $M_q(m,s)$ represents the number of solutions $(\mathbf{c}_j^{(i)}) \in \mathcal{C}$ of the vector equation (4.37). Since at least one h_{ij} is a nonzero element of F_q, we can choose $ms - 1$ vectors $\mathbf{c}_j^{(i)} \in F_q^m$ arbitrarily, and the remaining vector is then uniquely determined by (4.37). Therefore the number of solutions of (4.37) is $q^{(ms-1)m}$. Since $\text{card}(\mathcal{C}) = q^{m^2 s}$, it follows that

$$M_q(m,s) = q^{-m^2 s} q^{(ms-1)m} \sum_{H \neq 0} W_q(H) = \frac{1}{N} \sum_{H \neq 0} W_q(H).$$

If $q = 2$, then the second part of Lemma 3.13 yields

$$\sum_{H \neq 0} W_q(H) = \left(\frac{m}{2} + 1 \right)^s - 1 = \left(\frac{\log N}{\log 4} + 1 \right)^s - 1,$$

and the formula for $M_q(m,s)$ follows. For $q > 2$, the desired result is obtained from the first part of Lemma 3.13. $\square$

If we combine Lemma 4.32 and Theorem 4.33, then we see that, if q is a prime, $R = F_q$, and every η_{ij} is the identity map, and if $m \geq 1$ and $s \geq 1$ are fixed, then the construction of the point sets (4.25) yields on the average a point set P with $D_N^*(P) = O\left(N^{-1}(\log N)^s\right)$. We now show that the quantities $\rho(C)$ in Definition 4.27 and $R_q(C)$ in (4.35) are connected by the following inequalities.

THEOREM 4.34. *For $s \geq 2$ and any prime q, we have*

$$q^{-\rho(C)-1} \leq R_q(C) \leq \left(1 - \frac{1}{q} \right) k(q)^s \left((m+1)^s - \binom{\rho(C)+s}{s} \right) q^{-\rho(C)},$$

where $k(q) = 1$ if $q = 2$ and $k(q) = \csc(\pi/q) + 1$ if $q > 2$.

Proof. If $C = (\mathbf{c}_j^{(i)})$ is given and a nonzero $H = (h_{ij}) \in C(q)^{s \times m}$ is such that

$$(4.38) \qquad \sum_{i=1}^{s} \sum_{j=1}^{m} h_{ij} \mathbf{c}_j^{(i)} = \mathbf{0} \in F_q^m,$$

then the system $\{\mathbf{c}_j^{(i)} : 1 \le j \le d_i(H), 1 \le i \le s\}$ is linearly dependent over F_q, where $d_i(H) = d(h_{i1}, \ldots, h_{im})$ for $1 \le i \le s$ with the notation introduced in (3.15). From the definition of $\rho(C)$, it follows that $\sum_{i=1}^s d_i(H) \ge \rho(C) + 1$. We obtain the lower bound in the theorem from the fact that there is an H satisfying (4.38) and $\sum_{i=1}^s d_i(H) = \rho(C) + 1$.

To prove the upper bound, we put $D(H) = \sum_{i=1}^s d_i(H)$, and note that from (3.16), (3.17), and (3.18) we obtain

$$W_q(H) \le k(q)^s q^{-D(H)}.$$

Therefore

(4.39) $$R_q(C) \le k(q)^s \sum_H q^{-D(H)} =: k(q)^s S_q(C),$$

where the sum is extended over all nonzero $H = (h_{ij}) \in C(q)^{s \times m}$ satisfying (4.38). We have

(4.40) $$S_q(C) = \sum_{\mathbf{d}} A(\mathbf{d}) q^{-d_1 - \cdots - d_s},$$

where we sum over all $\mathbf{d} = (d_1, \ldots, d_s) \in \mathbb{Z}^s$ with $0 \le d_i \le m$ for $1 \le i \le s$ and $\sum_{i=1}^s d_i \ge \rho(C) + 1$, and where $A(\mathbf{d})$ is the number of $H = (h_{ij}) \in C(q)^{s \times m}$ satisfying (4.38) and $d_i(H) = d_i$ for $1 \le i \le s$. If $\mathbf{d}$ is fixed and H is counted by $A(\mathbf{d})$, then (4.38) attains the form

$$\sum_{i=1}^s \sum_{j=1}^{d_i} h_{ij} \mathbf{c}_j^{(i)} = \mathbf{0}.$$

Choose integers f_i with $0 \le f_i \le d_i$ for $1 \le i \le s$ and $\sum_{i=1}^s f_i = \rho(C)$. Then the last vector identity can be written in the form

(4.41) $$\sum_{i=1}^s \sum_{j=1}^{f_i} h_{ij} \mathbf{c}_j^{(i)} = -\sum_{i=1}^s \sum_{j=f_i+1}^{d_i} h_{ij} \mathbf{c}_j^{(i)}.$$

Suppose that we allow arbitrary choices for the coefficients h_{ij} on the right-hand side of (4.41), the only stipulation being that $h_{id_i} \ne 0$ whenever $d_i > f_i$. Since the vectors $\mathbf{c}_j^{(i)}$ on the left-hand side of (4.41) are linearly independent over F_q, there can be at most one choice for the coefficients h_{ij} on the left-hand side. Therefore

$$A(\mathbf{d}) \le \prod_{\substack{i=1 \\ d_i > f_i}}^s (q-1) q^{d_i - f_i - 1} = \prod_{\substack{i=1 \\ d_i > f_i}}^s \frac{q-1}{q} \cdot \prod_{i=1}^s q^{d_i - f_i} \le \left(1 - \frac{1}{q}\right) q^{d_1 + \cdots + d_s - \rho(C)}.$$

Together with (4.40), this yields

$$S_q(C) \le \left(1 - \frac{1}{q}\right) q^{-\rho(C)} \sum_{\mathbf{d}} 1 = \left(1 - \frac{1}{q}\right) q^{-\rho(C)} \left((m+1)^s - \binom{\rho(C) + s}{s}\right),$$

and, by invoking (4.39), we complete the proof. $\square$

It follows from the results already shown in this section that a point set constructed by (4.25) is a low-discrepancy point set precisely if $\rho(C)$ is large. The problem of maximizing the value of $\rho(C)$ for a given finite field F_q and for given integers $m \geq 1$ and $s \geq 1$ is an interesting combinatorial question for vector spaces over finite fields, which is also connected with a classical problem in algebraic coding theory; see Niederreiter [244, §7], [260]. An explicit construction of systems C with a large value of $\rho(C)$ will be given in §4.5.

We now give the description of a general principle for the construction of (t, s)-sequences in base b. Let the integers $s \geq 1$ and $b \geq 2$ be given. Then we choose the following:

(S1) A commutative ring R with identity and $\mathrm{card}(R) = b$;

(S2) Bijections $\psi_r : Z_b \to R$ for $r \geq 0$,
    with $\psi_r(0) = 0$ for all sufficiently large r;

(S3) Bijections $\eta_{ij} : R \to Z_b$ for $1 \leq i \leq s$ and $j \geq 1$;

(S4) Elements $c_{jr}^{(i)} \in R$ for $1 \leq i \leq s$, $j \geq 1$, and $r \geq 0$.

For $n = 0, 1, \ldots$, let

$$n = \sum_{r=0}^{\infty} a_r(n) b^r$$

be the digit expansion of n in base b, where $a_r(n) \in Z_b$ for $r \geq 0$ and $a_r(n) = 0$ for all sufficiently large r. We put

$$x_n^{(i)} = \sum_{j=1}^{\infty} y_{nj}^{(i)} b^{-j} \qquad \text{for } n \geq 0 \text{ and } 1 \leq i \leq s,$$

with

$$y_{nj}^{(i)} = \eta_{ij}\left(\sum_{r=0}^{\infty} c_{jr}^{(i)} \psi_r(a_r(n)) \right) \in Z_b \qquad \text{for } n \geq 0, \ 1 \leq i \leq s, \text{ and } j \geq 1.$$

Note that the sum over r is a finite sum, since $\psi_r(0) = 0$ and $a_r(n) = 0$ for all sufficiently large r. We now define the sequence

(4.42) $$\mathbf{x}_n = (x_n^{(1)}, \ldots, x_n^{(s)}) \qquad \text{for } n = 0, 1, \ldots .$$

To guarantee that the points $\mathbf{x}_n$ belong to I^s (and not just to $\bar{I}^s$), and also for the analysis of the sequence (4.42), we need the following condition:

(S5) For each $n \geq 0$ and $1 \leq i \leq s$, we have $y_{nj}^{(i)} < b - 1$ for infinitely many j.

This condition is always tacitly assumed when we consider the sequence (4.42). A sufficient condition for (S5) is:

(S6) $\eta_{ij}(0) = 0$ for $1 \leq i \leq s$ and all sufficiently large j, and for each $1 \leq i \leq s$ and $r \geq 0$, we have $c_{jr}^{(i)} = 0$ for all sufficiently large j.

Condition (S6) guarantees that, for each $n \geq 0$ and $1 \leq i \leq s$, we have $y_{nj}^{(i)} = 0$ for all sufficiently large j, and so each $x_n^{(i)}$ is given by a finite digit expansion in base b.

THEOREM 4.35. *Suppose that the integer $t \geq 0$ satisfies the following property: For any integers $m > t$ and $d_1, \ldots, d_s \geq 0$ with $\sum_{i=1}^{s} d_i = m - t$ and any $f_j^{(i)} \in R$, $1 \leq j \leq d_i$, $1 \leq i \leq s$, the system of $m - t$ linear equations*

$$\sum_{r=0}^{m-1} c_{jr}^{(i)} z_r = f_j^{(i)} \quad \text{for } 1 \leq j \leq d_i, \ 1 \leq i \leq s$$

in the unknowns $z_0, \ldots, z_{m-1}$ over R has exactly b^t solutions. Then the sequence (4.42) is a (t, s)-sequence in base b.

Proof. For integers $k \geq 0$ and $m > t$, consider the $\mathbf{x}_n$ with $kb^m \leq n < (k+1)b^m$. In this range, the digits $a_r(n)$ of n are prescribed for $r \geq m$, whereas the $a_r(n)$ with $0 \leq r \leq m - 1$ can vary freely over Z_b. Let

$$E = \prod_{i=1}^{s} [a_i b^{-d_i}, (a_i + 1) b^{-d_i})$$

be an elementary interval in base b with $\lambda_s(E) = b^{t-m}$; hence $\sum_{i=1}^{s} d_i = m - t$. Using condition (S5) and proceeding as in the proof of Theorem 4.26, we obtain that $\mathbf{x}_n \in E$ if and only if

$$\sum_{r=0}^{\infty} c_{jr}^{(i)} \psi_r(a_r(n)) = \eta_{ij}^{-1}(a_{ij}) \quad \text{for } 1 \leq j \leq d_i, \ 1 \leq i \leq s.$$

Since the $\psi_r(a_r(n))$ with $r \geq m$ are given, this reduces to

$$\sum_{r=0}^{m-1} c_{jr}^{(i)} \psi_r(a_r(n)) = f_j^{(i)} \quad \text{for } 1 \leq j \leq d_i, \ 1 \leq i \leq s,$$

with suitable $f_j^{(i)} \in R$. By hypothesis, this system of linear equations in the unknowns $\psi_r(a_r(n))$, $0 \leq r \leq m - 1$, over R has exactly b^t solutions. Each solution corresponds to a unique m-tuple $(a_0(n), \ldots, a_{m-1}(n))$, and each such m-tuple corresponds to a unique integer n with $kb^m \leq n < (k+1)b^m$. Therefore the points $\mathbf{x}_n$ with $kb^m \leq n < (k+1)b^m$ form a (t, m, s)-net in base b. The desired result is thus shown by Definition 4.2. $\square$

In the case of a prime power base q, there is an analogue of Theorem 4.28 for (t, s)-sequences. We must consider systems of vectors obtained from the elements $c_{jr}^{(i)}$ in (S4).

THEOREM 4.36. *Let q be a prime power, let $R = F_q$, and let $t \geq 0$ be an integer. If, for each integer $m > t$, the system $C^{(m)}$ consisting of the vectors*

$$\mathbf{c}_j^{(i)} = (c_{j0}^{(i)}, \ldots, c_{j,m-1}^{(i)}) \in F_q^m \quad \text{for } 1 \leq i \leq s, \ 1 \leq j \leq m,$$

satisfies $\rho(C^{(m)}) \geq m - t$, then the sequence (4.42) is a (t, s)-sequence in base q.

Proof. We verify the condition in Theorem 4.35 for the given value of t. Consider integers $m > t$ and $d_1, \ldots, d_s \geq 0$ with $\sum_{i=1}^{s} d_i = m - t$. From $\rho(C^{(m)}) \geq m - t$ and Definition 4.27, it follows that the coefficient matrix of the system of $m - t$ linear equations in Theorem 4.35 has rank $m - t$, and so the system always has exactly q^t solutions. $\square$

There is also an analogue of Theorem 4.29 for (t, s)-sequences. If the ring R is chosen as in that theorem, then the elements $c_{jr}^{(i)}$ in (S4) can again be written in the form (4.27).

THEOREM 4.37. *Let* $b = \prod_{v=1}^{h} q_v$ *be a product of prime powers* q_v, *let* $R = \prod_{v=1}^{h} F_{q_v}$, *and let* $t \geq 0$ *be an integer. Suppose that, for each integer* $m > t$ *and each* v *with* $1 \leq v \leq h$, *the system* $C_v^{(m)}$ *consisting of the vectors*

$$\mathbf{c}_{jv}^{(i)} = (c_{j0v}^{(i)}, \ldots, c_{j,m-1,v}^{(i)}) \in F_{q_v}^m \quad \text{for } 1 \leq i \leq s, \ 1 \leq j \leq m,$$

satisfies $\rho(C_v^{(m)}) \geq m - t$. *Then the sequence* (4.42) *is a* (t, s)-*sequence in base* b.

Proof. Proceed in analogy with the proofs of Theorems 4.29 and 4.36. $\square$

REMARK 4.38. The van der Corput sequence in base b (see Definition 3.2) arises as a special case from the general construction based on (S1) – (S5). Choose $s = 1$ and let the ring R be the residue class ring $\mathbb{Z}/b\mathbb{Z}$. Then R and Z_b can be identified, and so all bijections ψ_r and η_{ij} in (S2) and (S3), respectively, can be taken to be identity maps. Put $c_{jr}^{(1)} = 1$ if $r = j - 1$, and $c_{jr}^{(1)} = 0$ otherwise. Then condition (S6) is satisfied, and the sequence (4.42) is the van der Corput sequence in base b. It is a trivial verification that the condition in Theorem 4.35 is satisfied with $t = 0$. Thus the van der Corput sequence in base b is a $(0, 1)$-sequence in base b (compare also with the beginning of §4.1).

4.4.   A special construction of nets.

We discuss a special family of nets arising from the general construction based on (N1) – (N4) in §4.3. We choose the base to be a prime power q, and the ring R to be the finite field F_q with q elements. Let $F_q((x^{-1}))$ be the field of formal Laurent series over F_q in the variable x^{-1}. Thus the elements of $F_q((x^{-1}))$ are formal Laurent series

$$L = \sum_{k=w}^{\infty} t_k x^{-k},$$

where w is an arbitrary integer and all $t_k \in F_q$. The discrete exponential valuation ν on $F_q((x^{-1}))$ is defined by $\nu(L) = -w$ if $L \neq 0$ and w is the least index with $t_w \neq 0$, and by $\nu(0) = -\infty$. We have $\nu(f) = \deg(f)$ for all nonzero polynomials $f \in F_q[x]$. We also note that $F_q((x^{-1}))$ contains the field of rational functions over F_q as a subfield.

For a given dimension $s \geq 2$, choose $f \in F_q[x]$ with $\deg(f) = m \geq 1$ and let

$g_1, \ldots, g_s \in F_q[x]$. Consider the expansions

$$\frac{g_i(x)}{f(x)} = \sum_{k=w_i}^{\infty} u_k^{(i)} x^{-k} \in F_q((x^{-1})) \quad \text{for } 1 \le i \le s,$$

where $w_i \le 1$ for $1 \le i \le s$. Define the elements $c_{jr}^{(i)}$ in (N4) by

(4.43) $\quad c_{jr}^{(i)} = u_{r+j}^{(i)} \in F_q \quad$ for $1 \le i \le s$, $1 \le j \le m$, $0 \le r \le m-1$.

Choose the bijections in (N2) and (N3) arbitrarily. Then the general construction principle for nets described in §4.3 yields the point set (4.25) consisting of q^m points in I^s. We denote this point set by $P(\mathbf{g}, f)$, where we write $\mathbf{g} = (g_1, \ldots, g_s) \in F_q[x]^s$ for the s-tuple of polynomials $g_1, \ldots, g_s$. For an arbitrary $\mathbf{h} = (h_1, \ldots, h_s) \in F_q[x]^s$, we define the "inner product"

$$\mathbf{h} \cdot \mathbf{g} = \sum_{i=1}^{s} h_i g_i.$$

As usual, we write $f \mid g$ if f divides $g \in F_q[x]$. In the following, we use the convention $\deg(0) = -1$.

DEFINITION 4.39. For f and $\mathbf{g}$ as above, we define

$$\rho(\mathbf{g}, f) = s - 1 + \min \sum_{i=1}^{s} \deg(h_i),$$

where the minimum is extended over all nonzero $\mathbf{h} = (h_1, \ldots, h_s) \in F_q[x]^s$ with $\deg(h_i) < m$ for $1 \le i \le s$ and $f \mid \mathbf{h} \cdot \mathbf{g}$.

LEMMA 4.40. Let

$$\mathbf{c}_j^{(i)} = (c_{j0}^{(i)}, \ldots, c_{j,m-1}^{(i)}) \in F_q^m \quad \text{for } 1 \le i \le s, \ 1 \le j \le m,$$

where the $c_{jr}^{(i)}$ are given by (4.43). Then, for $h_{ij} \in F_q$, $1 \le i \le s$, $1 \le j \le m$, we have

(4.44) $$\sum_{i=1}^{s} \sum_{j=1}^{m} h_{ij} \mathbf{c}_j^{(i)} = \mathbf{0} \in F_q^m$$

if and only if $f \mid \mathbf{h} \cdot \mathbf{g}$, where $\mathbf{h} = (h_1, \ldots, h_s) \in F_q[x]^s$ with

(4.45) $$h_i(x) = \sum_{j=1}^{m} h_{ij} x^{j-1} \in F_q[x] \quad \text{for } 1 \le i \le s.$$

Proof. By comparing components, we see that (4.44) is equivalent to

(4.46) $$\sum_{i=1}^{s} \sum_{j=1}^{m} h_{ij} u_{r+j}^{(i)} = 0 \quad \text{for } 0 \le r \le m-1.$$

For $1 \leq i \leq s$, we have

$$\frac{h_i(x)g_i(x)}{f(x)} = \left(\sum_{j=1}^{m} h_{ij}x^{j-1}\right)\left(\sum_{k=w_i}^{\infty} u_k^{(i)}x^{-k}\right) = \sum_{j=1}^{m}\sum_{k=w_i}^{\infty} h_{ij}u_k^{(i)}x^{-k+j-1}$$

$$= \sum_{j=1}^{m} h_{ij}\sum_{r=w_i-j}^{\infty} u_{r+j}^{(i)}x^{-r-1}.$$

Thus, for $r \geq 0$, the coefficient of x^{-r-1} in $h_i g_i/f$ is $\sum_{j=1}^{m} h_{ij}u_{r+j}^{(i)}$. Therefore, condition (4.46) is equivalent to the following: For $0 \leq r \leq m-1$ the coefficient of x^{-r-1} in $\sum_{i=1}^{s} h_i g_i/f$ is 0. This means that

$$\frac{1}{f}\mathbf{h}\cdot\mathbf{g} = p + L,$$

where $p \in F_q[x]$ and $L \in F_q((x^{-1}))$ with $\nu(L) < -m$. The last identity is equivalent to

$$\mathbf{h}\cdot\mathbf{g} - pf = Lf.$$

On the left-hand side, we have a polynomial over F_q, whereas, on the right-hand side, we have $\nu(Lf) < 0$ since $\nu(f) = \deg(f) = m$. This is only possible if $Lf = 0$, i.e., if $f \mid \mathbf{h}\cdot\mathbf{g}$. $\square$

COROLLARY 4.41. *If C is the system of vectors $\mathbf{c}_j^{(i)}$ in Lemma 4.40 and $\rho(C)$ is as in Definition 4.27, then $\rho(C) = \rho(\mathbf{g}, f)$.*

Proof. By Definition 4.27, there exist integers $d_1, \ldots, d_s$ with $0 \leq d_i \leq m$ for $1 \leq i \leq s$ and $\sum_{i=1}^{s} d_i = \rho(C) + 1$ such that the system $\{\mathbf{c}_j^{(i)} : 1 \leq j \leq d_i, 1 \leq i \leq s\}$ is linearly dependent over F_q. Then there exist $h_{ij} \in F_q$, $1 \leq j \leq d_i$, $1 \leq i \leq s$, not all zero, such that

$$\sum_{i=1}^{s}\sum_{j=1}^{d_i} h_{ij}\mathbf{c}_j^{(i)} = \mathbf{0} \in F_q^m,$$

and, by putting $h_{ij} = 0$ for $d_i < j \leq m$, $1 \leq i \leq s$, we obtain an identity of the form (4.44). By Lemma 4.40 it follows that $f \mid \mathbf{h}\cdot\mathbf{g}$, where $\mathbf{h} = (h_1, \ldots, h_s) \neq \mathbf{0}$ with the polynomials h_i in (4.45). Hence, from Definition 4.39, we obtain

$$\rho(\mathbf{g}, f) \leq s - 1 + \sum_{i=1}^{s} \deg(h_i) \leq s - 1 + \sum_{i=1}^{s}(d_i - 1) = \rho(C).$$

On the other hand, by Definition 4.39, there exists a nonzero $\mathbf{h} = (h_1, \ldots, h_s) \in F_q[x]^s$ with $\deg(h_i) < m$ for $1 \leq i \leq s$ and $f \mid \mathbf{h}\cdot\mathbf{g}$ such that $\rho(\mathbf{g}, f) = s - 1 + \sum_{i=1}^{s} \deg(h_i)$. Then, by Lemma 4.40, we obtain (4.44) with the elements $h_{ij} \in F_q$, $1 \leq i \leq s$, $1 \leq j \leq m$, determined by (4.45). Thus the system $\{\mathbf{c}_j^{(i)} : 1 \leq j \leq \deg(h_i) + 1, 1 \leq i \leq s\}$ is linearly dependent over F_q, and so

$$\rho(C) \leq \sum_{i=1}^{s}(\deg(h_i) + 1) - 1 = \rho(\mathbf{g}, f).$$ $\square$

THEOREM 4.42. *The point set $P(\mathbf{g}, f)$ is a (t, m, s)-net in base q with $t = m - \rho(\mathbf{g}, f)$.*

Proof. This follows from Theorem 4.28 and Corollary 4.41. $\square$

It is clear from Theorem 4.42 that the larger the value of $\rho(\mathbf{g}, f)$, the better the distribution properties of the point set $P(\mathbf{g}, f)$. Therefore the number $\rho(\mathbf{g}, f)$ is called the *figure of merit*. From Corollary 4.41 and the remark following Definition 4.27, we see that we always have $0 \le \rho(\mathbf{g}, f) \le m$. From (4.31), Theorem 4.30, and Corollary 4.41, we obtain the discrepancy bounds

$$(4.47) \qquad \frac{q-1}{3q} q^{-\rho(\mathbf{g}, f)} \le D_N^*(P(\mathbf{g}, f)) \le B(s, q) q^{-\rho(\mathbf{g}, f)} (\log N)^{s-1}$$
$$+ O\big(q^{-\rho(\mathbf{g}, f)} (\log N)^{s-2}\big),$$

where the implied constant depends only on q and s. If $\eta_{ij}(0) = 0$ for $1 \le i \le s$, $1 \le j \le m$, then the factor $(q-1)/(3q)$ in the lower bound can be replaced by $(q-1)/(2q)$.

Another discrepancy bound is obtained from Lemma 4.32 in the case where q is prime and every η_{ij} is the identity map. If $\mathbf{h} = (h_1, \ldots, h_s) \in F_q[x]^s$ with $\deg(h_i) < m$ for $1 \le i \le s$, then we can use (4.45) and the fact that $C(q)$ forms a complete residue system $\bmod\, q$ to identify $\mathbf{h}$ with $H = (h_{ij}) \in C(q)^{s \times m}$, and we put $W_q(\mathbf{h}) = W_q(H)$. In analogy with the definition of $R_q(C)$, we then set

$$(4.48) \qquad R(\mathbf{g}, f) = \sum_{\mathbf{h}} W_q(\mathbf{h}),$$

where the sum is over all nonzero $\mathbf{h} = (h_1, \ldots, h_s) \in F_q[x]^s$ with $\deg(h_i) < m$ for $1 \le i \le s$ and $f \mid \mathbf{h} \cdot \mathbf{g}$. It follows from Lemma 4.40 that $R(\mathbf{g}, f) = R_q(C)$, where C is the system of vectors $\mathbf{c}_j^{(i)}$ in Lemma 4.40. Thus Lemma 4.32 shows that

$$(4.49) \qquad D_N^*(P(\mathbf{g}, f)) \le 1 - \left(1 - \frac{1}{N}\right)^s + R(\mathbf{g}, f) \le \frac{s}{N} + R(\mathbf{g}, f),$$

provided that q is prime and every η_{ij} is the identity map.

On the basis of (4.49), we will prove that the point sets $P(\mathbf{g}, f)$ are on the average low-discrepancy point sets. For $s \ge 2$ and $f \in F_q[x]$ with q prime and $\deg(f) = m \ge 1$, put

$$G_s(f) = \{\mathbf{g} = (g_1, \ldots, g_s) \in F_q[x]^s : \gcd(g_i, f) = 1 \text{ and } \deg(g_i) < m$$
$$\text{for } 1 \le i \le s\}.$$

Let

$$M_s(f) = \frac{1}{\operatorname{card}(G_s(f))} \sum_{\mathbf{g} \in G_s(f)} R(\mathbf{g}, f)$$

be the mean value of $R(\mathbf{g}, f)$ extended over the set $G_s(f)$. Note that $\operatorname{card}(G_s(f)) = \Phi_q(f)^s$, where Φ_q is the analogue of Euler's totient function for the ring $F_q[x]$. By a formula in [192, Lemma 3.69], we have

$$(4.50) \qquad \Phi_q(f) = q^m \prod_{k=1}^{r} (1 - q^{-n_k}),$$

where $n_1, \ldots, n_r$ are the degrees of the distinct monic irreducible polynomials over F_q dividing f.

The proof of the following theorem depends on the theory of arithmetic functions on $F_q[x]$ as developed by Carlitz [36] and on the theory of characters of $F_q((x^{-1}))$ as developed by Carlitz [37] and Hayes [131]. Henceforth, an *arithmetic function* is a real-valued function on the multiplicative semigroup S_q of monic polynomials over F_q. An arithmetic function E is called *multiplicative* (respectively, *additive*) if $E(gh) = E(g)E(h)$ (respectively, $E(gh) = E(g) + E(h)$) for all $g, h \in S_q$ with $\gcd(g, h) = 1$. We write $\sum_{v \bmod f}$ for a sum over all $v \in F_q[x]$ with $\deg(v) < \deg(f)$, and we write $\sum_{v \bmod f}^{*}$ if the additional condition $\gcd(v, f) = 1$ is imposed. Furthermore, $\sum_{d|f}$ denotes a sum over all $d \in S_q$ dividing f.

Let χ be a fixed nontrivial additive character of F_q. For $L \in F_q((x^{-1}))$, put $X_q(L) = \chi(t_1)$, where t_1 is the coefficient of x^{-1} in the expression for L. Then X_q is an additive character of $F_q((x^{-1}))$, that is trivial on $F_q[x]$. Consequently, $X_q(\cdot/f)$ is a nontrivial additive character of the residue class ring $F_q[x]/(f)$. For $g \in F_q[x]$ the orthogonality relations for characters yield

$$(4.51) \qquad \sum_{v \bmod f} X_q\left(\frac{vg}{f}\right) = \begin{cases} q^{\deg(f)} & \text{if } f \mid g, \\ 0 & \text{if } f \nmid g. \end{cases}$$

See, e.g., Car [35, p. 8] for this formula.

THEOREM 4.43. *Let q be a prime, let $s \geq 2$ be an integer, let $f \in F_q[x]$ with $\deg(f) = m \geq 1$, and put $N = q^m$. Then*

$$M_s(f) = \frac{1}{N}(c_q \log N + d_q)^s - c_q s \frac{\log N}{N} + O\left(\frac{(\log \log N)^2}{N}\right),$$

where the implied constant depends only on q and s and where $d_2 = 1$, $d_q = 1/q$ for $q > 2$, $c_2 = 1/\log 4$, and

$$c_q = \frac{1}{q \log q}\left(q - 1 + \sum_{z \in C^*(q)} \csc \frac{\pi|z|}{q}\right) \qquad \text{for } q > 2.$$

Proof. We can assume without loss of generality that f is monic. Inserting the definition of $R(\mathbf{g}, f)$ in (4.48) into the expression for $M_s(f)$ and interchanging the order of summation, we obtain

$$M_s(f) = \frac{1}{\Phi_q(f)^s} \sum_{\mathbf{h} \neq 0} A(\mathbf{h}) W_q(\mathbf{h}).$$

where the sum is over all nonzero $\mathbf{h} = (h_1, \ldots, h_s) \in F_q[x]^s$ with $\deg(h_i) < m$ for $1 \le i \le s$ and where $A(\mathbf{h})$ is the number of $\mathbf{g} \in G_s(f)$ with $f \mid \mathbf{h} \cdot \mathbf{g}$. Since $A(\mathbf{0}) = \Phi_q(f)^s$ and $W_q(\mathbf{0}) = 1$, we can write

$$(4.52) \qquad M_s(f) = \frac{1}{\Phi_q(f)^s} \sum_{\mathbf{h}} A(\mathbf{h}) W_q(\mathbf{h}) - 1,$$

where the sum is over all $\mathbf{h} = (h_1, \ldots, h_s) \in F_q[x]^s$ with $\deg(h_i) < m$ for $1 \le i \le s$. For any such $\mathbf{h}$, we have

$$A(\mathbf{h}) = \sum_{\mathbf{g} \in G_s(f)} q^{-m} \sum_{v \bmod f} X_q\left(\frac{v}{f} \mathbf{h} \cdot \mathbf{g}\right)$$

by (4.51). By the definition of $W_q(\mathbf{h})$, we can write

$$W_q(\mathbf{h}) = \prod_{i=1}^{s} Q_q(h_i),$$

where we use (4.45) to identify h_i with $(h_{i1}, \ldots, h_{im}) \in C_m(q)$, and we define $Q_q(h_i)$ to be the quantity $Q_q(h_{i1}, \ldots, h_{im})$ in (3.16) und (3.17). Then we obtain

$$\sum_{\mathbf{h}} A(\mathbf{h}) W_q(\mathbf{h}) = \frac{1}{N} \sum_{v \bmod f} \sum_{\mathbf{h}} \sum_{\mathbf{g} \in G_s(f)} X_q\left(\frac{v}{f} \mathbf{h} \cdot \mathbf{g}\right) W_q(\mathbf{h})$$

$$= \frac{1}{N} \sum_{v \bmod f} \sum_{h_1 \bmod f} \cdots \sum_{h_s \bmod f} {\sum_{g_1 \bmod f}}^* \cdots {\sum_{g_s \bmod f}}^* X_q\left(\frac{v}{f} h_1 g_1\right) \cdots X_q\left(\frac{v}{f} h_s g_s\right)$$

$$\cdot Q_q(h_1) \cdots Q_q(h_s)$$

$$= \frac{1}{N} \sum_{v \bmod f} Y_q(v, f)^s$$

with

$$Y_q(v, f) = \sum_{h \bmod f} {\sum_{g \bmod f}}^* X_q\left(\frac{v}{f} hg\right) Q_q(h).$$

Now

$$Y_q(0, f) = \Phi_q(f) \sum_{h \bmod f} Q_q(h);$$

thus

$$(4.53) \qquad \sum_{\mathbf{h}} A(\mathbf{h}) W_q(\mathbf{h}) = \frac{1}{N} \Phi_q(f)^s \left(\sum_{h \bmod f} Q_q(h)\right)^s + \frac{1}{N} \sum_{\substack{v \bmod f \\ v \ne 0}} Y_q(v, f)^s.$$

Let μ_q be the Möbius function on S_q (see [36] and [192, p. 145]), and note that μ_q is multiplicative. We abbreviate $\gcd(g, f)$ by (g, f) in this proof. Then, for fixed $v \in F_q[x]$ with $0 \le \deg(v) < m$, we obtain

$$Y_q(v, f) = \sum_{h \bmod f} Q_q(h) \sum_{g \bmod f} X_q\left(\frac{v}{f}hg\right) \sum_{d|(g,f)} \mu_q(d)$$

$$= \sum_{h \bmod f} Q_q(h) \sum_{d|f} \mu_q(d) \sum_{\substack{g \bmod f \\ d|g}} X_q\left(\frac{v}{f}hg\right)$$

$$= \sum_{h \bmod f} Q_q(h) \sum_{d|f} \mu_q(d) \sum_{a \bmod f/d} X_q\left(\frac{v}{f}had\right)$$

$$= \sum_{h \bmod f} Q_q(h) \sum_{d|f} \mu_q\left(\frac{f}{d}\right) \sum_{a \bmod d} X_q\left(\frac{v}{d}ha\right),$$

where, in the last step, we changed d into f/d. Applying (4.51) to the innermost sum, we obtain

$$Y_q(v, f) = \sum_{h \bmod f} Q_q(h) \sum_{\substack{d|f \\ d|vh}} \mu_q\left(\frac{f}{d}\right) q^{\deg(d)} = \sum_{d|f} \mu_q\left(\frac{f}{d}\right) q^{\deg(d)} \sum_{\substack{h \bmod f \\ d|vh}} Q_q(h).$$

Now $d \mid vh$ if and only if $d/(d, v)$ divides h; thus

$$(4.54) \qquad Y_q(v, f) = \sum_{d|f} \mu_q\left(\frac{f}{d}\right) q^{\deg(d)} E_q\left(\frac{d}{(d, v)}, f\right),$$

where, for an $a \in S_q$ dividing f, we put

$$E_q(a, f) = \sum_{\substack{h \bmod f \\ a|h}} Q_q(h).$$

If $a = f$, then

$$E_q(a, f) = Q_q(0) = 1.$$

Now let $a \ne f$; then

$$E_q(a, f) = 1 + \sum_{\substack{b \bmod f/a \\ b \ne 0}} Q_q(ab).$$

For $q = 2$, we have

$$\sum_{\substack{b \bmod f/a \\ b \ne 0}} Q_q(ab) = \sum_{\substack{b \bmod f/a \\ b \ne 0}} 2^{-\deg(ab)-1} = 2^{-\deg(a)-1} \sum_{k=0}^{\deg(f/a)-1} 2^{-k} 2^k$$

$$= \deg\left(\frac{f}{a}\right) 2^{-\deg(a)-1}.$$

For $q > 2$ and for $h \in F_q[x]$ with $0 \le \deg(h) < m$, we have

$$Q_q(h) = q^{-\deg(h)-1}\left(\csc\frac{\pi}{q}|\operatorname{sgn}(h)| + \sigma(\deg(h)+1, m)\right),$$

where $\operatorname{sgn}(h)$ is the leading coefficient of h, viewed as an element of $C^*(q)$. Since a is monic, we obtain

$$\sum_{\substack{b \bmod f/a \\ b \ne 0}} Q_q(ab) = \sum_{\substack{b \bmod f/a \\ b \ne 0}} q^{-\deg(ab)-1}\left(\csc\frac{\pi}{q}|\operatorname{sgn}(b)| + \sigma\left(\deg(b), \deg\left(\frac{f}{a}\right)-1\right)\right)$$

$$= q^{-\deg(a)-1}\sum_{k=0}^{\deg(f/a)-1} q^{-k}q^k \sum_{z \in C^*(q)}\left(\csc\frac{\pi|z|}{q} + \sigma\left(k, \deg\left(\frac{f}{a}\right)-1\right)\right)$$

$$= \deg\left(\frac{f}{a}\right)q^{-\deg(a)-1}\sum_{z \in C^*(q)}\csc\frac{\pi|z|}{q} + (q-1)\left(\deg\left(\frac{f}{a}\right)-1\right)q^{-\deg(a)-1}$$

$$= T_q\deg\left(\frac{f}{a}\right)q^{-\deg(a)} - \varepsilon_q q^{-\deg(a)},$$

where we put $T_q = c_q\log q$ for all q and $\varepsilon_q = (q-1)/q$ for $q > 2$. The case where $q = 2$ is also covered by this formula if we put $\varepsilon_2 = 0$. To include the case where $a = f$, we put

$$\delta_q(a, f) = \begin{cases} \varepsilon_q & \text{if } a = f, \\ 0 & \text{if } a \ne f. \end{cases}$$

Then, for all $a \in S_q$ dividing f, we have

$$(4.55) \quad E_q(a, f) = 1 + T_q\deg\left(\frac{f}{a}\right)q^{-\deg(a)} - (\varepsilon_q - \delta_q(a, f))q^{-\deg(a)}$$

$$= 1 + (mT_q - \varepsilon_q + \delta_q(a, f))q^{-\deg(a)} - T_q\deg(a)q^{-\deg(a)}.$$

Applying this formula with $a = d/(d, v)$ in (4.54), we obtain

$$Y_q(v, f) = \sum_{d|f}\mu_q\left(\frac{f}{d}\right)$$

$$\cdot\left(q^{\deg(d)} + \left(mT_q - \varepsilon_q + \delta_q\left(\frac{d}{(d, v)}, f\right)\right)q^{\deg((d,v))} - T_q\deg\left(\frac{d}{(d, v)}\right)q^{\deg((d,v))}\right);$$

thus

$$(4.56) \qquad Y_q(v, f) = \Phi_q\ (f) + (c_q\log N - \varepsilon_q)H_q^{(1)}(v, f)$$

$$- T_q H_q^{(2)}(v, f) + H_q^{(3)}(v, f)$$

with

$$H_q^{(1)}(v, f) = \sum_{d|f} \mu_q\left(\frac{f}{d}\right) q^{\deg((d,v))},$$

$$H_q^{(2)}(v, f) = \sum_{d|f} \mu_q\left(\frac{f}{d}\right) \deg\left(\frac{d}{(d,v)}\right) q^{\deg((d,v))},$$

$$H_q^{(3)}(v, f) = \sum_{d|f} \mu_q\left(\frac{f}{d}\right) \delta_q\left(\frac{d}{(d,v)}, f\right) q^{\deg((d,v))}.$$

In the remainder of the proof, p will always denote a monic irreducible polynomial over F_q. For a nonzero $v \in F_q[x]$, let $e_p(v)$ be the largest nonnegative integer such that $p^{e_p(v)}$ divides v. Now we consider $H_q^{(1)}(v, f)$ for a fixed $v \neq 0$. Since $q^{\deg((d,v))}$ is a multiplicative function of d, it follows that $H_q^{(1)}(v, f)$ is a multiplicative function of f. For any integer $k \geq 1$, we have

$$H_q^{(1)}(v, p^k) = q^{\deg((p^k,v))} - q^{\deg((p^{k-1},v))}.$$

Hence, if $e_p(v) < k$, then $H_q^{(1)}(v, p^k) = 0$. If $e_p(v) \geq k$, then

$$H_q^{(1)}(v, p^k) = q^{\deg(p^k)} - q^{\deg(p^{k-1})} = \Phi_q(p^k)$$

by (4.50). By multiplicativity, we obtain

(4.57) $$H_q^{(1)}(v, f) = \begin{cases} \Phi_q(f) & \text{if } f \mid v, \\ 0 & \text{if } f \nmid v. \end{cases}$$

Next, we consider $H_q^{(2)}(v, f)$ for a fixed $v \neq 0$. Since $\deg(d/(d,v))$ is an additive and $q^{\deg((d,v))}$ a multiplicative function of d, it follows by induction on the number of distinct polynomials p dividing f that

(4.58) $$H_q^{(2)}(v, f) = \sum_{p|f} H_q^{(2)}(v, p^{e_p(f)}) H_q^{(1)}(v, f/p^{e_p(f)}).$$

For any integer $k \geq 1$, we have

$$H_q^{(2)}(v, p^k) = \deg\left(\frac{p^k}{(p^k, v)}\right) q^{\deg((p^k,v))} - \deg\left(\frac{p^{k-1}}{(p^{k-1}, v)}\right) q^{\deg((p^{k-1},v))}.$$

Hence, if $e_p(v) \geq k$, then $H_q^{(2)}(v, p^k) = 0$. If $e_p(v) < k$, then

$$H_q^{(2)}(v, p^k) = \deg(p) q^{e_p(v) \deg(p)}.$$

By (4.57) and (4.58), we obtain

$$H_q^{(2)}(v, f) = \sum_p \deg(p) q^{e_p(v) \deg(p)} \Phi_q(f/p^{e_p(f)}),$$

where the sum is over all p satisfying the following two conditions: (i) $e_p(v) < e_p(f)$; (ii) $f/p^{e_p(f)}$ divides v. Note that (ii) means that $e_{p_1}(f) \leq e_{p_1}(v)$ for all monic irreducible polynomials p_1 over F_q with $p_1 \neq p$. Thus (i) and (ii) hold simultaneously if and only if there exists a unique p with $e_p(v) < e_p(f)$. If this condition is satisfied, then, with this p, we have

$$H_q^{(2)}(v, f) = \deg(p) q^{e_p(v) \deg(p)} \Phi_q(f/p^{e_p(f)}),$$

whereas $H_q^{(2)}(v, f) = 0$ otherwise.

Now we consider $H_q^{(3)}(v, f)$. Note that $\delta_q(d/(d,v), f) \neq 0$ only if $q > 2$ and $d/(d,v) = f$. Since d divides f, however, we have $d/(d,v) = f$ if and only if $d = f$ and $(f, v) = 1$. Thus, if $q > 2$ and $(f, v) = 1$, then $H_q^{(3)}(v, f) = (q-1)/q$. In all other cases, we have $H_q^{(3)}(v, f) = 0$.

For $v \in F_q[x]$ with $0 \leq \deg(v) < m$, we have $H_q^{(1)}(v, f) = 0$ by (4.57), and so, in view of (4.56) and the formula for $H_q^{(3)}(v, f)$, we obtain

$$Y_q(v, f) = \Phi_q(f) - T_q H_q^{(2)}(v, f) + O(1)$$

with an absolute implied constant. We combine this with (4.52) and (4.53) to obtain

$$M_s(f) = \frac{1}{N} E_q(1, f)^s + \frac{1}{N} \sum_{\substack{v \bmod f \\ v \neq 0}} \left(1 - T_q J_q(v, f) + O\left(\frac{1}{\Phi_q(f)}\right)\right)^s - 1,$$

where $J_q(v, f) = H_q^{(2)}(v, f)/\Phi_q(f)$. The formula for $H_q^{(2)}(v, f)$ shows that $J_q(v, f) = O(1)$; hence

(4.59)

$$M_s(f) = \frac{1}{N} E_q(1, f)^s + \frac{1}{N} \sum_{i=1}^{s} \binom{s}{i} (-T_q)^i \sum_{\substack{v \bmod f \\ v \neq 0}} J_q(v, f)^i + O\left(\frac{1}{\Phi_q(f)}\right)$$

with an implied constant depending only on q and s.

We now consider the sum over v in (4.59) for $1 \leq i \leq s$. From the formula for $H_q^{(2)}(v, f)$, we obtain

$$J_q(v, f) = \frac{\deg(p)}{\Phi_q(p^{e_p(f)-e_p(v)})}$$

if there exists a unique p with $e_p(v) < e_p(f)$, and $J_q(v, f) = 0$ otherwise. We put

$$H_i(f) = \sum_{\substack{v \bmod f \\ v \neq 0}} J_q(v, f)^i \quad \text{for } 1 \leq i \leq s.$$

Let $g, h \in S_q$ with $(g, h) = 1$ and let $v \in F_q[x]$ with $0 \leq \deg(v) < \deg(gh)$ be such that there exists a unique p with $e_p(v) < e_p(gh)$. Then since $e_p(gh) > 0$, p

divides exactly one of g and h, and so the sum $H_i(gh)$ can be split up into two subsums according to these two cases. If $p \mid g$, say, then $v = v_1 h$ with $v_1 \in F_q[x]$, $0 \leq \deg(v_1) < \deg(g)$, and $J_q(v, gh) = J_q(v_1 h, gh) = J_q(v_1, g)$. From this, it is easily seen that $H_i(gh) = H_i(g) + H_i(h)$; hence H_i is additive. For an integer $e \geq 1$ and any p, we have

$$H_i(p^e) = \deg(p)^i \sum_{k=0}^{e-1} \sum_{\substack{v \bmod p^e \\ e_p(v)=k}} \Phi_q(p^{e-k})^{-i}.$$

For $0 \leq k \leq e-1$, the number of $v \in F_q[x]$ with $0 \leq \deg(v) < \deg(p^e)$ and $e_p(v) = k$ is equal to $\Phi_q(p^{e-k})$, and so

(4.60) $$H_i(p^e) = \deg(p)^i \sum_{k=1}^{e} \Phi_q(p^k)^{1-i}.$$

For $i = 1$, this yields $H_1(p^e) = \deg(p)e = \deg(p^e)$, thus $H_1(f) = \deg(f) = m$ by additivity. For $i = 2$, we obtain

$$H_2(p^e) = \deg(p)^2 \sum_{k=1}^{e} q^{-k\deg(p)}(1 - q^{-\deg(p)})^{-1}$$

$$\leq 2\deg(p)^2 \sum_{k=1}^{e} q^{-k\deg(p)} < 4\deg(p)^2 q^{-\deg(p)},$$

and so, by additivity,

$$H_2(f) < 4 \sum_{p \mid f} \deg(p)^2 q^{-\deg(p)}.$$

Let n be the number of distinct monic irreducible polynomials over F_q dividing f, and let $p_1, \ldots, p_n$ be the first n in a list of all monic irreducible polynomials over F_q ordered by nondecreasing degrees. Then

$$H_2(f) < 4 \sum_{j=1}^{n} \deg(p_j)^2 q^{-\deg(p_j)} + O(1) \leq 4 \sum_{r=1}^{D(n)} r^2 q^{-r} I_q(r) + O(1),$$

where $D(n) = \deg(p_n)$ and $I_q(r)$ is the number of monic irreducible polynomials over F_q of degree r. Since $I_q(r) \leq q^r/r$ for $r \geq 1$ by [192, Cor. 3.21], it follows that

(4.61) $$H_2(f) < 4 \sum_{r=1}^{D(n)} r + O(1) = O(D(n)^2).$$

On the other hand, we have

$$m = \deg(f) \geq \sum_{j=1}^{n} \deg(p_j) \geq (D(n) - 1)I_q(D(n) - 1).$$

From [192, Exer. 3.27], we obtain $I_q(r) \geq cq^r/r$ for $r \geq 1$ with an absolute constant $c > 0$. Thus, if $D(n) \geq 2$, then $m \geq cq^{D(n)-1}$; hence $D(n) = O(1 + \log m)$, and this holds trivially if $D(n) = 1$. Combining this with (4.61), we obtain

$$(4.62) \qquad H_2(f) = O\big((\log\log N)^2\big).$$

For $i \geq 3$, it follows from (4.60) that

$$H_i(p^e) \leq \deg(p)^i \sum_{k=1}^{e} \Phi_q(p^k)^{-2} = \deg(p)^i \sum_{k=1}^{e} q^{-2k\deg(p)}(1 - q^{-\deg(p)})^{-2}$$
$$< 2\deg(p)^i (q^{\deg(p)} - 1)^{-2},$$

and so, by additivity,

$$H_i(f) < 2 \sum_{\substack{g \in S_q \\ \deg(g) \geq 1}} \deg(g)^i (q^{\deg(g)} - 1)^{-2} = 2 \sum_{k=1}^{\infty} k^i (q^k - 1)^{-2} q^k$$
$$\leq 4 \sum_{k=1}^{\infty} k^i (q^k - 1)^{-1} = O(1).$$

Now we use this information as well as (4.62) and $H_1(f) = m$ in formula (4.59). This yields

$$M_s(f) = \frac{1}{N} E_q(1, f)^s - c_q s \frac{\log N}{N} + O\left(\frac{(\log\log N)^2}{N}\right) + O\left(\frac{1}{\Phi_q(f)}\right).$$

By (4.55) we have $E_q(1, f) = mT_q + d_q = c_q \log N + d_q$, and [35, Prop. VI.11] yields $\Phi_q(f)^{-1} = O\big(N^{-1}\log\log(N+1)\big)$. Hence the desired result follows. $\square$

It follows from (4.49) and Theorem 4.43 that, if q is prime, every η_{ij} is the identity map, and if $s \geq 2$ and $f \in F_q[x]$ with $\deg(f) = m \geq 1$ are fixed, then, as $\mathbf{g}$ runs through $G_s(f)$, we get on the average $D_N^*(P(\mathbf{g}, f)) = O\big(N^{-1}(\log N)^s\big)$. We note that, for the number c_q in Theorem 4.43, we have the bound

$$c_q < \frac{2}{\pi} + \frac{7}{5\log q} - \frac{1}{q\log q} \qquad \text{for } q > 2,$$

according to (3.22).

REMARK 4.44. In the special case where f is irreducible over F_q, q prime, a result of the same type as Theorem 4.43 can be shown in a much easier fashion. Put $m = \deg(f)$ and let

$$G'_s(f) = \{\mathbf{g} = (g_1, \ldots, g_s) \in F_q[x]^s : \deg(g_i) < m \text{ for } 1 \leq i \leq s\},$$
$$M'_s(f) = \frac{1}{\operatorname{card}(G'_s(f))} \sum_{\mathbf{g} \in G'_s(f)} R(\mathbf{g}, f).$$

Then $\operatorname{card}(G'_s(f)) = q^{ms}$, and, in the same way as in the beginning of the proof of Theorem 4.43, we obtain

$$M'_s(f) = q^{-ms} \sum_{\mathbf{h} \neq 0} A'(\mathbf{h}) W_q(\mathbf{h}),$$

where $A'(\mathbf{h})$ is the number of $\mathbf{g} \in G'_s(f)$ with $f \mid \mathbf{h} \cdot \mathbf{g}$. For every $\mathbf{h}$ in the range of summation, we have $A'(\mathbf{h}) = q^{m(s-1)}$, since $s - 1$ entries of $\mathbf{g}$ can be prescribed arbitrarily and the remaining entry (for which the corresponding entry of $\mathbf{h}$ is $\neq 0$) is uniquely determined because of the irreducibility of f. Thus, with $N = q^m$, we obtain

$$M'_s(f) = \frac{1}{N} \sum_{\mathbf{h} \neq 0} W_q(\mathbf{h}),$$

and so Lemma 3.13 yields

$$M'_s(f) = \frac{1}{N} \left(\frac{\log N}{\log 4} + 1 \right)^s - \frac{1}{N} \quad \text{if } q = 2,$$

$$M'_s(f) = \frac{1}{N} \left(\frac{m}{q} \sum_{h \in C^*(q)} \csc \frac{\pi|h|}{q} + m - \frac{m-1}{q} \right)^s - \frac{1}{N}$$

$$< \frac{1}{N} \left(\left(\frac{2}{\pi} + \frac{7}{5 \log q} - \frac{1}{q \log q} \right) \log N + \frac{1}{q} \right)^s - \frac{1}{N} \quad \text{if } q > 2.$$

REMARK 4.45. If f is irreducible over F_q, then the $c_{jr}^{(i)}$ in (4.43) can also be represented as follows. We first note that the sequence $u_1^{(i)}, u_2^{(i)}, \cdots$ is a linear recurring sequence with characteristic polynomial f. Thus it follows from Theorem A.2 in Appendix A that there exist elements θ_i, $1 \leq i \leq s$, in the extension field F_N of order $N = q^m$ such that

$$u_k^{(i)} = \operatorname{Tr}(\theta_i \sigma^{k-1}) \quad \text{for } 1 \leq i \leq s \text{ and } k \geq 1,$$

where Tr is the trace function from F_N to F_q and where σ is a root of f in F_N. Hence (4.43) attains the form

$$c_{jr}^{(i)} = \operatorname{Tr}(\theta_i \sigma^{r+j-1}) \quad \text{for } 1 \leq i \leq s, \ 1 \leq j \leq m, \ 0 \leq r \leq m - 1.$$

Consequently, if q is prime, f is irreducible over F_q, and the bijections ψ_r and η_{ij} are identity maps, then the construction of the point sets $P(\mathbf{g}, f)$ is a special case of the construction in Niederreiter [239, p. 161], where, in the latter construction, we take $\beta_{ij} = \theta_i \sigma^{j-1} \in F_N$ for $1 \leq i \leq s, \ 1 \leq j \leq m$.

In the case where $s = 2$, there is a connection between the figure of merit $\rho(\mathbf{g}, f)$ introduced in Definition 4.39 and continued fractions for rational functions over F_q, where q is again an arbitrary prime power. Let $\mathbf{g} = (g_1, g_2) \in F_q[x]^2$ with $\gcd(g_i, f) = 1$ for $i = 1, 2$. Then the condition $\mathbf{h} \cdot \mathbf{g} = h_1 g_1 + h_2 g_2 \equiv 0 \bmod f$ in Definition 4.39 is equivalent to

$h_1 + h_2 g_1^* g_2 \equiv 0 \bmod f$, where $g_1^* \in F_q[x]$ is such that $g_1 g_1^* \equiv 1 \bmod f$. Therefore the figure of merit is the same for the original $\mathbf{g}$ and for the pair $(1, g_1^* g_2)$. Thus it suffices to consider the figure of merit for pairs $\mathbf{g}$ of the form $\mathbf{g} = (1, g)$ with $g \in F_q[x]$ and $\gcd(g, f) = 1$. Let

$$\frac{g}{f} = [A_0; A_1, A_2, \ldots, A_l]$$

be the continued fraction expansion of the rational function g/f, with partial quotients $A_n \in F_q[x]$ satisfying $\deg(A_n) \geq 1$ for $1 \leq n \leq l$. Put

(4.63)
$$K\left(\frac{g}{f}\right) = \max_{1 \leq n \leq l} \deg(A_n).$$

Then we have the following formula.

THEOREM 4.46. *If $f \in F_q[x]$ with $\deg(f) = m \geq 1$ and $\mathbf{g} = (1, g) \in F_q[x]^2$ with $\gcd(g, f) = 1$, then*

$$\rho(\mathbf{g}, f) = m + 1 - K\left(\frac{g}{f}\right).$$

Proof. If $\mathbf{h} = (h_1, h_2) \in F_q[x]^2$ satisfies the conditions in Definition 4.39, then we must have $h_2 \neq 0$; hence $0 \leq \deg(h_2) < m$. From $h_1 + h_2 g \equiv 0 \bmod f$, it follows that $h_1 = pf - h_2 g$ for some $p \in F_q[x]$, and actually p is chosen so that $\deg(h_1)$ is minimal. Therefore

$$\rho(\mathbf{g}, f) = 1 + \min_{\mathbf{h}}(\deg(h_1) + \deg(h_2)) = 1 + \min_{h_2, p}(\deg(pf - h_2 g) + \deg(h_2))$$

$$= m + 1 + \min_{h_2, p}\left(\nu\left(\frac{g}{f} - \frac{p}{h_2}\right) + 2\deg(h_2)\right),$$

where the last two minima are extended over all $h_2 \in F_q[x]$ with $0 \leq \deg(h_2) < m$ and all $p \in F_q[x]$. Now we use notation and results from Appendix B. For arbitrary h_2 and p, as above, there exists n with $1 \leq n \leq l$ such that $\deg(Q_{n-1}) \leq \deg(h_2) < \deg(Q_n)$. Then

$$\nu\left(\frac{g}{f} - \frac{p}{h_2}\right) + 2\deg(h_2) \geq \nu\left(\frac{g}{f} - \frac{P_{n-1}}{Q_{n-1}}\right) + 2\deg(Q_{n-1})$$

$$= \deg(Q_{n-1}) - \deg(Q_n) = -\deg(A_n),$$

with equality if $p = P_{n-1}$, $h_2 = Q_{n-1}$. Thus

$$\rho(\mathbf{g}, f) = m + 1 + \min_{1 \leq n \leq l}(-\deg(A_n)) = m + 1 - K\left(\frac{g}{f}\right). \qquad \square$$

It follows from Theorem 4.46 that the desirable pairs $\mathbf{g} = (1, g)$ are those with a small value of $K(g/f)$. The least possible value of $K(g/f)$ is 1. For any prescribed $m \geq 1$, we can obtain $f, g \in F_q[x]$ with $\deg(f) = m$, $\gcd(g, f) = 1$, and $K(g/f) = 1$, namely, by choosing partial quotients $A_0, \ldots, A_m$ with $\deg(A_r) = 1$ for $1 \le r \le m$ and letting g/f be the resulting rational function (A_0 can be arbitrary, the simplest choice being $A_0 = 0$). If $K(g/f) = 1$, then, from Theorem 4.46, we obtain $\rho(\mathbf{g}, f) = m$ for $\mathbf{g} = (1, g)$. With such a choice of $\mathbf{g}$ and f, we obtain a two-dimensional point set $P(\mathbf{g}, f)$ satisfying $D_N^*(P(\mathbf{g}, f)) = O(N^{-1} \log N)$, according to (4.47). By the general lower bound mentioned after (3.8), this is the smallest order of magnitude that can be achieved by the star discrepancy of a two-dimensional point set.

A construction analogous to that of the point sets $P(\mathbf{g}, f)$ can also be applied to sequences. A formal Laurent series $L \in F_q((x^{-1}))$ is called *irrational* if it is not the expansion of a rational function over F_q. Now let $s \ge 1$ be a given dimension and choose irrational $L_1, \ldots, L_s \in F_q((x^{-1}))$, say

$$L_i = \sum_{k=w_i}^{\infty} u_k^{(i)} x^{-k} \qquad \text{for } 1 \le i \le s,$$

where $w_i \le 1$ for $1 \le i \le s$. Then define the elements $c_{jr}^{(i)}$ in (S4) by

(4.64) $c_{jr}^{(i)} = u_{r+j}^{(i)} \in F_q \qquad \text{for } 1 \le i \le s,\ j \ge 1,\ r \ge 0.$

The bijections in (S2) are chosen arbitrarily, subject only to the condition imposed in (S2). Then the general construction principle for sequences described in §4.3 yields the sequence (4.42). It remains to guarantee that condition (S5) holds. The following is a sufficient condition for (S5) to be satisfied. Here η_{ij}^{-1} denotes again the inverse map of the bijection η_{ij}.

LEMMA 4.47. *If the bijections η_{ij} are such that $\eta_{ij}^{-1}(q-1)$ is $\ne 0$ and independent of j for all sufficiently large j, then, for each $n \ge 0$ and $1 \le i \le s$, we have $y_{nj}^{(i)} < q - 1$ for infinitely many j.*

Proof. Suppose that for some n and i we had $y_{nj}^{(i)} = q - 1$ for all sufficiently large j. Since, for a suitable integer $R_n \ge 0$, we have $\psi_r(a_r(n)) = 0$ for all $r > R_n$, it follows from (4.64) and the definition of the $y_{nj}^{(i)}$ that

$$\sum_{r=0}^{R_n} u_{r+j}^{(i)} \psi_r(a_r(n)) = \eta_{ij}^{-1}(q-1) \qquad \text{for all sufficiently large } j.$$

By hypothesis there exists a nonzero $m_i \in F_q$ such that $\eta_{ij}^{-1}(q-1) = m_i$ for all sufficiently large j. Thus, with a suitable integer $j_0 \ge 1$, we have

$$\sum_{r=0}^{R_n} \psi_r(a_r(n)) u_{r+j}^{(i)} = m_i \qquad \text{for all } j \ge j_0.$$

Hence, if we put $v_k = u_{k+j_0}^{(i)}$ for $k \ge 0$, then the sequence $v_0, v_1, \ldots$ of elements of F_q satisfies a nontrivial linear recursion and is thus ultimately periodic (compare with Appendix A). Consequently, the sequence $u_1^{(i)}, u_2^{(i)}, \ldots$ is ultimately periodic, and so L_i is the expansion of a rational function over F_q, which is a contradiction. $\square$

To illustrate the analysis of these sequences, we consider the simplest case where $s = 1$. For an irrational $L_1 \in F_q((x^{-1}))$ as above, let

$$L_1 = [A_0; A_1, A_2, \ldots]$$

be its continued fraction expansion, with partial quotients $A_d \in F_q[x]$, $d = 0, 1, \ldots$, satisfying $\deg(A_d) \geq 1$ for $d \geq 1$. Put

$$K(L_1) = \sup_{d \geq 1} \deg(A_d).$$

The hypothesis of Lemma 4.47 is assumed in the construction to guarantee the validity of condition (S5).

THEOREM 4.48. *If $K(L_1) < \infty$, then the above construction based on (4.64) with $s = 1$ yields a $(t,1)$-sequence in base q with $t = K(L_1) - 1$.*

Proof. By Theorem 4.36, it suffices to verify that, for each integer $m > t$, the vectors

$$c_j^{(1)} = (c_{j0}^{(1)}, \ldots, c_{j,m-1}^{(1)}) \in F_q^m, \qquad 1 \leq j \leq m - t,$$

are linearly independent over F_q. Suppose that, for some $m > t$, we had

$$\sum_{j=1}^{m-t} h_j c_j^{(1)} = \mathbf{0} \in F_q^m,$$

where not all $h_j \in F_q$ are zero. Then

$$\sum_{j=1}^{m-t} h_j u_{r+j}^{(1)} = 0 \qquad \text{for } 0 \leq r \leq m - 1.$$

With $h(x) = \sum_{j=1}^{m-t} h_j x^{j-1} \in F_q[x]$ we obtain

$$hL_1 = \left(\sum_{j=1}^{m-t} h_j x^{j-1} \right) \left(\sum_{k=w_1}^{\infty} u_k^{(1)} x^{-k} \right) = \sum_{j=1}^{m-t} h_j \sum_{k=w_1}^{\infty} u_k^{(1)} x^{-k+j-1}$$

$$= \sum_{j=1}^{m-t} h_j \sum_{r=w_1-j}^{\infty} u_{r+j}^{(1)} x^{-r-1},$$

and so the coefficient of x^{-r-1} in hL_1 is zero for $0 \leq r \leq m-1$. Thus $\nu(hL_1 - p) < -m$ for a suitable $p \in F_q[x]$. Since $\deg(h) \leq m - t - 1$, it follows that

(4.65) $$\deg(h) + \nu(hL_1 - p) < -t - 1 = -K(L_1).$$

On the other hand, with notation and results from Appendix B, we see that there exists a $d \geq 1$ with $\deg(Q_{d-1}) \leq \deg(h) < \deg(Q_d)$ and that

$$\deg(h) + \nu(hL_1 - p) = 2\deg(h) + \nu\left(L_1 - \frac{p}{h} \right) \geq 2\deg(Q_{d-1}) + \nu\left(L_1 - \frac{P_{d-1}}{Q_{d-1}} \right)$$

$$= \deg(Q_{d-1}) - \deg(Q_d) = -\deg(A_d) \geq -K(L_1).$$

This is a contradiction to (4.65). $\square$

4.5. A special construction of (t,s)-sequences.

We first consider a prime power base q and we choose the ring R to be the finite field F_q in the general construction based on (S1)–(S4) in §4.3. To obtain suitable elements $c_{jr}^{(i)} \in F_q$ in (S4), we again use the method of formal Laurent series employed in §4.4. In the following, we describe the most interesting special case of a construction introduced in Niederreiter [247].

For a given dimension $s \geq 1$, let $p_1, \ldots, p_s \in F_q[x]$ be distinct monic irreducible polynomials over F_q. Put $e_i = \deg(p_i)$ for $1 \leq i \leq s$. For $1 \leq i \leq s$ and integers $j \geq 1$ and $0 \leq k < e_i$, consider the expansions

$$(4.66) \qquad \frac{x^k}{p_i(x)^j} = \sum_{r=0}^{\infty} a^{(i)}(j,k,r) x^{-r-1} \in F_q((x^{-1})).$$

Then define the elements $c_{jr}^{(i)}$ in (S4) by

$$(4.67) \qquad c_{jr}^{(i)} = a^{(i)}(Q+1,k,r) \in F_q \qquad \text{for } 1 \leq i \leq s,\; j \geq 1,\; r \geq 0,$$

where $j - 1 = Qe_i + k$ with integers $Q = Q(i,j)$ and $k = k(i,j)$ satisfying $0 \leq k < e_i$. We assume that the bijections η_{ij} in (S3) are chosen in such a way that $\eta_{ij}(0) = 0$ for $1 \leq i \leq s$ and all sufficiently large j. The bijections in (S2) are selected arbitrarily, subject only to the condition imposed in (S2). For each $1 \leq i \leq s$ and $r \geq 0$, the elements in (4.67) satisfy $c_{jr}^{(i)} = 0$ for all sufficiently large j. Thus condition (S6) holds, and so (4.42) yields a sequence of points in I^s.

THEOREM 4.49. *The above construction, with the $c_{jr}^{(i)}$ defined by (4.67), yields a (t,s)-sequence in base q with $t = \sum_{i=1}^{s}(e_i - 1)$.*

Proof. By Theorem 4.36 and Definition 4.27, it suffices to verify the following property: For any integer $m > \sum_{i=1}^{s}(e_i - 1)$ and any integers $d_1, \ldots, d_s \geq 0$ with $1 \leq \sum_{i=1}^{s} d_i \leq m - \sum_{i=1}^{s}(e_i - 1)$, the vectors

$$\mathbf{c}_j^{(i)} = (c_{j0}^{(i)}, \ldots, c_{j,m-1}^{(i)}) \in F_q^m \qquad \text{for } 1 \leq j \leq d_i,\; 1 \leq i \leq s,$$

are linearly independent over F_q. Suppose that we have

$$\sum_{i=1}^{s} \sum_{j=1}^{d_i} f_j^{(i)} \mathbf{c}_j^{(i)} = \mathbf{0} \in F_q^m$$

for some $f_j^{(i)} \in F_q$, where we can assume without loss of generality that all $d_i \geq 1$. By comparing components, we obtain

$$(4.68) \qquad \sum_{i=1}^{s} \sum_{j=1}^{d_i} f_j^{(i)} c_{jr}^{(i)} = 0 \qquad \text{for } 0 \leq r \leq m - 1.$$

Consider the rational function

$$L = \sum_{i=1}^{s} \sum_{j=1}^{d_i} f_j^{(i)} \frac{x^{k(i,j)}}{p_i(x)^{Q(i,j)+1}} = \sum_{r=0}^{\infty} \left(\sum_{i=1}^{s} \sum_{j=1}^{d_i} f_j^{(i)} c_{jr}^{(i)} \right) x^{-r-1},$$

where we used (4.66) and (4.67) in the second identity. In view of (4.68), we have $\nu(L) < -m$. If we put $Q_i = \lfloor (d_i - 1)/e_i \rfloor$ for $1 \leq i \leq s$, then a common denominator of L is $g(x) = \prod_{i=1}^{s} p_i(x)^{Q_i+1}$, and so Lg is a polynomial. On the other hand, we have

$$\nu(Lg) < -m + \deg(g) = -m + \sum_{i=1}^{s}(Q_i+1)e_i \leq -m + \sum_{i=1}^{s}(d_i - 1 + e_i) \leq 0.$$

Thus $Lg = 0$; hence $L = 0$, and so

$$\sum_{i=1}^{s} \sum_{j=1}^{d_i} f_j^{(i)} \frac{x^{k(i,j)}}{p_i(x)^{Q(i,j)+1}} = 0.$$

The left-hand side is the partial fraction decomposition of a rational function, and so it follows from the uniqueness of the partial fraction decomposition that all $f_j^{(i)} = 0$. $\square$

In the general construction of Niederreiter [247], $p_1, \ldots, p_s$ can be any pairwise relatively prime polynomials over F_q of positive degrees. Furthermore, in (4.66) we can replace $x^k/p_i(x)^j$ by $x^k g_{ij}(x)/p_i(x)^j$, where $g_{ij} \in F_q[x]$ with $\gcd(g_{ij}, p_i) = 1$ for $1 \leq i \leq s$ and $j \geq 1$ and

$$\lim_{j \to \infty} (j \deg(p_i) - \deg(g_{ij})) = \infty \quad \text{for } 1 \leq i \leq s.$$

Now we return to the special case considered in Theorem 4.49, and we note that, for fixed s and q, the minimum value of t is obtained by choosing $p_1, \ldots, p_s$ as the "first s" monic irreducible polynomials over F_q. This means that we list all monic irreducible polynomials over F_q in a sequence according to nondecreasing degrees, and then we let $p_1, \ldots, p_s$ be the first s terms of this sequence. With such a choice for $p_1, \ldots, p_s$, we put

(4.69)
$$T_q(s) = \sum_{i=1}^{s} (\deg(p_i) - 1).$$

The polynomials $p_1, \ldots, p_s$ are not uniquely determined, but the number $T_q(s)$ is, of course, well defined. We then obtain the following consequences.

COROLLARY 4.50. *For every dimension $s \geq 1$ and every prime power q, there exists a $(T_q(s), s)$-sequence in base q.*

COROLLARY 4.51. *Let $b = \prod_{v=1}^{h} q_v$ be a product of prime powers q_v. Then, for every dimension $s \geq 1$, there exists a (t,s)-sequence in base b with*

$$t = \max_{1 \leq v \leq h} T_{q_v}(s).$$

Proof. For each v with $1 \leq v \leq h$, we choose elements $c_{jrv}^{(i)} \in F_{q_v}$ for $1 \leq i \leq s$, $j \geq 1$, and $r \geq 0$ as in (4.67), with $p_{1v}, \ldots, p_{sv} \in F_{q_v}[x]$ being selected in such a way that

$$\sum_{i=1}^{s} (\deg(p_{iv}) - 1) = T_{q_v}(s).$$

Then we define the elements $c_{jr}^{(i)} \in R = \prod_{v=1}^{h} F_{q_v}$ for $1 \le i \le s$, $j \ge 1$, and $r \ge 0$ by (4.27). By the proof of Theorem 4.49, the system $C_v^{(m)}$ in Theorem 4.37 satisfies $\rho(C_v^{(m)}) \ge m - T_{q_v}(s)$ for each integer $m > T_{q_v}(s)$ and each v with $1 \le v \le h$. Thus the condition in Theorem 4.37 holds with $t = \max_{1 \le v \le h} T_{q_v}(s)$; hence the result. $\square$

REMARK 4.52. If q is a prime power and s is an arbitrary dimension $\le q$, then we can choose for $p_1, \dots, p_s$ the linear polynomials $p_i(x) = x - b_i$ for $1 \le i \le s$, where $b_1, \dots, b_s$ are distinct elements of F_q. Thus we have $T_q(s) = 0$ for $s \le q$. Furthermore, (4.67) reduces to

$$c_{jr}^{(i)} = a^{(i)}(j, 0, r) \quad \text{for } 1 \le i \le s, \ j \ge 1, \ r \ge 0,$$

and these elements are obtained from the expansion

$$\frac{1}{p_i(x)^j} = \frac{1}{x^j(1 - b_i x^{-1})^j} = x^{-j} \sum_{r=0}^{\infty} \binom{r+j-1}{j-1} b_i^r x^{-r}$$

$$= \sum_{r=j-1}^{\infty} \binom{r}{j-1} b_i^{r-j+1} x^{-r-1}.$$

Thus, for $1 \le i \le s$ and $j \ge 1$, we have

$$c_{jr}^{(i)} = 0 \qquad\qquad \text{for } 0 \le r < j - 1,$$

$$c_{jr}^{(i)} = \binom{r}{j-1} b_i^{r-j+1} \qquad \text{for } r \ge j - 1,$$

where we use the convention $0^0 = 1 \in F_q$. This choice of the $c_{jr}^{(i)}$ yields the $(0, s)$-sequences in base q constructed in Niederreiter [244], and, if we specialize further to q being a prime, then this yields the sequences introduced by Faure [95]. Note that, as far as the construction of $(0, s)$-sequences in base q is concerned, the condition $s \le q$ on the dimension s is best possible, since Corollary 4.24 shows that $s \le q$ is a necessary condition for the existence of a $(0, s)$-sequence in base q. We obtain the choice of the $c_{jr}^{(i)}$ leading to the van der Corput sequence in a prime base q (see Remark 4.38) if we put $s = 1$ and $p_1(x) = x$.

We now consider in more detail the quantity $T_q(s)$ defined in (4.69). Let $I_q(n)$ be the number of monic irreducible polynomials over F_q of degree n, and let $J_q(n)$ be the number of monic irreducible polynomials over F_q of degree $\le n$, with $J_q(0) = 0$. For given $s \ge 1$, let $n = n_q(s)$ be the largest integer with $J_q(n) \le s$. Then it follows from the definition of $T_q(s)$ that

$$(4.70) \qquad T_q(s) = \sum_{h=1}^{n_q(s)} (h-1)I_q(h) + n_q(s)(s - J_q(n_q(s))).$$

The values of $T_q(s)$ for $q = 2, 3, 5$ and $1 \le s \le 30$ are given in the following tables. A general upper bound for $T_q(s)$ is shown in Theorem 4.54.

TABLE 4.1
Values of $T_2(s)$ for $1 \leq s \leq 30$.

s	1	2	3	4	5	6	7	8	9	10	11	12	13	14	15
$T_2(s)$	0	0	1	3	5	8	11	14	18	22	26	30	34	38	43

s	16	17	18	19	20	21	22	23	24	25	26	27	28	29	30
$T_2(s)$	48	53	58	63	68	73	78	83	89	95	101	107	113	119	125

TABLE 4.2
Values of $T_3(s)$ for $1 \leq s \leq 30$.

s	1	2	3	4	5	6	7	8	9	10	11	12	13	14	15
$T_3(s)$	0	0	0	1	2	3	5	7	9	11	13	15	17	19	22

s	16	17	18	19	20	21	22	23	24	25	26	27	28	29	30
$T_3(s)$	25	28	31	34	37	40	43	46	49	52	55	58	61	64	67

TABLE 4.3
Values of $T_5(s)$ for $1 \leq s \leq 30$.

s	1	2	3	4	5	6	7	8	9	10	11	12	13	14	15
$T_5(s)$	0	0	0	0	0	1	2	3	4	5	6	7	8	9	10

s	16	17	18	19	20	21	22	23	24	25	26	27	28	29	30
$T_5(s)$	12	14	16	18	20	22	24	26	28	30	32	34	36	38	40

LEMMA 4.53. *For any prime power q, we have*

$$J_q(n) \geq \frac{1}{n}q^n \quad \text{for all } n \geq 1.$$

Proof. By Appendix A, we have

$$I_q(n) = \frac{1}{n}\sum_{d|n}\mu\left(\frac{n}{d}\right)q^d \quad \text{for all } n \geq 1,$$

where μ is the Möbius function. This formula immediately yields the lower bound in the lemma for $n = 1, 2, 3$. For $n \geq 3$ we use induction to obtain

$$J_q(n+1) = J_q(n) + I_q(n+1) \geq \frac{1}{n}q^n + \frac{1}{n+1}\left(q^{n+1} - \sum_{d=1}^{\lfloor (n+1)/2 \rfloor} q^d\right)$$

$$> \frac{1}{n+1}q^{n+1} + \frac{1}{n}(q^n - q^{(n+3)/2}) \geq \frac{1}{n+1}q^{n+1}. \qquad \square$$

THEOREM 4.54. *Let q be any prime power. Then, for $1 \leq s \leq q$, we have $T_q(s) = 0$, and, for $s > q$, we have*

$$T_q(s) < s(\log_q s + \log_q \log_q s + 1),$$

where $\log_q$ denotes the logarithm to the base q.

Proof. The first part of the theorem was already noted in Remark 4.52. For $s > q$, we have

(4.71) $$T_q(s) < n_q(s)s$$

by (4.70). Put

$$k = \lfloor \log_q s + \log_q \log_q s \rfloor + 2.$$

If either $q = 2$, $y \geq 4$, or $q \geq 3$, $y > 1$, then

$$(q - 1)y \geq \log_q y + 2.$$

With $y = \log_q s$, we obtain

$$q \log_q s \geq \log_q s + \log_q \log_q s + 2 \geq k$$

if either $q = 2$, $s \geq 16$, or $q \geq 3$, $s > q$. In these cases, it follows that

$$k > \log_q s + \log_q \log_q s + 1 \geq \log_q s + \log_q k,$$

and so Lemma 4.53 yields

$$J_q(k) \geq \frac{1}{k} q^k > s.$$

By the definition of $n_q(s)$, we then see that

$$n_q(s) \leq k - 1 \leq \log_q s + \log_q \log_q s + 1,$$

and the bound for $T_q(s)$ follows from (4.71). In the remaining case where $q = 2$, $3 \leq s \leq 15$, the bound for $T_q(s)$ is checked directly by using Table 4.1. $\square$

We now discuss the important question of finding a sequence S of points in I^s, whose star discrepancy satisfies

$$ND_N^*(S) \leq C_s(\log N)^s + o\big((\log N)^s\big) \qquad \text{for all } N \geq 2,$$

where the constant C_s is as small as possible. The case where $s = 1$ has already been considered in §3.1, and so we take $s \geq 2$. For any prime power q, there exists a $(T_q(s), s)$-sequence in base q by Corollary 4.50, and, for such a sequence S, we have

$$ND_N^*(S) \leq C(s, q)q^{T_q(s)}(\log N)^s + O\big((\log N)^{s-1}\big) \qquad \text{for all } N \geq 2$$

by Theorem 4.17, where the implied constant depends only on q and s. If we optimize in this family of sequences, then we arrive at the value

(4.72) $$C_s = \min_q C(s, q)q^{T_q(s)},$$

where the minimum is extended over all prime powers q. Thus, for any $s \geq 2$, there exists a sequence S with

(4.73) $ND_N^*(S) \leq C_s (\log N)^s + O\big((\log N)^{s-1}\big)$ for all $N \geq 2$,

where C_s is given by (4.72) and where the implied constant depends only on s. For $s = 2$, we have

$$C_2 = C(2,2) = \frac{1}{8(\log 2)^2}.$$

For $s \geq 3$, let $q_1(s)$ be the least even prime power $\geq s$, let $q_2(s)$ be the least odd prime power $\geq s$, and put

$$C_s' = \min_{q<s} C(s,q) q^{T_q(s)},$$

where the minimum is extended over all prime powers $q < s$. Then

$$C_s = \min\big(C_s', \min_{q \geq s} C(s,q)\big)$$

since $T_q(s) = 0$ for $q \geq s$. Therefore, for $s \geq 3$, we obtain

(4.74) $C_s = \min\left(C_s', \frac{1}{s!}\left(1 - \frac{1}{q_1(s)}\right)\left(\frac{q_1(s)}{2\log q_1(s)}\right)^s, \frac{1}{s!}\left(\frac{q_2(s)-1}{2\log q_2(s)}\right)^s\right).$

This expresses C_s as a minimum of finitely many numbers. We tabulate the values of C_s for $2 \leq s \leq 20$. We again note that each value of C_s is obtained by considering a $(T_q(s), s)$-sequence in a suitable prime power base q. The appropriate value of q is listed in Table 4.4. For comparison, we also tabulate the constants A_s appearing in the discrepancy bound (3.6) for Halton sequences. The values of A_s and C_s in Table 4.4 have been rounded to three significant digits.

TABLE 4.4

Values of A_s, C_s for $2 \le s \le 20$.

s	A_s	C_s	q	s	A_s	C_s	q
				11	$(3.37) \cdot 10^3$	$(8.12) \cdot 10^{-5}$	11
2	$(6.57) \cdot 10^{-1}$	$(2.60) \cdot 10^{-1}$	2	12	$(1.68) \cdot 10^4$	$(5.60) \cdot 10^{-5}$	13
3	$(8.16) \cdot 10^{-1}$	$(1.26) \cdot 10^{-1}$	3	13	$(9.06) \cdot 10^4$	$(1.01) \cdot 10^{-5}$	13
4	$(1.26) \cdot 10^0$	$(8.58) \cdot 10^{-2}$	3	14	$(5.06) \cdot 10^5$	$(2.19) \cdot 10^{-5}$	13
5	$(2.62) \cdot 10^0$	$(2.47) \cdot 10^{-2}$	5	15	$(3.02) \cdot 10^6$	$(4.42) \cdot 10^{-6}$	17
6	$(6.14) \cdot 10^0$	$(1.86) \cdot 10^{-2}$	7	16	$(1.98) \cdot 10^7$	$(7.80) \cdot 10^{-7}$	17
7	$(1.73) \cdot 10^1$	$(4.11) \cdot 10^{-3}$	7	17	$(1.41) \cdot 10^8$	$(1.30) \cdot 10^{-7}$	17
8	$(5.30) \cdot 10^1$	$(2.99) \cdot 10^{-3}$	9	18	$(1.03) \cdot 10^9$	$(8.47) \cdot 10^{-8}$	19
9	$(1.86) \cdot 10^2$	$(6.05) \cdot 10^{-4}$	9	19	$(8.06) \cdot 10^9$	$(1.36) \cdot 10^{-8}$	19
10	$(7.72) \cdot 10^2$	$(4.28) \cdot 10^{-4}$	11	20	$(6.62) \cdot 10^{10}$	$(3.28) \cdot 10^{-8}$	23

To obtain information about the asymptotic behavior of C_s as $s \to \infty$, we use (4.74) and $q_1(s) < 2s$ to derive

$$C_s < \frac{1}{s!} \left(\frac{q_1(s)}{2 \log q_1(s)} \right)^s < \frac{1}{s!} \left(\frac{s}{\log(2s)} \right)^s.$$

Together with Stirling's formula, this yields

$$\varlimsup_{s \to \infty} \frac{\log C_s}{s \log \log s} \le -1.$$

Thus $C_s \to 0$ at a superexponential rate as $s \to \infty$. This should be compared with the observation at the beginning of this chapter that $A_s \to \infty$ at a superexponential rate as $s \to \infty$. The sequences satisfying (4.73) have asymptotically the smallest upper bound for the star discrepancy that is currently known.

The (t, s)-sequences in base q constructed in this section permit a particularly convenient implementation in the case where $q = 2$, since then the digits $y_{nj}^{(i)}$ are obtained by binary arithmetic and the coordinates $x_n^{(i)}$ are dyadic rationals. For the base $q = 2$, Sobol' [323] constructed (t, s)-sequences in base 2 for any dimension s. Let $U(s)$ denote the least value of t that can be achieved by the construction of Sobol' for given s. By Corollary 4.50, the construction in this section yields a $(T_2(s), s)$-sequence in base 2 for any s. A comparison with the formula for $U(s)$ given in [323, Thm. 3.4] shows that $T_2(s) = U(s)$ for $1 \le s \le 7$ and $T_2(s) < U(s)$ for all $s \ge 8$. Therefore, for all dimensions $s \ge 8$, the construction in this section yields dyadic sequences having a smaller upper bound for the star discrepancy than the sequences of Sobol'.

The construction in this section also has implications for the problem of determining the number $t_b(s)$ in Definition 4.25. By Corollary 4.50, we derive $t_q(s) \leq T_q(s)$ for all prime powers q and all s. In particular, the first part of Theorem 4.54 then implies that $t_q(s) = 0$ for all $s \leq q$. Furthermore, the remarks following Definition 4.25 show that $t_q(s) \geq 1$ for $s \geq q+1$. Since $T_q(q+1) = 1$, we obtain $t_q(q+1) = 1$ for all prime powers q. For an arbitrary base $b \geq 2$, it follows from Corollary 4.51 that, in the notation of this result, we have

$$(4.75) \qquad t_b(s) \leq \max_{1 \leq v \leq h} T_{q_v}(s) \qquad \text{for all } s \geq 1.$$

If q denotes the least prime power appearing in the canonical factorization of b into a product of prime powers, then $t_b(s) = 0$ for all $s \leq q$. For $s > q$, it follows from (4.75) and Theorem 4.54 that

$$t_b(s) < s(\log_q s + \log_q \log_q s + 1).$$

Another exact value of $t_b(s)$ is known for $b = 6$. By the remarks following Definition 4.25, we have $t_6(s) \geq 1$ for $s \geq 3$, and so (4.75) shows that $t_6(3) = 1$.

The construction of (t,s)-sequences in this section also yields information about the existence of nets. Indeed, by combining Lemma 4.22 and Corollary 4.51, we obtain the following result.

COROLLARY 4.55. *Let* $b = \prod_{v=1}^{h} q_v$ *be a product of prime powers* q_v, *let* $s \geq 2$, *and let* $t = \max_{1 \leq v \leq h} T_{q_v}(s-1)$. *Then, for every* $m \geq t$, *there exists a* (t,m,s)-*net in base* b.

By the device in Lemma 3.7, the low-discrepancy sequences constructed in this section can be used to obtain low-discrepancy point sets. For given $s \geq 3$, let S be a sequence of points $\mathbf{x}_0, \mathbf{x}_1, \ldots$ in I^{s-1} for which

$$ND_N^*(S) \leq C_{s-1}(\log N)^{s-1} + O\big((\log N)^{s-2}\big) \qquad \text{for all } N \geq 2,$$

where C_{s-1} is given by (4.72) and where the implied constant depends only on s (compare with (4.73)). For fixed $N \geq 2$, let P be the point set consisting of $(n/N, \mathbf{x}_n) \in I^s$ for $n = 0, 1, \ldots, N-1$. Then, by Lemma 3.7, we have

$$ND_N^*(P) \leq C_{s-1}(\log N)^{s-1} + O\big((\log N)^{s-2}\big),$$

where the implied constant depends only on s. For $s = 2$, we get low-discrepancy point sets by using the one-dimensional low-discrepancy sequences in §3.1 and the device in Lemma 3.7.

We briefly describe a method for the construction of $(0,s)$-sequences in a prime power base q, which uses the theory of hyperderivatives and was introduced in Niederreiter [251]. For an integer $k \geq 0$, the kth *hyperderivative* is the F_q-linear operator $H^{(k)}$ on the polynomial ring $F_q[x]$ defined by $H^{(k)}(x^r) = \binom{r}{k}x^{r-k}$ for $r \geq k$ and $H^{(k)}(x^r) = 0$ for $0 \leq r < k$. We again use the general principle for the construction of (t,s)-sequences based on (S1)–(S4) in §4.3, with $R = F_q$.

THEOREM 4.56. *For* $s \leq q$, *let* $b_1, \ldots, b_s$ *be* s *distinct elements of* F_q. *For* $1 \leq i \leq s$, *let* $g_i \in F_q[x]$ *with* $g_i(b_i) \neq 0$. *Define*

$$c_{jr}^{(i)} = [H^{(j-1)}(x^r g_i(x))](b_i) \qquad \text{for } 1 \leq i \leq s, \; j \geq 1, \; r \geq 0,$$

and suppose that the bijections η_{ij} are such that $\eta_{ij}(0) = 0$ for $1 \leq i \leq s$ and all sufficiently large j. Then the sequence (4.42) is a $(0, s)$-sequence in base q.

Proof. It is clear that condition (S6) in §4.3 is satisfied. To prove that the given sequence is a $(0, s)$-sequence in base q, it suffices to show by Theorem 4.36 that, for any integers $m \geq 1$ and $d_1, \ldots, d_s \geq 0$ with $\sum_{i=1}^s d_i = m$, the vectors

$$(c_{j0}^{(i)}, \ldots, c_{j,m-1}^{(i)}) \in F_q^m \quad \text{for } 1 \leq j \leq d_i, \ 1 \leq i \leq s,$$

are linearly independent over F_q. Suppose that the columns of the $m \times m$ matrix formed by these row vectors satisfy a linear dependence relation. Then there exist $f_0, \ldots, f_{m-1} \in F_q$ such that

$$\sum_{r=0}^{m-1} f_r [H^{(j-1)}(x^r g_i(x))](b_i) = 0 \quad \text{for } 1 \leq j \leq d_i, \ 1 \leq i \leq s.$$

With $f(x) = \sum_{r=0}^{m-1} f_r x^r \in F_q[x]$, this yields

$$[H^{(k)}(fg_i)](b_i) = 0 \quad \text{for } 0 \leq k \leq d_i - 1, \ 1 \leq i \leq s.$$

For $1 \leq i \leq s$, this implies by [192, Lemma 6.51] that b_i is a root of fg_i of multiplicity at least d_i. Since $g_i(b_i) \neq 0$, it follows that b_i is a root of f of multiplicity at least d_i. However, $\deg(f) < m = \sum_{i=1}^s d_i$, and so we must have $f = 0$, i.e., $f_r = 0$ for $0 \leq r \leq m-1$. $\square$

Notes.

The basic paper for the theory of (t, m, s)-nets and (t, s)-sequences is Niederreiter [244]. The results of §§4.1 and 4.2 and most of the results in §4.3 stem from this paper. For base 2, earlier results are due to Sobol' [323]. Surveys of the work of Sobol' can be found in Niederreiter [225, §3] and Sobol' [324]. A construction of $(0, 2)$-sequences in base 2 is also given in Srinivasan [333]. For a general background on latin squares, we refer to the book of Dénes and Keedwell [59]. Converses of Theorems 4.28 and 4.36 are shown in [244, §6]. Note that our definition of $\rho(C)$ is slightly different from that in [244]. Theorem 4.30, Lemma 4.32, and Theorem 4.33 are due to Niederreiter [261]. Theorem 4.34 is a special case of a result in Niederreiter [241], and Theorem 4.37 was shown in Niederreiter [247].

The construction of nets in §4.4 was introduced in Niederreiter [261], whereas the idea of using formal Laurent series for the construction of nets and (t, s)-sequences was previously established in Niederreiter [247]. Theorem 4.43 is a new result. Theorem 4.46 is shown in the same way as a special case that was considered in Niederreiter [241]. The quantity $K(g/f)$ was studied in detail in Niederreiter [243]. Calculations of the figure of merit $\rho(\mathbf{g}, f)$ have been carried out in certain special cases, e.g., for $\mathbf{g}$ of the form $\mathbf{g} = (1, x^m, x^{2m}, \ldots, x^{(s-1)m})$; see André, Mullen, and Niederreiter [8] and Mullen and Niederreiter [215]. This figure of merit also occurs in the context of pseudorandom number generation (compare with §9.1). The analysis of the sequences constructed in §4.4

leads to interesting connections with problems of diophantine approximation in $F_q((x^{-1}))$, which are further explored by Larcher and Niederreiter [180]. For the construction in §4.5, we need tables of irreducible polynomials over finite fields; we refer to [192, Chap. 10] for such tables. An interesting application of (t,s)-sequences to the numerical solution of integro-differential equations occurs in Lécot [184]. Fox [107] described a computer implementation of Faure sequences and compared their efficiency with that of Halton sequences and pseudorandom numbers; see also Sarkar and Prasad [301] for another comparative study. A computer implementation of Sobol' sequences was carried out by Antonov and Saleev [9], and an improved scheme was developed by Bratley and Fox [33].

CHAPTER 5

Lattice Rules for Numerical Integration

The quasi-Monte Carlo methods for numerical integration that we have discussed are based on low-discrepancy point sets and sequences. An inspection of the appropriate error bounds in §2.2 reveals a feature that may be construed as a drawback of these techniques, namely, that once the integrand is sufficiently regular, say of bounded variation in the sense of Hardy and Krause, then any additional regularity of the integrand is not reflected in the order of magnitude of the error bound. This is in marked contrast to classical one-dimensional integration methods such as Gaussian formulas and Newton-Cotes rules, which can be tailored to the regularity class of the integrand so that they become more efficient for more regular integrands.

The quasi-Monte Carlo methods presented in this chapter enjoy the property that the degree of regularity of the integrand is reflected in the order of magnitude of the error bound. To achieve this desirable goal, we must actually assume that the integrand is periodic with period interval $\bar{I}^s$ so that the underlying Fourier analysis makes sense, but this is no serious restriction since a nonperiodic integrand can always be periodized (see §5.1). The integration rules discussed here can be viewed as multidimensional analogues of the one-dimensional trapezoidal rule for periodic integrands. Historically, these integration rules first arose in the special form of the *method of good lattice points* introduced by Korobov in 1959, whereas the general class of *lattice rules* (or *lattice methods*) was defined and analyzed more recently. Particularly in the last few years, intensive research activities were devoted to these numerical integration techniques.

In §5.1 we present the fundamentals of the method of good lattice points, which serve as a stepping stone for the general theory of lattice rules. Theorems guaranteeing the existence of good parameters in the method of good lattice points are shown in §5.2, where we also discuss the interesting connections with continued fractions arising in the two-dimensional case. General lattice rules with their intriguing group-theoretic and geometric facets are studied in §5.3, while §5.4 is devoted to existence theorems for good parameters in the context of general lattice rules.

5.1.   The method of good lattice points.

In §3.1 we mentioned the uniformly distributed sequences $S(\mathbf{z})$ of fractional parts $\mathbf{x}_n = \{n\mathbf{z}\} \in I^s$, $n = 0, 1, \ldots$, where $\mathbf{z} = (z_1, \ldots, z_s) \in \mathbb{R}^s$ is such that $1, z_1, \ldots, z_s$ are linearly independent over the rationals. Discrete versions of these sequences are obtained if we consider points $\mathbf{z}$ with rational coordinates. If $\mathbf{z} \in \mathbb{Q}^s$ is such a point and the positive integer N is a common denominator of its coordinates, then $\mathbf{z} = N^{-1}\mathbf{g}$ with $\mathbf{g} \in \mathbb{Z}^s$. We are thus led to the point set

$$(5.1) \qquad \mathbf{x}_n = \left\{ \frac{n}{N}\mathbf{g} \right\} \in I^s \quad \text{for } n = 0, 1, \ldots, N-1.$$

Note that it is not necessary to consider the points $\mathbf{x}_n$ for $n \geq N$, since they just replicate the points in (5.1). With the points in (5.1), we get the quasi-Monte Carlo approximation

$$(5.2) \qquad \int_{\bar{I}^s} f(\mathbf{u})\, d\mathbf{u} \approx \frac{1}{N} \sum_{n=0}^{N-1} f\left(\left\{ \frac{n}{N}\mathbf{g} \right\}\right).$$

This approximation is particularly suited for periodic integrands. Let f be a periodic function on $\mathbb{R}^s$ with period interval $\bar{I}^s$ (or, equivalently, with period 1 in each of its s variables). Then, first of all, we can drop the fractional parts in (5.2) to get the simpler form

$$(5.3) \qquad \int_{\bar{I}^s} f(\mathbf{u})\, d\mathbf{u} \approx \frac{1}{N} \sum_{n=0}^{N-1} f\left(\frac{n}{N}\mathbf{g} \right).$$

Furthermore, suppose that f is represented by the absolutely convergent Fourier series

$$f(\mathbf{u}) = \sum_{\mathbf{h} \in \mathbb{Z}^s} \hat{f}(\mathbf{h}) e(\mathbf{h} \cdot \mathbf{u}) \quad \text{for } \mathbf{u} \in \mathbb{R}^s$$

with Fourier coefficients

$$\hat{f}(\mathbf{h}) = \int_{\bar{I}^s} f(\mathbf{u}) e(-\mathbf{h} \cdot \mathbf{u})\, d\mathbf{u} \quad \text{for } \mathbf{h} \in \mathbb{Z}^s,$$

where as usual $e(u) = e^{2\pi\sqrt{-1}u}$ for $u \in \mathbb{R}$ and $\mathbf{x} \cdot \mathbf{y}$ denotes the standard inner product of $\mathbf{x}, \mathbf{y} \in \mathbb{R}^s$. Then, since the exact value of the integral in (5.3) is given by $\hat{f}(\mathbf{0})$, we obtain

$$\frac{1}{N} \sum_{n=0}^{N-1} f\left(\frac{n}{N}\mathbf{g} \right) - \int_{\bar{I}^s} f(\mathbf{u})\, d\mathbf{u} = \frac{1}{N} \sum_{n=0}^{N-1} \sum_{\mathbf{h} \in \mathbb{Z}^s} \hat{f}(\mathbf{h}) e\left(\frac{n}{N}\mathbf{h} \cdot \mathbf{g} \right) - \hat{f}(\mathbf{0})$$

$$= \frac{1}{N} \sum_{\mathbf{h} \in \mathbb{Z}^s} \hat{f}(\mathbf{h}) \sum_{n=0}^{N-1} e\left(\frac{n}{N}\mathbf{h} \cdot \mathbf{g} \right) - \hat{f}(\mathbf{0})$$

$$= \frac{1}{N} \sum_{\substack{\mathbf{h} \in \mathbb{Z}^s \\ \mathbf{h} \neq \mathbf{0}}} \hat{f}(\mathbf{h}) \sum_{n=0}^{N-1} e\left(\frac{n}{N}\mathbf{h} \cdot \mathbf{g} \right).$$

Now the last inner sum is equal to 0 if $\mathbf{h} \cdot \mathbf{g} \not\equiv 0 \bmod N$ and equal to N if $\mathbf{h} \cdot \mathbf{g} \equiv 0 \bmod N$, and so

$$(5.4) \qquad \frac{1}{N} \sum_{n=0}^{N-1} f\left(\frac{n}{N}\mathbf{g}\right) - \int_{\bar{I}^s} f(\mathbf{u})\, d\mathbf{u} = \sum_{\mathbf{h}} \hat{f}(\mathbf{h}),$$

where the sum on the right-hand side is over all nonzero $\mathbf{h} \in \mathbb{Z}^s$ with $\mathbf{h} \cdot \mathbf{g} \equiv 0 \bmod N$. Thus the integration error in (5.3) can be expressed as a sum of certain Fourier coefficients of f.

According to the s-dimensional Riemann–Lebesgue lemma, $\hat{f}(\mathbf{h})$ tends to zero as $\mathbf{h}$ moves away from the origin. The rate of convergence of $\hat{f}(\mathbf{h})$ toward zero serves as a regularity condition on f. For $h \in \mathbb{Z}$, we put

$$r(h) = \max(1, |h|),$$

and, for $\mathbf{h} = (h_1, \ldots, h_s) \in \mathbb{Z}^s$, we set

$$r(\mathbf{h}) = \prod_{i=1}^{s} r(h_i).$$

DEFINITION 5.1. Let $\alpha > 1$ and $C > 0$ be real numbers. Then $\mathcal{E}_\alpha^s(C)$ is defined to be the class of all continuous periodic functions f on $\mathbb{R}^s$ with period interval $\bar{I}^s$ and with

$$|\hat{f}(\mathbf{h})| \leq Cr(\mathbf{h})^{-\alpha} \qquad \text{for all nonzero } \mathbf{h} \in \mathbb{Z}^s.$$

Furthermore, $\mathcal{E}_\alpha^s$ is the class of all f with $f \in \mathcal{E}_\alpha^s(C)$ for some $C > 0$.

It is easily seen that if $f \in \mathcal{E}_\alpha^s$, then its Fourier series is absolutely convergent and represents f. An important sufficient condition for the membership of a periodic function f on $\mathbb{R}^s$ with period interval $\bar{I}^s$ in the regularity class $\mathcal{E}_\alpha^s$ is the following. Let $\alpha > 1$ be an integer and suppose that all partial derivatives

$$\frac{\partial^{m_1 + \cdots + m_s} f}{\partial u_1^{m_1} \cdots \partial u_s^{m_s}} \qquad \text{with } 0 \leq m_i \leq \alpha - 1 \text{ for } 1 \leq i \leq s$$

exist and are of bounded variation on $\bar{I}^s$ in the sense of Hardy and Krause; then $f \in \mathcal{E}_\alpha^s(C)$ with a value of C which can be given explicitly (see Zaremba [363]). A more restrictive sufficient condition is the following: If $\alpha > 1$ is an integer and all partial derivatives

$$\frac{\partial^{m_1 + \cdots + m_s} f}{\partial u_1^{m_1} \cdots \partial u_s^{m_s}} \qquad \text{with } 0 \leq m_i \leq \alpha \text{ for } 1 \leq i \leq s$$

exist and are continuous on $\mathbb{R}^s$, then $f \in \mathcal{E}_\alpha^s(C)$ with an explicit value of C.

DEFINITION 5.2. For a real number $\alpha > 1$, for $\mathbf{g} \in \mathbb{Z}^s$, and for an integer $N \geq 1$, we put

$$P_\alpha(\mathbf{g}, N) = \sum_{\mathbf{h}} r(\mathbf{h})^{-\alpha},$$

where the sum is over all nonzero $\mathbf{h} \in \mathbb{Z}^s$ with $\mathbf{h} \cdot \mathbf{g} \equiv 0 \bmod N$.

THEOREM 5.3. *For any real numbers $\alpha > 1$ and $C > 0$, for any $\mathbf{g} \in \mathbb{Z}^s$ and any integer $N \geq 1$, we have*

$$\max_{f \in \mathcal{E}_\alpha^s(C)} \left| \frac{1}{N} \sum_{n=0}^{N-1} f\left(\frac{n}{N}\mathbf{g}\right) - \int_{\bar{I}^s} f(\mathbf{u})\, d\mathbf{u} \right| = C P_\alpha(\mathbf{g}, N).$$

Proof. For $f \in \mathcal{E}_\alpha^s(C)$, the bound

$$\left| \frac{1}{N} \sum_{n=0}^{N-1} f\left(\frac{n}{N}\mathbf{g}\right) - \int_{\bar{I}^s} f(\mathbf{u})\, d\mathbf{u} \right| \leq C P_\alpha(\mathbf{g}, N)$$

follows immediately from (5.4) and Definitions 5.1 and 5.2. Now let f_0 be the special function

$$f_0(\mathbf{u}) = C \sum_{\mathbf{h} \in \mathbb{Z}^s} r(\mathbf{h})^{-\alpha} e(\mathbf{h} \cdot \mathbf{u}) \quad \text{for } \mathbf{u} \in \mathbb{R}^s.$$

Then $f_0 \in \mathcal{E}_\alpha^s(C)$, and

$$\frac{1}{N} \sum_{n=0}^{N-1} f_0\left(\frac{n}{N}\mathbf{g}\right) - \int_{\bar{I}^s} f_0(\mathbf{u})\, d\mathbf{u} = C P_\alpha(\mathbf{g}, N)$$

by (5.4) and Definition 5.2. $\square$

Theorem 5.3 shows that, for given α and N, the lattice point $\mathbf{g}$ should be chosen in such a way that $P_\alpha(\mathbf{g}, N)$ is small. We now introduce a related quantity that does not depend on the regularity parameter α. The idea for its definition stems from the observation that the main contributions to the sum defining $P_\alpha(\mathbf{g}, N)$ come from the lattice points $\mathbf{h}$ close to $\mathbf{0}$. In the following definition, we use the set $C_s^*(N)$ introduced in §3.2.

DEFINITION 5.4. *For $\mathbf{g} \in \mathbb{Z}^s$, $s \geq 2$, and an integer $N \geq 2$, we put*

$$R(\mathbf{g}, N) = \sum_{\mathbf{h}} r(\mathbf{h})^{-1},$$

where the sum is over all $\mathbf{h} \in C_s^*(N)$ with $\mathbf{h} \cdot \mathbf{g} \equiv 0 \bmod N$.

Next, we establish a bound for $P_\alpha(\mathbf{g}, N)$ in terms of $R(\mathbf{g}, N)$ in an important special case. A more general, but somewhat weaker, bound will be proved in Theorem 5.26. Let $\zeta(\alpha) = \sum_{m=1}^\infty m^{-\alpha}$ for $\alpha > 1$ be the Riemann zeta-function.

THEOREM 5.5. *Let $N \geq 2$ be an integer and let $\mathbf{g} = (g_1, \ldots, g_s) \in \mathbb{Z}^s$, $s \geq 2$, with $\gcd(g_i, N) = 1$ for $1 \leq i \leq s$. Then, for any real $\alpha > 1$, we have*

$$P_\alpha(\mathbf{g}, N) < R(\mathbf{g}, N)^\alpha + (1 + 2\zeta(\alpha)N^{-\alpha})^s - 1$$
$$+ \frac{1}{N}(1 + 2\zeta(\alpha) + 2^\alpha \zeta(\alpha)N^{1-\alpha})^s - \frac{1}{N}(1 + 2\zeta(\alpha))^s.$$

Proof. Every $\mathbf{h} \in \mathbf{Z}^s$ can be uniquely written in the form $\mathbf{h} = \mathbf{k} + N\mathbf{m}$ with $\mathbf{k} \in C_s(N)$, $\mathbf{m} \in \mathbf{Z}^s$. Thus we can write

(5.5)
$$P_\alpha(\mathbf{g}, N) = \sum_{\substack{\mathbf{m} \in \mathbf{Z}^s \\ \mathbf{m} \neq 0}} r(N\mathbf{m})^{-\alpha} + \sum_{\substack{\mathbf{k} \in C_s^*(N) \\ \mathbf{k} \cdot \mathbf{g} \equiv 0 \bmod N}} \sum_{\mathbf{m} \in \mathbf{Z}^s} r(\mathbf{k} + N\mathbf{m})^{-\alpha} =: S_1 + S_2.$$

Now

(5.6) $$S_1 = \sum_{\mathbf{m} \in \mathbf{Z}^s} r(N\mathbf{m})^{-\alpha} - 1 = \left(\sum_{m \in \mathbf{Z}} r(Nm)^{-\alpha} \right)^s - 1$$

$$= \left(1 + 2 \sum_{m=1}^{\infty} (Nm)^{-\alpha} \right)^s - 1 = (1 + 2\zeta(\alpha)N^{-\alpha})^s - 1.$$

Furthermore,

(5.7) $$S_2 = \sum_{\substack{\mathbf{k} \in C_s^*(N) \\ \mathbf{k} \cdot \mathbf{g} \equiv 0 \bmod N}} \prod_{i=1}^{s} \left(\sum_{m \in \mathbf{Z}} r(k_i + Nm)^{-\alpha} \right),$$

where $\mathbf{k} = (k_1, \ldots, k_s)$. For $k = 0$, we have

$$\sum_{m \in \mathbf{Z}} r(k + Nm)^{-\alpha} = \sum_{m \in \mathbf{Z}} r(Nm)^{-\alpha} = 1 + 2\zeta(\alpha)N^{-\alpha}.$$

For $0 < |k| \leq N/2$, we have

$$\sum_{m \in \mathbf{Z}} r(k + Nm)^{-\alpha} = \sum_{m \in \mathbf{Z}} |k + Nm|^{-\alpha}$$

$$= |k|^{-\alpha} + \sum_{m=1}^{\infty} (k + Nm)^{-\alpha} + \sum_{m=1}^{\infty} (-k + Nm)^{-\alpha}$$

$$\leq |k|^{-\alpha} + \sum_{m=1}^{\infty} (Nm)^{-\alpha} + \sum_{m=1}^{\infty} \left(-\frac{N}{2} + Nm \right)^{-\alpha}$$

$$= |k|^{-\alpha} + 2^\alpha N^{-\alpha} \sum_{m=1}^{\infty} (2m)^{-\alpha} + 2^\alpha N^{-\alpha} \sum_{m=1}^{\infty} (2m - 1)^{-\alpha}$$

$$= |k|^{-\alpha} + 2^\alpha \zeta(\alpha)N^{-\alpha}.$$

Thus, in both cases,

$$\sum_{m \in \mathbf{Z}} r(k + Nm)^{-\alpha} \leq r(k)^{-\alpha} + 2^\alpha \zeta(\alpha)N^{-\alpha},$$

and so from (5.7) we obtain

$$S_2 \le \sum_{\substack{\mathbf{k} \in C_s^*(N) \\ \mathbf{k} \cdot \mathbf{g} \equiv 0 \bmod N}} \prod_{i=1}^{s} (r(k_i)^{-\alpha} + 2^\alpha \zeta(\alpha) N^{-\alpha})$$

$$< R_\alpha(\mathbf{g}, N) + 2^{\alpha s} \zeta(\alpha)^s N^{-\alpha s} \#\{\mathbf{k} \in C_s(N) : \mathbf{k} \cdot \mathbf{g} \equiv 0 \bmod N\}$$

$$+ \sum_{j=1}^{s-1} 2^{\alpha(s-j)} \zeta(\alpha)^{s-j} N^{-\alpha(s-j)} \sum_{1 \le i_1 < \cdots < i_j \le s} \sum_{\substack{\mathbf{k} \in C_s(N) \\ \mathbf{k} \cdot \mathbf{g} \equiv 0 \bmod N}} r(k_{i_1})^{-\alpha} \cdots r(k_{i_j})^{-\alpha}$$

with

$$R_\alpha(\mathbf{g}, N) = \sum_{\substack{\mathbf{k} \in C_s^*(N) \\ \mathbf{k} \cdot \mathbf{g} \equiv 0 \bmod N}} r(\mathbf{k})^{-\alpha}.$$

For fixed $1 \le j \le s-1$ and $1 \le i_1 < \cdots < i_j \le s$, we have

$$\sum_{\substack{\mathbf{k} \in C_s(N) \\ \mathbf{k} \cdot \mathbf{g} \equiv 0 \bmod N}} r(k_{i_1})^{-\alpha} \cdots r(k_{i_j})^{-\alpha} =$$

$$\sum_{\mathbf{h} \in C_j(N)} r(\mathbf{h})^{-\alpha} \#\{\mathbf{k} \in C_s(N) : \mathbf{k} \cdot \mathbf{g} \equiv 0 \bmod N \text{ and } k_{i_d} = h_d \text{ for } 1 \le d \le j\},$$

where $\mathbf{h} = (h_1, \ldots, h_j)$. The last counting function can be determined explicitly. If in the congruence

$$\mathbf{k} \cdot \mathbf{g} = k_1 g_1 + \cdots + k_s g_s \equiv 0 \bmod N$$

the values of $k_{i_1}, \ldots, k_{i_j}$ are prescribed, then $s - j - 1$ of the remaining coordinates of $\mathbf{k}$ can be chosen arbitrarily, and the last remaining coordinate of $\mathbf{k}$ is then uniquely determined since $\gcd(g_i, N) = 1$ for $1 \le i \le s$. Thus the counting function is given by N^{s-j-1}. Similarly, we have $\#\{\mathbf{k} \in C_s(N) : \mathbf{k} \cdot \mathbf{g} \equiv 0 \bmod N\} = N^{s-1}$. We obtain

$$\sum_{\substack{\mathbf{k} \in C_s(N) \\ \mathbf{k} \cdot \mathbf{g} \equiv 0 \bmod N}} r(k_{i_1})^{-\alpha} \cdots r(k_{i_j})^{-\alpha} = N^{s-j-1} \sum_{\mathbf{h} \in C_j(N)} r(\mathbf{h})^{-\alpha} < (1 + 2\zeta(\alpha))^j N^{s-j-1},$$

and so

$$S_2 < R_\alpha(\mathbf{g}, N) + 2^{\alpha s} \zeta(\alpha)^s N^{-\alpha s + s - 1}$$

$$+ \sum_{j=1}^{s-1} \binom{s}{j} 2^{\alpha(s-j)} \zeta(\alpha)^{s-j} (1 + 2\zeta(\alpha))^j N^{(1-\alpha)(s-j)-1}$$

$$= R_\alpha(\mathbf{g}, N) + \frac{1}{N} (1 + 2\zeta(\alpha) + 2^\alpha \zeta(\alpha) N^{1-\alpha})^s - \frac{1}{N} (1 + 2\zeta(\alpha))^s.$$

Together with (5.5) and (5.6), this yields

$$(5.8) \quad P_\alpha(\mathbf{g}, N) < R_\alpha(\mathbf{g}, N) + (1 + 2\zeta(\alpha)N^{-\alpha})^s - 1$$
$$+ \frac{1}{N}(1 + 2\zeta(\alpha) + 2^\alpha\zeta(\alpha)N^{1-\alpha})^s - \frac{1}{N}(1 + 2\zeta(\alpha))^s.$$

The result of the theorem follows from the inequality $R_\alpha(\mathbf{g}, N) \leq R(\mathbf{g}, N)^\alpha$. $\square$

We infer from Theorem 5.5 that, if $R(\mathbf{g}, N)$ is small, then $P_\alpha(\mathbf{g}, N)$ is small for all $\alpha > 1$. The quantity $R(\mathbf{g}, N)$ can also be used to provide an upper bound for the discrepancy of the point set (5.1). For $s \geq 2$ and $N \geq 2$, we use the notation in §3.2 to define

$$(5.9) \qquad R_1(\mathbf{g}, N) = \sum_{\mathbf{h}} r(\mathbf{h}, N)^{-1},$$

where we sum over all $\mathbf{h} \in C_s^*(N)$ with $\mathbf{h} \cdot \mathbf{g} \equiv 0 \bmod N$.

THEOREM 5.6. *For* $\mathbf{g} \in \mathbb{Z}^s$, $s \geq 2$, *and an integer* $N \geq 2$, *let* P *be the point set* (5.1). *Then*

$$D_N(P) \leq 1 - \left(1 - \frac{1}{N}\right)^s + R_1(\mathbf{g}, N) \leq \frac{s}{N} + \frac{1}{2}R(\mathbf{g}, N).$$

Proof. By Theorem 3.10 with $M = N$ and $\mathbf{y}_n = n\mathbf{g}$ for $0 \leq n \leq N - 1$, we obtain

$$D_N(P) \leq 1 - \left(1 - \frac{1}{N}\right)^s + \sum_{\mathbf{h} \in C_s^*(N)} \frac{1}{r(\mathbf{h}, N)} \left| \frac{1}{N} \sum_{n=0}^{N-1} e\left(\frac{n}{N}\mathbf{h} \cdot \mathbf{g}\right) \right|$$
$$= 1 - \left(1 - \frac{1}{N}\right)^s + R_1(\mathbf{g}, N).$$

The second inequality of the theorem is obtained from $r(\mathbf{h}, N) \geq 2r(\mathbf{h})$ for $\mathbf{h} \in C_s^*(N)$, which follows, in turn, from $\sin(\pi t) \geq 2t$ for $0 \leq t \leq \frac{1}{2}$. $\square$

On the basis of the discrepancy bound in Theorem 5.6, the point set (5.1) can also be used for the numerical integration of nonperiodic functions of low regularity, e.g., of bounded variation on $\bar{I}^s$ in the sense of Hardy and Krause. However, the full power of the point set (5.1) is achieved only for periodic integrands belonging to a function class $\mathcal{E}_\alpha^s$. There are methods for *periodization*, i.e., for transforming a sufficiently regular nonperiodic integrand into an integrand belonging to a suitable $\mathcal{E}_\alpha^s$ without changing the value of the integral. A simple periodization technique is the replacement of a given function f on $\bar{I}^s$ by the function

$$\bar{f}(u_1, \ldots, u_s) = 2^{-s} \sum_{\varepsilon_1=0}^{1} \cdots \sum_{\varepsilon_s=0}^{1} f(\varepsilon_1 + (-1)^{\varepsilon_1}u_1, \ldots, \varepsilon_s + (-1)^{\varepsilon_s}u_s)$$

for $(u_1, \ldots, u_s) \in \bar{I}^s$. This technique may be viewed as an analogue of the method of antithetic variates described in §1.2, but it is of limited usefulness because of a possible lack of regularity of the periodic extension of $\bar{f}$ to $\mathbb{R}^s$ at the boundary of $\bar{I}^s$. More satisfactory techniques are based on suitable changes of variables or on the device of adding functions to f that are obtained from Bernoulli polynomials and certain partial derivatives of f. We refer to Hua and Wang [145, Chap. 6], Korobov [160, Chap. 1], and Zaremba [365] for detailed discussions of periodization methods.

Another quantity measuring the quality of lattice points $\mathbf{g}$ is the positive integer introduced in Definition 5.7 below. The idea is that $P_\alpha(\mathbf{g}, N)$ and $R(\mathbf{g}, N)$ will be small if the nonzero lattice points $\mathbf{h}$ with $\mathbf{h} \cdot \mathbf{g} \equiv 0 \bmod N$ are rather far from $\mathbf{0}$.

DEFINITION 5.7. For $\mathbf{g} \in \mathbb{Z}^s$, $s \geq 2$, and an integer $N \geq 2$, the *figure of merit* $\rho(\mathbf{g}, N)$ is defined by

$$\rho(\mathbf{g}, N) = \min_{\mathbf{h}} r(\mathbf{h}),$$

where the minimum is extended over all nonzero $\mathbf{h} \in \mathbb{Z}^s$ with $\mathbf{h} \cdot \mathbf{g} \equiv 0 \bmod N$.

LEMMA 5.8. *We always have* $1 \leq \rho(\mathbf{g}, N) \leq N/2$.

Proof. If $\mathbf{g} = (g_1, \ldots, g_s)$ with $\gcd(g_1, N) = 1$, then $hg_1 + g_2 \equiv 0 \bmod N$ for some $h \in \mathbb{Z}$ with $-N/2 < h \leq N/2$, and so $\rho(\mathbf{g}, N) \leq r(h) \leq N/2$. If $\gcd(g_1, N) > 1$, then there exists a proper divisor d of N with $dg_1 \equiv 0 \bmod N$, and so $\rho(\mathbf{g}, N) \leq r(d) \leq N/2$. $\square$

REMARK 5.9. It follows from Lemma 5.8 that it suffices to extend the minimum in Definition 5.7 over all $\mathbf{h} \in C_s^*(N)$ with $\mathbf{h} \cdot \mathbf{g} \equiv 0 \bmod N$. If a nonzero $\mathbf{h} \in \mathbb{Z}^s$ is such that $\mathbf{h} \cdot \mathbf{g} \equiv 0 \bmod N$ and $\rho(\mathbf{g}, N) = r(\mathbf{h})$, then Lemma 5.8 implies that not all coordinates of $\mathbf{h}$ are divisible by N. Thus, if we reduce all coordinates of $\mathbf{h}$ modulo N to obtain a point $\mathbf{h}_0 \in C_s^*(N)$, then $\mathbf{h}_0 \cdot \mathbf{g} \equiv 0 \bmod N$ and $r(\mathbf{h}_0) \leq r(\mathbf{h})$; hence $\rho(\mathbf{g}, N) = r(\mathbf{h}_0)$.

The quantities $P_\alpha(\mathbf{g}, N)$ and $R(\mathbf{g}, N)$ can be bounded from below and above in terms of the figure of merit $\rho(\mathbf{g}, N)$. In detail, for any $\mathbf{g} \in \mathbb{Z}^s$, $s \geq 2$, and any integer $N \geq 2$, we have

(5.10)
$$\frac{2}{\rho(\mathbf{g}, N)^\alpha} \leq P_\alpha(\mathbf{g}, N) \leq \frac{c(s, \alpha)\,(1 + \log \rho(\mathbf{g}, N))^{s-1}}{\rho(\mathbf{g}, N)^\alpha} \qquad \text{for all } \alpha > 1,$$

where the constant $c(s, \alpha)$ depends only on s and α. The lower bound in (5.10) is trivial, and the upper bound is a special case of Theorem 5.34. Similarly, we have

(5.11)
$$\frac{1}{\rho(\mathbf{g}, N)} \leq R(\mathbf{g}, N) \leq \frac{c(s)(\log N)^s}{\rho(\mathbf{g}, N)},$$

where the constant $c(s)$ depends only on s. The lower bound in (5.11) follows from Remark 5.9, and the upper bound is a special case of Theorem 5.35. For the discrepancy of the point set P in (5.1), we have the bounds

(5.12)
$$\frac{c_1(s)}{\rho(\mathbf{g}, N)} \leq D_N(P) \leq \frac{c_2(s)(\log N)^s}{\rho(\mathbf{g}, N)},$$

where the constants $c_1(s) > 0$ and $c_2(s)$ depend only on s. The lower bound in (5.12) is a special case of Theorem 5.37 and the upper bound follows from Theorem 5.6, Lemma 5.8, and (5.11). We infer from (5.10), (5.11), and (5.12) that, for a given $N \geq 2$, the lattice points $\mathbf{g} \in \mathbb{Z}^s$, $s \geq 2$, which are suitable for numerical integration—in the sense of yielding a small integration error—are those for which $\rho(\mathbf{g}, N)$ is large. Such a $\mathbf{g}$ is informally called a *good lattice point* mod N, hence the name "method of good lattice points."

Good lattice points in large dimensions automatically yield good lattice points in smaller dimensions. Concretely, for a given dimension $s \geq 3$, let

$$\mathbf{g}^{(s)} = (g_1, \ldots, g_s) \in \mathbb{Z}^s,$$

and, for any dimension t with $2 \leq t < s$, put

$$\mathbf{g}^{(t)} = (g_1, \ldots, g_t) \in \mathbb{Z}^t.$$

Then, from Definition 5.7, we immediately obtain

(5.13)
$$\rho(\mathbf{g}^{(t)}, N) \geq \rho(\mathbf{g}^{(s)}, N) \quad \text{for any integer } N \geq 2.$$

Thus, if $\mathbf{g}^{(s)}$ is an s-dimensional good lattice point mod N, then $\mathbf{g}^{(t)}$ is a t-dimensional good lattice point mod N. However, there is no obvious way of constructing higher-dimensional good lattice points from lower-dimensional good lattice points. In analogy with (5.13), we have

$$P_\alpha(\mathbf{g}^{(t)}, N) \leq P_\alpha(\mathbf{g}^{(s)}, N) \quad \text{for any } N \geq 2 \text{ and } \alpha > 1$$

and

$$R(\mathbf{g}^{(t)}, N) \leq R(\mathbf{g}^{(s)}, N) \quad \text{for any } N \geq 2.$$

5.2. Existence theorems for good lattice points.

To guarantee that the method of good lattice points is practicable, we need results that demonstrate that, for given $s \geq 2$ and $N \geq 2$, there exist points $\mathbf{g} \in \mathbb{Z}^s$ such that $\rho(\mathbf{g}, N)$ is large and $P_\alpha(\mathbf{g}, N)$ and $R(\mathbf{g}, N)$ are small. We start with the last quantity and show that the average value of $R(\mathbf{g}, N)$, taken over a well-chosen set of lattice points $\mathbf{g}$, is small. We first note that $\mathbf{g}$ is only relevant modulo N, so that it suffices to take $\mathbf{g} \in C_s(N)$. We put

$$G_s(N) = \{\mathbf{g} = (g_1, \ldots, g_s) \in C_s(N) : \gcd(g_i, N) = 1 \text{ for } 1 \leq i \leq s\}.$$

Recall that the Euler–Mascheroni constant is given by

$$\gamma = \lim_{n \to \infty} \left(\sum_{m=1}^{n} \frac{1}{m} - \log n \right) = 0.577\ldots.$$

THEOREM 5.10. *For any integers $s \geq 2$ and $N \geq 2$, put*

$$M_s(N) = \frac{1}{\operatorname{card}(G_s(N))} \sum_{\mathbf{g} \in G_s(N)} R(\mathbf{g}, N).$$

Then we have

$$M_s(N) = \frac{1}{N}(2 \log N + c)^s - \frac{2s \log N}{N} + O\left(\frac{(\log \log N)^2}{N}\right),$$

where $c = 2\gamma - \log 4 + 1 = 0.768\ldots$ and where the implied constant depends only on s.

Proof. Note that $\operatorname{card}(G_s(N)) = \phi(N)^s$, where ϕ is Euler's totient function. By the definition of $R(\mathbf{g}, N)$, we then derive

$$M_s(N) = \frac{1}{\phi(N)^s} \sum_{\substack{\mathbf{g} \in G_s(N)}} \sum_{\substack{\mathbf{h} \in C_s^*(N) \\ \mathbf{h} \cdot \mathbf{g} \equiv 0 \bmod N}} r(\mathbf{h})^{-1} = \frac{1}{\phi(N)^s} \sum_{\mathbf{h} \in C_s^*(N)} A(\mathbf{h}) r(\mathbf{h})^{-1},$$

where $A(\mathbf{h})$ is the number of $\mathbf{g} \in G_s(N)$ with $\mathbf{h} \cdot \mathbf{g} \equiv 0 \bmod N$. Since $A(\mathbf{0}) = \phi(N)^s$ and $r(\mathbf{0}) = 1$, we obtain

$$(5.14) \qquad M_s(N) = \frac{1}{\phi(N)^s} \sum_{\mathbf{h} \in C_s(N)} A(\mathbf{h}) r(\mathbf{h})^{-1} - 1.$$

For any $\mathbf{h}$, we have

$$A(\mathbf{h}) = \sum_{\mathbf{g} \in G_s(N)} \frac{1}{N} \sum_{k=0}^{N-1} e\left(\frac{k}{N} \mathbf{h} \cdot \mathbf{g}\right).$$

In this proof, we write (m, n) for $\gcd(m, n)$. Then

$$\sum_{\mathbf{h} \in C_s(N)} A(\mathbf{h}) r(\mathbf{h})^{-1} = \frac{1}{N} \sum_{k=0}^{N-1} \sum_{\mathbf{h} \in C_s(N)} \sum_{\mathbf{g} \in G_s(N)} e\left(\frac{k}{N} \mathbf{h} \cdot \mathbf{g}\right) r(\mathbf{h})^{-1}$$

$$= \frac{1}{N} \sum_{k=0}^{N-1} \sum_{h_1 \in C(N)} \cdots \sum_{h_s \in C(N)} \sum_{\substack{g_1 \in C(N) \\ (g_1, N) = 1}} \cdots \sum_{\substack{g_s \in C(N) \\ (g_s, N) = 1}} \frac{e((k/N) h_1 g_1) \cdots e((k/N) h_s g_s)}{r(h_1) \cdots r(h_s)}$$

$$= \frac{1}{N} \sum_{k=0}^{N-1} T(k, N)^s$$

with

$$T(k, N) = \sum_{h \in C(N)} \sum_{\substack{g \in C(N) \\ (g, N) = 1}} e\left(\frac{k}{N} hg\right) r(h)^{-1}.$$

If we put

$$L(N) = \sum_{h \in C^*(N)} r(h)^{-1} = \sum_{h \in C^*(N)} |h|^{-1},$$

then $T(0, N) = \phi(N)(1 + L(N))$, and so

$$(5.15) \qquad \sum_{h \in C_s(N)} A(\mathbf{h}) r(\mathbf{h})^{-1} = \frac{1}{N} \phi(N)^s (1 + L(N))^s + \frac{1}{N} \sum_{k=1}^{N-1} T(k, N)^s.$$

For fixed $1 \le k \le N - 1$, we have

$$T(k, N) = \sum_{h \in C(N)} r(h)^{-1} \sum_{g \in C(N)} e\left(\frac{k}{N} hg\right) \sum_{d|(g,N)} \mu(d),$$

where μ is the Möbius function and d is restricted to positive divisors; if we also fix $h \in C(N)$, then

$$\sum_{g \in C(N)} e\left(\frac{k}{N} hg\right) \sum_{d|(g,N)} \mu(d) = \sum_{d|N} \mu(d) \sum_{\substack{g \in C(N) \\ d|g}} e\left(\frac{k}{N} hg\right)$$

$$= \sum_{d|N} \mu(d) \sum_{a \in C(N/d)} e\left(\frac{k}{N} had\right) = \sum_{d|N} \mu\left(\frac{N}{d}\right) \sum_{a \in C(d)} e\left(\frac{k}{d} ha\right) = \sum_{\substack{d|N \\ d|kh}} \mu\left(\frac{N}{d}\right) d.$$

Therefore

$$T(k, N) = \sum_{d|N} \mu\left(\frac{N}{d}\right) d \sum_{\substack{h \in C(N) \\ d|kh}} r(h)^{-1}.$$

Now d divides kh if and only if $d/(d, k)$ divides h; hence

$$(5.16) \qquad T(k, N) = \sum_{d|N} \mu\left(\frac{N}{d}\right) dL\left(\frac{d}{(d, k)}, N\right),$$

where, for a positive divisor b of N, we put

$$L(b, N) = \sum_{\substack{h \in C(N) \\ b|h}} r(h)^{-1}.$$

If $b < N$, then

$$L(b, N) = 1 + \sum_{\substack{h \in C^*(N) \\ b|h}} |h|^{-1} = 1 + \sum_{a \in C^*(N/b)} |ab|^{-1} = 1 + \frac{1}{b} L\left(\frac{N}{b}\right).$$

If we put $L(1) = 0$, then this formula for $L(b, N)$ also holds for $b = N$. Together with (5.16), this yields

$$(5.17) \qquad T(k, N) = \sum_{d \mid N} \mu\left(\frac{N}{d}\right) d\left(1 + \frac{(d, k)}{d} L\left(\frac{N(d, k)}{d}\right)\right)$$

$$= \phi(N) + \sum_{d \mid N} \mu\left(\frac{N}{d}\right)(d, k) L\left(\frac{N(d, k)}{d}\right).$$

By [226, Lemmas 1, 2] we have, for any integer $m \geq 1$,

$$(5.18) \qquad L(m) = 2 \log m + c - 1 + \varepsilon(m) \quad \text{with } |\varepsilon(m)| < 4m^{-2}.$$

Consequently,

$$\sum_{d \mid N} \mu\left(\frac{N}{d}\right)(d, k) L\left(\frac{N(d, k)}{d}\right) = (2 \log N + c - 1) B(k, N) - 2H(k, N) + V(k, N)$$

with

$$B(k, N) = \sum_{d \mid N} \mu\left(\frac{N}{d}\right)(d, k),$$

$$H(k, N) = \sum_{d \mid N} \mu\left(\frac{N}{d}\right)(d, k) \log \frac{d}{(d, k)},$$

$$V(k, N) = \sum_{d \mid N} \mu\left(\frac{N}{d}\right)(d, k) \varepsilon\left(\frac{N(d, k)}{d}\right).$$

For a prime power p^m with $m \geq 1$, we have $B(k, p^m) = (p^m, k) - (p^{m-1}, k)$; hence $B(k, p^m) = p^m - p^{m-1} = \phi(p^m)$ if $p^m \mid k$ and $B(k, p^m) = 0$ otherwise. For fixed k, we note that (d, k) is a multiplicative function of d, and so $B(k, N)$ is a multiplicative function of N. Thus, for any positive integers k and N, we obtain

$$(5.19) \qquad B(k, N) = \begin{cases} \phi(N) & \text{if } N \mid k, \\ 0 & \text{otherwise.} \end{cases}$$

In particular, for $1 \leq k \leq N - 1$, we have $B(k, N) = 0$, and so

$$(5.20) \quad T(k, N) = \phi(N) - 2H(k, N) + V(k, N) \quad \text{for } 1 \leq k \leq N - 1.$$

In the rest of the proof, p will always denote a prime number. For a positive integer n, let $e_p(n)$ be the largest nonnegative integer such that $p^{e_p(n)}$ divides n. We now consider $H(k, N)$ for a fixed k. Since (d, k) is a multiplicative and $\log(d/(d, k))$ an additive function of d, it follows by induction on the number of distinct prime factors of N that

$$(5.21) \qquad H(k, N) = \sum_{p \mid N} H(k, p^{e_p(N)}) B(k, N/p^{e_p(N)}).$$

For an integer $m \geq 1$, we have

$$H(k, p^m) = (p^m, k) \log \frac{p^m}{(p^m, k)} - (p^{m-1}, k) \log \frac{p^{m-1}}{(p^{m-1}, k)}.$$

If $m \leq e_p(k)$, then $(p^m, k) = p^m$ and $(p^{m-1}, k) = p^{m-1}$; hence $H(k, p^m) = 0$. If $m > e_p(k)$, then $(p^m, k) = (p^{m-1}, k) = p^{e_p(k)}$; hence $H(k, p^m) = p^{e_p(k)} \log p$. Together with (5.19) and (5.21), this yields

$$(5.22) \qquad H(k, N) = \sum_p p^{e_p(k)} \phi(N/p^{e_p(N)}) \log p,$$

where the sum runs over all p satisfying the following two conditions: (i) $e_p(N) > e_p(k)$; (ii) $N/p^{e_p(N)}$ divides k. Note that (ii) means that $e_{p_1}(N) \leq e_{p_1}(k)$ for all primes $p_1 \neq p$. Therefore (i) and (ii) hold simultaneously if and only if there exists a unique p with $e_p(N) > e_p(k)$. Hence it follows from (5.22) that if there exists a unique prime p with $e_p(N) > e_p(k)$, then

$$H(k, N) = p^{e_p(k)} \phi(N/p^{e_p(N)}) \log p,$$

and $H(k, N) = 0$ otherwise.

To treat $V(k, N)$, we use the bound for $\varepsilon(m)$ in (5.18) to obtain

$$|V(k, N)| \leq 4 \sum_{d|N} \left| \mu\left(\frac{N}{d}\right) \right| \left(\frac{d}{N}\right)^2 = 4 \sum_{d|N} \frac{|\mu(d)|}{d^2} = O(1)$$

with an absolute implied constant. Combining this with (5.14), (5.15), and (5.20), we obtain

$$M_s(N) = \frac{1}{N}(1 + L(N))^s + \frac{1}{N} \sum_{k=1}^{N-1} \left(1 - 2J(k, N) + O\left(\frac{1}{\phi(N)}\right)\right)^s - 1,$$

where $J(k, N) = H(k, N)/\phi(N)$. The formula for $H(k, N)$, given above, shows that $J(k, N) = O(1)$; hence

$$(5.23)$$
$$M_s(N) = \frac{1}{N}(1 + L(N))^s + \frac{1}{N} \sum_{i=1}^{s} \binom{s}{i} (-2)^i \sum_{k=1}^{N-1} J(k, N)^i + O\left(\frac{1}{\phi(N)}\right)$$

with an implied constant depending only on s.

We now consider the sum over k in (5.23) for $1 \leq i \leq s$. From the formula for $H(k, N)$, we obtain

$$J(k, N) = \frac{\log p}{\phi\left(p^{e_p(N) - e_p(k)}\right)}$$

if there exists a unique prime p with $e_p(k) < e_p(N)$, and $J(k, N) = 0$ otherwise. We put

$$Q_i(N) = \sum_{k=1}^{N-1} J(k, N)^i \quad \text{for } 1 \leq i \leq s,$$

and we claim that Q_i is an additive function. Let N_1 and N_2 be positive integers with $(N_1, N_2) = 1$. If $1 \leq k \leq N_1 N_2 - 1$ is such that there exists a unique p with $e_p(k) < e_p(N_1 N_2)$, then $e_p(N_1 N_2) > 0$, and so p divides exactly one of N_1 and N_2. Consequently, the sum $Q_i(N_1 N_2)$ can be split up into two subsums according to these two cases. If $p \mid N_1$, say, then $k = k_1 N_2$ with $1 \leq k_1 \leq N_1 - 1$ and $J(k, N_1 N_2) = J(k_1 N_2, N_1 N_2) = J(k_1, N_1)$. From this, it is easily seen that $Q_i(N_1 N_2) = Q_i(N_1) + Q_i(N_2)$; hence Q_i is additive. For an integer $m \geq 1$ and any prime p, we have

$$Q_i(p^m) = (\log p)^i \sum_{j=0}^{m-1} \sum_{\substack{k=1 \\ e_p(k)=j}}^{p^m-1} \phi(p^{m-j})^{-i}.$$

For $0 \leq j \leq m - 1$, the number of k with $1 \leq k \leq p^m - 1$ and $e_p(k) = j$ is equal to $\phi(p^{m-j})$, and so

$$(5.24) \qquad Q_i(p^m) = (\log p)^i \sum_{j=1}^{m} \phi(p^j)^{1-i}.$$

For $i = 1$, this yields $Q_1(p^m) = \log(p^m)$; hence $Q_1(N) = \log N$ by additivity. For $i = 2$, we obtain

$$Q_2(p^m) = (\log p)^2 \sum_{j=1}^{m} p^{-j}(1 - p^{-1})^{-1} \leq 2(\log p)^2 \sum_{j=1}^{m} p^{-j} < 4(\log p)^2 p^{-1},$$

and so, by additivity,

$$Q_2(N) < 4 \sum_{p \mid N} (\log p)^2 p^{-1}.$$

If n is the number of distinct prime factors of N and $p_1, \ldots, p_n$ are the first n prime numbers, then

$$Q_2(N) < 4 \sum_{t=1}^{n} (\log p_t)^2 p_t^{-1} + O(1)$$

with an absolute implied constant. By the prime number theorem, we have $c_1 t \log(t + 1) \leq p_t \leq c_2 t \log(t + 1)$ for $1 \leq t \leq n$ with absolute constants $c_1, c_2 > 0$, and so

$$Q_2(N) = O\left(\sum_{t=1}^{n} \frac{\log(t + 1)}{t} \right) = O\left((\log(n + 1))^2\right)$$

with absolute implied constants. From the trivial bound $\log N \geq n \log 2$, we see that

(5.25) $$Q_2(N) = O\big((\log \log N)^2\big)$$

with an absolute implied constant. For $i \geq 3$, it follows from (5.24) that

$$Q_i(p^m) \leq (\log p)^i \sum_{j=1}^{m} \phi(p^j)^{-2} = (\log p)^i \sum_{j=1}^{m} p^{-2j}(1 - p^{-1})^{-2}$$
$$< 2(\log p)^i (p - 1)^{-2},$$

and so, by additivity,

$$Q_i(N) < 2 \sum_{p|N} (\log p)^i (p - 1)^{-2} < 2 \sum_{j=1}^{\infty} \frac{(\log(j + 1))^i}{j^2} = O(1)$$

with an implied constant depending only on i.

Now we use this information as well as (5.25) and $Q_1(N) = \log N$ in formula (5.23). This yields

$$M_s(N) = \frac{1}{N}(1 + L(N))^s - \frac{2s \log N}{N} + O\left(\frac{(\log \log N)^2}{N}\right) + O\left(\frac{1}{\phi(N)}\right)$$
$$= \frac{1}{N}(1 + L(N))^s - \frac{2s \log N}{N} + O\left(\frac{(\log \log N)^2}{N}\right)$$

with an implied constant depending only on s, where we used $\phi(N)^{-1} = O\big(N^{-1} \log \log(N + 1)\big)$. The rest follows from (5.18). $\square$

Theorem 5.10 is an improved version of an earlier result in Niederreiter [226], according to which we have

$$M_s(N) < \frac{1}{N}\left(2 \log N + \frac{7}{5}\right)^s \qquad \text{for all } s \geq 2 \text{ and } N \geq 2.$$

Note that, for any $s \geq 2$ and $N \geq 2$, there exists a $\mathbf{g} \in G_s(N)$ with $R(\mathbf{g}, N) \leq M_s(N)$. It follows then from Theorem 5.6 that, for any $s \geq 2$ and $N \geq 2$, there exists a $\mathbf{g} \in G_s(N)$ such that the point set P in (5.1) has discrepancy

$$D_N(P) = O\big(N^{-1}(\log N)^s\big),$$

where the implied constant depends only on s. Theorem 5.10 shows that the average order of magnitude of $R(\mathbf{g}, N)$ for $\mathbf{g} \in G_s(N)$ is $N^{-1}(\log N)^s$, but there is even a general lower bound due to Larcher [175], which says that

$$R(\mathbf{g}, N) \geq c_s N^{-1}(\log N)^s$$

for all $\mathbf{g} \in \mathbb{Z}^s$, $s \geq 2$, and for all $N \geq 2$, where the constant $c_s > 0$ depends only on s.

We now consider the question of the existence of lattice points $\mathbf{g}$ for which the figure of merit $\rho(\mathbf{g}, N)$ is large. Here the relevant existence theorem is due to Zaremba [366]. For $s \geq 2$ and $N \geq 2$, let $E_s(N)$ be the set of all $\mathbf{g} = (g_1, \ldots, g_s) \in C_s(N)$ with $g_1 = 1$. The following auxiliary result from Zaremba [366, eq. (27)] is basic.

LEMMA 5.11. *For integers $s \geq 2$, $t \geq 2$, and $N \geq 2$, let $F_s(t, N)$ be the number of $\mathbf{g} \in E_s(N)$ with $\rho(\mathbf{g}, N) \leq t$. Then*

$$F_s(t, N) \leq \frac{2^{s-1}}{(s-1)!} N^{s-2} t (\log t)^{s-1} \left(1 + O\left(\frac{(\log \log(N+1))^{b(s)}}{\log t} \right) \right),$$

where the implied constant depends only on s and where $b(s) = 3$ for $s = 2$ and $b(s) = s - 1$ for $s \geq 3$.

It is clear that if t_0 is of the form $t_0 = c_s N/(\log N)^{s-1}$ with a suitable $c_s > 0$ depending only on s, then $F_s(t_0, N) < N^{s-1}$ for all sufficiently large N, and so for such N there exists a $\mathbf{g} \in E_s(N)$ with $\rho(\mathbf{g}, N) > t_0$. By a somewhat more refined argument, Zaremba [366] established the following result.

THEOREM 5.12. *For every dimension $s \geq 2$ and every sufficiently large integer N, there exists a $\mathbf{g} \in E_s(N)$ such that*

$$\rho(\mathbf{g}, N) > \frac{(s-1)! \, N}{(2 \log N)^{s-1}}.$$

It follows from (5.10) and Theorem 5.12 that, for every $s \geq 2$ and $N \geq 2$, there exists a $\mathbf{g} \in E_s(N)$ such that

$$(5.26) \qquad P_\alpha(\mathbf{g}, N) = O\left(N^{-\alpha} (\log N)^{(\alpha+1)(s-1)} \right) \qquad \text{for all } \alpha > 1,$$

with an implied constant depending only on s and α. Furthermore, Theorems 5.5 and 5.10 show that, for every $s \geq 2$ and $N \geq 2$, there exists a $\mathbf{g} \in G_s(N)$ such that

$$(5.27) \qquad P_\alpha(\mathbf{g}, N) = O\left(N^{-\alpha} (\log N)^{\alpha s} \right) \qquad \text{for all } \alpha > 1,$$

where the implied constant depends only on s and α and grows exponentially with s. Disney [66] and Disney and Sloan [67] have developed an approach that yields the bound in (5.27) for a suitable $\mathbf{g} \in G_s(N)$ depending also on α, but with the coefficient of the leading term being $(2e/s)^{\alpha s}$, which decreases superexponentially as s increases and α is fixed. On the other hand, there is a general lower bound of Sharygin [308], which shows that $P_\alpha(\mathbf{g}, N)$ is always at least of the order of magnitude $N^{-\alpha} (\log N)^{s-1}$. The following two results of Niederreiter [264] are currently the best general existence theorems for small values of $P_\alpha(\mathbf{g}, N)$.

THEOREM 5.13. *For any integers $s \geq 2$ and $N \geq 2$ and any real $\alpha > 1$, there exists a $\mathbf{g} \in G_s(N)$ with*

$$P_\alpha(\mathbf{g}, N) = O\left(N^{-\alpha} (\log N)^{\alpha(s-1)+1} \left(\frac{N}{\phi(N)} \right)^{(\alpha-1)(s-1)} \right),$$

where the implied constant depends only on s and α.

Proof. As in the proof of Theorem 5.5, we put

$$R_\alpha(\mathbf{g}, N) = \sum_{\substack{\mathbf{h} \in C_s^*(N) \\ \mathbf{h} \cdot \mathbf{g} \equiv 0 \bmod N}} r(\mathbf{h})^{-\alpha} \quad \text{for } \alpha > 1.$$

For fixed s, N, and α, consider now

$$M = M(s, N, \alpha) := \sum_{\mathbf{g} \in G_s(N)} \rho(\mathbf{g}, N)^{\alpha-1} R_\alpha(\mathbf{g}, N).$$

Inserting the definition of $R_\alpha(\mathbf{g}, N)$ and interchanging the order of summation, we obtain

$$M = \sum_{\mathbf{h} \in C_s^*(N)} r(\mathbf{h})^{-\alpha} \sum_{\substack{\mathbf{g} \in G_s(N) \\ \mathbf{h} \cdot \mathbf{g} \equiv 0 \bmod N}} \rho(\mathbf{g}, N)^{\alpha-1}.$$

If, for an $\mathbf{h} \in C_s^*(N)$, we have $\mathbf{h} \cdot \mathbf{g} \equiv 0 \bmod N$, then $\rho(\mathbf{g}, N) \le r(\mathbf{h})$ by Definition 5.7. Thus, for every $\mathbf{g}$ in the inner sum, we have $\rho(\mathbf{g}, N)^{\alpha-1} \le r(\mathbf{h})^{\alpha-1}$, and so

$$M \le \sum_{\mathbf{h} \in C_s^*(N)} r(\mathbf{h})^{-1} \sum_{\substack{\mathbf{g} \in G_s(N) \\ \mathbf{h} \cdot \mathbf{g} \equiv 0 \bmod N}} 1 = \sum_{\mathbf{g} \in G_s(N)} R(\mathbf{g}, N).$$

By Theorem 5.10, we then obtain

$$(5.28) \qquad M = O\big(\phi(N)^s N^{-1} (\log N)^s\big).$$

For an integer $t \ge 2$, let $K(s, N, t)$ be the number of $\mathbf{g} \in G_s(N)$ with $\rho(\mathbf{g}, N) > t$. If we choose t such that $K(s, N, t) > 0$, then it follows from the definition of M that

$$M > t^{\alpha-1} \sum_{\substack{\mathbf{g} \in G_s(N) \\ \rho(\mathbf{g}, N) > t}} R_\alpha(\mathbf{g}, N).$$

Together with (5.28), this yields

$$\sum_{\substack{\mathbf{g} \in G_s(N) \\ \rho(\mathbf{g}, N) > t}} R_\alpha(\mathbf{g}, N) = O\big(t^{1-\alpha} \phi(N)^s N^{-1} (\log N)^s\big),$$

and so there exists a $\mathbf{g} \in G_s(N)$ with $\rho(\mathbf{g}, N) > t$ and

$$(5.29) \qquad R_\alpha(\mathbf{g}, N) = O\big(K(s, N, t)^{-1} t^{1-\alpha} \phi(N)^s N^{-1} (\log N)^s\big),$$

where the implied constant depends only on s. Since $G_s(N)$ has $\phi(N)^s$ elements, we can write

$$K(s, N, t) = \phi(N)^s - \text{card}(\{\mathbf{g} \in G_s(N) : \rho(\mathbf{g}, N) \le t\}).$$

Now $\mathbf{g} = (g_1, \dots, g_s) \in G_s(N)$ satisfies the congruence $\mathbf{h} \cdot \mathbf{g} \equiv 0 \bmod N$ if and only if $\bar{g}_1 \mathbf{g}$ satisfies the same congruence, where $\bar{g}_1$ is determined by $g_1 \bar{g}_1 \equiv$

$1 \bmod N$. Furthermore, $\bar{g}_1 \mathbf{g}$ is congruent modulo N to a unique element of $E_s(N)$. Thus

$$(5.30) \qquad\qquad K(s, N, t) \geq \phi(N)^s - \phi(N) F_s(t, N).$$

If we put

$$B = \frac{c(s)\phi(N)^{s-1}}{N^{s-2}} \quad \text{and} \quad t_0 = \left\lfloor \frac{B}{(\log B)^{s-1}} \right\rfloor$$

with a constant $c(s) > 0$, then $t_0 \geq 2$ and $B \geq e$ for all sufficiently large N; hence $t_0(\log t_0)^{s-1} \leq B$ for such N. If $c(s)$ is chosen suitably, then it follows from (5.30) and Lemma 5.11 that

$$K(s, N, t_0) \geq c_1(s)\phi(N)^s$$

for a constant $c_1(s) > 0$ and all sufficiently large N. In particular, we have $K(s, N, t_0) > 0$ for all sufficiently large N, and so (5.29) is applicable with $t = t_0$. For a $\mathbf{g} \in G_s(N)$ satisfying (5.29), we then obtain

$$R_\alpha(\mathbf{g}, N) = O\left(N^{-\alpha}(\log N)^{\alpha(s-1)+1} \left(\frac{N}{\phi(N)} \right)^{(\alpha-1)(s-1)} \right).$$

Since by (5.8) we have

$$P_\alpha(\mathbf{g}, N) < R_\alpha(\mathbf{g}, N) + O(N^{-\alpha}),$$

the result of the theorem follows. $\quad \Box$

If we carefully keep track of the constants in the above proof, as is done in the original paper [264], then we obtain the bound for $P_\alpha(\mathbf{g}, N)$ in Theorem 5.13 with the coefficient of the leading term being

$$2^{\alpha(s-1)+1} \alpha \left(\frac{\alpha}{(s-1)!\,(\alpha-1)} \right)^{\alpha-1},$$

which decreases superexponentially as s increases and α is fixed. Using $\phi(N)^{-1} = O(N^{-1}\log\log(N+1))$, we may also write the bound in Theorem 5.13 in the form

$$P_\alpha(\mathbf{g}, N) = O\left(N^{-\alpha}(\log N)^{\alpha(s-1)+1} (\log\log(N+1))^{(\alpha-1)(s-1)} \right).$$

THEOREM 5.14. *For any integers $s \geq 2$ and $N \geq 2$ and any real $\alpha > 1$, there exists a $\mathbf{g} \in E_s(N)$ with*

$$P_\alpha(\mathbf{g}, N) = O\left(N^{-\alpha}(\log N)^{\alpha(s-1)} \left(1 + \frac{\tau(N)}{(\log N)^{s-1}} \right) \right) \qquad \text{if } s \geq 3,$$

$$P_\alpha(\mathbf{g}, N) = O\left(N^{-\alpha}(\log N)^\alpha \left(\frac{N}{\phi(N)} + \frac{\tau(N)}{\log N} \right) \right) \qquad \text{if } s = 2,$$

where the implied constants depend only on s and α and where $\tau(N)$ denotes the number of positive divisors of N.

Proof. For fixed s, N, and α and an integer $t \geq 2$, consider

$$H(t) = H(s, N, \alpha, t) := \sum_{\substack{\mathbf{g} \in E_s(N) \\ \rho(\mathbf{g}, N) > t}} P_\alpha(\mathbf{g}, N).$$

For $\mathbf{h} \in \mathbf{Z}^s$, let $D(\mathbf{h}, N)$ be the number of $\mathbf{g} \in E_s(N)$ with $\mathbf{h} \cdot \mathbf{g} \equiv 0 \bmod N$. Then, using the definition of $P_\alpha(\mathbf{g}, N)$ and the fact that, if $\rho(\mathbf{g}, N) > t$, then a nonzero $\mathbf{h} \in \mathbf{Z}^s$ can satisfy $\mathbf{h} \cdot \mathbf{g} \equiv 0 \bmod N$ only if $r(\mathbf{h}) > t$, we see that

$$(5.31) \qquad H(t) \leq \sum_{\substack{\mathbf{h} \in \mathbf{Z}^s \\ r(\mathbf{h}) > t}} r(\mathbf{h})^{-\alpha} D(\mathbf{h}, N).$$

To determine $D(\mathbf{h}, N)$ for any $\mathbf{h} = (h_1, \cdots, h_s) \in \mathbf{Z}^s$, we note that, if $\mathbf{g} = (1, g_2, \ldots, g_s) \in E_s(N)$ is a solution of

$$\mathbf{h} \cdot \mathbf{g} = h_1 + h_2 g_2 + \cdots + h_s g_s \equiv 0 \bmod N,$$

then $d = \gcd(N, h_2, \ldots, h_s)$ must divide h_1. In this case, we divide the congruence by d and obtain

$$(5.32) \qquad k_1 + k_2 g_2 + \cdots + k_s g_s \equiv 0 \bmod m$$

with $m = N/d$ and $\gcd(m, k_2, \ldots, k_s) = 1$. If $m > 1$, then let p^a be a prime power in the canonical factorization of m. Since at least one k_i, $2 \leq i \leq s$, is not divisible by p, the number of solutions $\bmod\, p^a$ of (5.32) is $p^{a(s-2)}$. By combining the solutions by the Chinese remainder theorem, the number of solutions $\bmod\, m$ of (5.32) is m^{s-2}, and this holds for $m = 1$ as well. Thus $D(\mathbf{h}, N) = (N/m)^{s-1} m^{s-2} = N^{s-2} d$ if d divides h_1, and $D(\mathbf{h}, N) = 0$ otherwise. Using this formula in (5.31), we obtain

$$H(t) \leq N^{s-2} \sum_{\mathbf{h}} \gcd(N, h_2, \ldots, h_s) r(\mathbf{h})^{-\alpha},$$

where the sum is over all $\mathbf{h} = (h_1, \ldots, h_s) \in \mathbf{Z}^s$ for which $r(\mathbf{h}) > t$ and $d = \gcd(N, h_2, \ldots, h_s)$ divides h_1. By splitting up the sum according to the value of d, we obtain

$$(5.33) \qquad H(t) \leq N^{s-2} \sum_{d \mid N} d T_d(t)$$

with

$$T_d(t) = \sum_{\substack{\mathbf{h} \in \mathbf{Z}^s \\ r(d\mathbf{h}) > t}} r(d\mathbf{h})^{-\alpha}.$$

We split up the last sum according to the number i of nonzero coordinates of $\mathbf{h}$ and the position of these nonzero coordinates. This yields

$$(5.34) \qquad T_d(t) = \sum_{i=1}^{s} \binom{s}{i} d^{-\alpha i} V_i\left(\frac{t}{d^i}\right),$$

where

$$V_i(u) = \sum_{\substack{(h_1,\cdots,h_i)\in\mathbb{Z}^i \\ |h_1\cdots h_i|>u}} |h_1\cdots h_i|^{-\alpha} \quad \text{for } u > 0.$$

For integers $1 \le i \le s$ and $k \ge 1$, let $A_i(k)$ be the number of $(h_1,\ldots,h_i) \in \mathbb{Z}^i$ with $0 < |h_1\cdots h_i| \le k$, and put $A_i(0) = 0$. Then

$$V_i(u) = \sum_{k>u} k^{-\alpha}(A_i(k) - A_i(k-1)) \le \sum_{k>u}(k^{-\alpha} - (k+1)^{-\alpha})A_i(k)$$

$$< \alpha \sum_{k>u} k^{-\alpha-1} A_i(k).$$

In the remainder of the proof, the implied constants in the Landau symbols always depend only on s and α. By induction on i, we see that

$$A_i(k) = O\big(k(\log(k+1))^{i-1}\big),$$

and so

$$V_i(u) = O\left(\sum_{k>u} k^{-\alpha}(\log(k+1))^{i-1}\right) = O\big(u^{1-\alpha}(\log(u+1))^{i-1}\big).$$

Thus, from (5.34),

$$T_d(t) = O\left(t^{1-\alpha}\sum_{i=1}^s d^{-i}(\log t)^{i-1}\right),$$

and so, by (5.33),

(5.35) $$H(t) = O\left(N^{s-2}t^{1-\alpha}\sum_{i=1}^s (\log t)^{i-1}\sum_{d|N} d^{1-i}\right).$$

For $i = 1$, we have $\sum_{d|N} d^{1-i} = \tau(N)$, and, for $i = 2$, we have $\sum_{d|N} d^{1-i} = \sum_{d|N} d^{-1} < N/\phi(N)$, where the inequality is obtained by comparing the two arithmetic functions at prime powers and using multiplicativity. For $i \ge 3$, we have $\sum_{d|N} d^{1-i} = O(1)$. For $s \ge 3$, we thus obtain from (5.35),

(5.36) $$H(t) = O\left(N^{s-2}t^{1-\alpha}\left((\log t)^{s-1} + \frac{N}{\phi(N)}\log t + \tau(N)\right)\right).$$

Let $L(s, N, t)$ be the numbers of $\mathbf{g} \in E_s(N)$ with $\rho(\mathbf{g}, N) > t$. Then $L(s, N, t) = N^{s-1} - F_s(t, N)$; hence if we put

$$t_0 = \left\lfloor \frac{c(s)N}{(\log c(s)N)^{s-1}} \right\rfloor$$

with a suitable constant $c(s) > 0$, then $t_0 \geq 2$ and $L(s, N, t_0) \geq c_1(s)N^{s-1}$ for all sufficiently large N and some constant $c_1(s) > 0$, by Lemma 5.11. It follows then from the definition of $H(t)$ and from (5.36) that, for $s \geq 3$, there exists a $\mathbf{g} \in E_s(N)$ with $\rho(\mathbf{g}, N) > t_0$ and

$$P_\alpha(\mathbf{g}, N) = O\left(\frac{N^{s-2}t_0^{1-\alpha}}{L(s, N, t_0)}\left((\log t_0)^{s-1} + \frac{N}{\phi(N)}\log t_0 + \tau(N)\right)\right)$$

$$= O\left(N^{-\alpha}(\log N)^{\alpha(s-1)}\left(1 + \frac{\tau(N)}{(\log N)^{s-1}}\right)\right).$$

For $s = 2$, we see, from (5.35), that

$$H(t) = O\left(t^{1-\alpha}\left(\frac{N}{\phi(N)}\log t + \tau(N)\right)\right).$$

By choosing t_0 as above and using a similar argument, we obtain the result of the theorem for $s = 2$. $\square$

The more detailed analysis performed in [264] yields the bounds in Theorem 5.14 with explicit coefficients of the main terms. These coefficients decrease superexponentially as s increases and α is fixed. Since $\tau(N)$ has the average order of magnitude $\log N$ by [188, Thm. 6.30], the result of Theorem 5.14 is usually better than that of Theorem 5.13. However, there exist sequences of values of N through which $\tau(N)$ grows faster than any given power of $\log N$ (see [188, p. 164]), and, for such values of N, Theorem 5.13 yields the better result.

The lattice points $\mathbf{g}$ satisfying the bounds in Theorems 5.13 and 5.14 depend, in particular, on α, so that these theorems can guarantee only that $P_\alpha(\mathbf{g}, N)$ is small for the chosen value of α. However, the proofs of these theorems yield the additional property that the figure of merit $\rho(\mathbf{g}, N)$ is large, and on the basis of this information it can be shown that $P_\beta(\mathbf{g}, N)$ is small for all $\beta > 1$ (see [264]).

For $s = 2$, there is an interesting connection between good lattice points and continued fractions for rational numbers, which can be used for the explicit construction of good lattice points. For an integer $N \geq 2$, let $\mathbf{g} = (1, g) \in \mathbb{Z}^2$ with $\gcd(g, N) = 1$. Let the rational number g/N have the continued fraction expansion

$$(5.37) \qquad\qquad \frac{g}{N} = [a_0; a_1, a_2, \dots, a_l],$$

where the a_j are integers with $a_j \geq 1$ for $1 \leq j \leq l$ and where $a_l = 1$ for the sake of uniqueness (compare with Appendix B). Recall that the convergents to g/N are defined by

$$\frac{p_j}{q_j} = [a_0; a_1, a_2, \dots, a_j] \qquad \text{for } 0 \leq j \leq l.$$

The integers p_j and q_j are uniquely determined if we impose the conditions $q_j \geq 1$ and $\gcd(p_j, q_j) = 1$. Then we have the following explicit formula for the figure of merit due to Borosh and Niederreiter [30].

THEOREM 5.15. *If $N \geq 2$ is an integer and $\mathbf{g} = (1, g) \in \mathbb{Z}^2$ with $\gcd(g, N) = 1$, then*

$$\rho(\mathbf{g}, N) = \min_{0 \leq j < l} q_j |q_j g - p_j N|.$$

Proof. Because of Lemma 5.8, it suffices to extend the minimum in Definition 5.7 over all nonzero $\mathbf{h} = (h_1, h_2) \in \mathbb{Z}^2$ with $|h_1| < N$, $|h_2| < N$, and $\mathbf{h} \cdot \mathbf{g} \equiv 0 \bmod N$. For such $\mathbf{h}$, we also have $h_1 h_2 \neq 0$. Therefore, we can write

$$\rho(\mathbf{g}, N) = \min h_2 |h_2 g - tN|,$$

where the minimum is extended over all integers h_2 with $1 \leq h_2 < N$ and over all integers t. If $1 \leq h_2 < N$, then for some j with $0 \leq j < l$ we have $q_j \leq h_2 < q_{j+1}$. Then, by an inequality in Appendix B, we obtain

$$h_2 |h_2 g - tN| \geq q_j |q_j g - p_j N|,$$

hence the result. $\square$

DEFINITION 5.16. For integers $N \geq 2$ and g with $\gcd(g, N) = 1$, let

$$K\left(\frac{g}{N}\right) = \max_{1 \leq j \leq l} a_j,$$

where $a_1, \ldots, a_l$ are the partial quotients in the continued fraction expansion of g/N given by (5.37).

In the case considered in Theorem 5.15, the figure of merit $\rho(\mathbf{g}, N)$ can be bounded in terms of $K(g/N)$, as was shown by Zaremba [361].

THEOREM 5.17. *If $N \geq 2$ is an integer and $\mathbf{g} = (1, g) \in \mathbb{Z}^2$ with $\gcd(g, N) = 1$, then*

$$\frac{N}{K(g/N) + 2} \leq \rho(\mathbf{g}, N) \leq \frac{N}{K(g/N)}.$$

Proof. From the theory of continued fractions (see Appendix B), we derive

$$\frac{1}{q_j(q_j + q_{j+1})} \leq \left| \frac{g}{N} - \frac{p_j}{q_j} \right| \leq \frac{1}{q_j q_{j+1}} \qquad \text{for } 0 \leq j < l,$$

and so

$$\frac{Nq_j}{q_j + q_{j+1}} \leq q_j |q_j g - p_j N| \leq \frac{Nq_j}{q_{j+1}} \qquad \text{for } 0 \leq j < l.$$

Now $q_j + q_{j+1} = (a_{j+1} + 1)q_j + q_{j-1} \leq (K(g/N) + 2)q_j$ for $0 \leq j < l$, and together with Theorem 5.15 this yields the desired lower bound. If we choose j with $0 \leq j < l$ and $a_{j+1} = K(g/N)$, then $q_{j+1} = a_{j+1} q_j + q_{j-1} \geq K(g/N)q_j$, and, in view of Theorem 5.15, we obtain the desired upper bound. $\square$

From Theorem 5.17, we infer the principle that two-dimensional good lattice points $\mathbf{g} = (1, g) \bmod N$ are obtained by choosing rational numbers g/N with small partial quotients in their continued fraction expansion. This principle leads, in particular, to the following explicit construction based on Fibonacci numbers. Recall that the sequence $F_1, F_2, \ldots$ of *Fibonacci numbers* is defined recursively by $F_1 = F_2 = 1$ and $F_m = F_{m-1} + F_{m-2}$ for $m \geq 3$. Now let $N = F_m$ for some $m \geq 3$ and $\mathbf{g} = (1, F_{m-1})$. Since all partial quotients of F_{m-1}/F_m used in Definition 5.16 are equal to 1, we have $K(F_{m-1}/F_m) = 1$, and so $\rho(\mathbf{g}, N)$ is of the order of magnitude N by Theorem 5.17. In fact, we have $\rho(\mathbf{g}, F_m) = F_{m-2}$ according to a formula of Zaremba [361]. From (5.10), we obtain $P_\alpha(\mathbf{g}, N) = O(N^{-\alpha} \log N)$ for all $\alpha > 1$ with an implied constant depending only on α, a result due to Bakhvalov [13]. This paper is also the first to contain this explicit construction of two-dimensional good lattice points. From (5.11), we infer that $R(\mathbf{g}, N) = O(N^{-1}(\log N)^2)$, where the implied constant is absolute. Note that these bounds for $P_\alpha(\mathbf{g}, N)$ and $R(\mathbf{g}, N)$ are the best possible that can be obtained for any two-dimensional lattice point with any modulus, according to the general lower bounds for $P_\alpha(\mathbf{g}, N)$ and $R(\mathbf{g}, N)$ due to Sharygin [308] and Larcher [175], respectively, which were mentioned earlier in this section.

It is an interesting question as to whether the orders of magnitude of $\rho(\mathbf{g}, N)$, $P_\alpha(\mathbf{g}, N)$, and $R(\mathbf{g}, N)$ achieved by the above construction can be obtained for any integer $N \geq 2$ in the two-dimensional case. This question leads to the consideration of the quantity

$$(5.38) \qquad K_N = \min_{\substack{g \in \mathbb{Z} \\ \gcd(g, N) = 1}} K\left(\frac{g}{N}\right) \qquad \text{for } N \geq 2.$$

It is clear from the above arguments that, if there exists an absolute constant C such that $K_N \leq C$ for all $N \geq 2$, then our question has an affirmative answer. In this context, we draw the attention to *Zaremba's conjecture* from [365, p. 76], which amounts to suggesting that $K_N \leq 5$ for all $N \geq 2$. The constant 5 cannot be replaced by a smaller one, since $K_{54} = K_{150} = 5$ (these are the only known values of K_N that are equal to 5). Borosh calculated K_N for $2 \leq N \leq 10^4$ (see [225, p. 989]), and Knuth [154, p. 548] extended this calculation to all $N < 2 \cdot 10^6$, the result being that Zaremba's conjecture is valid in this range. Borosh and Niederreiter [30] conjectured that $K_N \leq 3$ for all sufficiently large N. Zaremba's conjecture has been verified for some sequences of values of N. It is trivial that $K_N = 1$ if and only if N is a Fibonacci number. Niederreiter [238] established the following results by constructive proofs: if $N = 2^m$ or 3^m, $m \geq 1$, then $K_N \leq 3$, and $K_N = 2$ for infinitely many m; if $N = 5^m$, $m \geq 1$, then $K_N \leq 4$, and $K_N \leq 3$ for infinitely many m.

Consider again a point $\mathbf{g} = (1, g) \in \mathbb{Z}^2$ with $\gcd(g, N) = 1$ and $N \geq 2$. Let the continued fraction expansion of g/N be given by (5.37). Then the discrepancy $D_N(P)$ of the two-dimensional point set P in (5.1) satisfies

$$(5.39) \qquad N D_N(P) \leq \sum_{j=1}^{l} a_j + 1.$$

This is shown by adapting the method in the proof of Theorem 3.3 for rational z and by using an analogue of Lemma 3.7 for the discrepancy $D_N(P)$; also compare with Niederreiter [225, pp. 1024–1025]. The quantity

$$S\left(\frac{g}{N}\right) := \sum_{j=1}^{l} a_j$$

is connected with $K(g/N)$ in Definition 5.16 by the inequality $S(g/N) \le cK(g/N)\log N$ with an absolute constant $c > 0$, since we have $l \le c\log N$. Together with (5.39), this yields

$$ND_N(P) = O\left(K\left(\frac{g}{N}\right)\log N\right)$$

with an absolute implied constant, and a slightly more refined bound is obtained by adapting the method in the proof of Corollary 3.5. In analogy with (5.38), we define

$$S_N = \min_{\substack{g\in\mathbb{Z}\\ \gcd(g,N)=1}} S\left(\frac{g}{N}\right) \quad \text{for } N \ge 2.$$

Then we have $S_N \le cK_N\log N$ for all $N \ge 2$. It is conjectured that $S_N = O(\log N)$ with an absolute implied constant, and this conjecture would, of course, follow from the validity of Zaremba's conjecture. On the other hand, it is easily seen that S_N is at least of the order of magnitude $\log N$ (see Niederreiter [245]). For sequences of values of N for which $S_N = O(\log N)$, such as for the sequence of Fibonacci numbers, we obtain two-dimensional point sets P with $D_N(P) = O(N^{-1}\log N)$. Note that by a remark following (3.8), this is the least possible order of magnitude for the discrepancy of a two-dimensional point set. The best general bound on S_N that is currently known is

$$S_N = O\left(\frac{N}{\phi(N)}(\log N)\log\log(N+1)\right) = O\left((\log N)(\log\log N)^2\right),$$

which was shown by Larcher [173].

We now return to the consideration of an arbitrary dimension $s \ge 2$. Korobov [159] suggested the use of special lattice points of the form $(1, g, g^2, \dots, g^{s-1}) \in \mathbb{Z}^s$ to restrict the number of candidates that must be inspected in the search for good lattice points $\bmod N$. It turns out that, at least for prime moduli N, it is possible to prove existence theorems for these special lattice points, which are basically of the same quality as the existence theorems shown earlier in this section. We include the proof of the following theorem as an example.

THEOREM 5.18. *For any integer $s \ge 2$ and any prime N, put*

$$m_s(N) = \frac{1}{N}\sum_{g=0}^{N-1} R((1, g, g^2, \dots, g^{s-1}), N).$$

Then we have

$$m_s(N) < \frac{s-1}{N}(2\log N + 1)^s.$$

Proof. Inserting the definition of $R(\mathbf{g}, N)$ into the expression for $m_s(N)$ and interchanging the order of summation, we obtain

$$m_s(N) = \frac{1}{N} \sum_{\mathbf{h} \in C_s^*(N)} a(\mathbf{h}) r(\mathbf{h})^{-1},$$

where $a(\mathbf{h})$ is the number of integers g with $0 \le g \le N - 1$ and

$$\mathbf{h} \cdot (1, g, g^2, \dots, g^{s-1}) \equiv 0 \bmod N.$$

If we put $\mathbf{h} = (h_1, \dots, h_s)$, then the last congruence can be written as

$$\sum_{i=1}^{s} h_i g^{i-1} \equiv 0 \bmod N.$$

For $\mathbf{h} \in C_s^*(N)$, this is a nonzero polynomial congruence of degree $\le s - 1$ in the unknown g, and, since N is a prime, we conclude that $a(\mathbf{h}) \le s - 1$. Hence we obtain

$$m_s(N) \le \frac{s-1}{N} \sum_{\mathbf{h} \in C_s^*(N)} r(\mathbf{h})^{-1} < \frac{s-1}{N} \left(\sum_{h \in C(N)} r(h)^{-1} \right)^s$$

$$= \frac{s-1}{N} \left(\sum_{h \in C^*(N)} |h|^{-1} + 1 \right)^s < \frac{s-1}{N} (2 \log N + 1)^s. \qquad \square$$

It follows from Theorem 5.18 that, for any dimension $s \ge 2$ and any prime N, there exists a lattice point $\mathbf{g} \in \mathbb{Z}^s$ of the form $\mathbf{g} = (1, g, g^2, \dots, g^{s-1})$ for which

$$R(\mathbf{g}, N) < \frac{s-1}{N} (2 \log N + 1)^s.$$

We also have results guaranteeing the existence of lattice points $\mathbf{g}$ of this form for which $P_\alpha(\mathbf{g}, N)$ is small and $\rho(\mathbf{g}, N)$ is large, provided that N is a prime; compare with Hua and Wang [145, Chap. 7]. For $s = 2$, the earlier existence theorems in this section yield good lattice points $\mathbf{g}$ mod N of the form $\mathbf{g} = (1, g)$ for any integer $N \ge 2$. For $s = 3$ and any prime power N, a result showing the existence of small values of $R(\mathbf{g}, N)$ for $\mathbf{g} = (1, g, g^2)$ was proved by Larcher [171], and a result showing the existence of large values of $\rho(\mathbf{g}, N)$ for $\mathbf{g} = (1, g, g^2)$ was established by Larcher and Niederreiter [179].

5.3. General lattice rules and their classification.

For the point set $\mathbf{x}_0, \mathbf{x}_1, \dots, \mathbf{x}_{N-1}$ in (5.1), consider the corresponding residue classes $\mathbf{x}_n + \mathbb{Z}^s = (n/N)\mathbf{g} + \mathbb{Z}^s$, $0 \le n \le N-1$, in the additive group $\mathbb{R}^s/\mathbb{Z}^s$. These residue classes form a finite cyclic subgroup of $\mathbb{R}^s/\mathbb{Z}^s$ generated by $(1/N)\mathbf{g} + \mathbb{Z}^s$. If the point set in (5.1) is viewed in this way, then the following generalization is obvious. Let $L/\mathbb{Z}^s$ be *any* finite subgroup of $\mathbb{R}^s/\mathbb{Z}^s$ and let $\mathbf{x}_n + \mathbb{Z}^s$ with $\mathbf{x}_n \in I^s$ for $0 \le n \le N - 1$ be the distinct residue classes making up the group

$L/\mathbf{Z}^s$. The s-dimensional *lattice rule* L is then given by the quasi-Monte Carlo approximation

$$(5.40) \qquad \int_{\bar{I}^s} f(\mathbf{u})\,d\mathbf{u} \approx \frac{1}{N}\sum_{n=0}^{N-1} f(\mathbf{x}_n).$$

The set $\{\mathbf{x}_0, \mathbf{x}_1, \ldots, \mathbf{x}_{N-1}\}$ is called the *node set* of the lattice rule L. If we want to emphasize that the node set has cardinality N, then we refer to an N-*point lattice rule*.

The name "lattice rule" stems from a geometric interpretation of the above approach. If we view $L = \bigcup_{n=0}^{N-1}(\mathbf{x}_n + \mathbf{Z}^s)$ as a subset of $\mathbf{R}^s$, then L is an s-dimensional lattice. Here an s-dimensional *lattice* is meant to be a discrete additive subgroup of $\mathbf{R}^s$ not contained in any proper linear subspace of $\mathbf{R}^s$. Equivalently, an s-dimensional lattice is obtained by taking s linearly independent vectors $\mathbf{y}_1, \ldots, \mathbf{y}_s \in \mathbf{R}^s$ and forming the set $L = \{\sum_{i=1}^{s} a_i \mathbf{y}_i : a_i \in \mathbf{Z} \text{ for } 1 \le i \le s\}$ of all $\mathbf{Z}$-linear combinations. The lattices corresponding to lattice rules have the property that they contain $\mathbf{Z}^s$; a lattice containing $\mathbf{Z}^s$ is called an s-dimensional *integration lattice*. If we start from an s-dimensional integration lattice L, then the corresponding node set is determined as the intersection $L \cap I^s$, which is always a finite set.

REMARK 5.19. The point set in (5.1) leads to a lattice rule, but it need not be an N-point lattice rule because of a possible repetition of points. However, it is an easy exercise to show that this point set yields an N-point lattice rule if and only if $\mathbf{g} = (g_1, \ldots, g_s)$ satisfies $\gcd(g_1, \ldots, g_s, N) = 1$.

The error in the approximation (5.40) can be analyzed in the same way as for the method of good lattice points. The following definition and the subsequent lemma are basic. Definition 5.22 is an analogue of Definition 5.2.

DEFINITION 5.20. The *dual lattice* $L^\perp$ of the s-dimensional integration lattice L is defined by

$$L^\perp = \{\mathbf{h} \in \mathbf{Z}^s : \mathbf{h} \cdot \mathbf{x} \in \mathbf{Z} \text{ for all } \mathbf{x} \in L\}.$$

LEMMA 5.21. *Let* $\mathbf{x}_0, \mathbf{x}_1, \ldots, \mathbf{x}_{N-1}$ *be the nodes of an s-dimensional N-point lattice rule L, and let $\mathbf{h} \in \mathbf{Z}^s$. Then*

$$\sum_{n=0}^{N-1} e(\mathbf{h} \cdot \mathbf{x}_n) = \begin{cases} N & \text{if } \mathbf{h} \in L^\perp, \\ 0 & \text{if } \mathbf{h} \notin L^\perp. \end{cases}$$

Proof. If we put $A = L/\mathbf{Z}^s$ and $\chi_{\mathbf{h}}(\mathbf{x} + \mathbf{Z}^s) = e(\mathbf{h} \cdot \mathbf{x})$ for all $\mathbf{x} \in L$, then $\chi_{\mathbf{h}}$ is a well-defined character of the additive group A. We have

$$\sum_{n=0}^{N-1} e(\mathbf{h} \cdot \mathbf{x}_n) = \sum_{a \in A} \chi_{\mathbf{h}}(a),$$

and the last sum, being a character sum for the finite abelian group A, is equal to N if $\chi_{\mathbf{h}}$ is trivial and equal to zero if $\chi_{\mathbf{h}}$ is nontrivial. Furthermore, $\chi_{\mathbf{h}}$ is trivial if and only if $\mathbf{h} \cdot \mathbf{x} \in \mathbb{Z}$ for all $\mathbf{x} \in L$, i.e., if and only if $\mathbf{h} \in L^{\perp}$. □

DEFINITION 5.22. For a real number $\alpha > 1$ and for a lattice rule L, we put

$$P_{\alpha}(L) = \sum_{\mathbf{h}} r(\mathbf{h})^{-\alpha},$$

where the sum is over all nonzero $\mathbf{h} \in L^{\perp}$.

THEOREM 5.23. For any real numbers $\alpha > 1$ and $C > 0$ and for an s-dimensional lattice rule L with node set $\{\mathbf{x}_0, \mathbf{x}_1, \ldots, \mathbf{x}_{N-1}\}$, we have

$$\max_{f \in \mathcal{E}_{\alpha}^{s}(C)} \left| \frac{1}{N} \sum_{n=0}^{N-1} f(\mathbf{x}_n) - \int_{\bar{I}^s} f(\mathbf{u}) \, d\mathbf{u} \right| = C P_{\alpha}(L).$$

Proof. Any $f \in \mathcal{E}_{\alpha}^{s}(C)$ is represented by its absolutely convergent Fourier series

$$f(\mathbf{u}) = \sum_{\mathbf{h} \in \mathbb{Z}^s} \hat{f}(\mathbf{h}) e(\mathbf{h} \cdot \mathbf{u}) \quad \text{for } \mathbf{u} \in \mathbb{R}^s.$$

Then

$$\frac{1}{N} \sum_{n=0}^{N-1} f(\mathbf{x}_n) - \int_{\bar{I}^s} f(\mathbf{u}) \, d\mathbf{u} = \frac{1}{N} \sum_{n=0}^{N-1} \sum_{\mathbf{h} \in \mathbb{Z}^s} \hat{f}(\mathbf{h}) e(\mathbf{h} \cdot \mathbf{x}_n) - \hat{f}(\mathbf{0})$$

$$= \frac{1}{N} \sum_{\substack{\mathbf{h} \in \mathbb{Z}^s \\ \mathbf{h} \neq \mathbf{0}}} \hat{f}(\mathbf{h}) \sum_{n=0}^{N-1} e(\mathbf{h} \cdot \mathbf{x}_n) = \sum_{\substack{\mathbf{h} \in L^{\perp} \\ \mathbf{h} \neq \mathbf{0}}} \hat{f}(\mathbf{h})$$

by Lemma 5.21. The bound

$$\left| \frac{1}{N} \sum_{n=0}^{N-1} f(\mathbf{x}_n) - \int_{\bar{I}^s} f(\mathbf{u}) \, d\mathbf{u} \right| \leq C P_{\alpha}(L)$$

follows now from Definitions 5.1 and 5.22. The proof is completed by using the special function $f_0 \in \mathcal{E}_{\alpha}^{s}(C)$ as in the proof of Theorem 5.3. □

Theorem 5.23, which is due to Sloan and Kachoyan [316], shows that, for given α, the integration lattice L should be chosen in such a way that $P_{\alpha}(L)$ is small. The following definition is analogous to Definition 5.4.

DEFINITION 5.24. For an s-dimensional N-point lattice rule L with $s \geq 2$ and $N \geq 2$, we put

$$R(L) = \sum_{\mathbf{h} \in E(L)} r(\mathbf{h})^{-1},$$

where $E(L) = C_s^{*}(N) \cap L^{\perp}$.

REMARK 5.25. By the proof of Lemma 5.21, the dual group (or character group) of $L/\mathbb{Z}^s$ is $\mathbb{Z}^s/L^\perp$. Thus, since $L/\mathbb{Z}^s$ has order N, so has $\mathbb{Z}^s/L^\perp$. It follows that $N\mathbf{h} \in L^\perp$ for all $\mathbf{h} \in \mathbb{Z}^s$; hence $L^\perp$ contains $(N\mathbb{Z})^s$. Furthermore, $L^\perp/(N\mathbb{Z})^s$ has order $N^s/N = N^{s-1}$. Since $C_s(N)$ is a complete system of representatives for $\mathbb{Z}^s/(N\mathbb{Z})^s$, the set $C_s(N) \cap L^\perp$ has N^{s-1} elements, and so $\operatorname{card}(E(L)) = N^{s-1} - 1$. In particular, if $s \geq 2$ and $N \geq 2$, then $E(L)$ is nonempty.

THEOREM 5.26. *Let L be an s-dimensional N-point lattice rule with $s \geq 2$ and $N \geq 2$. Then, for any real $\alpha > 1$, we have*

$$P_\alpha(L) < (1+\zeta(\alpha)s)R(L)^\alpha + (1+2\zeta(\alpha)N^{-\alpha})^s - 1 + 2^{\alpha s}\zeta(\alpha)^s N^{-\alpha s + s - 1}$$
$$+ \sum_{j=1}^{s-2} \binom{s}{j} 2^{\alpha(s-j)}\zeta(\alpha)^{s-j}(1+2\zeta(\alpha))^j N^{(1-\alpha)(s-j)}.$$

In particular, if either $s = 2$ or $\alpha \geq 2$, then

$$P_\alpha(L) < (1+\zeta(\alpha)s)R(L)^\alpha + O(N^{-\alpha})$$

with an implied constant depending only on s and α.

Proof. Every $\mathbf{h} \in \mathbb{Z}^s$ can be uniquely represented in the form $\mathbf{h} = \mathbf{k} + N\mathbf{m}$ with $\mathbf{k} \in C_s(N)$, $\mathbf{m} \in \mathbb{Z}^s$. Since $L^\perp \supseteq (N\mathbb{Z})^s$ (see Remark 5.25), we have $\mathbf{h} \in L^\perp$ if and only if $\mathbf{k} \in L^\perp$. Separating the cases where $\mathbf{k} = \mathbf{0}$ and $\mathbf{k} \neq \mathbf{0}$, we obtain

$$(5.41) \quad P_\alpha(L) = \sum_{\substack{\mathbf{m} \in \mathbb{Z}^s \\ \mathbf{m} \neq \mathbf{0}}} r(N\mathbf{m})^{-\alpha} + \sum_{\mathbf{k} \in E(L)} \sum_{\mathbf{m} \in \mathbb{Z}^s} r(\mathbf{k} + N\mathbf{m})^{-\alpha} =: S_1 + S_2.$$

As in the proof of Theorem 5.5, we see that

$$S_2 < R_\alpha(L) + 2^{\alpha s}\zeta(\alpha)^s N^{-\alpha s}\operatorname{card}(C_s(N) \cap L^\perp)$$
$$+ \sum_{j=1}^{s-1} 2^{\alpha(s-j)}\zeta(\alpha)^{s-j}N^{-\alpha(s-j)} \sum_{1 \leq i_1 < \cdots < i_j \leq s} \sum_{\mathbf{k} \in E(L)} r(k_{i_1})^{-\alpha} \cdots r(k_{i_j})^{-\alpha},$$

where $\mathbf{k} = (k_1, \ldots, k_s)$ and

$$R_\alpha(L) = \sum_{\mathbf{k} \in E(L)} r(\mathbf{k})^{-\alpha}.$$

Now $\operatorname{card}(C_s(N) \cap L^\perp) = N^{s-1}$, as shown in Remark 5.25. Furthermore, for fixed $1 \leq j \leq s - 2$ and $1 \leq i_1 < \cdots < i_j \leq s$, we have

$$\sum_{\mathbf{k} \in E(L)} r(k_{i_1})^{-\alpha} \cdots r(k_{i_j})^{-\alpha}$$
$$= \sum_{\mathbf{h} \in C_j(N)} r(\mathbf{h})^{-\alpha}\#\{\mathbf{k} \in E(L) : k_{i_d} = h_d \text{ for } 1 \leq d \leq j\},$$

where $\mathbf{h} = (h_1, \ldots, h_j)$. A trivial upper bound for the last counting function is N^{s-j}; thus

$$\sum_{\mathbf{k} \in E(L)} r(k_{i_1})^{-\alpha} \cdots r(k_{i_j})^{-\alpha} < (1 + 2\zeta(\alpha))^j N^{s-j}.$$

For $j = s - 1$ and fixed $1 \le i_1 < \cdots < i_{s-1} \le s$, let i be the integer determined by $\{i_1, \ldots, i_{s-1}\} \cup \{i\} = \{1, 2, \ldots, s\}$. Then

$$\sum_{\mathbf{k} \in E(L)} r(k_{i_1})^{-\alpha} \cdots r(k_{i_{s-1}})^{-\alpha} = \sum_{\mathbf{k} \in E(L)} \frac{r(k_i)^{\alpha}}{r(\mathbf{k})^{\alpha}} \le \left(\frac{N}{2}\right)^{\alpha} R_{\alpha}(L).$$

Altogether, we obtain

$$S_2 < (1 + \zeta(\alpha)s) R_{\alpha}(L) + 2^{\alpha s} \zeta(\alpha)^s N^{-\alpha s + s - 1}$$
$$+ \sum_{j=1}^{s-2} \binom{s}{j} 2^{\alpha(s-j)} \zeta(\alpha)^{s-j} (1 + 2\zeta(\alpha))^j N^{(1-\alpha)(s-j)}.$$

In view of (5.6) and (5.41) and the inequality $R_{\alpha}(L) \le R(L)^{\alpha}$, this yields the first part of the theorem, and the second part is an immediate consequence. $\square$

For arbitrary $s \ge 2$ and $\alpha > 1$, we can derive an inequality of the type occurring in the second part of Theorem 5.26 by the following argument. As in the proof of Theorem 5.5, we obtain

$$S_2 \le \sum_{\mathbf{k} \in E(L)} \prod_{i=1}^{s} (r(k_i)^{-\alpha} + 2^{\alpha} \zeta(\alpha) N^{-\alpha}).$$

Now

$$\prod_{i=1}^{s} (r(k_i)^{-\alpha} + 2^{\alpha} \zeta(\alpha) N^{-\alpha}) = \prod_{i=1}^{s} r(k_i)^{-\alpha} \prod_{i=1}^{s} \left(1 + \zeta(\alpha) \left(\frac{2r(k_i)}{N}\right)^{\alpha}\right)$$
$$\le r(\mathbf{k})^{-\alpha} (1 + \zeta(\alpha))^s,$$

and so

$$S_2 \le (1 + \zeta(\alpha))^s R_{\alpha}(L).$$

Together with (5.6) and (5.41), this yields

(5.42)
$$P_{\alpha}(L) \le (1 + \zeta(\alpha))^s R_{\alpha}(L) + (1 + 2\zeta(\alpha)N^{-\alpha})^s - 1$$
$$\le (1 + \zeta(\alpha))^s R(L)^{\alpha} + (1 + 2\zeta(\alpha)N^{-\alpha})^s - 1$$
$$= (1 + \zeta(\alpha))^s R(L)^{\alpha} + O(N^{-\alpha})$$

with an implied constant depending only on s and α.

For an s-dimensional N-point lattice rule L with $s \ge 2$ and $N \ge 2$, we define in analogy with (5.9) the quantity

(5.43)
$$R_1(L) = \sum_{\mathbf{h} \in E(L)} r(\mathbf{h}, N)^{-1}.$$

The following discrepancy bound was shown by Niederreiter and Sloan [273].

THEOREM 5.27. *Let P be the node set of an s-dimensional N-point lattice rule L with $s \geq 2$ and $N \geq 2$. Then*

$$D_N(P) \leq 1 - \left(1 - \frac{1}{N}\right)^s + R_1(L) \leq \frac{s}{N} + \frac{1}{2}R(L).$$

Proof. If $P = \{\mathbf{x}_0, \mathbf{x}_1, \ldots, \mathbf{x}_{N-1}\}$, then, from the fact that the group $L/\mathbb{Z}^s$ has order N, it follows that $N\mathbf{x}_n \in \mathbb{Z}^s$ for $0 \leq n \leq N - 1$. Thus we can apply Theorem 3.10, which yields

$$D_N(P) \leq 1 - \left(1 - \frac{1}{N}\right)^s + \sum_{\mathbf{h} \in C_s^*(N)} \frac{1}{r(\mathbf{h}, N)} \left| \frac{1}{N} \sum_{n=0}^{N-1} e(\mathbf{h} \cdot \mathbf{x}_n) \right|$$

$$= 1 - \left(1 - \frac{1}{N}\right)^s + R_1(L),$$

where we applied Lemma 5.21 in the second step. The second inequality in the theorem is obtained as in the proof of Theorem 5.6. □

A fundamental classification theorem for lattice rules is due to Sloan and Lyness [317]. This result is based on the structure theory for finite abelian groups.

THEOREM 5.28. *For every s-dimensional N-point lattice rule with $N \geq 2$, the node set consists exactly of all fractional parts*

$$\left\{ \sum_{i=1}^r \frac{k_i}{n_i} \mathbf{g}_i \right\} \quad \text{with integers } 0 \leq k_i < n_i \text{ for } 1 \leq i \leq r,$$

where the integer r with $1 \leq r \leq s$ and the integers $n_1, \ldots, n_r \geq 2$ with n_{i+1} dividing n_i for $1 \leq i \leq r - 1$ and $n_1 \cdots n_r = N$ are uniquely determined. Furthermore, the vectors $\mathbf{g}_1, \ldots, \mathbf{g}_r \in \mathbb{Z}^s$ are linearly independent, and, for each $1 \leq i \leq r$, the coordinates of $\mathbf{g}_i$ and n_i are relatively prime.

Proof. Let $A = L/\mathbb{Z}^s$ be the finite abelian group corresponding to the lattice rule L. By the primary decomposition theorem, A is the direct sum of cyclic groups of prime-power order. Let n_1 be the maximum order of elements of A. Then all orders of elements of A divide n_1, and, from the primary decomposition, we obtain a decomposition $A = C_1 \oplus A_2$, where C_1 is a cyclic group of order n_1. If n_2 is the maximum order of elements of A_2, then n_2 divides n_1, and A_2 has a cyclic direct summand of order n_2. Continuing in this way, we obtain a decomposition $A = C_1 \oplus \cdots \oplus C_r$, where C_i is a cyclic group of order $n_i \geq 2$ for $1 \leq i \leq r$, and n_{i+1} divides n_i for $1 \leq i \leq r - 1$. A comparison of orders yields $N = n_1 \cdots n_r$. The number r and the orders $n_1, \ldots, n_r$ of the direct summands in this decomposition are uniquely determined by the orders of the direct summands in the primary decomposition, and the latter orders are, in turn, uniquely determined by A.

For $1 \leq i \leq r$, let $\mathbf{c}_i \in \mathbb{R}^s$ be such that $\mathbf{c}_i + \mathbb{Z}^s$ is a generator of C_i. Then $n_i \mathbf{c}_i \in \mathbb{Z}^s$; thus $\mathbf{c}_i = (1/n_i)\mathbf{g}_i$ for some $\mathbf{g}_i \in \mathbb{Z}^s$. Since $\mathbf{c}_i + \mathbb{Z}^s$ has order n_i, the coordinates of $\mathbf{g}_i$ and n_i are relatively prime (compare with Remark 5.19). From $A = C_1 \oplus \cdots \oplus C_r$, it follows that the node set of L is as indicated in the theorem. If $\mathbf{c}_1, \ldots, \mathbf{c}_r$ were linearly dependent, then $\mathbf{0}$ could be written as a nontrivial linear combination of $\mathbf{c}_1, \ldots, \mathbf{c}_r$ with rational coefficients. By clearing denominators, we get $\sum_{i=1}^r j_i \mathbf{c}_i = \mathbf{0}$ with integers $j_1, \ldots, j_r$ satisfying $\gcd(j_1, \ldots, j_r) = 1$. This yields the identity

$$\sum_{i=1}^r j_i (\mathbf{c}_i + \mathbb{Z}^s) = \mathbb{Z}^s$$

in the group A, and $A = C_1 \oplus \cdots \oplus C_r$ implies that n_i divides j_i for $1 \leq i \leq r$. Then, however, $n_r \geq 2$ divides $j_1, \ldots, j_r$, a contradiction. Thus $\mathbf{c}_1, \ldots, \mathbf{c}_r$, and so $\mathbf{g}_1, \ldots, \mathbf{g}_r$, are linearly independent. In particular, it follows that $r \leq s$. $\square$

DEFINITION 5.29. The integer r in Theorem 5.28 is called the *rank* of the lattice rule and the integers $n_1, \ldots, n_r$ in Theorem 5.28 are called the *invariants* of the lattice rule.

If we choose a node set (5.1) with $\mathbf{g} = (g_1, \ldots, g_s)$ satisfying $\gcd(g_1, \ldots, g_s, N) = 1$, then we obtain a lattice rule of rank 1 (compare with Remark 5.19). If we consider the Cartesian product of s trapezoidal rules in (1.2) for periodic integrands, then we get a lattice rule with node set

$$\left\{ \left(\frac{k_1}{m}, \ldots, \frac{k_s}{m} \right) : k_i \in \mathbb{Z} \text{ and } 0 \leq k_i < m \text{ for } 1 \leq i \leq s \right\}.$$

This lattice rule has rank s and invariants $n_i = m$ for $1 \leq i \leq s$.

For every s-dimensional lattice, there exists a *lattice basis*, i.e., a set $\{\mathbf{b}_1, \ldots, \mathbf{b}_s\}$ of linearly independent vectors such that the lattice consists exactly of all $\mathbb{Z}$-linear combinations of $\mathbf{b}_1, \ldots, \mathbf{b}_s$. The $s \times s$ matrix B with rows $\mathbf{b}_1, \ldots, \mathbf{b}_s$ is called a *generator matrix* of the lattice. A lattice has more than one generator matrix, since any matrix of the form UB with U being an $s \times s$ unimodular matrix with integer entries is also a generator matrix. However, for any lattice L, the absolute value $|\det(B)|$ of the determinant of a generator matrix B of L is invariant, and this number is called the *determinant* of L and is denoted by $\det(L)$. Geometrically, $\det(L)$ is the volume of the parallelepiped spanned by the vectors in a lattice basis of L. The following result is due to Sloan and Kachoyan [316].

THEOREM 5.30. *If L is an integration lattice yielding an N-point lattice rule, then $\det(L) = 1/N$. If B is a generator matrix of L, then $(B^T)^{-1}$ is a generator matrix of the dual lattice $L^\perp$ and $\det(L^\perp) = N$.*

Proof. If the dimension of L is s, then, for every positive integer k, the cube $[0, k)^s$ contains exactly $k^s N$ points of L. On the other hand, the geometric interpretation of $\det(L)$ shows that, as $k \to \infty$, the number of points of L in $[0, k)^s$ is asymptotically equal to $k^s / \det(L)$. A comparison implies that $\det(L) = 1/N$.

If $\mathbf{b}_1, \dots, \mathbf{b}_s$ are the rows of B and $\mathbf{a}_1, \dots, \mathbf{a}_s$ are the rows of $(B^{\mathrm{T}})^{-1}$, then $\mathbf{a}_i \cdot \mathbf{b}_j = \delta_{ij}$ for $1 \le i, j \le s$. Thus $\mathbf{a}_i \in L^{\perp}$ for $1 \le i \le s$ by Definition 5.20. If $\mathbf{h} \in L^{\perp}$ is arbitrary, then

$$\mathbf{h} = \mathbf{h} B^{\mathrm{T}} (B^{\mathrm{T}})^{-1} = \sum_{i=1}^{s} (\mathbf{h} \cdot \mathbf{b}_i) \mathbf{a}_i.$$

Since $\mathbf{h} \cdot \mathbf{b}_i \in \mathbb{Z}$ for $1 \le i \le s$, $\mathbf{h}$ is a $\mathbb{Z}$-linear combination of $\mathbf{a}_1, \dots, \mathbf{a}_s$. Hence these vectors form a lattice basis of $L^{\perp}$ and $(B^{\mathrm{T}})^{-1}$ is a generator matrix of $L^{\perp}$. Furthermore,

$$\det(L^{\perp}) = |\det((B^{\mathrm{T}})^{-1})| = |\det(B)|^{-1} = \det(L)^{-1} = N. \qquad \square$$

If L is an integration lattice, then any generator matrix of $L^{\perp}$ has integer entries. It follows from the theory of integer matrices (see Newman [216, Chap. 2]) that $L^{\perp}$ has a unique generator matrix in *Hermite normal form*, i.e., a lower triangular matrix with positive diagonal elements and with the elements of any column lying in the least residue system modulo the diagonal element. Consequently, the number of distinct s-dimensional N-point lattice rules is equal to the number $\nu_s(N)$ of $s \times s$ integer matrices in Hermite normal form with determinant N. By [216, p. 20], $\nu_s(N)$ is a multiplicative arithmetic function of N and is thus determined by its values at prime powers p^k, which are given by

$$\nu_s(p^k) = \prod_{i=1}^{s-1} \frac{p^{k+i} - 1}{p^i - 1}.$$

Compare also with Lyness and Sørevik [200] for this formula.

For an s-dimensional lattice rule L, the d-dimensional projection $\pi_d : \mathbb{R}^s \to \mathbb{R}^d$ with $1 \le d \le s$ defined by

$$\pi_d(u_1, \dots, u_s) = (u_1, \dots, u_d)$$

induces a group homomorphism $\varphi_d : L/\mathbb{Z}^s \to \mathbb{R}^d/\mathbb{Z}^d$ given by

$$\varphi_d(\mathbf{x} + \mathbb{Z}^s) = \pi_d(\mathbf{x}) + \mathbb{Z}^d \quad \text{for all } \mathbf{x} \in L.$$

The image of φ_d is a finite subgroup of $\mathbb{R}^d/\mathbb{Z}^d$ and hence corresponds to a d-dimensional lattice rule L_d. The nodes of L_d are obtained by omitting the last $s - d$ coordinates of each node of L and by dropping repeated nodes. Since $L_d/\mathbb{Z}^d$ is isomorphic to a factor group of $L/\mathbb{Z}^s$, it follows that, if L has rank r and invariants $n_1, \dots, n_r$, then L_d has rank $t \le \min(r, d)$ and invariants $m_1, \dots, m_t$ with m_i dividing n_i for $1 \le i \le t$ (see Sloan and Lyness [317, Thm. 5.1]). In particular, if N_d is the cardinality of the node set of L_d, then

$$N_d = m_1 \cdots m_t \le n_1 \cdots n_t \le n_1 \cdots n_{\min(r,d)}.$$

The lattice rule L is called *projection regular* if $N_d = n_1 \cdots n_{\min(r,d)}$ for $1 \le d \le s$. An obviously equivalent condition is $N_d = n_1 \cdots n_d$ for $1 \le d \le r$. A detailed study of projection-regular lattice rules was carried out by Sloan and

Lyness [318]. One of the main results of this paper is the following characterization of projection-regular lattice rules: L is projection regular if and only if the vectors $\mathbf{g}_i = (g_i^{(1)}, \ldots, g_i^{(s)})$, $1 \le i \le r$, in Theorem 5.28 can be chosen in such a way that $g_i^{(i)} = 1$ for $1 \le i \le r$ and $g_i^{(j)} = 0$ for $1 \le j < i \le r$. Furthermore, projection-regular lattice rules can be expressed in a uniquely determined canonical form.

DEFINITION 5.31. For any s-dimensional N-point lattice rule L with $s \ge 2$ and $N \ge 2$, the *figure of merit* $\rho(L)$ is defined by

$$\rho(L) = \min_{\mathbf{h}} r(\mathbf{h}),$$

where the minimum is extended over all nonzero $\mathbf{h} \in L^\perp$.

LEMMA 5.32. *We always have* $1 \le \rho(L) \le n_1$, *where* n_1 *is the first invariant of* L.

Proof. Since the invariants $n_2, \ldots, n_r$ are divisors of n_1, it follows from the description of the node set of L in Theorem 5.28 that the coordinates of all points of L are rationals with denominator n_1. Therefore $L^\perp$ contains $(n_1 \mathbb{Z})^s$. In particular, we have $\mathbf{h}_0 = (n_1, 0, \ldots, 0) \in L^\perp$; hence $\rho(L) \le r(\mathbf{h}_0) = n_1$. □

REMARK 5.33. If L has rank ≥ 2, then it follows from Lemma 5.32 that $\rho(L) \le N/2$, and, if L has rank 1, then the same inequality is obtained from Lemma 5.8. Thus it can be shown as in Remark 5.9 that it suffices to extend the minimum in Definition 5.31 over all $\mathbf{h} \in E(L)$, where $E(L)$ is as in Definition 5.24.

The quantities $P_\alpha(L)$ and $R(L)$ can be bounded in terms of the figure of merit $\rho(L)$. The lower bound

$$(5.44) \qquad\qquad P_\alpha(L) \ge \frac{2}{\rho(L)^\alpha} \qquad \text{for all } \alpha > 1$$

is trivial, and the bound

$$(5.45) \qquad\qquad R(L) \ge \frac{1}{\rho(L)}$$

follows from Remark 5.33. The corresponding upper bounds were established by Sloan and Kachoyan [316] and Niederreiter and Sloan [273], respectively.

THEOREM 5.34. *For any s-dimensional N-point lattice rule L with $s \ge 2$ and $N \ge 2$, we have*

$$P_\alpha(L) \le c(s, \alpha) \rho(L)^{-\alpha} (1 + \log \rho(L))^{s-1} \qquad \text{for all } \alpha > 1,$$

where the constant $c(s, \alpha)$ depends only on s and α.

Proof. Put $I_0 = (-\infty, 0]$, $I_1 = (0, \infty)$, and, for $\mathbf{d} = (d_1, \ldots, d_s) \in \{0, 1\}^s$, define

$$Q(\mathbf{d}) = \{\mathbf{h} = (h_1, \ldots, h_s) \in L^\perp : h_i \in I_{d_i} \text{ for } 1 \le i \le s \text{ and } \mathbf{h} \ne \mathbf{0}\}.$$

Then we can write

$$P_\alpha(L) = \sum_{\mathbf{d}} S(\mathbf{d}) \quad \text{with} \quad S(\mathbf{d}) = \sum_{\mathbf{h} \in Q(\mathbf{d})} r(\mathbf{h})^{-\alpha}.$$

We now consider $S(\mathbf{d})$ for fixed $\mathbf{d}$. Let μ be the largest integer with $2^\mu < \rho(L)$; we can assume that $\mu \geq 0$, since the case where $\rho(L) = 1$ is trivial. For $\mathbf{q} = (q_2, \dots, q_s) \in \mathbb{Z}^{s-1}$ with $q_i \geq 1$ for $2 \leq i \leq s$, we define

$$M(\mathbf{q}) = \{(h_2, \dots, h_s) \in \mathbb{Z}^{s-1} : 2^{q_i-1} \leq r(h_i) < 2^{q_i} \text{ for } 2 \leq i \leq s\}.$$

Then we may write $S(\mathbf{d})$ as the sum over all permissible $\mathbf{q}$ of

$$S(\mathbf{d}, \mathbf{q}) = \sum_{\substack{\mathbf{h} \in Q(\mathbf{d}) \\ (h_2, \dots, h_s) \in M(\mathbf{q})}} r(\mathbf{h})^{-\alpha}.$$

Case 1. $q_2 + \cdots + q_s \leq \mu + s - 1$. Put

$$\Delta(\mathbf{q}) = 2^{-q_2 - \cdots - q_s + s - 1} \rho(L) > 1,$$
$$K(\mathbf{q}, b) = \{h \in \mathbb{Z} : b\Delta(\mathbf{q}) \leq r(h) < (b+1)\Delta(\mathbf{q})\} \quad \text{for integers } b \geq 0.$$

We claim that, if $\mathbf{q} = (q_2, \dots, q_s)$ belonging to Case 1 and an integer $b \geq 0$ are given, then there exists at most one $\mathbf{h} = (h_1, \dots, h_s) \in Q(\mathbf{d})$ such that $h_1 \in K(\mathbf{q}, b)$ and $(h_2, \dots, h_s) \in M(\mathbf{q})$. Suppose that $\mathbf{h}' = (h_1', \dots, h_s') \neq \mathbf{h}$ are two points satisfying all these conditions. Then $b\Delta(\mathbf{q}) \leq r(h_1)$, $r(h_1') < (b+1)\Delta(\mathbf{q})$ and $h_1, h_1' \in I_{d_1}$; hence $r(h_1 - h_1') < \Delta(\mathbf{q})$. For $2 \leq i \leq s$, we have $2^{q_i-1} \leq r(h_i)$, $r(h_i') < 2^{q_i}$ and $h_i, h_i' \in I_{d_i}$; hence $r(h_i - h_i') \leq 2^{q_i-1}$. Therefore

$$r(\mathbf{h} - \mathbf{h}') = \prod_{i=1}^{s} r(h_i - h_i') < \Delta(\mathbf{q}) 2^{q_2 + \cdots + q_s - s + 1} = \rho(L).$$

On the other hand, $\mathbf{h} - \mathbf{h}' \in L^\perp$ and $\mathbf{h} - \mathbf{h}' \neq \mathbf{0}$; thus $r(\mathbf{h} - \mathbf{h}') \geq \rho(L)$ by Definition 5.31. This contradiction proves the claim.

Consider the contribution to $S(\mathbf{d}, \mathbf{q})$ arising from those $\mathbf{h} = (h_1, \dots, h_s) \in Q(\mathbf{d})$ with $(h_2, \dots, h_s) \in M(\mathbf{q})$ for which $h_1 \in K(\mathbf{q}, b)$. We trivially have $r(\mathbf{h}) \geq \rho(L)$ if $b = 0$, and, for $b \geq 1$, we obtain

$$r(\mathbf{h}) \geq b\Delta(\mathbf{q}) 2^{q_2 + \cdots + q_s - s + 1} = b\rho(L).$$

Summing over b, we obtain

$$S(\mathbf{d}, \mathbf{q}) \leq \rho(L)^{-\alpha} \left(1 + \sum_{b=1}^{\infty} b^{-\alpha}\right) = (1 + \zeta(\alpha))\rho(L)^{-\alpha}.$$

Since there are $\binom{\mu+s-1}{s-1}$ choices for $\mathbf{q}$ in Case 1, it follows that the sum $S_1(\mathbf{d})$ of those $S(\mathbf{d}, \mathbf{q})$ for which $\mathbf{q}$ belongs to Case 1 satisfies

$$(5.46) \qquad S_1(\mathbf{d}) \leq \quad (1 + \zeta(\alpha)) \rho(L)^{-\alpha} \binom{\mu + s - 1}{s - 1}$$
$$\leq \quad c_1(s, \alpha) \rho(L)^{-\alpha} (1 + \log \rho(L))^{s-1}.$$

Case 2. $q_2 + \cdots + q_s > \mu + s - 1$. Choose integers $\nu_2, \ldots, \nu_s$ with $0 \le \nu_i < q_i$ for $2 \le i \le s$ and $\nu_2 + \cdots + \nu_s = \mu$. For every $\mathbf{a} = (a_2, \ldots, a_s) \in \mathbb{Z}^{s-1}$ with $0 \le a_i < 2^{q_i - \nu_i - 1}$ for $2 \le i \le s$, let

$$M(\mathbf{q}, \mathbf{a}) = \{(h_2, \ldots, h_s) \in \mathbb{Z}^{s-1} : 2^{q_i - 1} + a_i 2^{\nu_i} \le r(h_i) < 2^{q_i - 1} + (a_i + 1)2^{\nu_i}$$
$$\text{for } 2 \le i \le s\}.$$

Then $M(\mathbf{q})$ defined above is the disjoint union of the sets $M(\mathbf{q}, \mathbf{a})$. Put

$$K(b) = \{h \in \mathbb{Z} : 2b \le r(h) \le 2b + 1\} \quad \text{for integers } b \ge 0.$$

We claim that, if $\mathbf{q} = (q_2, \ldots, q_s)$ belonging to Case 2, $\mathbf{a} = (a_2, \ldots, a_s)$ satisfying the restrictions above, and an integer $b \ge 0$ are given, then there exists at most one $\mathbf{h} = (h_1, \ldots, h_s) \in Q(\mathbf{d})$ such that $h_1 \in K(b)$ and $(h_2, \ldots, h_s) \in M(\mathbf{q}, \mathbf{a})$. Suppose that $\mathbf{h}' = (h_1', \ldots, h_s') \ne \mathbf{h}$ are two points satisfying all these conditions. Then $h_1, h_1' \in K(b) \cap I_{d_1}$; hence $r(h_1 - h_1') = 1$, and, for $2 \le i \le s$, we have $r(h_i - h_i') \le 2^{\nu_i}$. Therefore

$$r(\mathbf{h} - \mathbf{h}') = \prod_{i=1}^{s} r(h_i - h_i') \le 2^{\nu_2 + \cdots + \nu_s} = 2^{\mu} < \rho(L).$$

On the other hand, $\mathbf{h} - \mathbf{h}' \in L^{\perp}$ and $\mathbf{h} - \mathbf{h}' \ne \mathbf{0}$; thus $r(\mathbf{h} - \mathbf{h}') \ge \rho(L)$ by Definition 5.31. This contradiction proves the claim.

Since there are $\prod_{i=2}^{s} 2^{q_i - \nu_i - 1} = 2^{q_2 + \cdots + q_s - \mu - s + 1}$ choices for $\mathbf{a}$, it follows that, if b is given as above, then there are at most $2^{q_2 + \cdots + q_s - \mu - s + 1}$ points $\mathbf{h} = (h_1, \ldots, h_s) \in Q(\mathbf{d})$ such that $h_1 \in K(b)$ and $(h_2, \ldots, h_s) \in M(\mathbf{q})$. Therefore

$$S(\mathbf{d}, \mathbf{q}) \le 2^{q_2 + \cdots + q_s - \mu - s + 1} 2^{-\alpha(q_2 + \cdots + q_s - s + 1)} \left(1 + 2^{-\alpha} \sum_{b=1}^{\infty} b^{-\alpha}\right)$$

$$= 2^{-\alpha\mu} 2^{(1-\alpha)(q_2 + \cdots + q_s - \mu - s + 1)} (1 + 2^{-\alpha}\zeta(\alpha))$$

$$\le (2^{\alpha} + \zeta(\alpha))\rho(L)^{-\alpha} 2^{(1-\alpha)(q_2 + \cdots + q_s - \mu - s + 1)},$$

where we used $2^{\mu+1} \ge \rho(L)$ in the last step. If $S_2(\mathbf{d})$ is the sum of those $S(\mathbf{d}, \mathbf{q})$ for which $\mathbf{q}$ belongs to Case 2, then

$$S_2(\mathbf{d}) \le (2^{\alpha} + \zeta(\alpha))\rho(L)^{-\alpha} \sum_{q_2 + \cdots + q_s > \mu + s - 1} 2^{(1-\alpha)(q_2 + \cdots + q_s - \mu - s + 1)}$$

$$= (2^{\alpha} + \zeta(\alpha))\rho(L)^{-\alpha} \sum_{k=1}^{\infty} 2^{(1-\alpha)k} \binom{k + \mu + s - 2}{s - 2}$$

$$\le (2^{\alpha} + \zeta(\alpha))\rho(L)^{-\alpha}(\mu + 1)^{s-2} \sum_{k=1}^{\infty} 2^{(1-\alpha)k}(k+1)^{s-2}$$

$$\le c_2(s, \alpha)\rho(L)^{-\alpha}(1 + \log \rho(L))^{s-2}.$$

Together with (5.46) and $S(\mathbf{d}) = S_1(\mathbf{d}) + S_2(\mathbf{d})$, this yields

$$S(\mathbf{d}) \leq c_3(s, \alpha)\rho(L)^{-\alpha} (1 + \log \rho(L))^{s-1}.$$

Since there are 2^s choices for $\mathbf{d}$, the desired result follows. $\square$

THEOREM 5.35. *For any s-dimensional N-point lattice rule L with $s \geq 2$ and $N \geq 2$, we have*

$$R(L) < \frac{1}{\rho(L)} \left(\frac{2}{\log 2} \right)^{s-1} (2(\log N)^s + 3(\log N)^{s-1}).$$

Proof. Put $I_0 = (-N/2, 0]$, $I_1 = (0, N/2]$, and, for $\mathbf{d} = (d_1, \ldots, d_s) \in \{0, 1\}^s$, define

$$Q(\mathbf{d}) = \{\mathbf{h} = (h_1, \ldots, h_s) \in L^\perp : h_i \in I_{d_i} \text{ for } 1 \leq i \leq s \text{ and } \mathbf{h} \neq \mathbf{0}\}.$$

Then we can write

$$R(L) = \sum_{\mathbf{d}} S(\mathbf{d}) \quad \text{with } S(\mathbf{d}) = \sum_{\mathbf{h} \in Q(\mathbf{d})} r(\mathbf{h})^{-1}.$$

We now consider $S(\mathbf{d})$ for fixed $\mathbf{d}$. Let ω be the smallest integer with $2^\omega > N/2$ and let μ be the largest integer with $2^\mu < \rho(L)$; we can assume that $\mu \geq 0$, since the case where $\rho(L) = 1$ can easily be dealt with by using a trivial bound on $R(L)$. For $\mathbf{q} = (q_2, \ldots, q_s) \in \mathbb{Z}^{s-1}$ with $1 \leq q_i \leq \omega$ for $1 \leq i \leq s$, let $M(\mathbf{q})$ be as in the proof of Theorem 5.34 and define

$$S(\mathbf{d}, \mathbf{q}) = \sum_{\substack{\mathbf{h} \in Q(\mathbf{d}) \\ (h_2, \ldots, h_s) \in M(\mathbf{q})}} r(\mathbf{h})^{-1}.$$

We distinguish two cases as in the proof of Theorem 5.34. In Case 1, we use the same argument as in that proof, but now it suffices to consider integers b with $0 \leq b < \lfloor N/2 \rfloor$. This yields

$$(5.47) \qquad S(\mathbf{d}, \mathbf{q}) \leq \frac{1}{\rho(L)} \left(1 + \sum_{b=1}^{\lfloor N/2 \rfloor - 1} \frac{1}{b} \right) < \frac{1}{\rho(L)}(1 + \log N),$$

where we used [224, Lemma 3.7] in the last step. In Case 2, it suffices to consider integers b with $0 \leq b \leq \lfloor N/4 \rfloor$, but otherwise the argument in the proof of Theorem 5.34 can again be applied. This yields

$$S(\mathbf{d}, \mathbf{q}) \leq 2^{q_2 + \cdots + q_s - \mu - s + 1} 2^{-q_2 - \cdots - q_s + s - 1} \left(1 + \sum_{b=1}^{\lfloor N/4 \rfloor} \frac{1}{2b} \right) = 2^{-\mu} \left(1 + \sum_{b=1}^{\lfloor N/4 \rfloor} \frac{1}{2b} \right)$$

$$\leq \frac{1}{\rho(L)} \left(2 + \sum_{b=1}^{\lfloor N/4 \rfloor} \frac{1}{b} \right) < \frac{1}{\rho(L)} \left(\frac{3}{2} + \log N \right),$$

where the last inequality is valid as long as $N \neq 4$. By (5.47) this bound can also be used in Case 1. Since there are w^{s-1} choices for $\mathbf{q}$, we obtain

$$S(\mathbf{d}) < \frac{1}{\rho(L)} w^{s-1} \left(\frac{3}{2} + \log N \right),$$

and there are 2^s possibilities for $\mathbf{d}$; hence

$$R(L) < \frac{1}{\rho(L)} (2w)^{s-1} (3 + 2 \log N),$$

provided that $N \neq 4$. Since the definition of w implies that $2^w \leq N$, we obtain the desired bound on $R(L)$ for $N \neq 4$. For $N = 4$, we use the trivial bound

$$R(L) \leq \sum_{\mathbf{h} \in C_s^*(4)} r(\mathbf{h})^{-1} = \left(\sum_{h=-1}^{2} r(h)^{-1} \right)^s - 1 = \left(\frac{7}{2} \right)^s - 1.$$

Since $\rho(L) \leq 2$ by Remark 5.33, it is easily seen that $R(L)$ again satisfies the inequality in the theorem. $\square$

We can combine Theorems 5.27 and 5.35 to obtain an upper bound for the discrepancy of the node set P of an s-dimensional N-point lattice rule L with $s \geq 2$ and $N \geq 2$, namely,

$$D_N(P) < \frac{s}{N} + \frac{1}{\rho(L)} \left(\frac{2}{\log 2} \right)^{s-1} \left((\log N)^s + \frac{3}{2} (\log N)^{s-1} \right).$$

There is also a lower bound for $D_N(P)$ in terms of the figure of merit, which was shown by Niederreiter and Sloan [273].

LEMMA 5.36. *Let* $\mathbf{t}_0, \mathbf{t}_1, \ldots, \mathbf{t}_{N-1} \in \mathbb{R}^s$ *and suppose that there exist an* $\mathbf{h} = (h_1, \ldots, h_s) \in \mathbb{Z}^s$ *with* $\sum_{i=1}^s |h_i| \geq 2$ *and a* $\theta \in [0, 1)$ *such that* $\{\mathbf{h} \cdot \mathbf{t}_n\} = \theta$ *for* $0 \leq n \leq N - 1$. *Then the point set* P *consisting of the fractional parts* $\{\mathbf{t}_0\}, \{\mathbf{t}_1\}, \ldots, \{\mathbf{t}_{N-1}\}$ *satisfies*

$$D_N(P) \geq \frac{1}{m^m r(\mathbf{h})},$$

where m *is the number of nonzero coordinates of* $\mathbf{h}$.

Proof. Consider the interval $J = \prod_{i=1}^s J_i \subseteq I^s$ with

$$J_i = \left(\frac{\theta}{mh_i}, \frac{\theta+1}{mh_i} \right) \qquad \text{if } h_i > 0,$$

$$J_i = (0, 1) \qquad \text{if } h_i = 0,$$

$$J_i = \left(1 + \frac{\theta+1}{mh_i}, 1 + \frac{\theta}{mh_i} \right) \qquad \text{if } h_i < 0.$$

If $\mathbf{t} = (t_1, \dots, t_s) \in J$, then

$$\frac{\theta}{m} < h_i t_i < \frac{\theta + 1}{m} \qquad \text{if } h_i > 0,$$

$$h_i t_i = 0 \qquad \text{if } h_i = 0,$$

$$h_i + \frac{\theta}{m} < h_i t_i < h_i + \frac{\theta + 1}{m} \qquad \text{if } h_i < 0,$$

and so

$$\sum_{\substack{i=1 \\ h_i < 0}}^{s} h_i + \theta < \mathbf{h} \cdot \mathbf{t} < \sum_{\substack{i=1 \\ h_i < 0}}^{s} h_i + \theta + 1.$$

Thus $\{\mathbf{h} \cdot \mathbf{t}\} \neq \theta$ for $\mathbf{t} \in J$; hence no point $\{\mathbf{t}_n\}$ is in J. Consequently,

$$D_N(P) \geq \lambda_s(J) = \frac{1}{m^m r(\mathbf{h})}. \qquad \square$$

THEOREM 5.37. *The discrepancy of the node set P of an s-dimensional N-point lattice rule L with $s \geq 2$ and $N \geq 2$ satisfies*

$$D_N(P) \geq \frac{1}{c_s \rho(L)}$$

with $c_2 = 4$, $c_3 = 27$, and $c_s = \frac{2}{\pi}((\pi + 1)^s - 1)$ for $s \geq 4$.

Proof. By Definition 5.31, there exists a nonzero $\mathbf{h} = (h_1, \dots, h_s) \in L^\perp$ with $r(\mathbf{h}) = \rho(L)$. If $P = \{\mathbf{x}_0, \mathbf{x}_1, \dots, \mathbf{x}_{N-1}\}$, then $\mathbf{h} \cdot \mathbf{x}_n \in \mathbb{Z}$ for $0 \leq n \leq N - 1$, and so an application of Theorem 3.16 with $\mathbf{t}_n = \mathbf{x}_n$ for $0 \leq n \leq N - 1$ and $\theta = 0$ yields

$$1 \leq \frac{2}{\pi}((\pi + 1)^s - 1)\rho(L)D_N(P).$$

This is the desired result for $s \geq 4$. If $\sum_{i=1}^{s} |h_i| \geq 2$, then we apply Lemma 5.36 with $\mathbf{t}_n = \mathbf{x}_n$ for $0 \leq n \leq N - 1$ and $\theta = 0$ to obtain

(5.48)
$$D_N(P) \geq \frac{1}{s^s \rho(L)}.$$

If $\sum_{i=1}^{s} |h_i| = 1$, then, for some i with $1 \leq i \leq s$, we have $h_i = \pm 1$ and $h_j = 0$ for all $j \neq i$. From $\mathbf{h} \cdot \mathbf{x}_n \in \mathbb{Z}$ it follows then that the ith coordinate of each $\mathbf{x}_n$ is 0. This yields $D_N(P) = 1$, and so (5.48) holds trivially. From (5.48), we obtain the desired result for $s = 2$ and $s = 3$. $\square$

5.4.   Existence theorems for efficient lattice rules.

Let L be an s-dimensional N-point lattice rule with $s \geq 2$ and $N \geq 2$, and let r be its rank and $n_1, \dots, n_r$ its invariants. The following result from Niederreiter [262] is an analogue of Lemma 5.32 and shows that the first invariant n_1 must be large for an efficient lattice rule.

THEOREM 5.38. *The following bounds are valid:*

(i) $P_\alpha(L) \geq \left(1 + 2\zeta(\alpha)n_1^{-\alpha}\right)^s - 1 > 2s\zeta(\alpha)n_1^{-\alpha}$ *for all* $\alpha > 1$;

(ii) $R(L) \geq c(s)n_1^{-1}\log(N/n_1)$, *where* $c(s) > 0$ *depends only on* s;

(iii) $D_N^*(P) \geq 1 - \left(1 - n_1^{-1}\right)^s \geq n_1^{-1}$, *where* P *is the node set of* L.

Proof. (i) Since $L^\perp \supseteq (n_1\mathbb{Z})^s$ by the proof of Lemma 5.32, we see that, for $\alpha > 1$,

$$
P_\alpha(L) \geq \sum_{\mathbf{h}\in(n_1\mathbb{Z})^s} r(\mathbf{h})^{-\alpha} - 1 = \left(\sum_{h\in\mathbb{Z}} r(n_1 h)^{-\alpha}\right)^s - 1
$$

$$
= \left(1 + 2\sum_{h=1}^\infty (n_1 h)^{-\alpha}\right)^s - 1 = (1 + 2\zeta(\alpha)n_1^{-\alpha})^s - 1 > 2s\zeta(\alpha)n_1^{-\alpha}.
$$

(ii) From $L^\perp \supseteq (n_1\mathbb{Z})^s$, we obtain $E(L) \supseteq C_s^*(N) \cap (n_1\mathbb{Z})^s$ in the notation of Definition 5.24. The elements of this intersection are exactly all points $n_1\mathbf{h}$ with $\mathbf{h} \in C_s^*(N/n_1)$. Therefore

$$
R(L) \geq \sum_{\mathbf{h}\in C_s(N/n_1)} r(n_1\mathbf{h})^{-1} - 1 = \left(\sum_{h\in C(N/n_1)} r(n_1 h)^{-1}\right)^s - 1
$$

$$
= \left(1 + n_1^{-1}\sum_{h\in C^*(N/n_1)} |h|^{-1}\right)^s - 1 \geq c(s)n_1^{-1}\log(N/n_1).
$$

(iii) By the proof of Lemma 5.32, the coordinates of all points of P are rationals with denominator n_1. Thus the desired result follows from Theorem 3.14. $\square$

Existence theorems for efficient lattice rules of rank 1 have already been shown in §5.2. These theorems can be used to obtain results for higher ranks by a method of extending lattice rules.

LEMMA 5.39. *For* $s \geq 2$, *let a rank* r *with* $1 \leq r \leq s$ *and invariants* $n_1,\dots,n_r \geq 2$ *with* n_{i+1} *dividing* n_i *for* $1 \leq i \leq r-1$ *be given, and let* L_1 *be an* s-*dimensional* n_1-*point lattice rule of rank 1 generated by* $\mathbf{g}_1 = (g_1^{(1)},\dots,g_1^{(s)}) \in \mathbb{Z}^s$ *with* $\gcd(g_1^{(1)},n_1) = 1$. *Then there exists an* s-*dimensional lattice rule* L *with rank* r *and invariants* $n_1,\dots,n_r$ *such that the node set of* L *contains the node set of* L_1.

Proof. We may assume that $r \geq 2$. We construct L by putting

$$
\mathbf{g}_i = (g_i^{(1)},\dots,g_i^{(s)}) \in \mathbb{Z}^s \quad \text{for } 2 \leq i \leq r
$$

with $g_i^{(j)} = 0$ for $1 \leq j \leq i-1$ and $\gcd(g_i^{(i)},n_i) = 1$ and letting the nodes of L be all fractional parts

$$
\left\{\sum_{i=1}^r \frac{k_i}{n_i}\mathbf{g}_i\right\} \quad \text{with } 0 \leq k_i < n_i \text{ for } 1 \leq i \leq r.
$$

Consider the mapping ψ on the finite abelian group $A = (\mathbb{Z}/n_1\mathbb{Z}) \oplus \cdots \oplus (\mathbb{Z}/n_r\mathbb{Z})$ defined by

$$\psi : (k_1 + n_1\mathbb{Z}, \ldots, k_r + n_r\mathbb{Z}) \longmapsto \sum_{i=1}^{r} \frac{k_i}{n_i} \mathbf{g}_i + \mathbb{Z}^s \in L/\mathbb{Z}^s.$$

Then ψ is a surjective group homomorphism. We claim that the kernel of ψ is trivial, i.e., that

$$(5.49) \qquad\qquad \sum_{i=1}^{r} \frac{k_i}{n_i} \mathbf{g}_i \equiv \mathbf{0} \bmod \mathbb{Z}^s$$

implies that $k_i \equiv 0 \bmod n_i$ for $1 \leq i \leq r$. By comparing the first coordinates in (5.49), we derive $(k_1/n_1)g_1^{(1)} \equiv 0 \bmod 1$; hence $k_1 g_1^{(1)} \equiv 0 \bmod n_1$, and thus $k_1 \equiv 0 \bmod n_1$ since $\gcd(g_1^{(1)}, n_1) = 1$. Thus (5.49) reduces to $\sum_{i=2}^{r} (k_i/n_i)\mathbf{g}_i \equiv \mathbf{0} \bmod \mathbb{Z}^s$, and, comparing second coordinates, we obtain $k_2 \equiv 0 \bmod n_2$. By continuing in this manner, we establish the claim. Consequently, $L/\mathbb{Z}^s$ is isomorphic to A, and so L has rank r and invariants $n_1, \ldots, n_r$. Clearly, the node set of L contains the node set of L_1. $\square$

LEMMA 5.40. *For $s \geq 2$, let $L_1 \subseteq L_2$ be two s-dimensional integration lattices, and let N_1 and N_2 be the number of nodes of the corresponding lattice rules L_1 and L_2, respectively, with $N_1 \geq 2$. Then*

(i) $\rho(L_2) \geq \rho(L_1)$;

(ii) $P_\alpha(L_2) \leq P_\alpha(L_1)$ *for all* $\alpha > 1$;

(iii) $R(L_2) < \left(\left(2 + \log \dfrac{N_2}{N_1}\right)^s - \left(1 + \log \dfrac{N_2}{N_1}\right)^s\right) R(L_1) + \dfrac{2^s}{N_1}\left(1 + \log \dfrac{N_2}{N_1}\right)^s$

$\qquad\qquad + \left(1 + \dfrac{2}{N_1} \log \dfrac{2N_2}{N_1}\right)^s - 1;$

(iv) $R(L_2) < R(L_1) + \dfrac{1}{N_1}\left((2\log N_2 + 3)^s - (2\log N_1 + 1)^s\right)$

$\qquad\qquad + \left(1 + \dfrac{2}{N_1} \log \dfrac{2N_2}{N_1}\right)^s - 1$

if L_1 is a lattice rule of rank 1 generated by a point $\mathbf{g} \in G_s(N_1)$.

Proof. (i) From $L_1 \subseteq L_2$, we obtain $L_1^\perp \supseteq L_2^\perp$, and so the desired inequality follows immediately from the definition of the figure of merit.

(ii) Use $L_1^\perp \supseteq L_2^\perp$ and the definitions of $P_\alpha(L_1)$ and $P_\alpha(L_2)$.

(iii) Note that N_1 divides N_2, since $L_1/\mathbb{Z}^s$ is a subgroup of order N_1 of the group $L_2/\mathbb{Z}^s$ of order N_2. Every $\mathbf{h} \in C_s(N_2)$ can be written in the form $\mathbf{h} = \mathbf{k} + N_1\mathbf{m}$ with $\mathbf{k} \in C_s(N_1)$, $\mathbf{m} \in M_s := [-N_2/(2N_1), N_2/(2N_1)]^s \cap \mathbb{Z}^s$.

Since $N_1\mathbf{m} \in L_1^\perp$ by Remark 5.25, we have $\mathbf{h} \in L_1^\perp$ if and only if $\mathbf{k} \in L_1^\perp$. Also using $L_1^\perp \supseteq L_2^\perp$, we see that

$$(5.50) \qquad R(L_2) \leq \sum_{\mathbf{h} \in C_s(N_2) \cap L_1^\perp} r(\mathbf{h})^{-1} - 1$$

$$\leq \sum_{\mathbf{m} \in M_s} r(N_1\mathbf{m})^{-1} - 1 + \sum_{\mathbf{k} \in E(L_1)} \sum_{\mathbf{m} \in M_s} r(\mathbf{k} + N_1\mathbf{m})^{-1}$$

with the notation in Definition 5.24. Now

$$(5.51) \qquad \sum_{\mathbf{m} \in M_s} r(N_1\mathbf{m})^{-1} - 1 = \left(1 + 2 \sum_{m=1}^{\lfloor N_2/(2N_1) \rfloor} \frac{1}{N_1 m}\right)^s - 1$$

$$< \left(1 + \frac{2}{N_1} \log \frac{2N_2}{N_1}\right)^s - 1.$$

Furthermore,

$$T := \sum_{\mathbf{k} \in E(L_1)} \sum_{\mathbf{m} \in M_s} r(\mathbf{k} + N_1\mathbf{m})^{-1} = \sum_{\mathbf{k} \in E(L_1)} \prod_{i=1}^{s} \left(\sum_{|m| \leq N_2/(2N_1)} r(k_i + N_1 m)^{-1}\right),$$

where $\mathbf{k} = (k_1, \ldots, k_s)$. By proceeding as in the argument following (5.7), we obtain

$$\sum_{|m| \leq N_2/(2N_1)} r(k + N_1 m)^{-1} \leq r(k)^{-1} + \frac{2}{N_1} \log \frac{eN_2}{N_1} \qquad \text{for } k \in C(N_1),$$

and so

$$(5.52)$$

$$T \leq \sum_{\mathbf{k} \in E(L_1)} \prod_{i=1}^{s} \left(r(k_i)^{-1} + \frac{2}{N_1} \log \frac{eN_2}{N_1}\right)$$

$$= R(L_1) + \frac{2^s}{N_1^s} \left(\log \frac{eN_2}{N_1}\right)^s \operatorname{card}(E(L_1))$$

$$+ \sum_{j=1}^{s-1} \left(\frac{2}{N_1} \log \frac{eN_2}{N_1}\right)^{s-j} \sum_{1 \leq i_1 < \cdots < i_j \leq s} \sum_{\mathbf{k} \in E(L_1)} r(k_{i_1})^{-1} \cdots r(k_{i_j})^{-1}.$$

For fixed $1 \leq j \leq s-1$ and $1 \leq i_1 < \cdots < i_j \leq s$ and any $\mathbf{k} \in E(L_1)$, we have

$$r(k_{i_1})^{-1} \cdots r(k_{i_j})^{-1} \leq \left(\frac{N_1}{2}\right)^{s-j} r(\mathbf{k})^{-1},$$

and so

$$\sum_{\mathbf{k} \in E(L_1)} r(k_{i_1})^{-1} \cdots r(k_{i_j})^{-1} \leq \left(\frac{N_1}{2}\right)^{s-j} \sum_{\mathbf{k} \in E(L_1)} r(\mathbf{k})^{-1} = \left(\frac{N_1}{2}\right)^{s-j} R(L_1).$$

Since $\mathrm{card}(E(L_1)) = N_1^{s-1} - 1$ by Remark 5.25, it follows from (5.52) that

$$T < R(L_1) \sum_{j=1}^{s} \binom{s}{j} \left(1 + \log \frac{N_2}{N_1}\right)^{s-j} + \frac{2^s}{N_1}\left(1 + \log \frac{N_2}{N_1}\right)^s,$$

and, together with (5.50) and (5.51), this yields (iii).

(iv) If L_1 is as in (iv), then, for fixed $1 \le j \le s-1$ and $1 \le i_1 < \cdots < i_j \le s$, we obtain, as in the proof of Theorem 5.5,

$$\sum_{\mathbf{k} \in E(L_1)} r(k_{i_1})^{-1} \cdots r(k_{i_j})^{-1} \le N_1^{s-j-1} \sum_{\mathbf{h} \in C_j(N_1)} r(\mathbf{h})^{-1} < N_1^{s-j-1}(2 \log N_1 + 1)^j.$$

Using this in (5.52), we derive

$$T < R(L_1) + \frac{2^s}{N_1}\left(1 + \log \frac{N_2}{N_1}\right)^s + \frac{1}{N_1} \sum_{j=1}^{s-1} \binom{s}{j}\left(2 \log \frac{N_2}{N_1} + 2\right)^{s-j} (2 \log N_1 + 1)^j$$

$$= R(L_1) + \frac{1}{N_1}((2 \log N_2 + 3)^s - (2 \log N_1 + 1)^s),$$

and, together with (5.50) and (5.51), this yields (iv). □

THEOREM 5.41. *For $s \ge 2$, let a rank r with $1 \le r \le s$ and invariants $n_1, \ldots, n_r \ge 2$ with n_{i+1} dividing n_i for $1 \le i \le r - 1$ be given. Then, for every $\alpha > 1$, there exists an s-dimensional lattice rule L with this rank and these invariants such that*

$$P_\alpha(L) = O\left(n_1^{-\alpha}(\log n_1)^{\alpha(s-1)+1}\left(\frac{n_1}{\phi(n_1)}\right)^{(\alpha-1)(s-1)}\right),$$

where the implied constant depends only on s and α.

Proof. By Theorem 5.13, there exists a $\mathbf{g}_1 \in G_s(n_1)$ such that $P_\alpha(\mathbf{g}_1, n_1)$ satisfies the bound in Theorem 5.13 with $N = n_1$. Let L_1 be the corresponding s-dimensional n_1-point lattice rule of rank 1 and let L be as in Lemma 5.39. Then $L_1 \subseteq L$, and so $P_\alpha(L) \le P_\alpha(L_1) = P_\alpha(\mathbf{g}_1, n_1)$ by part (ii) of Lemma 5.40. By the construction of $\mathbf{g}_1$, we get the desired result. □

THEOREM 5.42. *For $s \ge 2$, let a rank r and invariants $n_1, \ldots, n_r$ be given as in Theorem 5.41. Then, for every $\alpha > 1$, there exists an s-dimensional lattice rule L with this rank and these invariants such that*

$$P_\alpha(L) = O\left(n_1^{-\alpha}(\log n_1)^{\alpha(s-1)}\left(1 + \frac{\tau(n_1)}{(\log n_1)^{s-1}}\right)\right) \qquad \text{if } s \ge 3,$$

$$P_\alpha(L) = O\left(n_1^{-\alpha}(\log n_1)^{\alpha}\left(\frac{n_1}{\phi(n_1)} + \frac{\tau(n_1)}{\log n_1}\right)\right) \qquad \text{if } s = 2,$$

where $\tau(n_1)$ is the number of positive divisors of n_1 and where the implied constants depend only on s and α.

Proof. Proceed as in the proof of Theorem 5.41, but use Theorem 5.14 instead of Theorem 5.13. □

The remarks following Theorem 5.14 apply, with the necessary changes having been made, to Theorems 5.41 and 5.42 as well. Analogous existence theorems for large values of $\rho(L)$ and small values of $R(L)$ for lattice rules L with prescribed rank and invariants can be deduced from parts (i), (iii), and (iv) of Lemma 5.40 and from the corresponding existence theorems concerning $\rho(\mathbf{g}, N)$ and $R(\mathbf{g}, N)$ in §5.2.

Theorems 5.41 and 5.42 have been obtained by a method that is in a sense indirect, since, in the proof, we first consider efficient lattice rules of rank 1. There is also a direct method of establishing existence theorems for efficient lattice rules in which we immediately look at lattice rules of the desired rank. For a dimension $s \geq 2$, let a rank r with $1 \leq r \leq s$ and invariants $n_1, \ldots, n_r \geq 2$ with n_{i+1} dividing n_i for $1 \leq i \leq r - 1$ be given. We put

$$Z_i = \{g \in \mathbb{Z} : 0 \leq g < n_i \text{ and } \gcd(g, n_i) = 1\} \quad \text{for } 1 \leq i \leq r.$$

Let $\mathcal{L} = \mathcal{L}(s; n_1, \ldots, n_r)$ be the family of all s-dimensional lattice rules L for which the node set consists exactly of all fractional parts

$$\left\{ \sum_{i=1}^{r} \frac{k_i}{n_i} \mathbf{g}_i \right\} \quad \text{with integers } 0 \leq k_i < n_i \text{ for } 1 \leq i \leq r,$$

where the $\mathbf{g}_i$ have the special form $\mathbf{g}_i = (g_i^{(1)}, \ldots, g_i^{(s)})$ with $g_i^{(j)} = 0$ for $1 \leq j \leq i - 1$ and $g_i^{(j)} \in Z_i$ for $i \leq j \leq s$. It follows from the proof of Lemma 5.39 that each $L \in \mathcal{L}$ has rank r and invariants $n_1, \ldots, n_r$. Let

$$M(\mathcal{L}) = \frac{1}{\operatorname{card}(\mathcal{L})} \sum_{L \in \mathcal{L}} R(L)$$

be the average value of $R(L)$ as L runs through $\mathcal{L}$. Note that $\operatorname{card}(\mathcal{L}) = \prod_{i=1}^{r} \phi(n_i)^{s-i+1}$. Inserting the definition of $R(L)$ and interchanging the order of summation, we obtain

$$M(\mathcal{L}) = \frac{1}{\operatorname{card}(\mathcal{L})} \sum_{\mathbf{h} \in C_s(N)} A(\mathbf{h}) r(\mathbf{h})^{-1} - 1,$$

where $N = n_1 \cdots n_r$ and $A(\mathbf{h})$ is the number of $L \in \mathcal{L}$ with $\mathbf{h} \in L^{\perp}$. We now invoke Lemma 5.21 to express $A(\mathbf{h})$ in terms of exponential sums, and we use the special form of the node set of each $L \in \mathcal{L}$ to obtain

$$A(\mathbf{h}) = \frac{1}{N} \sum_{k_1=0}^{n_1-1} \cdots \sum_{k_r=0}^{n_r-1} \prod_{j=1}^{s} \prod_{i=1}^{\min(j,r)} \left(\sum_{g \in Z_i} e\left(\frac{k_i}{n_i} h_j g \right) \right)$$

for $\mathbf{h} = (h_1, \ldots, h_s) \in C_s(N)$. Therefore

$$\sum_{\mathbf{h} \in C_s(N)} \frac{A(\mathbf{h})}{r(\mathbf{h})} = \frac{1}{N} \sum_{k_1=0}^{n_1-1} \cdots \sum_{k_r=0}^{n_r-1} \prod_{j=1}^{s} \left(\sum_{h \in C(N)} \frac{1}{r(h)} \prod_{i=1}^{\min(j,r)} \left(\sum_{g \in Z_i} e\left(\frac{k_i}{n_i} hg \right) \right) \right).$$

The innermost sum is calculated by the method following (5.15), which yields

$$\sum_{g \in Z_i} e\left(\frac{k_i}{n_i} hg\right) = \sum_{\substack{d|n_i \\ d|k_i h}} \mu\left(\frac{n_i}{d}\right) d.$$

The resulting expression for $M(\mathcal{L})$ is rather complicated. Even in the simplest higher-rank case where $r = 2$, very elaborate number-theoretic arguments are needed to deal with this expression. The following result is obtained in Niederreiter [259] for this case.

THEOREM 5.43. *For every $s \geq 2$ and any prescribed invariants $n_1, n_2 \geq 2$ with n_2 dividing n_1, we have*

$$M(\mathcal{L}) < c_s \left(\frac{(\log N)^s}{N} + \frac{\log N}{n_1}\right)$$

with a constant c_s depending only on s. In particular, there exists an s-dimensional lattice rule L of rank 2 with invariants n_1 and n_2 such that

$$R(L) < c_s \left(\frac{(\log N)^s}{N} + \frac{\log N}{n_1}\right).$$

By combining this result with Theorem 5.27, we see that there always exists a lattice rule of rank 2 with prescribed invariants for which the node set has a discrepancy of an order of magnitude close to that of the lower bound in part (iii) of Theorem 5.38. Similarly, by virtue of Theorem 5.26 or (5.42), we get a value of $P_\alpha(L)$ of an order of magnitude close to that of the lower bound in part (i) of Theorem 5.38.

Efficient lattice rules can also be obtained by considering suitable s-dimensional lattice rules of maximal rank $r = s$, with *copy rules* offering the most promising option. If L is an s-dimensional lattice rule and $k \geq 2$ is an integer, then the k^s-*copy* of L is the lattice rule with integration lattice $k^{-1}L$, i.e., the lattice L scaled by a factor k^{-1}. The k^s-copy of L may also be described as the lattice rule obtained by partitioning I^s into k^s cubes of side k^{-1} and applying a properly scaled version of the lattice rule L to each of these smaller cubes. Thus the use of copy rules may be viewed as a special deterministic version of the Monte Carlo technique of stratified sampling (compare with §1.2). In the following theorem, we collect the basic information on copy rules.

THEOREM 5.44. *If L is an s-dimensional N-point lattice rule and $k \geq 2$ is an integer, then $k^{-1}L$ is a $k^s N$-point lattice rule of rank s with dual lattice $(k^{-1}L)^\perp = kL^\perp$.*

Proof. The number of nodes of $k^{-1}L$ is equal to the number of points of the integration lattice L in $[0, k)^s$, which is $k^s N$. Furthermore, $k^{-1}L$ contains $(k^{-1}\mathbb{Z})^s$, and the group $(k^{-1}\mathbb{Z})^s/\mathbb{Z}^s$ is the direct sum of s cyclic groups of order k. Hence $(k^{-1}\mathbb{Z})^s$ has rank s, and so has $k^{-1}L$ by [317, Thm. 3.3]. Finally, from the definition of the dual lattice, we immediately obtain that $(k^{-1}L)^\perp$ contains $kL^\perp$. Now $\mathbb{Z}^s/(k^{-1}L)^\perp$ has order $k^s N$ by Remark 5.25, and, from

$\mathbb{Z}^s \supseteq L^\perp \supseteq kL^\perp$ and Remark 5.25, we see that $\mathbb{Z}^s/(kL^\perp)$ also has order $k^s N$. Therefore $(k^{-1}L)^\perp = kL^\perp$. $\square$

On the basis of the identity $(k^{-1}L)^\perp = kL^\perp$, corresponding quantities for $k^{-1}L$ and L can be related. For instance, we have

$$P_\alpha(k^{-1}L) = \sum_{\mathbf{h}} r(k\mathbf{h})^{-\alpha} \quad \text{for any } \alpha > 1,$$

where the sum is over all nonzero $\mathbf{h} \in L^\perp$, and this expression is closely connected with $P_\alpha(L)$. This connection can be effectively exploited in the case where L is a lattice rule of rank 1. Disney and Sloan [68] calculated the mean value of $P_\alpha(k^{-1}L)$ when L ranges over all s-dimensional N-point lattice rules of rank 1 generated by a point $\mathbf{g} \in G_s(N)$, where N is a prime number, and showed that for $k = 2$ this mean value is asymptotically smaller than the corresponding mean value of $P_\alpha(L)$ for a comparable number of nodes. This suggests that there are lattice rules of higher rank that yield smaller error bounds than lattice rules of rank 1 with a comparable number of nodes.

One of the principal problems in the area is to find general constructions of efficient lattice rules. Except for the case where $s = 2$, in which the connection with continued fractions can be used (see §5.2), no explicit constructions of infinite families of efficient lattice rules are known. Some attempts have been made by Hua and Wang [144] and Zinterhof [370] for lattice rules of rank 1, but the results fall far short of the levels that are set by the existence theorems. Thus, at present, we still must resort to computer searches to find efficient lattice rules for dimensions $s \geq 3$. The search for good lattice points mod N may proceed by two strategies, namely, an elimination method in which the points $\mathbf{g} \bmod N$ with a small value of $\rho(\mathbf{g}, N)$ are systematically eliminated, and a random search method in which points $\mathbf{g} \bmod N$ are chosen at random and a good lattice point mod N is obtained after sufficiently many trials. Sometimes the search is restricted to points of the special form $(1, g, g^2, \ldots, g^{s-1})$ proposed by Korobov [159]. Extensive tables of good lattice points were compiled by Maisonneuve [203], and these were complemented more recently by the tables in the book of Hua and Wang [145] and in the papers of Bourdeau and Pitre [31] and Haber [123]. The search for efficient lattice rules of higher rank is based on similar strategies. The most ambitious search project involving higher-rank lattice rules was undertaken by Sloan and Walsh [321] and yielded many practically useful lattice rules of rank 2.

Notes.

The method of good lattice points was introduced by Korobov [158], and further pioneering papers on the subject include Bakhvalov [13], Hlawka [135], and Korobov [159]. Expository accounts of this method can be found in the books of Korobov [160] and Hua and Wang [145] and in the survey articles of Zaremba [365] and Niederreiter [225]; see Niederreiter [251] for an update of the latter paper. Theorem 5.5 is from Niederreiter [264]. By averaging the quantity $R_1(\mathbf{g}, N)$ in (5.9) over suitable sets of points $\mathbf{g} \bmod N$ and using the first inequality in

Theorem 5.6, improved existence theorems for the discrepancy $D_N(P)$ of the point set P in (5.1) are obtained; see Niederreiter [239] for primes N and Niederreiter [237] for arbitrary $N \geq 2$. Algorithms for the determination of good lattice points modulo powers of 2 were described by Korobov [161]. Computer implementations of the method of good lattice points are discussed in Genz [113] and Kahaner [149]. A widely available software implementation is routine D01GCF in the NAG library. Several open problems on good lattice points are stated in Niederreiter [233]. Further existence theorems for good lattice points of the form $(1, g, g^2, \ldots, g^{s-1})$ can be found in Larcher [171] and Temlyakov [343].

A report on calculations in connection with Zaremba's conjecture is given in Borosh and Niederreiter [30]. For theoretical results related to Zaremba's conjecture, see Cusick [46], [47], [48], Hensley [133], and Sander [300]. Cusick [49] considered a higher-dimensional analogue of Zaremba's conjecture. Temlyakov [344] proved the optimality of the two-dimensional lattice point $\mathbf{g} = (1, F_{m-1}) \bmod F_m$ for numerical integration in a class of functions with bounded mixed derivative.

The first steps in the direction of lattice rules were taken by Frolov [111]. Sloan [314] and Sloan and Kachoyan [315] again approached the subject, and a systematic theory of lattice rules was developed by Sloan and Kachoyan [316]. For a background on lattices, we refer to the book of Cassels [38]. Lyness [198] and Sloan and Walsh [320] gave brief surveys of lattice rules from the viewpoints of generator matrices and classification theory, respectively. Lyness [197] discussed various ways of assessing the quality of lattice rules. Further results on ranks and invariants can be found in Sloan and Lyness [317], and a detailed study of lattice rules of rank 2 is carried out in Lyness and Sloan [199]. Structural results on integration lattices and their dual lattices are established in Lyness, Sørevik, and Keast [201]. For lattice rules of rank 1, Theorem 5.34 was shown by Zaremba [365], and Theorem 5.35, in a somewhat weaker form, by Niederreiter [224] (see also Niederreiter [234]). The method of obtaining the lower bound for the discrepancy in Theorem 5.37 can also be traced to [234]. Lemmas 5.39 and 5.40 are derived from Niederreiter [262]. Further information on copy rules, in particular, on their invariants, can be found in Sloan and Lyness [317]. Joe [148] extended the randomization procedure of Cranley and Patterson [45] from lattice rules of rank 1 to arbitrary lattice rules. Analogues of lattice rules for integration over $\mathbb{R}^s$ were considered by Joe [147], Sloan and Osborn [319], and Sugihara [336]. A generalization of lattice rules for Haar integrals over compact groups was introduced by Niederreiter [262].

CHAPTER 6

Quasi-Monte Carlo Methods for Optimization

Another basic problem of numerical analysis to which quasi-Monte Carlo methods can be applied is global optimization. The standard Monte Carlo method for finding global optima is random search, and it is employed in situations where the objective function has a low degree of regularity, e.g., in the case of a nondifferentiable objective function in which the usual gradient methods fail. The deterministic analogue of random search is the quasi-Monte Carlo method of quasirandom search. The analysis of quasi-Monte Carlo optimization follows the same approach as for quasi-Monte Carlo integration: We first establish an effective error bound in terms of a suitable quantity depending on the deterministically selected points (in this case, the relevant quantity is the dispersion rather than the discrepancy), and then we strive to find deterministic point sets or sequences that make this quantity as small as possible.

Both random search and quasirandom search can be described in a quite general setting, and this is done in §6.1. In the standard case where the objective function is defined on a bounded subset of a Euclidean space, more concrete information can be given. Since a straightforward quasirandom search method is usually inefficient, we also discuss more refined techniques, such as localization of search. In all these variants of quasirandom search, a basic role is played by low-dispersion point sets and sequences, which are studied in §6.2.

6.1. General theory of quasirandom search methods.

Let X be a separable topological space and let the objective function f be a real-valued function on X for which we want to calculate a global optimum. It suffices, of course, to restrict the attention to the case where we are interested in the global supremum (or maximum) of f. Thus we assume that f is bounded from above, and we put

$$m(f) = \sup_{x \in X} f(x).$$

The Monte Carlo method of *random search* proceeds as follows. Put a probability measure λ on X, take a sequence S of independent λ-distributed random samples $x_1, x_2, \ldots \in X$, and use the estimate

(6.1) $$m(f) \approx m_N(f; S) := \max_{1 \le n \le N} f(x_n).$$

The sequence $m_N(f; S)$, $N = 1, 2, \ldots$ is nondecreasing, and we would expect that it converges to $m(f)$. In fact, this can be shown to happen with probability 1 if f is continuous and the measure λ is suitable.

THEOREM 6.1. *If f is continuous on X and if the measure λ is such that $\lambda(A) > 0$ for every nonempty open subset A of X, then*

$$\lim_{N \to \infty} m_N(f; S) = m(f) \qquad \lambda^\infty\text{-}a.e.$$

Proof. For given $\varepsilon > 0$, the nonempty set $A_\varepsilon = \{x \in X : f(x) > m(f) - \varepsilon\}$ is open by the continuity of f. Furthermore, we have $m_N(f; S) > m(f) - \varepsilon$ if and only if at least one of $x_1, \ldots, x_N$ lies in A_ε. The probability of the latter event is $1 - (1 - \lambda(A_\varepsilon))^N$ by the independence of the samples. Thus, if X^∞ denotes the set of all sequences of elements of X, then

$$\lambda^\infty(\{S \in X^\infty : m_N(f; S) > m(f) - \varepsilon \text{ for all sufficiently large } N\})$$
$$\geq 1 - (1 - \lambda(A_\varepsilon))^h \qquad \text{for } h = 1, 2, \ldots .$$

Letting $h \to \infty$ and using $\lambda(A_\varepsilon) > 0$, we obtain

$$\lambda^\infty(\{S \in X^\infty : m_N(f; S) > m(f) - \varepsilon \text{ for all sufficiently large } N\}) = 1.$$

Applying this with $\varepsilon = 1/k$, $k = 1, 2, \ldots$, we get the desired result. □

In the quasi-Monte Carlo method of *quasirandom search*, we use a deterministic sequence S of points $x_1, x_2, \ldots$ in X and employ approximation (6.1). We clearly have

$$\lim_{N \to \infty} m_N(f; S) = m(f)$$

whenever f is continuous on X and the sequence S is dense in X. For the purpose of error analysis, let (X, d) be a bounded metric space, which means that the metric d satisfies $\sup_{x,y \in X} d(x, y) < \infty$.

DEFINITION 6.2. *If (X, d) is a bounded metric space and the point set P consists of $x_1, \ldots, x_N \in X$, then the* dispersion *of P in X is defined by*

$$d_N(P; X) = \sup_{x \in X} \min_{1 \leq n \leq N} d(x, x_n).$$

Note that the boundedness of (X, d) implies that the dispersion $d_N(P; X)$ is finite. If $B(x; r)$ denotes the closed ball with center $x \in X$ and radius r, then $d_N(P; X)$ may also be described as the infimum of all radii $r \geq 0$ such that the balls $B(x_1; r), \ldots, B(x_N; r)$ cover X. If P is as in Definition 6.2, then we also write $m_N(f; P)$ for the maximum in (6.1). Let

$$\omega(f; t) = \sup_{\substack{x, y \in X \\ d(x,y) \leq t}} |f(x) - f(y)| \qquad \text{for } t \geq 0$$

be the *modulus of continuity* of f.

THEOREM 6.3. *If (X, d) is a bounded metric space, then, for any point set P of N points in X with dispersion $d_N = d_N(P; X)$, we have*

$$m(f) - m_N(f; P) \leq \omega(f; d_N).$$

Proof. Choose $\varepsilon > 0$ and let $y \in X$ be such that $f(y) > m(f) - \varepsilon$. For some k with $1 \leq k \leq N$, we have

$$d(y, x_k) = \min_{1 \leq n \leq N} d(y, x_n),$$

where $x_1, \ldots, x_N$ are the points of P. It follows that $d(y, x_k) \leq d_N$. Furthermore, we have $f(y) - f(x_k) \leq \omega(f; d_N)$, and so

$$m(f) - \varepsilon < f(y) \leq f(x_k) + \omega(f; d_N) \leq m_N(f; P) + \omega(f; d_N),$$

which implies the result of the theorem.   □

Theorem 6.3 shows that suitable deterministic point sets for quasirandom search are those with small dispersion. If S is a sequence of elements of X, then we write $d_N(S; X)$ for the dispersion of the first N terms of S. For a sequence S, the error bound $\omega(f; d_N(S; X))$ in Theorem 6.3 tends to zero as $N \to \infty$ if f is uniformly continuous on X and $d_N(S; X) \to 0$ as $N \to \infty$. The latter property is seen to be equivalent to the denseness of S in X, provided that (X, d) is totally bounded, which means that, for every $\varepsilon > 0$, X can be covered by finitely many closed balls of radius ε. Thus the dispersion may be viewed as a measure for the deviation from denseness.

To transform low-dispersion point sets and sequences from one domain to another, the following simple result is convenient.

THEOREM 6.4. *Let $T : (X, d) \to (Y, d')$ be a map from the bounded metric space (X, d) onto the metric space (Y, d') such that there exists a constant $L \geq 0$ with*

(6.2) $$d'(T(x), T(z)) \leq L d(x, z) \quad \text{for all } x, z \in X.$$

If P is the point set consisting of $x_1, \ldots, x_N \in X$ and P' is the point set consisting of $T(x_1), \ldots, T(x_N) \in Y$, then

$$d_N(P'; Y) \leq L d_N(P; X),$$

with equality holding if we have equality in (6.2).

Proof. Note first that, from (6.2) and the surjectivity of T, it follows that (Y, d') is also bounded. Furthermore,

$$d_N(P'; Y) = \sup_{y \in Y} \min_{1 \leq n \leq N} d'(y, T(x_n)) = \sup_{x \in X} \min_{1 \leq n \leq N} d'(T(x), T(x_n))$$
$$\leq \sup_{x \in X} \min_{1 \leq n \leq N} L d(x, x_n) = L d_N(P; X),$$

with equality throughout if we have equality in (6.2).   □

In most applications, the domain of the objective function will be a bounded subset E of a Euclidean space $\mathbb{R}^s$. In this case, there are two interesting metrics on E, namely, the standard Euclidean metric d and the maximum metric d' defined by

$$d'(\mathbf{u}, \mathbf{v}) = \max_{1 \leq i \leq s} |u_i - v_i|$$

for $\mathbf{u} = (u_1, \ldots, u_s)$ and $\mathbf{v} = (v_1, \ldots, v_s)$ in E. We write $d_N(P; E)$ for the dispersion of a point set P in (E, d) and $d'_N(P; E)$ for the dispersion in (E, d'), and similarly for sequences. Since $d'(\mathbf{u}, \mathbf{v}) \leq d(\mathbf{u}, \mathbf{v}) \leq s^{1/2} d'(\mathbf{u}, \mathbf{v})$ for all $\mathbf{u}, \mathbf{v} \in E$, it follows from Theorem 6.4 applied to the identity map on E that

$$d'_N(P; E) \leq d_N(P; E) \leq s^{1/2} d'_N(P; E).$$

Thus the two dispersions have the same order of magnitude, but, in certain circumstances, one might be easier to work with. For $d_N(P; E)$, we have the general lower bound

(6.3) $$d_N(P; E) \geq \left(\frac{\bar{\lambda}_s(E)}{\gamma_s} \right)^{1/s} N^{-1/s},$$

where $\bar{\lambda}_s$ is the s-dimensional outer Lebesgue measure and $\gamma_s = \pi^{s/2}/\Gamma(s/2+1)$ is the volume of the s-dimensional unit ball. This is shown by letting $\mathbf{x}_1, \ldots, \mathbf{x}_N \in E$ be the points of P and noting that the balls $B(\mathbf{x}_1; r), \ldots, B(\mathbf{x}_N; r)$ with radius $r = d_N(P; E)$ cover E. Comparing measures, we get $N\gamma_s r^s \geq \bar{\lambda}_s(E)$, which leads to (6.3). The analogous bound for $d'_N(P; E)$ is

(6.4) $$d'_N(P; E) \geq \tfrac{1}{2}\bar{\lambda}_s(E)^{1/s} N^{-1/s}.$$

REMARK 6.5. If $\bar{\lambda}_s(E) > 0$, then (6.3) and (6.4) show that $d_N(P; E)$ and $d'_N(P; E)$ are at least of the order of magnitude $N^{-1/s}$. On the other hand, we can construct point sets for which the dispersion attains this order of magnitude. Let E be a bounded subset of $\mathbb{R}^s$, so that E is contained in some cube $[a, b]^s$. For a positive integer k, we partition $[a, b]$ into the intervals $I_h = [a+h(b-a)/k, a + (h+1)(b-a)/k)$ for $0 \leq h \leq k - 2$ and $I_{k-1} = [b - (b-a)/k, b]$. Then the cubes $\prod_{i=1}^{s} I_{h_i}$, with the h_i, $1 \leq i \leq s$, running independently through the integers $0, 1, \ldots, k - 1$, form a partition of $[a, b]^s$. For each of those cubes C having a nonempty intersection with E, we select one point from $C \cap E$. In this way, we arrive at a point set P consisting, say, of $\mathbf{x}_1, \ldots, \mathbf{x}_N \in E$. If $\mathbf{x} \in E$ is arbitrary, then $\mathbf{x}$ lies in some cube C_0 from above having a nonempty intersection with E, and also $\mathbf{x}_n \in C_0$ for some n with $1 \leq n \leq N$. Since $d'(\mathbf{x}, \mathbf{x}_n) \leq (b-a)/k$, we arrive at $d'_N(P; E) \leq (b-a)/k$. Now $N \leq k^s$, and therefore $d'_N(P; E) \leq (b-a)N^{-1/s}$.

The quasirandom search method already described is also known as *crude search*. This method has a limited usefulness, since its rate of convergence is, in general, very slow. Its inefficiency can also be seen from the fact that most of the time is spent calculating function values at points that are far from those points at which the function values are close to $m(f)$. A refinement of crude search was introduced by Niederreiter and Peart [269] and is called *localization of search*. To simplify the exposition, we assume that $E = \bar{I}^s$ with the maximum metric d'. For $B = B(\mathbf{a}; \delta)$ with $\mathbf{a} \in \bar{I}^s$ and $\delta > 0$, let $g_B : \bar{I}^s \to B$ be the function defined by

$$g_B(\mathbf{x}) = \mathbf{a} + \delta(2\mathbf{x} - (1, \dots, 1)) \quad \text{for } \mathbf{x} \in \bar{I}^s,$$

which is the canonical similarity transformation from $\bar{I}^s$ onto B. Now let $\mathbf{x}_1, \dots, \mathbf{x}_N$ be points in $\bar{I}^s$, put

$$S(B) = \{1 \le n \le N : g_B(\mathbf{x}_n) \in \bar{I}^s\},$$

and define

$$l_N(f; B) = \max\left(f(\mathbf{a}), \max_{n \in S(B)} f(g_B(\mathbf{x}_n))\right).$$

Furthermore, let $\mathbf{x}^*(B)$ be one of the points in the set $\{\mathbf{a}\} \cup \{g_B(\mathbf{x}_n) : n \in S(B)\}$ for which

$$l_N(f; B) = f(\mathbf{x}^*(B)).$$

Now choose a sequence $\varepsilon_1, \varepsilon_2, \dots$ of positive numbers converging monotonically to zero and define a sequence $B_0, B_1, \dots$ of balls (in the maximum metric, i.e., cubes in the usual geometry) as follows:

$$B_0 = \bar{I}^s, \quad B_1 = B(\mathbf{x}^*(B_0); \varepsilon_1),$$

and, for $j = 1, 2, \dots$,

$$B_{j+1} = \begin{cases} B(\mathbf{x}^*(B_j); \varepsilon_{j+1}) & \text{if } l_N(f; B_j) > l_N(f; B_{j-1}), \\ B(x^*(B_{j-1}); \varepsilon_{j+1}) & \text{otherwise.} \end{cases}$$

Then the sequence $l_N(f; B_j)$, $j = 0, 1, \dots$, is nondecreasing and, for suitably large j, the value of $l_N(f; B_j)$ is taken as an approximation to $m(f)$. In practice, we will usually set $\varepsilon_j = \varepsilon^j$ for $j = 1, 2, \dots$ with a fixed ε satisfying $0 < \varepsilon < \frac{1}{2}$. The point set P of initial points $\mathbf{x}_1, \dots, \mathbf{x}_N \in \bar{I}^s$ should then be chosen in such a way that $d'_N(P; \bar{I}^s) < \varepsilon$.

It should be noted that, contrary to what we know about the crude search method, the convergence of the method of localization of search cannot be guaranteed. Problems arise when f has a local maximum very close, but not equal, to $m(f)$. The difficulty of proving a rigorous convergence theorem for localization of search occurs even in the context of a stochastic model, as was noted by Solis and Wets [330, p. 21]. It is advisable to perform the method of localization of search several times, with different initial point sets and different values of ε, and then to take the maximum function value reached in all these calculations as the approximate value of $m(f)$.

It may also happen that the sequence $l_N(f; B_j)$, $j = 0, 1, \dots$, does not converge to $m(f)$ because the sequence $\varepsilon_1, \varepsilon_2, \dots$ converges too quickly to zero.

The following procedure of *outer iteration* may be used to countervail that tendency. We first run through a small number of steps in the localization of search method, thus obtaining a point $\mathbf{x}_1^*$ at which f has the largest computed value. Then we start a second localization of search method with a ball $B(\mathbf{x}_1^*; \delta_1)$ with δ_1 larger than the radius of the ball searched last. In general, having arrived after $k-1$ outer iterations at the point $\mathbf{x}_{k-1}^*$, we start the kth iteration with a ball $B(\mathbf{x}_{k-1}^*; \delta_{k-1})$ with δ_{k-1} by a constant factor (independent of k) larger than the radius of the ball searched last. We refer to Niederreiter and Peart [269] for a further discussion of this procedure.

If prior information on the function f is available, we could also employ *adaptive methods* to improve the performance of crude search. One idea is to use fewer points $\mathbf{x}_n$ in those regions where f varies slowly and more points in those regions where f oscillates strongly. Information on the oscillation of f can also be obtained from an initial crude search. Another possibility is to adapt the metric to the behavior of f. For instance, we may use the "weighted" maximum metric

$$d^{(w)}(\mathbf{u}, \mathbf{v}) = \max_{1 \leq i \leq s} c_i |u_i - v_i|$$

for $\mathbf{u} = (u_1, \dots, u_s)$ and $\mathbf{v} = (v_1, \dots, v_s)$ in E, where the positive weight c_i measures the oscillation of $f(u_1, \dots, u_s)$ as a function of u_i. If f had bounded partial derivatives on E, we could use for c_i the supremum of $|\partial f / \partial u_i|$ over E. In general, these suprema will not exist or will not be available numerically, but we may use a difference scheme based on a coarse grid to get approximate values for the c_i. See Niederreiter [235] for further comments on adaptive methods.

6.2.   Low-dispersion point sets and sequences.

We now normalize E to be $\bar{I}^s$. Instead of $d_N(P; \bar{I}^s)$ and $d_N'(P; \bar{I}^s)$, we simply write $d_N(P)$ and $d_N'(P)$, respectively, and similarly for sequences. The following result provides an easy connection between the dispersion and the discrepancy.

THEOREM 6.6.   *For any point set P consisting of N points in $\bar{I}^s$, we have*

$$d_N'(P) \leq D_N(P)^{1/s}.$$

Proof. Let $\mathbf{x}_1, \dots, \mathbf{x}_N$ be the points of P. For given ε with $0 < \varepsilon < r := d_N'(P)$ there exists an $\mathbf{x} \in \bar{I}^s$ such that $d'(\mathbf{x}, \mathbf{x}_n) > r - \varepsilon$ for $1 \leq n \leq N$. Thus the ball $B(\mathbf{x}; r - \varepsilon)$ in the metric d' contains none of the points of P. Now $\bar{J} = B(\mathbf{x}; r - \varepsilon) \cap \bar{I}^s$ is a closed interval with $\lambda_s(\bar{J}) \geq (r - \varepsilon)^s$, and so, for the half-open version J of $\bar{J}$, we have

$$D_N(P) \geq \left| \frac{A(J; P)}{N} - \lambda_s(J) \right| = \lambda_s(J) \geq (r - \varepsilon)^s,$$

which implies the desired inequality. $\square$

Thus every low-discrepancy point set (or sequence) is a low-dispersion point set (or sequence), but not conversely. If we had a general inequality of the form $D_N(P) \leq g(d_N'(P))$ with a function g satisfying $\lim_{u \to 0+} g(u) = 0$, then this would lead to the conclusion that every dense sequence in $\bar{I}^s$ is uniformly distributed in $\bar{I}^s$, which is obviously incorrect. The constructions of low-discrepancy point sets in Chapters 3 and 4 yield, in the s-dimensional case, point sets P with $D_N(P) = O(N^{-1}(\log N)^{s-1})$, and so, from the bound in Theorem 6.6, we obtain $d'_N(P) = O(N^{-1/s}(\log N)^{(s-1)/s})$, where the implied constants depend only on s. As we have seen in Remark 6.5, we can sometimes achieve a slightly smaller order of magnitude by a direct inspection of the dispersion.

In the case where $s = 1$, the two metrics d and d' are identical, and so $d_N(P) = d'_N(P)$. If we order the points $x_1, \ldots, x_N$ of P such that $0 \leq x_1 \leq x_2 \leq \cdots \leq x_N \leq 1$, then it is easily seen that we have the explicit formula

(6.5)
$$d_N(P) = \max\left(x_1, \tfrac{1}{2}(x_2 - x_1), \tfrac{1}{2}(x_3 - x_2), \ldots, \tfrac{1}{2}(x_N - x_{N-1}), 1 - x_N\right).$$

If $x_n = (2n-1)/(2N)$ for $1 \leq n \leq N$, then $d_N(P) = 1/(2N)$, and (6.4) shows that this is the minimum value of $d_N(P)$ for any point set P consisting on N points in $\bar{I}$. The corresponding question for one-dimensional sequences is already less trivial. Here we have, first, the following lower bound due to Niederreiter [230].

THEOREM 6.7. *For any sequence S of elements of $\bar{I}$, we have*

$$\overline{\lim_{N \to \infty}} \, N d_N(S) \geq \frac{1}{\log 4} = 0.721 \ldots .$$

Proof. Suppose that there exists a sequence S of elements of $\bar{I}$ with

$$\overline{\lim_{N \to \infty}} \, N d_N(S) < c = \frac{1}{\log 4}.$$

Then, for a sufficiently small $\varepsilon > 0$, we have

(6.6)
$$d_N(S) \leq \frac{c - \varepsilon}{N} \quad \text{for all sufficiently large } N.$$

For such an N, we order the first N terms of S so that $0 \leq x_1 \leq x_2 \leq \cdots \leq x_N \leq 1$. There are $N+1$ steps x_1, $x_{n+1} - x_n$ for $1 \leq n \leq N-1$, and $1 - x_N$, which we denote by $u_0, u_1, \ldots, u_N$ in such a way that $u_0 \geq u_1 \geq \cdots \geq u_N$. We note that $d_N(S) \geq u_0/2$ by (6.5). The $(N+1)$th term of S falls at best into the largest step; hence $d_{N+1}(S) \geq u_1/2$. Similarly, after having taken into account the $(N+1)$th and $(N+2)$th term, a step $\geq u_2$ will remain; thus $d_{N+2}(S) \geq u_2/2$. Continuing in this way, we get $d_{N+m}(S) \geq u_m/2$ for $0 \leq m \leq N$, and so, by (6.6),

$$u_m \leq \frac{2(c - \varepsilon)}{N + m} \quad \text{for } 0 \leq m \leq N.$$

It follows that

$$1 = \sum_{m=0}^{N} u_m \leq 2(c - \varepsilon) \sum_{m=0}^{N} \frac{1}{N + m} < 2(c - \varepsilon) \left(\frac{1}{N} + \int_N^{2N} \frac{dt}{t} \right)$$

$$= 1 - \varepsilon \log 4 + \frac{2(c - \varepsilon)}{N},$$

which is a contradiction for sufficiently large N. $\square$

The lower bound in Theorem 6.7 is the best possible, according to the following example given by Ruzsa (see Niederreiter [230]). Consider the sequence S defined by

(6.7) $x_1 = 1,$ $x_n = \left\{ \dfrac{\log(2n-3)}{\log 2} \right\}$ for $n = 2, 3, \dots$.

A straightforward argument shows that

$$d_N(S) = \frac{\log N - \log(N-1)}{\log 4} \quad \text{for } N \ge 2,$$

and so, for this sequence, we have

$$\lim_{N \to \infty} N d_N(S) = \frac{1}{\log 4}.$$

It is remarkable that this sequence S of asymptotically minimal dispersion is *not* uniformly distributed in $\bar{I}$, and so its discrepancy does not satisfy $\lim_{N \to \infty} D_N(S) = 0$. At any rate, the problem of constructing a sequence with asymptotically minimal dispersion can be solved in the one-dimensional case, whereas the corresponding problem for the discrepancy is far from being settled (compare with §3.1). This suggests that questions of irregularities of distribution are easier to handle for the dispersion than for the discrepancy.

In the multidimensional case, we can determine for every fixed N the minimum value of the dispersion $d'_N(P)$ relative to the maximum metric. The following result of Sukharev [337] contains the relevant information. The lower bound for $d'_N(P)$ is a slight refinement of (6.4).

THEOREM 6.8. *For any point set P of N points in $\bar{I}^s$, we have*

$$d'_N(P) \ge \frac{1}{2\lfloor N^{1/s} \rfloor}.$$

Furthermore, for every N and s, there exists a P for which equality holds.

Proof. Let the points of P be $\mathbf{x}_1, \dots, \mathbf{x}_N \in \bar{I}^s$ and let m be the positive integer with $m^s \le N < (m+1)^s$. If $r = d'_N(P)$, then the balls $B(\mathbf{x}_n; r)$, $1 \le n \le N$, in the metric d' cover $\bar{I}^s$. Consider the point set Q consisting of the $(m+1)^s$ points $(k_1/m, \dots, k_s/m)$ with the k_i running independently through the set $\{0, 1, \dots, m\}$. By the pigeon-hole principle, there exists an n with $1 \le n \le N$ such that $B(\mathbf{x}_n; r)$ contains two distinct points of Q, say $\mathbf{q}_1$ and $\mathbf{q}_2$. Then it follows that

$$\frac{1}{m} \le d'(\mathbf{q}_1, \mathbf{q}_2) \le d'(\mathbf{q}_1, \mathbf{x}_n) + d'(\mathbf{x}_n, \mathbf{q}_2) \le 2r;$$

hence

$$d'_N(P) = r \ge \frac{1}{2m} = \frac{1}{2\lfloor N^{1/s} \rfloor}.$$

To prove the second part, let N and s be given and choose m as above. Consider the m^s points $(h_1/(2m), \dots, h_s/(2m))$ with the h_i running independently through the set $\{1, 3, 5, \dots, 2m - 1\}$, and then repeat some of these points to obtain a point set P with N points. For this P, it is easily seen that

$$d'_N(P) = \frac{1}{2m} = \frac{1}{2\lfloor N^{1/s} \rfloor}.$$ □

The analogous problem of determining the minimum value of $d_N(P)$ for fixed N is equivalent to a difficult geometric problem, namely, that of finding the most economical covering of $\mathbb{R}^s$ by balls (in the Euclidean metric) of equal radius. This problem has been solved only in the trivial case where $s = 1$ and in the case where $s = 2$, where the solution is given by the circumscribed circles of a hexagonal tiling of $\mathbb{R}^2$ (see [102, pp. 58–59]).

Next, we consider the question of constructing low-dispersion sequences relative to the maximum metric in the multidimensional case. Currently, the best result on this problem is due to Niederreiter [235].

THEOREM 6.9. *For every $s \geq 1$, there exists a sequence S of points in $\bar{I}^s$ with*

$$\lim_{N \to \infty} N^{1/s} d'_N(S) = \frac{1}{\log 4}.$$

Proof. Let S_0 be the one-dimensional sequence defined in (6.7). Consider a sequence S of points $\mathbf{x}_1, \mathbf{x}_2, \dots \in \bar{I}^s$ such that, for any positive integer m, the first m^s terms of S consist exactly of all points $(u_1, \dots, u_s)$ with the u_i running independently through the set $\{x_1, \dots, x_m\}$. The precise order of the $\mathbf{x}_n$ is immaterial. For given $N \geq 1$, determine m by $m^s \leq N < (m + 1)^s$ and let $\mathbf{y} = (y_1, \dots, y_s) \in \bar{I}^s$ be arbitrary. Then, for each i with $1 \leq i \leq s$, there exists an integer n_i with $1 \leq n_i \leq m$ such that $|y_i - x_{n_i}| \leq d_m(S_0)$. The point $(x_{n_1}, \dots, x_{n_s})$ is among the points $\mathbf{x}_1, \dots, \mathbf{x}_N$; thus $d'_N(S) \leq d_m(S_0)$. Furthermore, there exists $t \in \bar{I}$ such that

$$\min_{1 \leq n \leq m+1} |t - x_n| = d_{m+1}(S_0).$$

Then the point $(t, \dots, t) \in \bar{I}^s$ has distance $\geq d_{m+1}(S_0)$ in the metric d' from all points $\mathbf{x}_1, \dots, \mathbf{x}_N$. This implies that $d'_N(S) \geq d_{m+1}(S_0)$. Consequently, we have

$$m d_{m+1}(S_0) \leq N^{1/s} d'_N(S) < (m + 1) d_m(S_0),$$

and so $\lim_{m \to \infty} m d_m(S_0) = 1/(\log 4)$ yields the desired conclusion.   □

Thus, for every dimension s, there is a sequence S of points in $\bar{I}^s$ with $d'_N(S) = O(N^{-1/s})$. In view of Theorem 6.8, this order of magnitude is the best possible. Note that the corresponding problem of determining the minimal order of magnitude for the discrepancy of s-dimensional sequences is unsolved for $s \geq 2$ (compare with §3.1). As to the dispersion $d'_N(S)$, there remains the problem of finding the asymptotically optimal constant in the bound $d'_N(S) = O(N^{-1/s})$. More precisely, we want to determine the constant

(6.8) $$D(\bar{I}^s) = \inf_S \varlimsup_{N \to \infty} N^{1/s} d'_N(S),$$

where the infimum is taken over all sequences S of points in $\bar{I}^s$. We infer from Theorems 6.8 and 6.9 that

$$\frac{1}{2} \leq D(\bar{I}^s) \leq \frac{1}{\log 4}.$$

The value of $D(\bar{I}^s)$ is only known in the case where $s = 1$, where it is equal to $1/(\log 4)$ by Theorem 6.7. In analogy with (6.8), we may define, for any bounded subset E of $\mathbb{R}^s$ with $\bar{\lambda}_s(E) > 0$, the constant

$$D(E) = \inf_S \varlimsup_{N \to \infty} N^{1/s} d_N'(S; E),$$

where the infimum is extended over all sequences S of points in E. It appears to be a rather challenging problem to determine the value of this constant.

We now analyze the dispersion of some typical low-discrepancy point sets and sequences to improve on the bound obtained by Theorem 6.6 in the cases considered. The following two results for nets and (t,s)-sequences (see Chapter 4) were shown by Niederreiter [247].

THEOREM 6.10. *For any (t,m,s)-net P in base b, we have*

$$d_N'(P) \leq b^{-\lfloor (m-t)/s \rfloor} \leq b^{(s-1+t)/s} N^{-1/s} \qquad \text{with } N = b^m.$$

Proof. Write $k = \lfloor (m-t)/s \rfloor$, so that $m - t = ks + h$ with $0 \leq h \leq s - 1$. Consider the partition of I^s into elementary intervals in base b of the form

$$\prod_{i=1}^{h} [a_i b^{-k-1}, (a_i + 1)b^{-k-1}) \times \prod_{i=h+1}^{s} [a_i b^{-k}, (a_i + 1)b^{-k})$$

with integers $0 \leq a_i < b^{k+1}$ for $1 \leq i \leq h$ and $0 \leq a_i < b^k$ for $h + 1 \leq i \leq s$. If $\mathbf{x} \in I^s$ is arbitrary, then $\mathbf{x}$ belongs to a unique interval J of that partition. Since

$$\lambda_s(J) = (b^{-k-1})^h (b^{-k})^{s-h} = b^{-ks-h} = b^{t-m},$$

it follows from Definition 4.1 that J contains at least one point $\mathbf{x}_n$ of P. Then $d'(\mathbf{x}, \mathbf{x}_n) < b^{-k}$; thus

$$d_N'(P) \leq b^{-k} \leq b^{(s-1+t)/s} b^{-m/s} = b^{(s-1+t)/s} N^{-1/s}. \qquad \square$$

THEOREM 6.11. *For any (t,s)-sequence S in base b, we have*

$$d_N'(S) < b^{(s+t)/s} N^{-1/s} \qquad \text{for all } N \geq 1.$$

Proof. For $N < b^{s+t}$, we have $d_N'(S) \leq 1 < b^{(s+t)/s} N^{-1/s}$. For $N \geq b^{s+t}$ let m be the largest integer with $b^m \leq N$, so that, in particular, $m > t$. By Definition 4.2, the first b^m terms of S form a (t,m,s)-net in base b. Using Theorem 6.10 and $N < b^{m+1}$, we therefore obtain

$$d_N'(S) \leq d_{b^m}'(S) \leq b^{(s-1+t)/s} b^{-m/s} < b^{(s+t)/s} N^{-1/s}. \qquad \square$$

Next, we present bounds for the dispersion of Halton sequences and Hammersley point sets (see §3.1). Theorem 6.12 is an analogue of a result of Mitchell [212] for the dispersion with respect to the Euclidean metric, and Theorem 6.13 was established by Bayrhamer [17] (see [212] for the "Euclidean" version).

THEOREM 6.12. *For the Halton sequence S in the pairwise relatively prime bases $b_1, \ldots, b_s$, we have*

$$d'_N(S) < N^{-1/s} \max_{1 \leq i \leq s} b_i \quad \text{for all } N \geq 1.$$

Proof. Fix $N \geq 1$, and, for $1 \leq i \leq s$, let f_i be the largest integer with $b_i^{f_i} \leq N^{1/s}$. Consider the partition of I^s into intervals of the form

$$\prod_{i=1}^{s} [c_i b_i^{-f_i}, (c_i + 1)b_i^{-f_i})$$

with integers $0 \leq c_i < b_i^{f_i}$ for $1 \leq i \leq s$. If $\mathbf{x} \in I^s$ is arbitrary, then $\mathbf{x}$ belongs to a unique interval J of that partition. In the proof of Theorem 3.6, we have shown that among any $b_1^{f_1} \cdots b_s^{f_s}$ consecutive terms of S exactly one lies in J. Since $N \geq b_1^{f_1} \cdots b_s^{f_s}$, it follows, in particular, that J contains at least one term $\mathbf{x}_n$ of S with $0 \leq n \leq N - 1$. Now $d'(\mathbf{x}, \mathbf{x}_n) < \max_{1 \leq i \leq s} b_i^{-f_i}$, and so

$$d'_N(S) \leq \max_{1 \leq i \leq s} b_i^{-f_i} < N^{-1/s} \max_{1 \leq i \leq s} b_i,$$

where we used $b_i^{f_i+1} > N^{1/s}$ for $1 \leq i \leq s$. $\square$

THEOREM 6.13. *If $s \geq 2$, then, for the N-element Hammersley point set P in the pairwise relatively prime bases $b_1, \ldots, b_{s-1}$, we have*

$$d'_N(P) < \left(1 + \max_{1 \leq i \leq s-1} b_i\right) N^{-1/s}.$$

Proof. For $1 \leq i \leq s - 1$, let f_i be the largest integer with $b_i^{f_i} \leq N^{1/s}$, and put $m = \prod_{i=1}^{s-1} b_i^{f_i}$. A given $\mathbf{x} \in \bar{I}^s$ has a distance $\leq m/N$ from a suitable interval of the form

$$J = \left[\frac{cm}{N}, \frac{(c+1)m}{N}\right) \times \prod_{i=1}^{s-1} [c_i b_i^{-f_i}, (c_i + 1)b_i^{-f_i})$$

with integers $0 \leq c < \lfloor N/m \rfloor$ and $0 \leq c_i < b_i^{f_i}$ for $1 \leq i \leq s - 1$. A point $\mathbf{x}_n$ of P lies in J if and only if $cm \leq n < (c + 1)m$ and the term with index n of the $(s - 1)$-dimensional Halton sequence in the bases $b_1, \ldots, b_{s-1}$ lies in $\prod_{i=1}^{s-1} [c_i b_i^{-f_i}, (c_i + 1)b_i^{-f_i})$. By the proof of Theorem 3.6, these two conditions on n are satisfied for exactly one value of n. With this n, we have

$$d'(\mathbf{x}, \mathbf{x}_n) \leq \frac{m}{N} + \max\left(\frac{m}{N}, \max_{1 \leq i \leq s-1} b_i^{-f_i}\right),$$

and the bound for $d'_N(P)$ follows. $\square$

Theorems 6.11 and 6.12 provide further examples of sequences S of points in $\bar{I}^s$ for which $d'_N(S) = O(N^{-1/s})$. A sequence S of dyadic points in $\bar{I}^2$ with $d_N(S) = O(N^{-1/2})$ was constructed by Lambert [167]. Good lattice points (see §5.1) can also be used to obtain s-dimensional point sets with a dispersion of minimal order of magnitude. In fact, it was shown by Niederreiter [240] that, for every s, there are infinitely many N for which an effective construction of a $\mathbf{g} \in \mathbb{Z}^s$ can be given such that the corresponding point set P in (5.1) satisfies $d'_N(P) = O(N^{-1/s})$.

Notes.

Expository accounts of random search methods can be found in the books of Evtushenko [92], Rubinstein [297], [298], Tőrn and Žilinskas [352], and Zhigljavsky [368]. Various stochastic models for random search have been analyzed by Devroye [61], Matyas [208], Pintér [282], and Solis and Wets [330], among others.

Quasirandom search methods have been used in numerical practice for a considerable time; see Aird and Rice [6], Artobolevskii et al. [10], [11], Sobol' [325], and Sobol' and Statnikov [329] for early published accounts. Sukharev [337] carried out the first theoretical analysis of quasirandom search for objective functions satisfying a Lipschitz condition. A general systematic analysis, including the error bound in Theorem 6.3, was first given in Niederreiter [228] (see also Niederreiter and McCurley [266]), where the term "dispersion" was also coined. The dispersion was studied in detail in Niederreiter [230], [235]. For the case of point sets in $\bar{I}^s$, Sobol' [326] proposed to take into account the dispersion of the projections of a point set on all lower-dimensional faces of $\bar{I}^s$ when assessing the suitability of a point set for quasirandom search. Sobol' [327], [328] investigated the dispersion with respect to weighted l^1 metrics on $\bar{I}^s$.

The lower bound (6.3) for the dispersion was shown in Niederreiter [228], where an improvement can be found for a tiling domain E, i.e., for a bounded subset E of $\mathbb{R}^s$ with $\lambda_s(E) > 0$ such that $\mathbb{R}^s$ can be tiled by congruent copies of E (such as $E = \bar{I}^s$). An improvement on (6.3) for the case where E is a convex body was established by Gritzmann [115]. In the proof of Theorem 6.8, we followed Niederreiter [235]. For the special case of (t, m, s)-nets P in base 2, an analogue of Theorem 6.10 for the dispersion $d_N(P)$ was proved by Sobol' [326]. Bounds for the dispersion of nets with respect to weighted l^1 metrics were given in Sobol' [327], [328]. For $s = 2$, Peart [280] determined the exact value of $d_N(P)$ when P is an N-element Hammersley point set in base 2 with N being a power of 2. Again for $s = 2$, Larcher [174] gave a formula for $d'_N(P)$ when P is the N-element point set (5.1) generated by $\mathbf{g} = (1, g) \in \mathbb{Z}^2$. The related concept of the dispersion of a two-dimensional lattice was introduced and analyzed by Larcher [177]. The dispersion of the sequence of fractional parts $\{n\mathbf{z}\}$, $n = 1, 2, \ldots$, with $\mathbf{z} \in \mathbb{R}^s$ was studied by Drobot [71] and Niederreiter [230] in the one-dimensional case and by Niederreiter [235] in the multidimensional case. With suitable choices of $\mathbf{z}$ we arrive at s-dimensional sequences S with $d'_N(S) = O(N^{-1/s})$. General bounds for the dispersion in terms of exponential sums were shown by Mitchell [212] and Niederreiter [230], [240]. A result of Deheuvels [57] on maximal spacings for multivariate order statistics implies that $d'_N(S)$ is almost surely of the order of magnitude $N^{-1/s}(\log N)^{1/s}$ for random sequences S of points in $\bar{I}^s$.

Reports on comparative studies of the performance of various low-discrepancy point sets and sequences in quasirandom search methods can be found in Bandyopadhyay and Sarkar [15] and Niederreiter and Peart [267]. Tests with Halton sequences were carried out by Niederreiter and McCurley [266]. Numerical experiments for domains other than $\bar{I}^s$ were reported in Niederreiter and Peart [268], and this paper contains also Theorem 6.4 as well as methods of generating low-dispersion point sets and sequences in special domains such as balls, spheres, and simplices. Fedorenko [101] compared quasirandom search methods with other global optimization methods. Applications of quasirandom search methods to computational physics are discussed in Bandyopadhyay and Sarkar [14] and Khasnabis et al. [151].

Level sets of the objective function and their connections with quasirandom search were studied by Bayrhamer [16], [17]. A description of localization of search in the setting of metric spaces was given by Niederreiter [235]. Sukharev [338] analyzed sequential search strategies, i.e., procedures where the choice of a sample point depends on the previously calculated sample points and function values. Applications of quasirandom search to discrete optimization are discussed in Niederreiter [240].

CHAPTER 7

Random Numbers and Pseudorandom Numbers

Random sampling is at the heart of the Monte Carlo method, as we have seen in Chapter 1. The success of a Monte Carlo calculation depends, of course, on the appropriateness of the underlying stochastic model, but also, to a large extent, on how well the random numbers used in the computation simulate the random variables in the model. The specification of the requirements on random numbers and the discussion of the testing of these requirements are two of the topics of this chapter. In actual practice, random numbers are generated by a deterministic algorithm that is implemented in the computer, and so we are really working with pseudorandom numbers. Therefore our main attention in this and the following chapters will be focused on pseudorandom numbers. The emphasis will be on methods of pseudorandom number generation for which a theoretical analysis of the structural and statistical properties is possible.

In §7.1 we discuss the desirable properties of random numbers and some attempts at defining the rather elusive concept of a sequence of random numbers. Section 7.2 lays the foundations for our treatment of pseudorandom numbers, gives a brief account of some methods for the generation of nonuniform pseudorandom numbers, and describes randomness tests for uniform pseudorandom numbers. Some classical methods for the generation of uniform pseudorandom numbers, such as the linear congruential method, are briefly analyzed in §7.3.

7.1. Random number generation.

The task in random number generation is the following: Given a distribution function F on $\mathbb{R}$, generate a sequence of real numbers that simulates a sequence of independent and identically distributed random variables with distribution function F. Random numbers are needed in a wide range of areas; we have noted their applications in Monte Carlo methods and, more generally, in simulation methods, but they are also of basic importance in computational statistics, in the implementation of probabilistic algorithms, and in related problems of scientific computing that have a stochastic ingredient. In addition, random numbers are applied in areas of direct practical interest such as VLSI testing, cryptography, and computer games.

The requirements on random numbers may be classified into the following four categories: *structural, statistical, complexity-theoretic,* and *computational.*

Structural requirements refer to aspects such as period length, lattice structure, and so on. Statistical and complexity-theoretic requirements will be discussed more fully in the sequel. By computational requirements, we mean features relating to the computer implementation of random numbers, such as ease of coding, set-up time, running time, required memory space, and portability. Given the power of modern computers, the consideration of the efficiency, i.e., of the time and space requirements, of random number generation has a lower priority nowadays; we quote from James [146, p. 332]: "This [efficiency] was considered very important in the early days, but with the kind of computations being performed now, both the computer time and memory space taken by random number generation are increasingly insignificant and can almost always be neglected."

It is common to make a distinction between uniform and nonuniform random numbers. *Uniform random numbers* are random numbers for which the target distribution is the uniform distribution U on $\bar{I} = [0,1]$, i.e., the distribution function defined by $U(t) = 0$ for $t < 0$, $U(t) = t$ for $0 \le t \le 1$, and $U(t) = 1$ for $t > 1$. *Nonuniform random numbers* (also called *random variates*) have a target distribution different from U. Nonuniform random numbers are often generated by suitably transforming uniform random numbers; see §7.2 for a description of such methods in the context of pseudorandom number generation.

The statistical requirements imposed on random numbers relate mostly to distribution and statistical independence properties. Statistical tests for these properties will be discussed in §7.2 in connection with uniform pseudorandom numbers. Here we report on efforts of handling the vexing problem of defining the concept of a sequence of random numbers, a problem which, if explored to its full consequence, actually leads from the mathematical into the philosophical realm. A possible formalization of the statistical properties of uniform random numbers is based on the following extension of the notion of a uniformly distributed sequence (compare with §2.1).

DEFINITION 7.1. A sequence $x_0, x_1, \ldots$ of numbers in $\bar{I}$ is *completely uniformly distributed* if for every integer $s \ge 1$ the sequence of points $(x_n, x_{n+1}, \ldots, x_{n+s-1}) \in \bar{I}^s$, $n = 0, 1, \ldots$, is uniformly distributed in $\bar{I}^s$.

Knuth [154, §3.5] proposes a hierarchy of definitions for a sequence of uniform random numbers, and, on the lowest level of this hierarchy, is his Definition R1, according to which a sequence of numbers in $\bar{I}$ is random if it is completely uniformly distributed. The notion of complete uniform distribution attempts to formalize the requirement that successive random numbers should be statistically independent. However, this notion does not reflect the intuitively obvious principle that the distribution and statistical independence properties of a sequence of random numbers should be invariant under certain selection rules for subsequences. Clearly, we cannot insist that the sequence and *all* its subsequences be completely uniformly distributed, as this would lead to a void concept. Hence some restriction on the admissible selection rules has to be imposed. Definition R4 of Knuth [154, §3.5] proposes to call a sequence $x_0, x_1, \ldots$ of numbers in $\bar{I}$ random if, for every effective algorithm that specifies a sequence $s_0, s_1, \ldots$ of distinct nonnegative integers, the sequence $x_{s_0}, x_{s_1}, \ldots$ is completely uniformly distributed.

Explicit constructions of completely uniformly distributed sequences are known, and we refer to [225, p. 997] for a survey of such constructions. Note that, according to [163, p. 204, Thm. 3.13], λ^∞-almost all sequences of numbers in $\bar{I}$ are completely uniformly distributed, where λ is the Lebesgue measure on $\bar{I}$. A classical probabilistic result of Franklin [108] says that the sequence of fractional parts $\{\theta^n\}$, $n = 0, 1, \ldots$, is completely uniformly distributed for almost all real numbers $\theta > 1$ (in the sense of Lebesgue measure). Thus, in the indicated sense, almost all these specific sequences satisfy Knuth's Definition R1 of randomness. Knuth [154, §3.5] conjectured that these sequences satisfy his much stronger Definition R4 in the above probabilistic sense, and Niederreiter and Tichy [275] managed to prove this conjecture by combining several techniques of probabilistic number theory and results on the location of zeros of sparse polynomials. Concretely, the theorem of Niederreiter and Tichy states the following.

THEOREM 7.2. *The sequence of fractional parts* $\{\theta^n\}$, $n = 0, 1, \ldots$, *satisfies Knuth's Definition R4 of randomness for almost all real numbers* θ *with* $|\theta| > 1$ *(in the sense of Lebesgue measure).*

The approach to randomness based on the notion of complete uniform distribution can also be pursued for sequences of digits (see Knuth [154, §3.5]). In this case, there are interesting connections with the classical theory of normal numbers (see Knuth [154, §3.5] and Kuipers and Niederreiter [163, §1.8]).

A complexity-theoretic approach to a definition of randomness for finite strings of digits is due to Kolmogorov [156], Chaitin [39], and Martin-Löf [207]. If $b \geq 2$ is an integer and σ_N is a string, i.e., a finite sequence, of length N consisting of elements of $Z_b = \{0, 1, \ldots, b-1\}$, then its *Kolmogorov complexity* is defined as the shortest length of a program that generates σ_N on a Turing machine. The string σ_N is designated as random if it has the maximum Kolmogorov complexity among all strings of length N consisting of elements of Z_b. This is, of course, the worst concept of randomness from the viewpoint of practical random number generation, since it means that the random strings are those that are the least efficient with regard to computer implementation. On the other hand, this complexity-theoretic approach is of great relevance for random bit strings that are used for cryptographic purposes. In these applications, it is essential that the utilized bit strings have a sufficiently high complexity, so that the algorithms generating the strings cannot be "cracked." The procedures that have been devised for the generation of cryptographically strong pseudorandom bit strings have not yet made an impact on random number generation for simulation methods, one reason being that the secrecy aspect in cryptography is not a concern in simulation studies. On the contrary, it can be argued that, in the latter area, transparency and reproducibility of random numbers are virtues.

Efforts have also been made to produce *physical random numbers*, i.e., to generate random numbers by physical devices. The sources of random numbers that have been considered include coin flipping, roulette wheels, white noise, and counts of emitted particles. Some relevant references are given in [225, p. 998]. Although the use of physical random numbers may appeal to intuition, it must be emphasized that these types of random numbers are problematic in numerical practice. First, since no theoretical analysis of these random numbers is possible, they must be subjected to extensive statistical tests for randomness prior to actual use. Furthermore, the simulation studies now performed require huge amounts of random numbers, and since these must be available for the later validation of computations, this causes considerable storage difficulties in the case of physical random numbers. By way of comparison, in the case of standard algorithms for pseudorandom number generation, just a few parameters and some seed values must be stored. There is also a more philosophical standpoint that posits that calculations executed in a computer should be supported as much as possible by internal routines and should not have to rely on external sources for auxiliary data such as random numbers.

7.2. Pseudorandom numbers.

Early in the history of the Monte Carlo method, it already became clear that "truly random" numbers are fictitious from a practical point of view. Therefore users have resorted to pseudorandom numbers (abbreviated PRN) that can be readily generated in the computer by deterministic algorithms with relatively few input parameters. In this way, problems of storage and reproducibility do not arise. Furthermore, well-chosen algorithms for pseudorandom number generation can be subjected to a rigorous theoretical analysis. Naturally, the PRN must pass an assortment of statistical tests for randomness to be suitable for simulation purposes. It should be clear that a deterministic sequence of numbers cannot perform well under *all* imaginable tests for randomness. Therefore the user of PRN must be aware of the specific desirable statistical properties of the random samples in the current computational project and must choose PRN that are known to pass the corresponding statistical tests.

The standard algorithms for generating sequences of PRN are based on recursive procedures and yield sequences that are ultimately periodic. It is no serious loss of generality if we restrict the attention to (purely) periodic sequences. A sequence $y_0, y_1, \ldots$ of elements of a nonempty set is (purely) *periodic* if there exists a positive integer T such that $y_{n+T} = y_n$ for all $n \geq 0$. We write $\mathrm{per}(y_n)$ for the least value of T, i.e., for the least period length.

The desirable properties of a sequence of PRN may be summarized as follows: (i) the least period length should be sufficiently large; (ii) it should have little intrinsic structure (such as lattice structure); (iii) it should have good statistical properties; (iv) the computational requirements listed in §7.1 should be satisfied (e.g., the algorithm generating the sequence should be reasonably efficient).

As in the case of random numbers, we distinguish between *uniform pseudorandom numbers* and *nonuniform pseudorandom numbers*. Uniform PRN simulate the uniform distribution U on $\bar{I}$. Nonuniform PRN are usually generated by starting from uniform PRN and transforming them to fit a given target distribution $F \neq U$. In our exposition, we will concentrate on uniform PRN. Many methods have been developed for transforming uniform PRN into nonuniform PRN, and, in the following, we briefly discuss the most common ones.

(i) *Inversion method.* Let the distribution function F be strictly increasing and continuous on $\mathbb{R}$. Then F has an inverse function F^{-1}, which is defined at least on the open interval $(0, 1)$. Now take a sequence $x_0, x_1, \ldots$ of uniform PRN in $(0, 1)$ and define $y_n = F^{-1}(x_n)$, $n = 0, 1, \ldots$, as the sequence of nonuniform PRN. If F does not satisfy the two conditions above, then we may consider the generalized inverse function $G(u) = \min\{t \in \mathbb{R} : F(t) \geq u\}$ for $u \in (0, 1)$, which exists under the standard assumption that the distribution function F is continuous from the right, and then we put $y_n = G(x_n)$ for $n \geq 0$. Although this method is, in theory, universal, it is in many cases impractical since the (generalized) inverse function may not be available in a convenient form.

(ii) *Rejection method.* Suppose that F has a density f, i.e., $F(u) = \int_{-\infty}^{u} f(t) \, dt$ for $u \in \mathbb{R}$. Find a "nice" distribution G with density g such that $f(t) \leq cg(t)$ for all $t \in \mathbb{R}$ with a constant $c \geq 1$. Now generate two independent random samples, namely, x from the uniform distribution U and z from the distribution G. If $cx > f(z)/g(z)$, then reject z and try again with other x and z. This is repeated until finally $cx \leq f(z)/g(z)$, and then the random variate $y = z$ is the output. Note that

$$\text{Prob}(z \leq u \text{ and } z \text{ is accepted}) = \int_{-\infty}^{u} \frac{f(t)}{cg(t)} \, dG(t) = \int_{-\infty}^{u} \frac{f(t)}{cg(t)} g(t) \, dt$$

$$= \frac{1}{c} \int_{-\infty}^{u} f(t) \, dt = \frac{1}{c} F(u),$$

and, by taking $u \to \infty$, we see that

$$\text{Prob}(z \text{ is accepted}) = \frac{1}{c}.$$

Thus we obtain the conditional probability

$$\text{Prob}(z \leq u \mid z \text{ is accepted}) = \frac{c^{-1} F(u)}{c^{-1}} = F(u).$$

Consequently, the random variate y has the distribution function F. The constant c should be as close to 1 as possible so that the acceptance probability is large.

(iii) *Composition method.* We regard F as a mixture $F = \sum_{j=1}^{r} p_j F_j$ with distribution functions F_j on $\mathbb{R}$ and a discrete probability distribution $(p_1, \ldots, p_r)$ with $\sum_{j=1}^{r} p_j = 1$ and $p_j \geq 0$ for $1 \leq j \leq r$. Now we first sample j from the discrete distribution, and then y from the corresponding distribution F_j. The random variate y has the distribution function F. This method is often applied in the following form: Partition $\mathbb{R}$ into finitely many intervals $I_1, \ldots, I_r$ and let F_j be the distribution function with support I_j induced by F.

(iv) *Ratio-of-uniforms method* . Suppose that F has a density f, put $A = \{(u, v) \in \mathbb{R}^2 : 0 < u \leq f(v/u)^{1/2}\}$, and assume that A is contained in some compact interval $[0, a] \times [b_1, b_2]$. Now we generate two independent uniform random numbers x_1 and x_2, and we put $z_1 = ax_1$ and $z_2 = b_1 + (b_2 - b_1)x_2$. If $(z_1, z_2) \notin A$, then we try again with other x_1 and x_2. This is repeated until finally $(z_1, z_2) \in A$, and then the random variate $y = z_2/z_1$ is the output. It can be shown that y has the distribution function F (see [62, p. 195], [295, p. 66]).

There are quite a few other general techniques for transforming uniform PRN into nonuniform PRN, and there is a great abundance of methods tailored to special distributions such as normal distributions, beta distributions, gamma distributions, and so on. An encyclopedic account of methods for random variate generation is given in the book of Devroye [62].

We now discuss some typical statistical tests for the randomness of uniform PRN. Acceptable sequences of uniform PRN should pass a variety of such tests. Let $x_0, x_1, \ldots$ be a sequence of numbers in $\bar{I}$ to be tested for randomness and let N be a large integer; if the sequence is periodic, then it suffices to take $N \le \mathrm{per}(x_n)$.

A. *Uniformity test.* This is a goodness-of-fit test for the empirical distribution of an initial segment $x_0, x_1, \ldots, x_{N-1}$ of the sequence. The test is performed by calculating (or bounding) the discrepancy or the star discrepancy of $x_0, x_1, \ldots, x_{N-1}$. If $D_N^*(x_0, \ldots, x_{N-1})$ is taken as the test quantity, then this amounts to performing the two-sided Kolmogorov test in nonparametric statistics, which is a very well-studied procedure. For fixed N and random point sets $z_0, z_1, \ldots, z_{N-1} \in \bar{I}$, the distribution of $D_N^*(z_0, \ldots, z_{N-1})$ is known. Various formulas for $\mathrm{Prob}(D_N^*(z_0, \ldots, z_{N-1}) \le u)$, $0 \le u \le 1$, are given in [220, §5]. For random sequences $z_0, z_1, \ldots$ of numbers in $\bar{I}$, the star discrepancy $D_N^*(z_0, \ldots, z_{N-1})$ follows the Kolmogorov–Smirnov law

$$\lim_{N \to \infty} \mathrm{Prob}(N^{1/2} D_N^*(z_0, \ldots, z_{N-1}) \le u) = 1 - 2 \sum_{k=1}^{\infty} (-1)^{k+1} e^{-2k^2 u^2} \quad \text{for } u > 0.$$

Furthermore, we have the law of the iterated logarithm

$$(7.1) \qquad \overline{\lim_{N \to \infty}} \frac{(2N)^{1/2} D_N^*(z_0, \ldots, z_{N-1})}{(\log \log N)^{1/2}} = 1 \qquad \lambda^\infty\text{-a.e.,}$$

where λ is the Lebesgue measure on $\bar{I}$ (see Chung [41]). In a related test known as the *frequency test*, we partition $\bar{I}$ into finitely many subintervals, count the number of terms among $x_0, x_1, \ldots, x_{N-1}$ falling into the various subintervals, and perform a χ^2 test on these data.

B. *Gap test* . Let J be a fixed proper subinterval of $\bar{I}$. If, for some $n \ge 0$, we have $x_{n+j} \notin J$ for $0 \le j \le k-1$, but $x_{n+k} \in J$, then we refer to a *gap of length* k. These gap lengths are geometrically distributed with parameter $1 - \lambda_1(J)$. In the practical implementation of the gap test, we choose a positive integer h and count the number of gaps of lengths $0, 1, \ldots, h-1$, and $\ge h$ until a large total number of gaps is reached. Then we apply a χ^2 test to these data.

C. *Run test.* A segment of the sequence satisfying $x_n < x_{n+1} < \cdots < x_{n+k-1}$, but $x_{n-1} \ge x_n$ and $x_{n+k-1} \ge x_{n+k}$, is called a *run-up of length* k. We count the number of runs-up of lengths $1, 2, \ldots, h$, and $\ge h + 1$ in $x_0, x_1, \ldots, x_{N-1}$.

Since adjacent runs are not independent, we cannot use a straightforward χ^2 test for these data. A more complicated statistic given in [154, §3.3.2] must be computed. A similar test can be performed for runs-down.

D. *Permutation test.* We choose an integer $s \geq 2$ and consider the s-tuples $(x_n, x_{n+1}, \ldots, x_{n+s-1})$, $n = 0, 1, \ldots, N-1$. There are $s!$ possible relative orderings among the entries of such an s-tuple, and these orderings are equiprobable. We determine the frequency of each ordering and apply a χ^2 test to these data, using the probability $1/s!$ for each ordering. Alternatively, we may consider the maximal deviation of these frequencies from the expected number of occurrences.

E. *Serial correlation.* This is a rather weak test for the interdependence between x_n and x_{n+h}, where $h \geq 1$ is a given integer. The test is performed by calculating the *serial correlation coefficient*

$$\sigma_N^{(h)} = \frac{M_N(x_n x_{n+h}) - M_N(x_n)^2}{M_N(x_n^2) - M_N(x_n)^2},$$

where $M_N(u_n) = N^{-1} \sum_{n=0}^{N-1} u_n$ is the mean value of $u_0, u_1, \ldots, u_{N-1}$ and where we assume that the denominator is nonzero. If x_n and x_{n+h} are almost independent, then $|\sigma_N^{(h)}|$ is very small. It is a deficiency of this test that the converse does not necessarily hold.

F. *Serial test.* This is a more severe test for the statistical independence of successive PRN and is a multidimensional version of the uniformity test in A. The serial test can also be viewed as a way of measuring the deviation from the property of complete uniform distribution in Definition 7.1. It is therefore closely connected with Knuth's Definition R1 of randomness, stated in §7.1. For a fixed dimension $s \geq 2$, put

$$\mathbf{x}_n = (x_n, x_{n+1}, \ldots, x_{n+s-1}) \in \bar{I}^s \quad \text{for } n = 0, 1, \cdots, N-1.$$

Then consider the discrepancy

$$(7.2) \qquad\qquad D_N^{(s)} := D_N(\mathbf{x}_0, \ldots, \mathbf{x}_{N-1})$$

or the star discrepancy

$$(7.3) \qquad\qquad D_N^{*(s)} := D_N^*(\mathbf{x}_0, \ldots, \mathbf{x}_{N-1}).$$

For fixed N and random point sets $\mathbf{z}_0, \mathbf{z}_1, \ldots, \mathbf{z}_{N-1} \in \bar{I}^s$, we have the following result of Kiefer [152] on the distribution of the star discrepancy: For every $\varepsilon > 0$, there exists a constant $c > 0$ depending only on ε and s such that

$$\text{Prob}(N^{1/2} D_N^*(\mathbf{z}_0, \ldots, \mathbf{z}_{N-1}) \leq u) \geq 1 - ce^{-(2-\varepsilon)u^2} \quad \text{for all } u \geq 0.$$

For random sequences $\mathbf{z}_0, \mathbf{z}_1, \ldots$ of points in $\bar{I}^s$, the behavior of $D_N^*(\mathbf{z}_0, \ldots, \mathbf{z}_{N-1})$ is governed by the s-dimensional version of the law of the iterated logarithm in (7.1), namely,

$$(7.4) \qquad\qquad \varlimsup_{N \to \infty} \frac{(2N)^{1/2} D_N^*(\mathbf{z}_0, \ldots, \mathbf{z}_{N-1})}{(\log \log N)^{1/2}} = 1 \quad \lambda^\infty\text{-a.e.,}$$

where λ is now the Lebesgue measure on $\bar{I}^s$ (see [152]). This law serves as a benchmark for the orders of magnitude of $D_N^{(s)}$ and $D_N^{*(s)}$. The s-dimensional serial test has an added significance for numerical analysis, since upper bounds on $D_N^{*(s)}$ yield error bounds for quasi-Monte Carlo integrations using the nodes $\mathbf{x}_0, \ldots, \mathbf{x}_{N-1}$ (compare with §2.2). Moreover, further quantities of statistical relevance can be bounded in terms of $D_N^{*(s)}$. For instance, by the method in Niederreiter [233], we obtain

$$|\sigma_N^{(h)}| < 73 D_N^{*(h+1)}$$

for the serial correlation coefficient $\sigma_N^{(h)}$. Some authors have also considered the distribution of the nonoverlapping s-tuples $\mathbf{x}_{ns} = (x_{ns}, x_{ns+1}, \ldots, x_{ns+s-1}) \in \bar{I}^s$, $n = 0, 1, \ldots$. However, it should be noted that usually this does not make any difference, for, in the standard case where $x_0, x_1, \ldots$ is periodic and $N = \mathrm{per}(x_n)$, the point sets $\mathbf{x}_0, \mathbf{x}_1, \ldots, \mathbf{x}_{N-1}$ and $\mathbf{x}_0, \mathbf{x}_s, \ldots, \mathbf{x}_{(N-1)s}$ are identical whenever $\gcd(s, N) = 1$, since then the indices ns, $n = 0, 1, \ldots, N-1$, run modulo N through the set $\{0, 1, \ldots, N-1\}$. There is also an s-dimensional *frequency test*, which operates like the frequency test mentioned under A, namely, by starting from a partition of $\bar{I}^s$ into finitely many subintervals, counting the number of terms among $\mathbf{x}_0, \mathbf{x}_1, \ldots, \mathbf{x}_{N-1}$ falling into the various subintervals, and applying a χ^2 test to these data.

G. *Spectral test.* This test is applied to periodic sequences $x_0, x_1, \ldots$, where all x_n are rationals with common denominator M. If $\mathrm{per}(x_n) = T$, then, for $\mathbf{h} = (h_1, \ldots, h_s) \in \mathbb{Z}^s$, we define the exponential sums

$$X(\mathbf{h}) = \frac{1}{T} \sum_{n=0}^{T-1} e\left(\sum_{i=1}^{s} h_i x_{n+i-1}\right).$$

Ideally, we should have $X(\mathbf{h}) = 1$ if $\mathbf{h} \equiv \mathbf{0} \bmod M$ and $X(\mathbf{h}) = 0$ otherwise. The deviation from this behavior is a measure for the nonrandomness of the given sequence of PRN. The difficulty here is to find a convincing quantitative formulation of this idea. Coveyou and MacPherson [44] used an intuitive analogy with the theory of harmonic oscillation; in the case of linear congruential PRN, this proposal has a nice geometric interpretation (see §7.3).

7.3. Classical generators.

A classical and still very popular method for the generation of uniform PRN is the *linear congruential method* introduced by Lehmer [187]. As the parameters in this method, we choose a large positive integer M, an integer a with $1 \le a < M$ and $\gcd(a, M) = 1$, and an integer $c \in Z_M = \{0, 1, \ldots, M-1\}$. Then we select an initial value $y_0 \in Z_M$ and generate a sequence $y_0, y_1, \ldots \in Z_M$ by the recursion

$$(7.5) \qquad\qquad y_{n+1} \equiv a y_n + c \bmod M \qquad \text{for } n = 0, 1, \ldots .$$

From this sequence, we derive the *linear congruential pseudorandom numbers*

$$(7.6) \qquad x_n = \frac{y_n}{M} \in I = [0,1) \quad \text{for } n = 0, 1, \dots.$$

In this context, M is referred to as the *modulus* and a as the *multiplier*. The choice of the modulus is customarily accorded with the word length of the machine, typical values being $M = 2^{32}$ or the Mersenne prime $M = 2^{31} - 1$. For high-precision calculations, larger values such as $M = 2^{48}$ have also been used. A common distinction is between the *homogeneous case* where $c = 0$, also called the *multiplicative congruential method*, and the *inhomogeneous case* where $c \neq 0$, also called the *mixed congruential method*. Since the linear congruential method has been extensively treated in book form (see, e.g., [154], [295]), we limit our discussion to those aspects that are related to other material in these lecture notes.

It is clear from (7.5) and (7.6) that the sequences $x_0, x_1, \dots$ and $y_0, y_1, \dots$ are both periodic and that $\text{per}(x_n) = \text{per}(y_n) \leq M$. An elementary number-theoretic argument shows that $\text{per}(x_n) = M$ if and only if $\gcd(c, M) = 1$, $a \equiv 1 \bmod p$ for every prime p dividing M, and $a \equiv 1 \bmod 4$ whenever 4 divides M (see [154, §3.2.1]). The following are three standard cases that are considered in practical implementations of the linear congruential method (in all three cases $\text{per}(x_n)$ is reasonably close to M):

(i) M is prime, a is a primitive root modulo M (i.e., the multiplicative order of a modulo M is $M - 1$), $c = 0$, and $y_0 \neq 0$. Note that (7.5) implies that $y_n \equiv a^n y_0 \bmod M$ for $n = 0, 1, \dots$, and so $\text{per}(x_n) = M - 1$.

(ii) M is a power of 2, $a \equiv 5 \bmod 8$, and c is odd. From the above criterion, we get $\text{per}(x_n) = M$.

(iii) M is a power of 2, $a \equiv 5 \bmod 8$, $c = 0$, and y_0 is odd. Then, again, $y_n \equiv a^n y_0 \bmod M$ for $n = 0, 1, \dots$, and so $\text{per}(x_n)$ equals the multiplicative order of a modulo M, which yields $\text{per}(x_n) = M/4$ by an elementary argument (see [295, Thm. 2.2]).

The performance of linear congruential PRN under the uniformity test is easy to describe in the above three cases if we apply the test to the full period. Put $T = \text{per}(x_n)$ and first consider case (ii). Then the point set $x_0, x_1, \dots, x_{T-1}$ is equal to the set of rationals in I with denominator M, and so $D_T^*(x_0, \dots, x_{T-1}) = 1/M$ by Theorem 2.6. In case (i) the point set $x_0, x_1, \dots, x_{T-1}$ is equal to the equidistant point set $1/M, 2/M, \dots, (M-1)/M$, and so $D_T^*(x_0, \dots, x_{T-1}) = 1/M$ by Theorem 2.6. In case (iii), the point set $x_0, x_1, \dots, x_{T-1}$ is equal to the set of all rationals in I of the form b/M with an integer $b \equiv y_0 \bmod 4$, and so $D_T^*(x_0, \dots, x_{T-1}) = 3/M$ by Theorem 2.6. Thus, in all three cases, we have $D_T^*(x_0, \dots, x_{T-1}) = O(M^{-1})$ with an absolute implied constant. The situation is less trivial if we consider the uniformity test for parts of the period, i.e., for $1 \leq N < T$. Results of Niederreiter [221], [222] show that, in our three cases, we have

$$D_N^*(x_0, \dots, x_{N-1}) = O\left(N^{-1}M^{1/2}(\log M)^2\right) \quad \text{for } 1 \leq N < T$$

with an absolute implied constant and that this bound is, in general, the best possible, apart from the logarithmic factor.

Historically, the distribution of the s-tuples $\mathbf{x}_n = (x_n, x_{n+1}, \dots, x_{n+s-1}) \in I^s$, $n = 0, 1, \dots$, with $s \geq 2$ was first considered in the context of stochastic models. Franklin [108] studied the dynamics of the recursion $x_{n+1} = \{ax_n + \theta\}$, $n = 0, 1, \dots$, with an integer $a > 1$, a fixed $\theta \in I$, and a random initial value $x_0 \in I$, as well as the dynamics of the associated sequence $\mathbf{x}_0, \mathbf{x}_1, \dots$ of s-tuples. Although the sequence $\mathbf{x}_0, \mathbf{x}_1, \dots$ can never be uniformly distributed in $\bar{I}^s$, Franklin could prove that, for almost all $x_0 \in I$ (in the sense of Lebesgue measure), the sequence is "asymptotically" uniformly distributed in $\bar{I}^s$ as the integer a tends to infinity. For the case where $\theta = 0$, corresponding to the multiplicative congruential method, a quantitative refinement was established by Ermakov [91]. We refer also to [225, §11] for a brief discussion of these results.

The more important question of the performance of a concrete sequence $x_0, x_1, \dots$ of linear congruential PRN under the s-dimensional serial test was explored much later. To arrive at the crucial observation in a more leisurely way, we consider, for now, only case (i). Then $y_n \equiv a^n y_0 \bmod M$ for all $n \geq 0$, and so, for $\mathbf{y}_n = (y_n, y_{n+1}, \dots, y_{n+s-1}) \in Z_M^s$, we obtain

$$\mathbf{y}_n \equiv a^n y_0 \mathbf{g} \bmod M \quad \text{for } n \geq 0,$$

where $\mathbf{g} = (1, a, a^2, \dots, a^{s-1}) \in \mathbb{Z}^s$. Since a is a primitive root modulo M, $\gcd(y_0, M) = 1$, and $T = \operatorname{per}(x_n) = M - 1$, the integers $a^n y_0$, $n = 0, 1, \dots$, $T - 1$, run modulo M through the set $\{1, 2, \dots, M - 1\}$. Now $\mathbf{x}_n = M^{-1}\mathbf{y}_n$ for $n \geq 0$ by (7.6), and so the point set $\mathbf{x}_0, \mathbf{x}_1, \dots, \mathbf{x}_{T-1}$ is equal to the point set consisting of the fractional parts $\{(n/M)\mathbf{g}\}$, $n = 1, 2, \dots, M - 1$. This is a point set of the type (5.1), except that the point corresponding to $n = 0$ is missing (which is, of course, insignificant for large M). Therefore, by the theory developed in §5.1, the distribution behavior of the point set $\mathbf{x}_0, \mathbf{x}_1, \dots, \mathbf{x}_{T-1}$, and thus the performance of the full period of the sequence $x_0, x_1, \dots$ under the s-dimensional serial test, is governed by the quantities measuring the suitability of $\mathbf{g}$ as a good lattice point $\bmod M$. In particular, for the discrepancy $D_T^{(s)}$ of the point set $\mathbf{x}_0, \mathbf{x}_1, \dots, \mathbf{x}_{T-1}$, we obtain the following bound, which is a slight variant of a result of Niederreiter [223], [224].

THEOREM 7.3. *In case (i) of the linear congruential method, we have*

$$D_T^{(s)} \leq \frac{s+1}{M-1} + \frac{M}{M-1} R_1(\mathbf{g}, M) \quad \text{for every } s \geq 2,$$

where $R_1(\mathbf{g}, M)$ is defined by (5.9) and where $\mathbf{g} = (1, a, a^2, \dots, a^{s-1}) \in \mathbb{Z}^s$.

Proof. Let P be the point set consisting of $\{(n/M)\mathbf{g}\}$, $n = 0, 1, \dots, M - 1$, and let P^* be obtained from P by deleting $\mathbf{0}$. For every $J \in \mathcal{J}$ (see Definition 2.2), we have $A(J; P^*) = A(J; P) - \varepsilon(J)$ with $\varepsilon(J) = 0$ or 1, and so

$$|A(J; P^*) - (M-1)\lambda_s(J)| = |A(J; P) - \varepsilon(J) - M\lambda_s(J) + \lambda_s(J)|$$
$$\leq MD_M(P) + |\lambda_s(J) - \varepsilon(J)| \leq MD_M(P) + 1.$$

Consequently,

$$TD_T^{(s)} = (M-1)D_{M-1}(P^*) \leq MD_M(P) + 1.$$

We can bound $D_M(P)$ by Theorem 5.6, and this yields

$$TD_T^{(s)} \leq M\left(1 - \left(1 - \frac{1}{M}\right)^s + R_1(\mathbf{g}, M)\right) + 1 \leq s + 1 + MR_1(\mathbf{g}, M). \qquad \square$$

We may use the bound $R_1(\mathbf{g}, M) \leq \frac{1}{2}R(\mathbf{g}, M)$ (see the proof of Theorem 5.6), and then there arises the problem of the existence of a primitive root a modulo the prime M for which $R((1, a, a^2, \ldots, a^{s-1}), M)$ is small. This problem can be treated by the averaging technique in the proof of Theorem 5.18, although now the mean value is just taken over the primitive roots modulo M. This leads to the following theorem of Niederreiter [224].

THEOREM 7.4. *In case* (i) *of the linear congruential method, we have, for every* $s \geq 2$,

$$D_T^{(s)} = O\left(M^{-1}(\log M)^s \log\log(M+1)\right)$$

for an average multiplier a, *where the implied constant depends only on* s.

In analogy with the theory of good lattice points, the quality of a multiplier can also be assessed by an appropriate figure of merit. The following is a specialization of Definition 5.7.

DEFINITION 7.5. For every dimension $s \geq 2$ and any integers $M \geq 2$ and a, define the *figure of merit* $\rho^{(s)}(a, M)$ by $\rho^{(s)}(a, M) = \rho(\mathbf{g}, M)$ with $\mathbf{g} = (1, a, a^2, \ldots, a^{s-1}) \in \mathbb{Z}^s$.

In view of Theorem 7.3 and (5.11), the discrepancy $D_T^{(s)}$ can be bounded in terms of $\rho^{(s)}(a, M)$ in case (i) of the linear congruential method. For this case, the following result concerning large figures of merit was shown by Niederreiter [224]: For every $s \geq 2$ and every prime M, there exists a primitive root a modulo M with

$$(7.7) \qquad \rho^{(s)}(a, M) > \frac{c_s M}{(\log M)^{s-1} \log\log(M+1)},$$

where the constant $c_s > 0$ depends only on s.

If $s = 2$, then the quantities considered above, such as $\rho^{(s)}(a, M)$, are connected with continued fractions (compare with §5.2). In case (i), the favorable multipliers a for the two-dimensional serial test are the primitive roots a modulo M for which the number $K(a/M)$ introduced in Definition 5.16 is small. This then leads to the consideration of a quantity analogous to that in (5.38), namely,

$$Q_M = \min K\left(\frac{a}{M}\right) \qquad \text{for primes } M,$$

where the minimum is extended over all primitive roots a modulo M. In particular, there is the open problem of whether there exists an absolute constant C such that $Q_M \leq C$ for all primes M. From Theorem 5.17 and (7.7) with $s = 2$, we obtain $Q_M = O\big((\log M) \log \log(M + 1)\big)$ with an absolute implied constant.

Let us return to the crucial observation in the treatment of case (i), above, namely, that the point set $\mathbf{x}_0, \mathbf{x}_1, \ldots, \mathbf{x}_{T-1} \in I^s$ with $T = \mathrm{per}(x_n)$ is basically the same as a point set (5.1) with a suitable $\mathbf{g} \in \mathbb{Z}^s$. This brings us directly to the *lattice structure* of linear congruential PRN, i.e., to the phenomenon that the points $\mathbf{x}_n = (x_n, x_{n+1}, \ldots, x_{n+s-1})$ obtained from a sequence $x_0, x_1, \ldots$ of linear congruential PRN are bound to form a regular lattice pattern. We refer to §5.3 for the basics of the theory of lattices in $\mathbb{R}^s$. For $s \geq 2$, put $X_s = \{\mathbf{x}_0, \mathbf{x}_1, \ldots, \mathbf{x}_{T-1}\}$, where, again, $T = \mathrm{per}(x_n)$. Since the points $\mathbf{x}_n$, $0 \leq n \leq T - 1$, are distinct, X_s is the same as the point set consisting of $\mathbf{x}_0, \mathbf{x}_1, \ldots, \mathbf{x}_{T-1}$. For an integer $N \geq 1$ and a multiplier a, let $L_s(a, N)$ be the s-dimensional lattice with lattice basis

$$\mathbf{b}_1 = \frac{1}{N}(1, a, a^2, \ldots, a^{s-1}),$$
$$\mathbf{b}_i = \mathbf{e}_i \quad \text{for } 2 \leq i \leq s,$$

where $\mathbf{e}_i$ is the ith vector in the standard ordered basis of $\mathbb{R}^s$. Note that $L_s(a, N)$ contains $\mathbb{Z}^s$ and is thus an integration lattice in the sense of §5.3. The following result describes the lattice structure in the three standard cases of the linear congruential method.

THEOREM 7.6. *For every $s \geq 2$, we have*

$$X_s = L_s(a, M) \cap (0, 1)^s \qquad \text{in case (i)},$$
$$X_s = \big(\mathbf{x}_0 + L_s(a, M)\big) \cap I^s \qquad \text{in case (ii)},$$
$$X_s = \big(\mathbf{x}_0 + L_s\big(a, \frac{M}{4}\big)\big) \cap I^s \qquad \text{in case (iii)}.$$

Proof. In case (i), we have already seen that $X_s \subseteq L_s(a, M) \cap I^s$, and, since no $\mathbf{x}_n$ has a zero coordinate, we get $X_s \subseteq L_s(a, M) \cap (0, 1)^s$. On the other hand, $L_s(a, M)$ has determinant $1/M$, and so Theorem 5.30 shows that $\mathrm{card}(L_s(a, M) \cap I^s) = M$. Thus $\mathrm{card}(L_s(a, M) \cap (0, 1)^s) \leq M - 1$; hence $X_s = L_s(a, M) \cap (0, 1)^s$ since $\mathrm{card}(X_s) = M - 1$.

In general, we note that if, for fixed $n \geq 0$ we use induction on i and the recursion (7.5), we then obtain

$$(7.8) \qquad y_{n+i} - y_i \equiv a^i(y_n - y_0) \bmod M \quad \text{for } i = 0, 1, \ldots.$$

Therefore

$$(7.9) \quad \mathbf{x}_n - \mathbf{x}_0 \equiv (y_n - y_0)\frac{1}{M}(1, a, a^2, \ldots, a^{s-1}) \bmod \mathbb{Z}^s \quad \text{for all } n \geq 0,$$

and so always $X_s \subseteq (\mathbf{x}_0 + L_s(a, M)) \cap I^s$. In case (ii), both sets have cardinality M, and so they are equal. In case (iii), we have $y_n \equiv y_0 \bmod 4$ for all $n > 0$:

hence (7.9) can be written as

$$\mathbf{x}_n - \mathbf{x}_0 \equiv \frac{y_n - y_0}{4} \cdot \frac{1}{M/4}(1, a, a^2, \dots, a^{s-1}) \bmod \mathbb{Z}^s \qquad \text{for all } n \geq 0.$$

Thus $X_s \subseteq (\mathbf{x}_0 + L_s(a, \frac{M}{4})) \cap I^s$, and, since both sets have cardinality $M/4$, they are equal. $\square$

In the above proof, we have noted that X_s is always contained in $(\mathbf{x}_0 + L_s(a, M)) \cap I^s$. Thus all points $\mathbf{x}_n$ lie on a *grid*, i.e., a shifted lattice, with the determinant of the lattice being $1/M$. In case (iii), we can even get a determinant $4/M$. At any rate, the determinant is independent of s; we get what is called a "coarse" lattice structure. Theorem 7.6 can be used to give bounds on the discrepancy $D_T^{(s)}$ of the point set X_s, which are analogous to the bound in Theorem 7.3 (compare with Niederreiter [224], [234] for such bounds).

The lattice structure of linear congruential PRN provides a basis for *lattice tests* that can be applied to these PRN. Strictly speaking, "lattice tests" is a misnomer, since these are not statistical tests, but rather methods of checking structural properties of linear congruential PRN. Typical examples are the following (see [154, §3.3.4], [295, Chap. 2] for a fuller description):

L1. *Number of hyperplanes.* Determine the minimum number of parallel hyperplanes on which all points $\mathbf{x}_n$ lie. This number should be as large as possible.

L2. *Distance between hyperplanes.* Determine the maximum distance between adjacent hyperplanes, taken over all families of parallel hyperplanes with the property that they contain all points $\mathbf{x}_n$. This distance should be as small as possible. In certain cases, such as case (ii), this can be viewed as a geometric version of the spectral test (see test G in §7.2).

L3. *Basis test.* Consider the lattice $L_s(a, M)$ in cases (i) and (ii) and the lattice $L_s(a, M/4)$ in case (iii). Determine a "reduced" lattice basis of this lattice, such as a Minkowski-reduced lattice basis, and calculate the ratio of the lengths of the shortest and the longest basis vector. This ratio should be as close to 1 as possible.

Below, we list some *deficiencies of the linear congruential method*, which are of relevance when comparing this method with other methods to be discussed later:

(a) The modulus M, and therefore $\mathrm{per}(x_n)$, are bounded in terms of the word length of the machine. For instance, with a 32-bit processor we have $\mathrm{per}(x_n) \leq M \leq 2^{32}$, unless we are willing to use costly multiple-precision arithmetic.

(b) There is too much regularity in sequences of linear congruential PRN, which stems from the simple nature of the generation algorithm. For instance, in case (i), we have Theorem 7.4, which states that $D_{M-1}^{(s)} = O(M^{-1}(\log M)^s \log\log(M+1))$ for most choices of multipliers. Compare this with the law of the iterated logarithm in (7.4), according to which the discrepancy of $M - 1$ random points in $\bar{I}^s$ should have an order of magnitude around $M^{-1/2}$. Also, some long-range correlations in sequences of linear congruential PRN have recently been discovered; we mention the papers of de Matteis and Pagnutti [58], Eichenauer-Herrmann and Grothe [84], and Percus and Percus [281]. These regularities can create misleading results in simulations where "true randomness" is essential.

(c) The coarse lattice structure of linear congruential PRN is a strong element of nonrandomness and can be disruptive in simulations; see, e.g., Eichenauer and Lehn [78] and Ripley [295, pp. 55–59] for illustrations.

The idea of employing higher-order linear recursions for pseudorandom number generation is used in the *multiple-recursive method*. Let p be a large prime, let $k \geq 2$ be an integer that serves as the order of the linear recursion, and choose $a_0, \ldots, a_{k-1} \in Z_p$ with $a_0 \neq 0$. Then we generate a sequence $y_0, y_1, \ldots \in Z_p$ by the recursion

$$(7.10) \qquad y_{n+k} \equiv \sum_{l=0}^{k-1} a_l y_{n+l} \bmod p \qquad \text{for } n = 0, 1, \ldots,$$

where $y_0, \ldots, y_{k-1}$ are initial values that are not all zero. We obtain *multiple-recursive pseudorandom numbers* by the normalization

$$x_n = \frac{y_n}{p} \in I \qquad \text{for } n = 0, 1, \ldots.$$

The sequences $x_0, x_1, \ldots$ and $y_0, y_1, \ldots$ are both periodic and $\mathrm{per}(x_n) = \mathrm{per}(y_n)$. The k-tuples $(y_n, y_{n+1}, \ldots, y_{n+k-1}) \in Z_p^k$, $n = 0, 1, \ldots$, are all $\neq \mathbf{0}$ and cannot be repeated within the period. Therefore $\mathrm{per}(y_n) \leq p^k - 1$. The upper bound $p^k - 1$ can be achieved as follows. View $a_0, \ldots, a_{k-1}$ as elements of the finite field F_p of order p and let

$$f(x) = x^k - \sum_{l=0}^{k-1} a_l x^l \in F_p[x]$$

be the *characteristic polynomial* of the recursion (7.10). Now assume that f is a primitive polynomial over F_p in the sense of Definition A.1 in Appendix A. Then $\mathrm{per}(y_n) = p^k - 1$, and so $T = \mathrm{per}(x_n) = p^k - 1$.

Let $x_0, x_1, \ldots$ be a sequence of multiple-recursive PRN with primitive characteristic polynomial. Then, for every dimension $s \leq k$, the distribution of the points $\mathbf{x}_n = (x_n, x_{n+1}, \ldots, x_{n+s-1}) \in I^s$, $0 \leq n \leq T - 1$, or, equivalently, of the points $\mathbf{y}_n = (y_n, y_{n+1}, \ldots, y_{n+s-1}) \in Z_p^s$, $0 \leq n \leq T - 1$, can be described explicitly. For $\mathbf{c} \in Z_p^s$, let $A(\mathbf{c})$ be the number of integers n with $0 \leq n \leq T - 1$ and $\mathbf{y}_n = \mathbf{c}$. Then we have

$$(7.11) \qquad A(\mathbf{c}) = \begin{cases} p^{k-s} & \text{if } \mathbf{c} \neq \mathbf{0}, \\ p^{k-s} - 1 & \text{if } \mathbf{c} = \mathbf{0}. \end{cases}$$

For the proof, we observe that, since $T = p^k - 1$, the k-tuples $(y_n, y_{n+1}, \ldots, y_{n+k-1})$, $0 \leq n \leq T - 1$, run exactly through all nonzero points in Z_p^k. Therefore $A(\mathbf{c})$ is equal to the number of nonzero $\mathbf{b} \in Z_p^k$ that have $\mathbf{c}$

as the s-tuple of their first s coordinates. For $\mathbf{c} \neq \mathbf{0}$, we can have all possible combinations of elements of Z_p in the remaining $k - s$ coordinates of $\mathbf{b}$; hence $A(\mathbf{c}) = p^{k-s}$. For $\mathbf{c} = \mathbf{0}$, we must exclude the possibility that all remaining $k - s$ coordinates of $\mathbf{b}$ are 0; hence $A(\mathbf{c}) = p^{k-s} - 1$.

Formula (7.11) establishes an almost perfect equidistribution of the points $\mathbf{y}_n$, and so of the points $\mathbf{x}_n$. Nevertheless, multiple-recursive PRN have a serious weakness. Note that the coordinates of all points $\mathbf{x}_n$ are rationals with denominator p. Therefore the star discrepancy $D_N^{*(s)} = D_N^*(\mathbf{x}_0, \ldots, \mathbf{x}_{N-1})$ satisfies

$$D_N^{*(s)} \geq 1 - \left(1 - \frac{1}{p}\right)^s \geq \frac{1}{p} \quad \text{for all } s \geq 1 \text{ and } N \geq 1$$

by Theorem 3.14. In particular, with $N = T = p^k - 1$, we obtain that $D_T^{*(s)}$ is at least of the order of magnitude $T^{-1/k}$, which is too large for $k \geq 3$ (compare with (7.4)). The underlying reason for this deficiency is, of course, that compared to the least period length the discretization afforded by multiple-recursive PRN is too coarse.

Notes.

Expository accounts of random and pseudorandom number generation are given in the books of Bratley, Fox, and Schrage [34], Dagpunar [50], Deák [53], Devroye [62], Kalos and Whitlock [150], Knuth [154], and Ripley [295], and in the recent survey articles of Anderson [7], James [146], L'Ecuyer [186], and Niederreiter [257]. Refinements of Theorem 7.2 were obtained by Goldstern [114], Niederreiter and Tichy [276], and Tichy [350]. Interesting work on complete uniform distribution of sequences of digits was recently done by Flajolet, Kirschenhofer, and Tichy [105], [106] and Kirschenhofer and Tichy [153], among others. Further information on the complexity-theoretic approach to randomness can be found in Chaitin [40], Kolmogorov and Uspenskii [157], Schnorr [304], and Uspenskii, Semenov, and Shen' [355]. See Kranakis [162] for methods of generating cryptographically strong pseudorandom bit strings.

Further results on the uniformity test and the serial test for linear congruential PRN, also for parts of the period, can be found in Levin [189], Niederreiter [225], [231], [234], and Shparlinskii [313]. Detailed investigations of the two-dimensional serial test for the full period were carried out by Dieter [63] and Niederreiter [224]. Exact calculations of the discrepancy of linear congruential PRN were discussed by Bhavsar et al. [27] in the one-dimensional case, and by Afflerbach and Weilbächer [5] in the multidimensional case. Further existence theorems for large figures of merit are shown in Larcher and Niederreiter [179] and Niederreiter [224]; see also Larcher [171] for a related result. Various problems on figures of merit and on the discrepancies $D_T^{(s)}$ for linear congruential PRN are posed in Niederreiter [233]. Fishman and Moore [104] performed an exhaustive search for good multipliers with the prime modulus $M = 2^{31} - 1$, whereas Fishman [103] undertook an exhaustive search with the modulus $M = 2^{32}$ and a partial search with $M = 2^{48}$. A systematic search algorithm for optimal multipliers with respect to the two-dimensional serial test was developed by Borosh and

Niederreiter [30], and a different algorithm for this purpose is due to Denzer and Ecker [60]. Applications of linear congruential and other PRN to quasi-Monte Carlo integration were considered by Niederreiter [237].

The lattice structure of linear congruential PRN was noted by Marsaglia [204], and detailed investigations of the lattice structure were later done by Beyer [25], Beyer, Roof, and Williamson [26], Marsaglia [205], and Ripley [294]. The formulation of Theorem 7.6 stems from [294]. The proof of Theorem 7.6 shows that the formula for case (ii) holds whenever $\mathrm{per}(x_n) = M$. Sometimes the structure of X_s cannot be described by a single grid, and then a union of grids is needed. A recent paper on the lattice structure is Afflerbach [2]. In the implementation of lattice tests, an algorithm of Dieter [64] for calculating a shortest nonzero vector in a lattice is often useful. See Afflerbach and Grothe [3] and Eichenauer-Herrmann and Grothe [85] for recent work on lattice tests.

The uniformity test and the serial test for multiple-recursive PRN were studied by Niederreiter [222], [227] and Shparlinskii [312], and the lattice structure was investigated by Dieter [65] and Grube [119]. Interesting methods for pseudorandom number generation that are not discussed in these lecture notes include the combining of generators (see, e.g., Collings [43], L'Ecuyer [185], and Wichmann and Hill [358], [359]), shuffling techniques (see, e.g., MacLaren and Marsaglia [202]), and the use of cellular automata (see, e.g., Wolfram [360]).

CHAPTER 8

Nonlinear Congruential
Pseudorandom Numbers

To overcome some of the deficiencies of the linear congruential method, such as the coarse lattice structure, new methods for the generation of uniform PRN have recently been designed and analyzed. The basic idea is to consider recursions other than the linear recursion that is used for the generation of linear congruential PRN. The result is that, with suitable nonlinear recursions, the coarse lattice structure can be broken up.

The general nonlinear congruential method is described in §8.1, and the resulting PRN are analyzed by their lattice structure and by the serial test. In this section, we also briefly discuss the quadratic congruential method, which has a somewhat longer history than the general nonlinear congruential method. A particularly promising type of nonlinear congruential method is the inversive congruential method treated in §8.2. Here the nonlinearity is achieved by using multiplicative inversion in modular arithmetic. Inversive congruential PRN with a prime modulus are, in a sense, optimal with regard to the lack of a lattice structure, and they behave much better under the serial test than linear congruential PRN.

8.1. The general nonlinear congruential method.

The general framework for the methods to be discussed in this chapter is the following. Choose a large positive integer M, called the *modulus*, and define a *congruential generator* modulo M to be a sequence $y_0, y_1, \ldots$ of elements of $Z_M = \{0, 1, \ldots, M - 1\}$, that is generated by a congruential recursion (of arbitrary order and with an arbitrary feedback function). A very special instance of this is the sequence generated by the recursion (7.5) in the linear congruential method. From a congruential generator modulo M, we derive a sequence $x_0, x_1, \ldots$ of uniform PRN by the normalization $x_n = y_n/M$ for $n = 0, 1, \ldots$.

In the general *first-order congruential method*, the congruential generator modulo M is obtained by an arbitrary first-order (or one-step) recursion

$$(8.1) \qquad y_{n+1} \equiv f(y_n) \bmod M \qquad \text{for } n = 0, 1, \ldots,$$

where f is an integer-valued function on Z_M. In practice, f and the initial value y_0 are chosen in such a way that the sequence $y_0, y_1, \ldots$ is (purely) periodic and $\mathrm{per}(y_n)$ is large. We clearly have $\mathrm{per}(x_n) = \mathrm{per}(y_n) \leq M$. We can always achieve $\text{per}(y_n) = M$ by starting from a periodic sequence $y_0, y_1, \ldots$ with $\text{per}(y_n) = M$ and $\{y_0, y_1, \ldots, y_{M-1}\} = Z_M$ and defining $f(y_n) = y_{n+1}$ for $0 \leq n \leq M - 1$. In practical terms, however, this particular example is useless, since we want a function f that is computable without the prior knowledge of the sequence $y_0, y_1, \ldots$. Among first-order congruential methods, we can distinguish the linear congruential method and *nonlinear congruential methods*, which are all remaining methods. As in the linear congruential method, the most convenient moduli for first-order congruential methods are primes and powers of 2.

Now let M be a prime modulus and let us write $M = p$. In this case, we can identify Z_M with the finite field F_p of order p. Consider a periodic sequence $y_0, y_1, \ldots$ of elements of F_p with $\text{per}(y_n) = p$. Then the map $n \in F_p \mapsto y_n \in F_p$, like any self-map of a finite field, can be represented by a uniquely determined polynomial $g \in F_p[x]$ with $d := \deg(g) < p$. In other words, we have

$$(8.2) \qquad\qquad y_n = g(n) \in F_p \quad \text{for } n = 0, 1, \ldots,$$

where n is also viewed as an element of F_p. If $\{y_0, y_1, \ldots, y_{p-1}\} = F_p$, then g is a *permutation polynomial* of F_p, i.e., a polynomial over F_p with $\{g(0), g(1), \ldots, g(p-1)\} = F_p$. Conversely, if the sequence $y_0, y_1, \ldots$ is given by (8.2) with a permutation polynomial g of F_p, then the sequence is periodic with $\text{per}(y_n) = p$ and $\{y_0, y_1, \ldots, y_{p-1}\} = F_p$. We now restrict the attention to this case. Note that the sequence $y_0, y_1, \ldots$ can also be generated by (8.1) with a suitable f, as was shown in the previous paragraph. The degree d of the polynomial g plays an important role in the theory. Since g is a permutation polynomial of F_p, we must have $d \geq 1$. If $d = 1$, then the sequence $y_0, y_1, \ldots$ can be generated by (8.1) with f being a monic linear polynomial, and so we get the linear congruential method with modulus p and multiplier $a = 1$ (by the way, this is a very bad choice for the multiplier in the linear congruential method). If $d > 1$, then by a result from the theory of permutation polynomials (see [192, Cor. 7.5]) d cannot divide $p - 1$, and so $3 \leq d \leq p - 2$; note that this implies, in particular, that $p \geq 5$. If $d > 1$, then we speak of the sequence $y_0, y_1, \ldots$ as a (first-order) *nonlinear congruential generator* modulo p, and the corresponding PRN $x_n = y_n/p \in I$, $n = 0, 1, \ldots$, are called *nonlinear congruential pseudorandom numbers* (with modulus p). These PRN were first proposed by Eichenauer, Grothe, and Lehn [76], and the viewpoint based on permutation polynomials was introduced by Niederreiter [248].

The following basic definition makes sense for any congruential generator modulo a prime p. For $s \geq 1$, we view F_p^s as an s-dimensional vector space over F_p.

DEFINITION 8.1. For given $s \geq 1$, a congruential generator $y_0, y_1, \ldots$ modulo the prime p passes the *s-dimensional lattice test* if the vectors $\mathbf{y}_n - \mathbf{y}_0$, $n = 1, 2, \ldots$, span F_p^s, where

$$\mathbf{y}_n = (y_n, y_{n+1}, \ldots, y_{n+s-1}) \in F_p^s \quad \text{for } n = 0, 1, \ldots.$$

For comparison, we first consider the s-dimensional lattice test for a linear congruential generator $y_0, y_1, \ldots$ obtained from (7.5) with a prime modulus p.

From (7.8), we infer that

$$\mathbf{y}_n - \mathbf{y}_0 = (y_n - y_0)(1, a, a^2, \dots, a^{s-1}) \quad \text{for } n = 1, 2, \dots$$

in the vector space F_p^s. This shows that the vectors $\mathbf{y}_n - \mathbf{y}_0$, $n = 1, 2, \dots$, span a linear subspace of F_p^s of dimension at most 1. Consequently, a linear congruential generator with prime modulus can pass the s-dimensional lattice test at most for $s = 1$. This is another instance of the weakness of linear congruential PRN with regard to lattice structure.

The situation is quite different for nonlinear congruential generators modulo p. Here the importance of the number d, introduced above, becomes apparent. The theorem below was shown by Eichenauer, Grothe, and Lehn [76]; our proof follows Niederreiter [248].

THEOREM 8.2. *A nonlinear congruential generator modulo p passes the s-dimensional lattice test if and only if $s \leq d$.*

Proof. Since passing the s-dimensional lattice test implies passing any lower-dimensional lattice test, it suffices to show that a nonlinear congruential generator $y_0, y_1, \dots$ modulo p passes the d-dimensional lattice test and does not pass the $(d+1)$-dimensional lattice test. Equivalently, if we put

$$\mathbf{u}_j = (y_{j+1} - y_j, y_{j+2} - y_j, \dots, y_{j+p-1} - y_j) \in F_p^{p-1} \quad \text{for } j = 0, 1, \dots$$

and U_s is the $s \times (p-1)$ matrix with rows $\mathbf{u}_0, \mathbf{u}_1, \dots, \mathbf{u}_{s-1}$, then it suffices to show that $\mathrm{rank}(U_d) = \mathrm{rank}(U_{d+1}) = d$ (consider the columns of U_d and U_{d+1}). Let Δ^k be the k-fold iterate of the difference operator $\Delta t_n = t_{n+1} - t_n$ defined on a sequence $t_0, t_1, \dots$. For $i = 1, 2, \dots$, we have

$$\sum_{j=0}^{d} (-1)^{d-j} \binom{d}{j} (y_{j+i} - y_j) = \sum_{j=0}^{d} (-1)^{d-j} \binom{d}{j} \sum_{n=0}^{i-1} \Delta y_{n+j}$$

$$= \sum_{n=0}^{i-1} \Delta^d(\Delta y_n) = \sum_{n=0}^{i-1} \Delta^{d+1} y_n = 0,$$

where the last step follows from (8.2) and $\deg(g) = d$. Therefore

$$\sum_{j=0}^{d} (-1)^{d-j} \binom{d}{j} \mathbf{u}_j = \mathbf{0};$$

hence $\mathbf{u}_d$ is a linear combination of $\mathbf{u}_0, \dots, \mathbf{u}_{d-1}$, and so $\mathrm{rank}(U_{d+1}) \leq d$. Furthermore, $\Delta^d y_n = \Delta^d g(n) \neq 0$ and $\Delta^{d+1} y_n = 0$ for all $n \geq 0$; thus $y_0, y_1, \dots$ is a linear recurring sequence with minimal polynomial $(x-1)^{d+1}$ (compare with Appendix A). With

$$\mathbf{y}_j = (y_j, y_{j+1}, \dots, y_{j+d}) \in F_p^{d+1},$$

we claim that $\mathbf{y}_0, \mathbf{y}_1, \dots, \mathbf{y}_d$ are linearly independent over F_p. Suppose that there exist $b_0, b_1, \dots, b_d \in F_p$, not all zero, such that $\sum_{j=0}^{d} b_j \mathbf{y}_j = \mathbf{0}$. By comparing components, we see that

$$\sum_{j=0}^{d} b_j g(n+j) = 0 \quad \text{for } n = 0, 1, \dots, d.$$

This means that the polynomial $h(x) = \sum_{j=0}^{d} b_j g(x+j)$ has at least $d+1$ distinct roots in F_p. Now $\deg(h) \le d$, however, and so h is the zero polynomial. From this, we obtain

$$\sum_{j=0}^{d} b_j y_{n+j} = 0 \quad \text{for } n = 0, 1, \dots;$$

thus the sequence $y_0, y_1, \dots$ satisfies a linear recursion of order $\le d$, which is a contradiction. From the linear independence of $\mathbf{y}_0, \mathbf{y}_1, \dots, \mathbf{y}_d$, we deduce the linear independence of $\mathbf{y}_1 - \mathbf{y}_0, \dots, \mathbf{y}_d - \mathbf{y}_0$, and since the transposes of the latter vectors are the first d columns of U_{d+1}, we obtain $\operatorname{rank}(U_{d+1}) = d$. It follows that $\mathbf{u}_0, \dots, \mathbf{u}_{d-1}$ are linearly independent over F_p, and so $\operatorname{rank}(U_d) = d$. $\square$

Since $d \le p - 2$, it follows from Theorem 8.2 that a nonlinear congruential generator modulo p cannot pass the s-dimensional lattice test for $s \ge p-1$. From the viewpoint of the lattice test, a large value of d is preferable. The polynomial g determined by (8.2) can be written as

$$g(x) = \sum_{n=0}^{p-1} \left(1 - (x-n)^{p-1}\right) y_n = \sum_{k=0}^{p-2} (-1)^{k+1} \binom{p-1}{k} x^k \sum_{n=0}^{p-1} n^{p-1-k} y_n,$$

and so d is equal to the largest integer $k \le p - 2$ for which

$$\sum_{n=0}^{p-1} n^{p-1-k} y_n \not\equiv 0 \bmod p.$$

In particular, d has the maximal value $p - 2$ if and only if

(8.3) $$\sum_{n=0}^{p-1} n y_n \not\equiv 0 \bmod p.$$

This was used by Eichenauer and Niederreiter [81] to construct the following example. Consider the periodic sequence $y_0, y_1, \dots \in Z_p$ with $\operatorname{per}(y_n) = p$, which is given by $y_n = n$ for $0 \le n \le p-3$, $y_{p-2} = p-1$, and $y_{p-1} = p-2$. Then it is easily checked that (8.3) is satisfied, and so this nonlinear congruential generator modulo p passes the s-dimensional lattice test for all $s \le p - 2$ by Theorem 8.2. On the other hand, it is clear that this generator has extremely bad statistical properties (consider, e.g., the distribution of pairs (y_n, y_{n+1}) or the run test). Therefore the lattice test is rather weak and should only be used for the elimination of bad generators.

We now study the behavior of the full period of a sequence $x_0, x_1, \dots$ of nonlinear congruential PRN with modulus p under the uniformity test and the serial test. Since in the full period we find exactly all rationals in I with denominator p, we obviously get $D_p(x_0, \ldots, x_{p-1}) = 1/p$. To assess the performance under the serial test, we consider the discrepancy $D_p^{(s)}$ defined by (7.2). We have the following result of Niederreiter [249] in which the number d is again important.

THEOREM 8.3. *For nonlinear congruential PRN with modulus p, we have*

$$D_p^{(s)} \leq 1 - \left(1 - \frac{1}{p}\right)^s + (d-1)p^{-1/2}\left(\frac{4}{\pi^2}\log p + 1.72\right)^s \quad \textit{for } 2 \leq s \leq d.$$

Proof. If $y_0, y_1, \ldots \in F_p$ is the corresponding nonlinear congruential generator modulo p, then we have shown in the proof of Theorem 8.2 that this is a linear recurring sequence with minimal polynomial $(x - 1)^{d+1}$. For a given s with $2 \leq s \leq d$, put $\mathbf{y}_n = (y_n, y_{n+1}, \ldots, y_{n+s-1})$ for $n \geq 0$. For a fixed $\mathbf{h} = (h_1, \ldots, h_s) \in C_s^*(p)$, we consider

$$\mathbf{h} \cdot \mathbf{y}_n = \sum_{i=1}^{s} h_i y_{n+i-1}$$

as an element of F_p. Suppose that there would exist a $b \in F_p$ such that

$$\sum_{i=1}^{s} h_i y_{n+i-1} = b \quad \text{for all } n \geq 0.$$

Then, by applying the difference operator Δ on both sides, it follows that the sequence $y_0, y_1, \ldots$ satisfies a nontrivial linear recursion of order $\leq s$, which is a contradiction. Thus, in conjunction with (8.2), we see that there exists a polynomial $G \in F_p[x]$ with $1 \leq \deg(G) \leq d < p$ such that $\mathbf{h} \cdot \mathbf{y}_n = G(n)$ for all $n \geq 0$. From Weil's bound for character sums (see [192, Thm. 5.38]), we then obtain

$$\left|\sum_{n=0}^{p-1} e\left(\frac{1}{p}\mathbf{h} \cdot \mathbf{y}_n\right)\right| = \left|\sum_{n=0}^{p-1} e\left(\frac{G(n)}{p}\right)\right| \leq (d-1)p^{1/2} \quad \text{for all } \mathbf{h} \in C_s^*(p).$$

Therefore the hypothesis of Corollary 3.11 is satisfied with $B = (d-1)p^{1/2}$, and the result of the theorem follows. $\square$

Further results in [249] show that Theorem 8.3 is, in general, the best possible, in the sense that $D_p^{(s)}$ can be of an order of magnitude at least $p^{-1/2}$ and that the bound cannot hold for dimensions $s > d$. Similar theorems for parts of the period are also available in [249]. Note that the bound in Theorem 8.3 is only useful if d is at most of a somewhat smaller order of magnitude than $p^{1/2}$.

A special first-order congruential method that has received some attention is the *quadratic congruential method* proposed by Knuth [154, §3.2.2]. Here we use (8.1) with the modulus $M = 2^\alpha$, $\alpha \geq 2$, and with f being the quadratic polynomial $f(x) = ax^2 + bx + c$, where $a, b, c \in Z_M$. For the corresponding sequence $x_0, x_1, \ldots$ of *quadratic congruential pseudorandom numbers*, we have $\text{per}(x_n) = M$ if and only if a is even, $b \equiv a + 1 \mod 4$, and c is odd, according to a result in [154, §3.2.2]. In the following discussion, we always assume that $\mathrm{per}(x_n) = M$.

The lattice structure of quadratic congruential PRN was analyzed by Eichenauer and Lehn [79]. For a given dimension $s \geq 2$, the set of all nonoverlapping s-tuples $\mathbf{x}_{ns} = (x_{ns}, x_{ns+1}, \dots, x_{ns+s-1}) \in I^s$, $n = 0, 1, \dots, M - 1$, is the same as the intersection of I^s with a union of $2^{\omega - \eta}$ grids with explicitly known shift vectors and lattice bases. Here η and ω are determined by $\gcd(s, M) = 2^\eta$, $\gcd(a, M) = 2^\beta$, and $\omega = \max(\lfloor \frac{1}{2}(\alpha - \beta + 1) \rfloor, \eta)$.

Eichenauer-Herrmann and Niederreiter [88] investigated the performance of quadratic congruential PRN under the two-dimensional serial test. Let $D_M^{(s)}$ be the discrepancy defined by (7.2) for $s \geq 2$ and the full period, and let β be as above. Then, for $s = 2$, we have

$$D_M^{(2)} < \frac{2}{M} + \frac{4}{7}(2\sqrt{2} + 1)2^{\beta/2}M^{-1/2}\left(\frac{2}{\pi}\log M + \frac{2}{5}\right)^2.$$

This is the best possible in the sense that, if $\beta \leq \alpha - 2$ and $b \equiv 1 \bmod 2^{\beta+1}$, then

$$D_M^{(s)} \geq \frac{1}{(\pi + 2)\sqrt{2}} 2^{\beta/2}M^{-1/2} \quad \text{for all } s \geq 2.$$

The upper bound for $D_M^{(2)}$ suggests that it is reasonable to choose the parameter a in such a way that $\beta = 1$, i.e., that $a \equiv 2 \bmod 4$. Then the criterion for $\mathrm{per}(x_n) = M$ implies that $b \equiv 3 \bmod 4$, and, in this case, we have the lower bound

$$D_M^{(s)} \geq \frac{1}{3(\pi + 2)} M^{-1/2} \quad \text{for all } s \geq 2.$$

The resulting order of magnitude of $D_M^{(2)}$ is in line with the probabilistic law (7.4) for random sequences.

8.2. The inversive congruential method.

In the *inversive congruential method*, we use the recursion (8.1) with a simple class of functions f, which involve multiplicative inversion in modular arithmetic. As usual, convenient moduli are primes and powers of 2. We first consider the case of a prime modulus $M = p \geq 5$. For $c \in Z_p$, we define $\bar{c} \in Z_p$ by $c\bar{c} \equiv 1 \bmod p$ if $c \neq 0$ and $\bar{c} = 0$ if $c = 0$. Now we choose parameters $a, b \in Z_p$ with $a \neq 0$ and an initial value $y_0 \in Z_p$. Then the sequence $y_0, y_1, \dots \in Z_p$ generated by the recursion

(8.4) $y_{n+1} \equiv a\bar{y}_n + b \bmod p \quad \text{for } n = 0, 1, \dots$

is called an *inversive congruential generator* modulo p, and the corresponding PRN $x_n = y_n/p \in I$, $n = 0, 1, \dots$, are called *inversive congruential pseudorandom numbers* (with modulus p). These PRN were introduced by Eichenauer and Lehn [78]. Since $a \neq 0$, the congruence (8.4) can be solved uniquely for y_n if y_{n+1} is given, and so the sequence $y_0, y_1, \dots$ is periodic and $\mathrm{per}(x_n) = \mathrm{per}(y_n) \leq p$.

The following sufficient condition for $\text{per}(x_n) = p$ was shown in [78]. We again identify Z_p with the finite field F_p, and we recall the definition of a primitive polynomial over F_p from Appendix A.

THEOREM 8.4. *If* $a, b \in F_p$ *are such that* $x^2 - bx - a$ *is a primitive polynomial over* F_p, *then the sequence* $x_0, x_1, \ldots$ *of inversive congruential PRN with modulus* p *satisfies* $\text{per}(x_n) = p$.

Proof. The sequence $c_0, c_1, \ldots \in F_p$ defined by $c_0 = 0$, $c_1 = 1$, $c_{n+2} = bc_{n+1} + ac_n$ for $n \geq 0$ is a maximal period sequence in F_p (see Appendix A); hence it is periodic with $\text{per}(c_n) = p^2 - 1$. Let γ be a root of $x^2 - bx - a$ in F_{p^2}. Then, by Theorem A.2 in Appendix A, there exists a $\theta \in F_{p^2}$ with $\theta \neq 0$ such that

(8.5) $$c_n = \theta\gamma^n + \theta^p\gamma^{pn} \qquad \text{for } n = 0, 1, \ldots .$$

Since $c_0 = 0$, (8.5) shows that $\theta^{p-1} = -1$. Now suppose that we had $c_m = 0$ for some m with $1 \leq m \leq p$. Then (8.5) yields $\gamma^{(p-1)m} = -\theta^{1-p} = 1$. Again, by (8.5), we then get $c_{n+(p-1)m} = c_n$ for $n = 0, 1, \ldots$; thus $\text{per}(c_n) \leq (p-1)m \leq (p-1)p < p^2 - 1$, a contradiction. Thus $c_n \neq 0$ for $1 \leq n \leq p$.

Let $y_0, y_1, \ldots$ be generated by (8.4) and consider first the case where $y_0 = 0$. Then, using $c_n \neq 0$ for $1 \leq n \leq p$, we obtain by induction on n that $y_n = \bar{c}_n c_{n+1}$ for $0 \leq n \leq p$. Consequently, we have $y_n \neq 0$ for $1 \leq n \leq p-1$, and so $\text{per}(y_n) \geq p$; hence $\text{per}(x_n) = \text{per}(y_n) = p$. In particular, $\{y_0, y_1, \ldots, y_{p-1}\} = Z_p$. If we have an arbitrary initial value y_0, then the sequence $y_0, y_1, \ldots$ is a shifted version of the sequence with initial value 0, and so again $\text{per}(x_n) = \text{per}(y_n) = p$. $\square$

We henceforth assume that $a, b \in F_p$ have been chosen in such a way that $x^2 - bx - a$ is a primitive polynomial over F_p. Since $\text{per}(y_n) = p$, we are then in the framework developed in §8.1 for prime moduli. Inversive congruential generators modulo p behave very well under the lattice test. The following result of Niederreiter [248] represents a slight improvement on an earlier theorem of Eichenauer, Grothe, and Lehn [76].

THEOREM 8.5. *An inversive congruential generator modulo* p *passes the s-dimensional lattice test for all* $s \leq (p+1)/2$.

Proof. If $g \in F_p[x]$ is as in (8.2), then, by Theorem 8.2, it suffices to show that $d = \deg(g) \geq (p+1)/2$. Put $w_n = y_n y_{n+1} - by_n - a$ for $n \geq 0$; then w_n is represented by a polynomial over F_p of degree $2d$. From (8.4), it follows that $w_n = 0$ for $p - 1$ values $n \in F_p$, namely, for those with $y_n \neq 0$. Thus we must have $p - 1 \leq 2d$. Now $d = (p-1)/2$ is impossible by a property of permutation polynomials of F_p stated in §8.1, and so $d \geq (p+1)/2$. The fact that $d = (p-1)/2$ is impossible can also be seen directly as follows. If $d = (p-1)/2$, then $g(x)^2 = \sum_{j=0}^{p-1} a_j x^j$ with all $a_j \in F_p$ and $a_{p-1} \neq 0$. In F_p, however, we have

$$0 = \sum_{n=0}^{p-1} n^2 = \sum_{n=0}^{p-1} y_n^2 = \sum_{n=0}^{p-1} g(n)^2 = \sum_{j=0}^{p-1} a_j \sum_{n=0}^{p-1} n^j = -a_{p-1},$$

which gives a contradiction. $\square$

The following strong nonlinearity property of inversive congruential generators modulo p was shown by Eichenauer-Herrmann [82]. Here we view F_p^s as an affine space.

THEOREM 8.6. *For* $s \geq 2$ *and every inversive congruential generator* $y_0, y_1, \ldots$ *modulo* p, *any hyperplane in* F_p^s *contains at most* s *of the points* $\mathbf{y}_n = (y_n, y_{n+1}, \ldots, y_{n+s-1})$ *with* $0 \leq n \leq p - 1$ *and* $y_n \cdots y_{n+s-2} \neq 0$.

Proof. Let $u_0, u_1, \ldots \in F_p$ be generated by (8.4) with $u_0 = 0$ and put $d_j = -a\bar{u}_j \in F_p$ for $j \geq 0$. From $\{u_0, u_1, \ldots, u_{p-1}\} = F_p$, it follows that $d_0, d_1, \ldots, d_{p-1}$ are distinct. Define $\psi(n) = a\bar{n} + b \in F_p$ for $n \in F_p$ and let ψ^j be the jth iterate of the function ψ, with $\psi^0(n) = n$. By induction on j, we have

$$(8.6) \qquad \psi^j(n) = u_j \frac{n - d_j}{n - d_{j-1}} \qquad \text{for } 1 \leq j \leq p - 1$$

and whenever $n \neq d_i$ for $0 \leq i \leq j - 1$. Since the theorem is trivial for $s \geq p$, we can assume that $s < p$. We have

$$(8.7) \quad \{\mathbf{y}_n : 0 \leq n \leq p - 1\} = \{(\psi^0(n), \psi^1(n), \ldots, \psi^{s-1}(n)) : 0 \leq n \leq p - 1\},$$

and the condition $y_n \cdots y_{n+s-2} \neq 0$ amounts to the condition $n \neq d_i$ for $0 \leq i \leq s - 2$ in the second set. Now let a hyperplane H in F_p^s be defined by $\sum_{j=1}^s b_j z_j = b_0$ with $b_0, b_1, \ldots, b_s \in F_p$ and $(b_1, \ldots, b_s) \neq \mathbf{0}$. Then (8.6) shows that, for $n \neq d_i$, $0 \leq i \leq s - 2$, we have $(\psi^0(n), \psi^1(n), \ldots, \psi^{s-1}(n)) \in H$ if and only if

$$b_1 n + \sum_{j=2}^s b_j u_{j-1} \frac{n - d_{j-1}}{n - d_{j-2}} = b_0.$$

Clearing denominators, we see that this is equivalent to $h(n) = 0$, where the polynomial h over F_p is given by

$$h(x) = (b_1 x - b_0) \prod_{j=2}^s (x - d_{j-2}) + \sum_{j=2}^s b_j u_{j-1} (x - d_{j-1}) \prod_{\substack{i=2 \\ i \neq j}}^s (x - d_{i-2}).$$

Since $\deg(h) \leq s$, the result of the theorem follows if we can show that h is not the zero polynomial. If h were the zero polynomial, then, by looking at the coefficient of x^s, we would get $b_1 = 0$. Furthermore, for $2 \leq k \leq s$, we would obtain

$$0 = h(d_{k-2}) = b_k u_{k-1} (d_{k-2} - d_{k-1}) \prod_{\substack{i=2 \\ i \neq k}}^s (d_{k-2} - d_{i-2});$$

hence $b_k = 0$, a contradiction to $(b_1, \ldots, b_s) \neq \mathbf{0}$. $\square$

Note that any s points in F_p^s define a hyperplane or a lower-dimensional affine subspace, and so Theorem 8.6 is optimal in the sense that there do exist hyperplanes in F_p^s that contain exactly s of the points $\mathbf{y}_n$ considered in this theorem. We remark also that the condition $y_n \cdots y_{n+s-2} \neq 0$ in Theorem 8.6 eliminates exactly $s - 1$ of the points $\mathbf{y}_n$.

Since inversive congruential PRN with modulus p are, in particular, nonlinear congruential PRN with modulus p, we could hope to deal with the serial test for inversive congruential PRN by simply referring to Theorem 8.3. However, for these PRN, we have $d \geq (p+1)/2$ by the proof of Theorem 8.5, and so the bound in Theorem 8.3 becomes useless. Therefore the case of inversive congruential PRN must be treated by a specially adapted method. The following is a slight variant of a result of Niederreiter [252].

THEOREM 8.7. *For inversive congruential PRN with modulus p, we have*

$$D_p^{(s)} \leq 1 - \left(1 - \frac{1}{p}\right)^s + \left(\frac{2s-2}{p^{1/2}} + \frac{s-1}{p}\right)\left(\frac{4}{\pi^2}\log p + 1.72\right)^s \qquad \textit{for } s \geq 2.$$

Proof. Let $y_0, y_1, \ldots$ be the corresponding inversive congruential generator modulo p, and, for a given $s \geq 2$, put $\mathbf{y}_n = (y_n, y_{n+1}, \ldots, y_{n+s-1})$ for $n \geq 0$. Since the theorem is trivial for $s \geq p$, we can assume that $s < p$. For a fixed $\mathbf{h} = (h_1, \ldots, h_s) \in C_s^*(p)$, we use (8.7) to obtain

$$S(\mathbf{h}) := \sum_{n=0}^{p-1} e\left(\frac{1}{p}\mathbf{h} \cdot \mathbf{y}_n\right) = \sum_{n=0}^{p-1} e\left(\frac{1}{p}\sum_{j=1}^{s} h_j \psi^{j-1}(n)\right).$$

Let k be the least index with $h_k \neq 0$. If $k = s$, then, since ψ^{s-1} is a permutation of F_p, we get $S(\mathbf{h}) = 0$. For $k < s$, we simplify the writing by introducing the additive character $\chi(c) = e(c/p)$ for $c \in F_p$. We have

$$\sum_{j=1}^{s} h_j \psi^{j-1}(n) = \sum_{j=k}^{s} h_j \psi^{j-1}(n) = \sum_{j=k}^{s} h_j \psi^{j-k}\left(\psi^{k-1}(n)\right),$$

and, using $\psi^{k-1}(n)$ as a new summation variable, we derive

$$S(\mathbf{h}) = \sum_{n \in F_p} \chi\left(\sum_{j=k}^{s} h_j \psi^{j-k}(n)\right) = \sum_{n \in F_p} \chi\left(\sum_{j=0}^{s-k} h_{j+k}\psi^{j}(n)\right).$$

Now we apply (8.6) for $n \neq d_i$, $0 \leq i \leq s - k - 1$, which yields

$$\sum_{j=0}^{s-k} h_{j+k}\psi^{j}(n) = h_k n + \sum_{j=1}^{s-k} h_{j+k}u_j \frac{n - d_j}{n - d_{j-1}}.$$

The last expression is a rational function Q/R of n with $Q \in F_p[x]$ and $R(x) = \prod_{j=1}^{s-k}(x - d_{j-1}) \in F_p[x]$. Therefore

$$|S(\mathbf{h})| \leq s - k + \left|\sum_{\substack{n \in F_p \\ R(n) \neq 0}} \chi\left(\frac{Q(n)}{R(n)}\right)\right|.$$

The rational function Q/R has at most $s - k$ finite poles, each of multiplicity 1, and, since $\deg(Q) = \deg(R) + 1$, it has a pole at the point at infinity of multiplicity 1. Thus a well-known bound of Weil [357] (see also Stepanov [335] for an elementary proof) yields

$$\left| \sum_{\substack{n \in F_p \\ R(n) \neq 0}} \chi\left(\frac{Q(n)}{R(n)}\right) \right| \leq 2(s - k)p^{1/2} \leq (2s - 2)p^{1/2}.$$

Altogether, we obtain

$$|S(\mathbf{h})| \leq (2s - 2)p^{1/2} + s - 1 \qquad \text{for all } \mathbf{h} \in C_s^*(p).$$

Thus we can apply Corollary 3.11 with $B = (2s - 2)p^{1/2} + s - 1$, and this yields the desired result. $\square$

The upper bound in Theorem 8.7 has the order of magnitude $p^{-1/2}(\log p)^s$. This is, in general, the best possible up to the logarithmic factor, as the following result of Niederreiter [255] demonstrates. Note that $\phi(p^2 - 1)/2$ is the total number of primitive polynomials $x^2 - bx - a$ over F_p by [192, Thm. 3.5].

THEOREM 8.8. *Let $p \geq 5$ be a prime and let $0 < t < 1$. Then there are more than $A_p(t)\phi(p^2 - 1)/2$ primitive polynomials $x^2 - bx - a$ over F_p such that, for the corresponding inversive congruential PRN with modulus p, we have*

$$D_p^{(s)} > \frac{t}{2\pi + 4}p^{-1/2} \qquad \text{for all } s \geq 2,$$

where the numbers $A_p(t)$ satisfy

$$\lim_{p \to \infty} A_p(t) = \frac{1 - t^2}{4 - t^2} > 0 \qquad \text{for all } t.$$

A comparison between the linear congruential method and the inversive congruential method with prime modulus reveals that the latter has at least the following three advantages:

(i) Inversive congruential PRN are vastly superior with respect to lattice structure. Once $a, b \in F_p$ have been chosen such that $x^2 - bx - a$ is primitive over F_p, then Theorem 8.5 guarantees that the lattice test is passed for a very large range of dimensions, and Theorem 8.6 ensures strong nonlinearity properties. In contrast, for the linear congruential method, laborious calculations are needed to find multipliers that yield a nearly optimal lattice structure even for a modest range of dimensions. For instance, an inversive congruential generator modulo $p = 2^{31} - 1$ passes the s-dimensional lattice test for all $s \leq 2^{30}$, whereas, for the linear congruential method with this modulus, it is already difficult to guarantee a nearly optimal lattice structure for all $s \leq 10$ (compare with Fishman and Moore [104]).

(ii) Inversive congruential PRN show a better behavior under the serial test. Theorems 8.7 and 8.8 entail that, for a positive fraction of the possible pairs

$(a, b) \in F_p^2$ of parameters, and, in particular, on the average, $D_p^{(s)}$ has an order of magnitude between $p^{-1/2}$ and $p^{-1/2}(\log p)^s$ for every $s \geq 2$. This is in reasonable accordance with the law of the iterated logarithm in (7.4). On the other hand, in case (i) of the linear congruential method with prime modulus p and least period length $p - 1$, we have on the average $D_{p-1}^{(s)} = O(p^{-1}(\log p)^s \log \log(p + 1))$ for every $s \geq 2$ by Theorem 7.4. Thus sequences of inversive congruential PRN display more irregularity in their distribution and, in this sense, model truly random numbers more closely than linear congruential PRN.

(iii) The inversive congruential method allows a wide choice of parameters, all of which lead to guaranteed and comparable structural and statistical properties. It suffices to choose $a, b \in F_p$ such that $x^2 - bx - a$ is primitive over F_p, and then the properties in Theorems 8.5, 8.6, and 8.7 hold without any further restriction. This feature can be of great practical value in various parallelized simulation techniques in which many parallel streams of PRN are needed. In case (i) of the linear congruential method with prime modulus p, just choosing any primitive root a modulo p is certainly not enough. Rather, the multiplier a must be selected very carefully, and this selection process is a nontrivial computational task.

A computational issue that arises in connection with the recursion (8.4) is the efficient calculation of $\bar{c}$ for given $c \in F_p$. One method is based on the observations that $\bar{c} = c^{p-2}$ for all $c \in F_p$ and that c^{p-2} can be calculated with $O(\log p)$ multiplications in F_p by using the standard square-and-multiply technique (see [193, p. 347]). A second method calculates $\bar{c}$ for $c \neq 0$ by using the Euclidean algorithm with the integers c and p, and this algorithm will terminate after $O(\log p)$ steps (see [154, §4.5]).

The inversive congruential method can also be used with a composite modulus M. Let G_M be the set of $c \in Z_M$ with $\gcd(c, M) = 1$. For $c \in G_M$, let $\bar{c}$ be the unique element of G_M with $c\bar{c} \equiv 1 \bmod M$. With an initial value $y_0 \in G_M$ and parameters $a \in G_M$ and $b \in Z_M$, a sequence $y_0, y_1, \ldots \in G_M$ is generated by the recursion

$$(8.8) \qquad y_{n+1} \equiv a\bar{y}_n + b \bmod M \qquad \text{for } n = 0, 1, \ldots .$$

The integers a, b must be chosen in such a way that each y_n is guaranteed to be in G_M. In this case, the sequence $y_0, y_1, \ldots$ is called an *inversive congruential generator* modulo M, and the corresponding PRN $x_n = y_n/M \in I$, $n = 0, 1, \ldots$, are called *inversive congruential pseudorandom numbers* (with modulus M). In the case of greatest practical interest, namely, when M is a power of 2, these PRN were introduced by Eichenauer, Lehn, and Topuzoğlu [80]. Since $\gcd(a, M) = 1$, the sequence $y_0, y_1, \ldots$ generated by (8.8) is periodic and $\text{per}(x_n) = \text{per}(y_n) \leq \text{card}(G_M) = \phi(M)$.

Now let M be a power of 2. Then $a \equiv y_0 \equiv 1 \bmod 2$, and we have $y_n \in G_M$ for all $n \geq 0$ if and only if $b \equiv 0 \bmod 2$. From the above general bound, we obtain $\text{per}(x_n) \leq M/2$. The following criterion for $\text{per}(x_n) = M/2$ was established by Eichenauer, Lehn, and Topuzoğlu [80].

THEOREM 8.9. *If $M \geq 8$ is a power of 2, then a sequence $x_0, x_1, \ldots$ of inversive congruential PRN with modulus M satisfies $\mathrm{per}(x_n) = M/2$ if and only if $a \equiv 1 \bmod 4$ and $b \equiv 2 \bmod 4$.*

Proof. If $\mathrm{per}(x_n) = M/2$, then $\{y_0, y_1, \ldots, y_{(M/2)-1}\} = G_M$, and so we can assume that $y_0 = 1$. If we consider the sequence $y_0, y_1, \ldots$ modulo 4, then it has least period length 2; hence $y_2 \equiv 1 \bmod 4$. If we consider this sequence modulo 8, then it has least period length 4; hence $y_2 \not\equiv 1 \bmod 8$, and so $y_2 \equiv 5 \bmod 8$. Since $\bar{c} \equiv c \bmod 8$ for $c \in G_M$, it follows from (8.8) that

$$y_2 \equiv a(a+b) + b \equiv 1 + (a+1)b \bmod 8,$$

and so $(a+1)b \equiv 4 \bmod 8$. This implies that $a \equiv 1 \bmod 4$ and $b \equiv 2 \bmod 4$.

Conversely, suppose that $a \equiv 1 \bmod 4$ and $b \equiv 2 \bmod 4$ and consider first the case where $y_0 = 1$. For $M = 8$, it is checked by the above arguments that $\mathrm{per}(y_n) = 4$. Now let $M = 2^\alpha$ with $\alpha \geq 4$. Define the sequence $c_0, c_1, \ldots \in Z_M$ by $c_0 = c_1 = 1$ and

(8.9) $\qquad c_{n+2} \equiv bc_{n+1} + ac_n \bmod M \qquad$ for $n = 0, 1, \ldots$.

Then $c_n \equiv 1 \bmod 2$, and so $c_n \in G_M$ for all $n \geq 0$. By induction on n, we obtain

(8.10) $\qquad y_n \equiv \bar{c}_n c_{n+1} \bmod M \qquad$ for all $n \geq 0$.

With the integer matrix

$$A = \begin{pmatrix} 0 & 1 \\ a & b \end{pmatrix},$$

we see, from (8.9), that

$$\begin{pmatrix} c_{n+1} \\ c_{n+2} \end{pmatrix} \equiv A \begin{pmatrix} c_n \\ c_{n+1} \end{pmatrix} \bmod M \qquad \text{for all } n \geq 0,$$

and so

(8.11) $\qquad \begin{pmatrix} c_n \\ c_{n+1} \end{pmatrix} \equiv A^n \begin{pmatrix} 1 \\ 1 \end{pmatrix} \bmod M \qquad \text{for all } n \geq 0.$

By induction on $h \geq 4$ and using $a \equiv 1 \bmod 4$, $b \equiv 2 \bmod 4$, it is shown that

(8.12)
$$A^{2^{h-2}} \equiv \begin{pmatrix} 2^{h-1}k + 2^{h-2} + 1 & 2^{h-1}l + 3 \cdot 2^{h-2} \\ 2^{h-1}l + 3 \cdot 2^{h-2} & 2^{h-1}k + 3 \cdot 2^{h-2} + 1 \end{pmatrix} \bmod 2^h \qquad \text{for all } h \geq 4$$

with suitable $k, l \in \mathbb{Z}$. By applying (8.12) with $h = \alpha + 2$ and also using (8.11), we see that $c_{n+M} = c_n$ for all $n \geq 0$, and so $y_{n+M} = y_n$ for all $n \geq 0$ by (8.10). Thus $\mathrm{per}(y_n)$ divides M, and we already know that $\mathrm{per}(y_n) \leq M/2$. Hence, to prove that $\mathrm{per}(y_n) = M/2$, it suffices to show that $\mathrm{per}(y_n) > M/4$. If we had $\mathrm{per}(y_n) \leq M/4$, then $y_{M/4} = y_0 = 1$, and so $c_{(M/4)+1} = c_{M/4}$ by (8.10). From (8.11), however, with $n = M/4$ and (8.12) with $h = \alpha$, we obtain the contradiction $c_{(M/4)+1} \equiv c_{M/4} + (M/2) \bmod M$, and so $\mathrm{per}(y_n) = M/2$ is proved if $y_0 = 1$. In particular, $\{y_0, y_1, \ldots, y_{(M/2)-1}\} = G_M$. If we have an arbitrary initial value $y_0 \in G_M$, then the sequence $y_0, y_1, \ldots$ is a shifted version of the sequence with initial value 1, and so again $\mathrm{per}(x_n) = \mathrm{per}(y_n) = M/2$. $\square$

According to a result of Eichenauer-Herrmann et al. [87], the lattice structure of inversive congruential PRN with modulus $M = 2^\alpha$, $\alpha \geq 3$, and with $a \equiv 1 \bmod 4$ and $b \equiv 2 \bmod 4$ can be described as follows. For a given dimension $s \geq 2$, the set of all nonoverlapping s-tuples $\mathbf{x}_{ns} = (x_{ns}, x_{ns+1}, \ldots, x_{ns+s-1}) \in I^s$, $n = 0, 1, \ldots, (M/2) - 1$, is the same as the intersection of I^s with a union of $2^{\omega - \eta - 1}$ grids with explicitly known shift vectors and lattice bases. Here η and ω are determined by $\gcd(s, 2^{\alpha-1}) = 2^\eta$ and $\omega = \max(\lfloor \frac{1}{2}(\alpha + 1) \rfloor, \eta + 1)$.

Again for $M = 2^\alpha$, $\alpha \geq 3$, and $a \equiv 1 \bmod 4$, $b \equiv 2 \bmod 4$, the behavior of inversive congruential PRN with modulus M under the two-dimensional serial test was studied by Niederreiter [252]. If $D_{M/2}^{(s)}$ is the discrepancy defined by (7.2) for $s \geq 2$ and the full period, then, for $s = 2$, we have $D_{M/2}^{(2)} = O(M^{-1/2}(\log M)^2)$ with an absolute implied constant. Eichenauer-Herrmann and Niederreiter [89] have shown that this bound is the best possible in the sense that, for a positive fraction of all possible pairs (a, b) of parameters, the discrepancy $D_{M/2}^{(s)}$ is at least of the order of magnitude $M^{-1/2}$ for all $s \geq 2$.

Notes.

The s-dimensional lattice test in Definition 8.1 can be viewed as a special case of a lattice test proposed by Marsaglia [205]. For more information on permutation polynomials, we refer to [192, Chap 7]. Quadratic congruential PRN with arbitrary modulus were studied by Eichenauer and Lehn [79]. The least period length of sequences of inversive congruential PRN with an arbitrary prime power modulus was discussed by Eichenauer-Herrmann and Topuzoğlu [90], and Eichenauer-Herrmann [83] treated the two-dimensional serial test for odd prime power moduli. The proof of Theorem 8.8 depends on distribution properties of the values of Kloosterman sums over finite fields; see Niederreiter [256] for a detailed study of such properties. Parameters $a, b \in F_p$ such that $x^2 - bx - a$ is a primitive polynomial over F_p are tabulated in Grothe [118] for some large primes such as $p = 2^{31} - 1$. A generalization of the inversive congruential method, which is based on higher-order recursions, was introduced by Eichenauer et al. [77].

Shift-Register Pseudorandom Numbers

Pseudorandom numbers generated by higher-order linear recursions have already been considered briefly in §7.3 in the form of multiple-recursive PRN. However, the method we used there to transform a linear recurring sequence into a sequence of uniform PRN, namely normalization, is not quite satisfactory, and much better methods are available for this purpose. The basic idea of these methods is to employ a small prime modulus p (such as $p = 2$) for the generation of the linear recurring sequence and then take certain collections of terms of this sequence as digits of the PRN to be constructed. This has the advantages that modular arithmetic must be performed only with respect to a small modulus and that there is much flexibility as far as the discretization of the PRN is concerned. There are two methods of this type that have received much attention in the literature, namely, the digital multistep method and the GFSR (for "generalized feedback shift register") method. The PRN generated by these two methods have comparable properties, and these PRN are collectively known as *shift-register pseudorandom numbers*. One common feature of these PRN is that they tend to have strong uniformity properties, which can be made explicit in terms of the theory of nets described in Chapter 4. The reference to shift registers in the terminology stems from the fact that linear recurring sequences in finite fields can be generated by simple switching circuits called (linear feedback) shift registers (compare with [192, §8.1]).

In §9.1 we discuss the digital multistep method, and in §9.2 the GFSR method. In the latter section, we also perform a comparative analysis of linear congruential PRN and shift-register PRN.

9.1. The digital multistep method.

Let p be a small prime (usually $p = 2$), let $k \geq 2$ be an integer, and generate a kth-order (or k-step) linear recurring sequence $y_0, y_1, \ldots \in Z_p$ by

$$(9.1) \qquad y_{n+k} \equiv \sum_{l=0}^{k-1} a_l y_{n+l} \bmod p \qquad \text{for } n = 0, 1, \ldots,$$

where $y_0, \ldots, y_{k-1}$ are initial values that are not all zero. The integer coefficients $a_0, \ldots, a_{k-1}$ in (9.1) are chosen in such a way that, if they are viewed as elements of the finite field F_p, then the characteristic polynomial

$$f(x) = x^k - \sum_{l=0}^{k-1} a_l x^l \in F_p[x]$$

of the recursion (9.1) is a primitive polynomial over F_p. We then have $\operatorname{per}(y_n) = p^k - 1$ (compare with §7.3 and Appendix A).

In the *digital multistep method* due to Tausworthe [342], the sequence $y_0, y_1, \ldots$ is transformed into a sequence $x_0, x_1, \ldots$ of uniform PRN in the following way. Choose an integer m with $2 \le m \le k$ and put

(9.2)
$$x_n = \sum_{j=1}^{m} y_{mn+j-1} p^{-j} \qquad \text{for } n = 0, 1, \ldots .$$

In other words, the numbers x_n are obtained by splitting up the sequence $y_0, y_1, \ldots$ into consecutive blocks of length m and then interpreting each block as the digit expansion in base p of a number in $I = [0, 1)$. The numbers x_n are called *digital multistep pseudorandom numbers*, or *digital k-step pseudorandom numbers* if we want to emphasize the value of k.

LEMMA 9.1. *The sequence* $x_0, x_1, \ldots$ *defined by* (9.2) *is periodic with*

$$\operatorname{per}(x_n) = \frac{p^k - 1}{\gcd(m, p^k - 1)}.$$

Proof. Put $T = p^k - 1$ and $d = \gcd(m, T)$. Then, from (9.2) and $\operatorname{per}(y_n) = T$, we get $x_{n+(T/d)} = x_n$ for all $n \ge 0$; thus $x_0, x_1, \ldots$ is periodic and $T_1 = \operatorname{per}(x_n)$ divides T/d. From $x_{n+T_1} = x_n$ for all $n \ge 0$ and (9.2), we infer that

$$y_{mn+j-1+mT_1} = y_{mn+j-1} \qquad \text{for all } n \ge 0 \text{ and } 1 \le j \le m;$$

hence $y_{n+mT_1} = y_n$ for all $n \ge 0$. This implies that T divides mT_1; thus T/d divides T_1, and so $T_1 = T/d$. $\square$

We henceforth assume that $\gcd(m, p^k - 1) = 1$, and we thus guarantee by Lemma 9.1 that the sequence $x_0, x_1, \ldots$ of digital k-step PRN satisfies $\operatorname{per}(x_n) = p^k - 1 = T$. To study the behavior of these PRN under the uniformity test and the serial test, we consider, for a given dimension $s \ge 1$, the points

(9.3) $\mathbf{x}_n = (x_n, x_{n+1}, \ldots, x_{n+s-1}) \in I^s \qquad \text{for } n = 0, 1, \ldots, T - 1.$

For small dimensions, i.e., for $s \le k/m$, the distribution of these points can be described exactly. Note that the coordinates of all points $\mathbf{x}_n$ are rationals with denominator p^m.

THEOREM 9.2. *Let* $s \le k/m$ *and let* $\mathbf{t} \in I^s$ *be such that all coordinates of* $\mathbf{t}$ *are rationals with denominator* p^m. *If* $Z(\mathbf{t})$ *is the number of integers* n *with* $0 \le n \le T - 1$ *and* $\mathbf{x}_n = \mathbf{t}$, *then*

$$Z(\mathbf{t}) = \begin{cases} p^{k-ms} & \text{if } \mathbf{t} \ne \mathbf{0}, \\ p^{k-ms} - 1 & \text{if } \mathbf{t} = \mathbf{0}. \end{cases}$$

Proof. The sequence $\mathbf{y}_n = (y_n, y_{n+1}, \ldots, y_{n+ms-1}) \in Z_p^{ms}$, $n = 0, 1, \ldots,$ satisfies $\operatorname{per}(\mathbf{y}_n) = T$, and, from $\gcd(m, T) = 1$, it follows that the points $\mathbf{y}_{mn}$, $0 \le n \le T - 1$, form a rearrangement of the points $\mathbf{y}_n$, $0 \le n \le T - 1$. Since $ms \le k$, formula (7.11) can be applied with s replaced by ms, and the same formula also holds for the counting function referring to the points $\mathbf{y}_{mn}$, $0 \le n \le T - 1$. From (9.2) and (9.3), we see that $\mathbf{x}_n = \mathbf{t}$ if and only if $\mathbf{y}_{mn} = \mathbf{c}$ for a suitable $\mathbf{c} \in Z_p^{ms}$ depending only on $\mathbf{t}$, with $\mathbf{c} = \mathbf{0}$ if and only if $\mathbf{t} = \mathbf{0}$, and so we obtain the desired result. $\square$

If $D_T^{*(s)}$ denotes, as in (7.3), the star discrepancy of the point set in (9.3), then from Theorem 9.2 we obtain

$$(9.4) \qquad D_T^{*(s)} = 1 - (1 - p^{-m})^s \qquad \text{for } s \le k/m$$

by a straightforward argument; see Niederreiter [241] for the details.

For $s > k/m$, the distribution of the points in (9.3), and thus the s-dimensional serial test, can be analyzed by means of the theory of nets in Chapter 4. The only provision we must make is that we must add the point $\mathbf{0}$ to the point set in (9.3). Note that the characteristic polynomial f has a root α in the extension field F_q of F_p, where $q = p^k$. Consider the system

$$(9.5) \qquad C_1 = \{\alpha^{(i-1)m+j-1} : 1 \le i \le s, \ 1 \le j \le m\}$$

of elements of F_q. If we view F_q as a k-dimensional vector space over F_p, then we can assign to C_1 the number $\rho(C_1)$ according to Definition 4.27.

DEFINITION 9.3. For $s > k/m$, the *figure of merit* $r^{(s)}(f, m)$ depending on s, the characteristic polynomial f, and m is defined by

$$r^{(s)}(f, m) = \min(m, \rho(C_1)).$$

REMARK 9.4. The value of $r^{(s)}(f, m)$ does not depend on the choice of the root α of f. Note that f as a primitive polynomial over F_p is, in particular, irreducible over F_p. The residue class field $F_p[x]/(f)$ can be viewed as a vector space over F_p. Then a subsystem $\{\alpha^{(i-1)m+j-1} : 1 \le j \le d_i, \ 1 \le i \le s\}$ of C_1 is linearly independent over F_p if and only if the corresponding system $\{x^{(i-1)m+j-1} + (f) : 1 \le j \le d_i, \ 1 \le i \le s\}$ of residue classes is linearly independent over F_p. Now it suffices to observe that the latter statement does not depend on α.

THEOREM 9.5. *For* $s > k/m$, *the* p^k *points* $\mathbf{0}, \mathbf{x}_0, \mathbf{x}_1, \ldots, \mathbf{x}_{T-1}$ *form a* (t, k, s)-*net in base* p *with* $t = k - r^{(s)}(f, m)$.

Proof. We first show that the p^k points in the theorem can be obtained by the general construction of (t, k, s)-nets in base p leading to (4.25). In the notation of this construction, we obtain, from (9.2) and (9.3), that, for $1 \le n \le T$ and $1 \le i \le s$, we have

$$y_{nj}^{(i)} = y_{m(n+i-1)+j-1} \qquad \text{for } 1 \le j \le m,$$
$$y_{nj}^{(i)} = 0 \qquad \text{for } m < j \le k.$$

If Tr denotes the trace from F_q to F_p, then, by Theorem A.2 in Appendix A, there exists a $\theta \in F_q^*$ such that

$$y_n = \text{Tr}(\theta \alpha^n) \quad \text{for } n = 0, 1, \ldots .$$

It follows then that, for $1 \le n \le T$, $1 \le i \le s$, and $1 \le j \le m$, we have

$$y_{nj}^{(i)} = \text{Tr}(\theta \alpha^{mn} \alpha^{(i-1)m+j-1}).$$

Put $\gamma_n = \theta \alpha^{mn}$ and let $\{\beta_0, \ldots, \beta_{k-1}\}$ be a basis of F_q over F_p. Then

$$\gamma_n = \sum_{r=0}^{k-1} b_r(\gamma_n)\beta_r$$

with suitable $b_r(\gamma_n) \in F_p$, and so

$$y_{nj}^{(i)} = \sum_{r=0}^{k-1} b_r(\gamma_n) \text{Tr}(\beta_r \alpha^{(i-1)m+j-1})$$

for $1 \le n \le T$, $1 \le i \le s$, and $1 \le j \le m$. From $\gcd(m, T) = 1$, it follows that α^m is a generator of the cyclic group F_q^*, and so the γ_n, $1 \le n \le T$, run exactly through F_q^*. If we now put $\gamma_0 = 0$, then the k-tuples $(b_0(\gamma_n), \ldots, b_{k-1}(\gamma_n))$, $0 \le n \le T$, run exactly through F_p^k. Therefore we get the point set in the theorem if, in the construction of (t, k, s)-nets in base p leading to (4.25), we choose $R = F_p$ and the bijections in (N2) and (N3) to be identity maps, and if, for $1 \le i \le s$ and $0 \le r \le k - 1$, we put

$$c_{jr}^{(i)} = \text{Tr}(\beta_r \alpha^{(i-1)m+j-1}) \quad \text{for } 1 \le j \le m,$$
$$c_{jr}^{(i)} = 0 \quad \text{for } m < j \le k.$$

Note that the inclusion of $\gamma_0 = 0$ amounts to the inclusion of $\mathbf{0}$ in the point set.

Let $C = \{\mathbf{c}_j^{(i)} : 1 \le i \le s, 1 \le j \le k\}$ with $\mathbf{c}_j^{(i)} = (c_{j0}^{(i)}, \ldots, c_{j,k-1}^{(i)}) \in F_p^k$. Then, by virtue of Theorem 4.28, it suffices to show that $\rho(C) = r^{(s)}(f, m)$. Let $C' = \{\mathbf{c}_j^{(i)} : 1 \le i \le s, 1 \le j \le m\}$ and note that $\mathbf{c}_j^{(i)} = \mathbf{0}$ for $1 \le i \le s$ and $m < j \le k$. We claim that $\rho(C) = \min(m, \rho(C'))$. This is trivial if $\rho(C') \le m$. If $\rho(C') > m$, then, from the linear dependence of $\mathbf{c}_1^{(1)}, \ldots, \mathbf{c}_m^{(1)}, \mathbf{c}_{m+1}^{(1)} = \mathbf{0}$ over F_p, it follows that $\rho(C) \le m$; however, any system $\{\mathbf{c}_j^{(i)} : 1 \le j \le d_i, 1 \le i \le s\}$ with $d_i \ge 0$ for $1 \le i \le s$ and $\sum_{i=1}^s d_i = m$ is linearly independent over F_p, and so $\rho(C) = m$. Next we claim that $\rho(C') = \rho(C_1)$. Consider a subsystem $\{\mathbf{c}_j^{(i)} : 1 \le j \le d_i, 1 \le i \le s\}$ of C' with $0 \le d_i \le m$ for $1 \le i \le s$. It suffices to prove that this subsystem satisfies a linear dependence relation over F_p if and only if the corresponding subsystem $\{\alpha^{(i-1)m+j-1} : 1 \le j \le d_i, 1 \le i \le s\}$ of C_1 satisfies the same linear dependence relation. Suppose that we have

$$\sum_{i=1}^s \sum_{j=1}^{d_i} b_j^{(i)} \mathbf{c}_j^{(i)} = \mathbf{0} \quad \text{with all } b_j^{(i)} \in F_p.$$

By comparing components and using the formula for the $c_{jr}^{(i)}$, we see that the relation above is equivalent to

$$\sum_{i=1}^{s}\sum_{j=1}^{d_i} b_j^{(i)} \mathrm{Tr}(\beta_r \alpha^{(i-1)m+j-1}) = 0 \qquad \text{for } 0 \le r \le k-1.$$

By the F_p-linearity of the trace, this is, in turn, equivalent to

$$\mathrm{Tr}\left(\beta_r \sum_{i=1}^{s}\sum_{j=1}^{d_i} b_j^{(i)} \alpha^{(i-1)m+j-1}\right) = 0 \qquad \text{for } 0 \le r \le k-1.$$

Since $\{\beta_0, \dots, \beta_{k-1}\}$ is a basis of F_q over F_p and the trace is surjective, the last condition holds if and only if

$$\sum_{i=1}^{s}\sum_{j=1}^{d_i} b_j^{(i)} \alpha^{(i-1)m+j-1} = 0,$$

and the claim is verified. Altogether we have

$$\rho(C) = \min(m, \rho(C')) = \min(m, \rho(C_1)) = r^{(s)}(f, m). \qquad \square$$

COROLLARY 9.6. *For digital k-step PRN, we have, for $s > k/m$,*

$$\left(\frac{1}{2} - \frac{1}{2p}\right) p^{-r} \le D_T^{*(s)} = O(r^{s-1}p^{-r})$$

with $r = r^{(s)}(f, m)$, where the implied constant depends only on p and s.

Proof. In the proof of Theorem 9.5, we have shown that the points $0, x_0, x_1, \dots, x_{T-1}$ form a point set of the type in (4.25). Therefore the lower bound for the star discrepancy $D_T^{*(s)}$ of the point set consisting of $x_0, x_1, \dots, x_{T-1}$ follows from Theorem 4.30 and Remark 4.31. The upper bound is obtained from Theorems 4.5 and 4.6 and from the argument in the proof of Theorem 7.3, which takes care of the deletion of 0 from the net. $\square$

Theorem 9.5 and Corollary 9.6 are due to Niederreiter [244]. The upper bound in Corollary 9.6 can be made explicit by the results in §4.1 (compare also with [244, Thm. 9.4]). It is evident from Theorem 9.5 and Corollary 9.6 that the larger the figure of merit, the better the distribution properties of the points x_n. The following theorem, which is a special case of a result of Niederreiter [246], shows that large figures of merit can always be achieved by a suitable choice of f.

THEOREM 9.7. *For any prime p and any s, k, m with $s > k/m$, there exists a primitive polynomial f over F_p with $\deg(f) = k$ and*

$$r^{(s)}(f, m) \ge \min\left(m, \left\lfloor \log_p \frac{\phi(p^k - 1)}{(ms-1)(m+1)^{s-1}} \right\rfloor\right),$$

where $\log_p$ denotes the logarithm to the base p.

Proof. Put

$$d = \left\lfloor \log_p \frac{\phi(p^k - 1)}{(ms - 1)(m + 1)^{s-1}} \right\rfloor.$$

If $d \leq 0$, then there is nothing to prove, so we can assume that $d \geq 1$. It suffices to show that there exists a primitive polynomial over F_p of degree k for which the corresponding system C_1 in (9.5) satisfies $\rho(C_1) \geq d$. Fix an s-tuple $(d_1, \dots, d_s)$ of integers with $0 \leq d_i \leq m$ for $1 \leq i \leq s$ and $\sum_{i=1}^{s} d_i = d$. The system $\{x^{(i-1)m+j-1} + (f) : 1 \leq j \leq d_i, \ 1 \leq i \leq s\}$ in $F_p[x]/(f)$ is linearly dependent over F_p if and only if there exist $b_j^{(i)} \in F_p$, $1 \leq j \leq d_i$, $1 \leq i \leq s$, which are not all zero, such that $f(x)$ divides

$$\sum_{i=1}^{s} \sum_{j=1}^{d_i} b_j^{(i)} x^{(i-1)m+j-1}.$$

There are less than p^d choices for the $b_j^{(i)}$, and, for each such choice, there exist at most $(ms - 1)/k$ primitive polynomials f over F_p of degree k that divide the above polynomial. Furthermore, an upper bound for the number of s-tuples $(d_1, \dots, d_s)$ satisfying the above conditions is $(m + 1)^{s-1}$. Thus it follows from Remark 9.4 that the number $A_k(d)$ of primitive polynomials over F_p of degree k with $\rho(C_1) \leq d - 1$ satisfies

$$A_k(d) < \frac{ms - 1}{k}(m + 1)^{s-1} p^d.$$

From the definition of d, we obtain $A_k(d) < \phi(p^k - 1)/k$, which is the total number of primitive polynomials over F_p of degree k by [192, Thm. 3.5]. Consequently, there exists a primitive polynomial f over F_p with $\deg(f) = k$ that is not counted by $A_k(d)$, and for this f we have $\rho(C_1) \geq d$. $\square$

To obtain large values of $r^{(s)}(f, m)$, we first choose m to be maximal, i.e., we take $m = k$. Then $r^{(s)}(f, k) = \rho(C_1)$ by Definition 9.3, and we are in the case where $s > k/m$ if $s \geq 2$. In the remainder of this section, we assume that $m = k$. The following special case of a result of Niederreiter [246] provides information on the average order of magnitude of the star discrepancy $D_T^{*(s)}$ of the point set in (9.3).

THEOREM 9.8. *If $s \geq 2$, $m = k$, and $\gcd(k, T) = 1$, then, for digital k-step PRN, we have, on the average,*

$$D_T^{*(s)} = O\big(T^{-1}(\log T)^{s+1} \log \log T\big)$$

with an implied constant depending only on p and s, where the average is taken over all primitive polynomials f over F_p of degree k.

Proof. In the proof of Theorem 9.5, we have shown that the point set P consisting of $\mathbf{0}, \mathbf{x}_0, \mathbf{x}_1, \dots, \mathbf{x}_{T-1}$ can be obtained by the construction leading to (4.25), with the system $C = \{\mathbf{c}_j^{(i)} \in F_p^k : 1 \leq i \leq s, \ 1 \leq j \leq k\}$ given in that proof. Thus it follows from Lemma 4.32 that

$$D_N^*(P) \leq \frac{s}{N} + R_p(C)$$

with $N = p^k$. By the argument in the proof of Theorem 7.3, we obtain $TD_T^{*(s)} \leq ND_N^*(P) + 1$, and so

(9.6)
$$D_T^{*(s)} \leq \frac{s+1}{T} + \left(1 + \frac{1}{T}\right) R_p(C).$$

Note that C depends on f, so we write $C = C_f$. We have

$$R_p(C_f) = \sum_{H \in B_f} W_p(H),$$

where B_f is the set of all nonzero $H = (h_{ij}) \in C(p)^{s \times k}$ with

(9.7)
$$\sum_{i=1}^{s} \sum_{j=1}^{k} h_{ij} \mathbf{c}_j^{(i)} = \mathbf{0} \in F_p^k.$$

We now consider the average value R of $R_p(C_f)$ taken over the set Q of all primitive polynomials f over F_p of degree k. Since $\mathrm{card}(Q) = \phi(T)/k$, we obtain

$$R = \frac{k}{\phi(T)} \sum_{f \in Q} R_p(C_f) = \frac{k}{\phi(T)} \sum_{f \in Q} \sum_{H \in B_f} W_p(H)$$

$$= \frac{k}{\phi(T)} \sum_{H \neq 0} W_p(H) \sum_{\substack{f \in Q \\ H \in B_f}} 1.$$

For a fixed $H \neq 0$, the condition $H \in B_f$ is described by (9.7), and, by the proof of Theorem 9.5 and Remark 9.4, condition (9.7) is equivalent to

$$\sum_{i=1}^{s} \sum_{j=1}^{k} h_{ij} x^{(i-1)k+j-1} \equiv 0 \bmod f(x).$$

On the left-hand side, we have a nonzero polynomial of degree $\leq ks - 1$, and so there are at most $s - 1$ polynomials $f \in Q$ satisfying this condition. Therefore

$$R \leq \frac{(s-1)k}{\phi(T)} \sum_{H \neq 0} W_p(H) = O\left(\phi(T)^{-1} (\log T)^{s+1}\right)$$

by Lemma 3.13, and the result of the theorem follows from $\phi(T)^{-1} = O(T^{-1} \log \log T)$ and (9.6). $\quad\square$

Since we have assumed that $m = k$, the maximum possible value of $r^{(s)}(f, k)$ is k. If $r^{(s)}(f, k) = k$, then the point set in Theorem 9.5 forms a $(0, k, s)$-net in base p. However, by Corollary 4.21, a $(0, k, s)$-net in base p can only exist if $s \le p + 1$. Therefore, for $s \ge p + 2$, we must have $r^{(s)}(f, k) < k$.

We are led to the following computational problem: Given $s \ge 2$, $k \ge 2$, and the prime p, find a primitive polynomial f over F_p of degree k for which $r^{(s)}(f, k)$ is large. For practical implementations, the case where $p = 2$ is of the greatest interest. A straightforward argument shows that we have $r^{(s)}(f, k) \ge r^{(v)}(f, k)$ whenever $s \le v$. Therefore, to obtain large values of $r^{(s)}(f, k)$ for some $s \ge 2$, we first must make sure that we achieve large values of $r^{(2)}(f, k)$. The treatment of the latter problem is facilitated by the formula given in Theorem 9.9, below. Using the notation introduced in (4.63), we put $L(f) = K(f(x)/x^k)$.

THEOREM 9.9. *For any characteristic polynomial f of degree k, we have*

$$r^{(2)}(f, k) = k + 1 - L(f).$$

Proof. We have $r^{(2)}(f, k) = \rho(C_1)$, where, by Remark 9.4, we can take $C_1 = \{x^{(i-1)k+j-1} + (f) : 1 \le i \le 2, 1 \le j \le k\}$. Note that, for $0 \le d_1, d_2 \le k$ with $d_1 + d_2 > 0$, the subsystem $\{x^{(i-1)k+j-1} + (f) : 1 \le j \le d_i, 1 \le i \le 2\}$ of C_1 is linearly dependent over F_p if and only if there exist $h, h_1 \in F_p[x]$ not both zero with $h_1(x) + h(x)x^k \equiv 0 \bmod f(x)$ and $\deg(h_1) \le d_1 - 1$, $\deg(h) \le d_2 - 1$. Then we must have $h \ne 0$ and $h_1(x) + h(x)x^k = h_2(x)f(x)$ with $\deg(h_2) = \deg(h)$, and the congruence is equivalent to $h_1(x) - h_2(x)f(x) \equiv 0 \bmod x^k$. If we put $\mathbf{g} = (1, f) \in F_p[x]^2$, then the above argument shows that $\rho(C_1) = \rho(\mathbf{g}, x^k)$, where the latter quantity is defined in Definition 4.39. The desired formula for $r^{(2)}(f, k)$ now follows from Theorem 4.46. $\square$

It is a consequence of Theorem 9.9 that $r^{(2)}(f, k)$ is large if and only if $L(f)$ is small. The problem of finding primitive polynomials f over F_p for which $L(f)$ is small can be solved on the basis of results in Niederreiter [243]. The necessary computations were carried out for the case where $p = 2$ by Mullen and Niederreiter [215]. Polynomials f over F_2 with $L(f) = 1$ can be characterized completely (see [243]), and they are rarely irreducible, let alone primitive. However, if we consider the next larger value 2, then primitive polynomials f over F_2 of degree k with $L(f) = 2$ can be found for each k in the range $3 \le k \le 64$. A table of such polynomials is given in [215]. It is conjectured that such polynomials exist for all $k \ge 3$. For $s \ge 3$, the search for primitive polynomials f over F_2 of degree k with large $r^{(s)}(f, k)$ proceeds by finding many f with $L(f) \le 2$ and then maximizing the value of $r^{(s)}(f, k)$ among these. This program was carried out by André, Mullen, and Niederreiter [8] for dimensions $s = 3, 4, 5$ and degrees $k \le 32$.

9.2. The generalized feedback shift-register (GFSR) method.

The *generalized feedback shift-register* (GFSR) *method* due to Lewis and Payne [190] is another technique for transforming the sequence $y_0, y_1, \ldots$ in §9.1 into a sequence of uniform PRN. Again, let p be a small prime, let $k \ge 2$ be an integer, and define the sequence $y_0, y_1, \ldots \in Z_p$ by the recursion (9.1) with primitive characteristic polynomial f over F_p and with initial values $y_0, \ldots, y_{k-1}$ that are not all zero. Then we choose an integer $m \ge 2$ and integers $h_1, \ldots, h_m \ge 0$, and we put

(9.8)
$$x_n = \sum_{j=1}^{m} y_{n+h_j} p^{-j} \quad \text{for } n = 0, 1, \ldots .$$

The numbers x_n belong to the interval I and are called GFSR *pseudorandom numbers*. From $\text{per}(y_n) = p^k - 1$, it immediately follows that $\text{per}(x_n) = p^k - 1 = T$. A convenient implementation of GFSR PRN is based on the vectors $Y_n = (y_{n+h_1}, \ldots, y_{n+h_m})$, $n = 0, 1, \ldots$. It follows from (9.1) that the Y_n can be generated by the vector recursion

$$Y_{n+k} \equiv \sum_{l=0}^{k-1} a_l Y_{n+l} \bmod p \quad \text{for } n = 0, 1, \ldots,$$

and, if Y_n is interpreted as a block of digits in base p, then we obtain x_n due to (9.8).

In the treatment of digital multistep PRN in §9.1, we have seen that the cases where $s \leq k/m$ and $s > k/m$ must be distinguished. The corresponding distinction for GFSR PRN is given in the following definition. Let α again denote a root of f in the field F_q, where $q = p^k$, and let $s \geq 1$ be a given dimension.

DEFINITION 9.10. For GFSR PRN, we have the *low-dimensional case* if the ms elements α^{i-1+h_j}, $1 \leq i \leq s$, $1 \leq j \leq m$, of F_q are linearly independent over F_p and the *high-dimensional case* otherwise.

As in Remark 9.4, it is verified that this distinction does not depend on the choice of the root α. Note that, since F_q is a vector space over F_p of dimension k, the low-dimensional case can only arise if $s \leq k/m$. We now consider the points

(9.9) $\mathbf{x}_n = (x_n, x_{n+1}, \ldots, x_{n+s-1}) \in I^s \quad \text{for } n = 0, 1, \ldots, T - 1.$

In the low-dimensional case, we have the following analogue of Theorem 9.2.

THEOREM 9.11. *Let* $\mathbf{t} \in I^s$ *be such that all coordinates of* $\mathbf{t}$ *are rationals with denominator* p^m. *If* $Z(\mathbf{t})$ *is the number of integers* n *with* $0 \leq n \leq T - 1$ *and* $\mathbf{x}_n = \mathbf{t}$, *then, in the low-dimensional case of the GFSR method, we have*

$$Z(\mathbf{t}) = \begin{cases} p^{k-ms} & \text{if } \mathbf{t} \neq \mathbf{0}, \\ p^{k-ms} - 1 & \text{if } \mathbf{t} = \mathbf{0}. \end{cases}$$

Proof. If Y_n is as above, then we have $\mathbf{x}_n = \mathbf{t}$ if and only if $(Y_n, Y_{n+1}, \ldots, Y_{n+s-1}) = \mathbf{c}$ for a suitable $\mathbf{c} \in Z_p^{ms}$ depending only on $\mathbf{t}$, with $\mathbf{c} = \mathbf{0}$ if and only if $\mathbf{t} = \mathbf{0}$. If $\mathbf{c} = (c_{ij})$, $1 \leq i \leq s$, $1 \leq j \leq m$, is viewed as an element of F_p^{ms} and if we use the formula for y_n in terms of the trace stated in the proof of Theorem 9.5, then we see that $Z(\mathbf{t})$ is equal to the number of n with $0 \leq n \leq T - 1$ and

$$\text{Tr}(\theta \alpha^n \alpha^{i-1+h_j}) = c_{ij} \quad \text{for } 1 \leq i \leq s, \ 1 \leq j \leq m.$$

Since the $\theta\alpha^n$, $0 \leq n \leq T-1$, run exactly through F_q^*, it follows that $Z(\mathbf{t})$ equals the number of $\beta \in F_q^*$ with

(9.10) $\mathrm{Tr}(\beta\alpha^{i-1+h_j}) = c_{ij}$ for $1 \leq i \leq s$, $1 \leq j \leq m$.

Since the system $\{\alpha^{i-1+h_j} : 1 \leq i \leq s, 1 \leq j \leq m\}$ is linearly independent over F_p, it can form the first ms elements of an ordered basis of F_q over F_p. Let $\{\eta_1, \dots, \eta_k\}$ be the dual basis of this ordered basis (see Appendix A), and write $\beta = \sum_{l=1}^{k} b_l \eta_l$ with all $b_l \in F_p$. Then (9.10) states that the coefficients b_l, $1 \leq l \leq ms$, are uniquely determined by the c_{ij}, with all these $b_l = 0$ if and only if $\mathbf{c} = \mathbf{0}$, while the remaining b_l can be arbitrary. This leads to the formula for $Z(\mathbf{t})$ in the theorem. $\square$

If $D_T^{*(s)}$ denotes the star discrepancy of the point set in (9.9), then Theorem 9.11 shows that, in the low-dimensional case, we have the formula in (9.4). In the high-dimensional case, we proceed in analogy with the case where $s > k/m$ in §9.1. Consider the system

$$C_2 = \{\alpha^{i-1+h_j} : 1 \leq i \leq s, 1 \leq j \leq m\}$$

of elements of F_q, view F_q as a k-dimensional vector space over F_p, and let $\rho(C_2)$ be given by Definition 4.27.

DEFINITION 9.12. In the high-dimensional case of the GFSR method, the *figure of merit* $r^{(s)}(f, \mathbf{H})$ depending on s, the characteristic polynomial f, and the m-tuple $\mathbf{H} = (h_1, \dots, h_m)$ of parameters $h_1, \dots, h_m$ is defined by

$$r^{(s)}(f, \mathbf{H}) = \min(m, \rho(C_2)).$$

REMARK 9.13. As in Remark 9.4, we see that $r^{(s)}(f, \mathbf{H})$ is independent of the choice of α, since $\rho(C_2)$ may also be defined by considering the system $\{x^{i-1+h_j} + (f) : 1 \leq i \leq s, 1 \leq j \leq m\}$ of residue classes in $F_p[x]/(f)$.

THEOREM 9.14. *In the high-dimensional case of the GFSR method, the p^k points $\mathbf{0}, \mathbf{x}_0, \mathbf{x}_1, \dots, \mathbf{x}_{T-1}$ form a (t, k, s)-net in base p with $t = k - r^{(s)}(f, \mathbf{H})$.*

Proof. We proceed as in the proof of Theorem 9.5, and we again use the notation in the general construction of (t, k, s)-nets in base p leading to (4.25). From (9.8) and (9.9), we obtain that, for $1 \leq n \leq T$ and $1 \leq i \leq s$, we have

$$y_{nj}^{(i)} = y_{n+i-1+h_j} \qquad \text{for } 1 \leq j \leq m,$$
$$y_{nj}^{(i)} = 0 \qquad \text{for } m < j \leq k.$$

Continuing as in the proof of Theorem 9.5 and using the simpler expression $\gamma_n = \theta\alpha^n$, we arrive, for $1 \leq i \leq s$ and $0 \leq r \leq k - 1$, at the formulas

$$c_{jr}^{(i)} = \mathrm{Tr}(\beta_r \alpha^{i-1+h_j}) \qquad \text{for } 1 \leq j \leq m,$$
$$c_{jr}^{(i)} = 0 \qquad \text{for } m < j \leq k.$$

The proof is then completed as in the case of Theorem 9.5. $\square$

COROLLARY 9.15. *For GFSR PRN, we have, in the high-dimensional case,*

$$\left(\frac{1}{2} - \frac{1}{2p}\right)p^{-r} \le D_T^{*(s)} = O(r^{s-1}p^{-r})$$

with $r = r^{(s)}(f, \mathbf{H})$, where the implied constant depends only on p and s.

Proof. For the proof, proceed as in the proof of Corollary 9.6. □

Theorem 9.14 and Corollary 9.15 are due to Niederreiter [244]. The upper bound in Corollary 9.15 can be made explicit by the results in §4.1 (compare also with [244, Thm. 9.4]). Theorem 9.14 and Corollary 9.15 imply that a larger figure of merit guarantees better distribution properties of the points $\mathbf{x}_n$. The following result of Niederreiter [253] shows that, under reasonable conditions, a large value of $r^{(s)}(f, \mathbf{H})$ can be obtained by a suitable choice of $\mathbf{H}$.

THEOREM 9.16. *Let p be a prime, let $k \ge s \ge 2$ and $ms > k$, and let f be a primitive polynomial over F_p of degree k. Then there exists a choice of $\mathbf{H} = (h_1, \dots, h_m)$ such that*

$$r^{(s)}(f, \mathbf{H}) \ge \min(m, \lfloor k - (s-1)\log_p(m+1) \rfloor),$$

where $\log_p$ denotes the logarithm to the base p.

Proof. It suffices to show that there exist nonzero $\gamma_1, \dots, \gamma_m \in F_q$ such that the system $C = \{\alpha^{i-1}\gamma_j : 1 \le i \le s, \ 1 \le j \le m\}$ of elements of the vector space F_q over F_p satisfies

(9.11) $$\rho(C) \ge \lfloor k - (s-1)\log_p(m+1) \rfloor =: d.$$

The reason is that α, being a root of f, generates the cyclic group F_q^*; hence, if $\gamma_1, \dots, \gamma_m \in F_q^*$ as above have been found, then, for suitable integers $h_1, \dots, h_m \ge 0$, we have $\gamma_j = \alpha^{h_j}$ for $1 \le j \le m$, and so the result of the theorem follows from Definition 9.12 with $\mathbf{H} = (h_1, \dots, h_m)$. If $d \le 0$, then (9.11) holds trivially. For $d \ge 1$, let $G(d)$ be the number of m-tuples $(\gamma_1, \dots, \gamma_m)$ of elements of F_q^* such that the system $\{\alpha^{i-1}\gamma_j : 1 \le j \le d_i, \ 1 \le i \le s\}$ is linearly dependent over F_p for some s-tuple $(d_1, \dots, d_s)$ of integers with $0 \le d_i \le m$ for $1 \le i \le s$ and $\sum_{i=1}^{s} d_i = d$. Fix such an s-tuple $(d_1, \dots, d_s)$ and let $M(d_1, \dots, d_s)$ be the number of m-tuples $(\gamma_1, \dots, \gamma_m)$ of elements of F_q^* such that the system $\{\alpha^{i-1}\gamma_j : 1 \le j \le d_i, \ 1 \le i \le s\}$ is linearly dependent over F_p. Let

$$\sum_{i=1}^{s}\sum_{j=1}^{m} c_{ij}\alpha^{i-1}\gamma_j = 0$$

be a linear dependence relation with fixed $c_{ij} \in F_p$ not all zero and $c_{ij} = 0$ for $j > d_i$. With $\eta_j = \sum_{i=1}^{s} c_{ij}\alpha^{i-1}$ it can be written as

(9.12) $$\sum_{j=1}^{m} \eta_j \gamma_j = 0.$$

Since $k \geq s$, the system $\{\alpha^{i-1} : 1 \leq i \leq s\}$ is linearly independent over F_p, and so $\eta_j \neq 0$ for at least one j. It follows that the number of $(\gamma_1, \ldots, \gamma_m)$ satisfying (9.12) is at most $(q-1)^{m-1}$. Since the number of choices for the c_{ij} is $p^d - 1$, we obtain that

$$M(d_1, \ldots, d_s) \leq (p^d - 1)(q - 1)^{m-1}.$$

The number of $(d_1, \ldots, d_s)$ with $0 \leq d_i \leq m$ for $1 \leq i \leq s$ and $\sum_{i=1}^{s} d_i = d$ is at most $(m+1)^{s-1}$, and so

$$G(d) \leq (m+1)^{s-1}(p^d - 1)(q - 1)^{m-1}.$$

From the definition of d in (9.11), it follows that

$$G(d) \leq (m+1)^{s-1}\left(\frac{q}{(m+1)^{s-1}} - 1\right)(q-1)^{m-1} < (q-1)^m.$$

Thus there exists an m-tuple $(\gamma_1, \ldots, \gamma_m)$ of elements of F_q^* that is not counted by $G(d)$. For this m-tuple, we have $\rho(C) \geq d$, and so (9.11) holds. $\square$

As in §9.1, we now consider again the special case where $m = k$. The following is a special case of a result of Niederreiter [244], which provides information on the average order of magnitude of the star discrepancy $D_T^{*(s)}$ of the point set in (9.9).

THEOREM 9.17. *If f is a primitive polynomial over F_p of degree $k \geq s \geq 2$ and if $m = k$, then, for GFSR PRN, we have, on the average,*

$$D_T^{*(s)} = O\big(T^{-1}(\log T)^s\big)$$

with an implied constant depending only on p and s, where the average is taken over all $\mathbf{H} = (h_1, \ldots, h_k)$ with $0 \leq h_j \leq T - 1$ for $1 \leq j \leq k$.

Proof. By the argument leading to (9.6), we obtain

(9.13) $$D_T^{*(s)} \leq \frac{s+1}{T} + \left(1 + \frac{1}{T}\right)R_p(C).$$

Here C depends on $\mathbf{H}$, so we write $C = C_{\mathbf{H}}$. We have

$$R_p(C_{\mathbf{H}}) = \sum_{E \in B_{\mathbf{H}}} W_p(E),$$

where $B_{\mathbf{H}}$ is the set of all nonzero $E = (e_{ij}) \in C(p)^{s \times k}$ with

(9.14) $$\sum_{i=1}^{s} \sum_{j=1}^{k} e_{ij}\alpha^{i-1+h_j} = 0.$$

We now consider the average value R of $R_p(C_{\mathbf{H}})$ taken over the set Q of all $\mathbf{H} = (h_1, \ldots, h_k)$ with $0 \leq h_j \leq T - 1$ for $1 \leq j \leq k$. Then

$$R = T^{-k} \sum_{\mathbf{H} \in Q} R_p(C_{\mathbf{H}}) = T^{-k} \sum_{\mathbf{H} \in Q} \sum_{E \in B_{\mathbf{H}}} W_p(E),$$

and, by interchanging the order of summation, we obtain

$$(9.15) \qquad R = T^{-k} \sum_{E \neq 0} W_p(E) \sum_{\substack{\mathbf{H} \in Q \\ E \in B_{\mathbf{H}}}} 1.$$

For fixed $E \neq 0$, the inner sum in (9.15) is equal to the number of $\mathbf{H} = (h_1, \ldots, h_k) \in Q$ that satisfy (9.14). We write (9.14) in the form

$$\sum_{j=1}^{k} \eta_j \alpha^{h_j} = 0 \quad \text{with } \eta_j = \sum_{i=1}^{s} e_{ij} \alpha^{i-1} \quad \text{for } 1 \leq j \leq k.$$

Since $k \geq s$, the system $\{\alpha^{i-1} : 1 \leq i \leq s\}$ is linearly independent over F_p, and so $\eta_j \neq 0$ for at least one j. From this, it follows that the number of $\mathbf{H} \in Q$ satisfying (9.14) is at most T^{k-1}. Thus, from (9.15),

$$R \leq \frac{1}{T} \sum_{E \neq 0} W_p(E) = O\big(T^{-1}(\log T)^s\big),$$

where we applied Lemma 3.13 in the second step. The result of the theorem now follows from (9.13). □

For $m = k$, the maximum possible value of $r^{(s)}(f, \mathbf{H})$ is k. If $r^{(s)}(f, \mathbf{H}) = k$, then the point set in Theorem 9.14 forms a $(0, k, s)$-net in base p. However, by Corollary 4.21, a $(0, k, s)$-net in base p can only exist if $s \leq p + 1$. Thus, for $s \geq p + 2$, we must have $r^{(s)}(f, \mathbf{H}) < k$; in the special case where $p = 2$, this was proved in Tezuka [346] by a different method.

The results in this chapter demonstrate that shift-register PRN tend to have strong uniformity properties and small discrepancy, and, at least in the latter respect, they are thus similar to linear congruential PRN (compare with §7.3). There are, however, the following *advantages of shift-register* PRN over linear congruential PRN.

(i) Shift-register PRN can be generated by fast algorithms, since, in the standard case where $p = 2$, we use only binary arithmetic rather than modular arithmetic with a very large modulus.

(ii) The least period length of sequences of shift-register PRN is not bounded in terms of the word length of the machine. Note that, in the standard case where $p = 2$, the least period length is $2^k - 1$ and that the value of k can be chosen far beyond the word length. The value of k is, in principle, limited only by memory restrictions.

(iii) Shift-register PRN are preferable with regard to lattice structure. It is a consequence of Theorems 9.5 and 9.14 that the digital multistep method and the GFSR method with well-chosen parameters yield PRN with very little lattice structure. We have, of course, the trivial lattice structure, which stems from the fact that all generated PRN are rationals with fixed denominator p^m.

Notes.

Proofs of elementary facts about digital multistep PRN, such as least period
length and low-dimensional distribution properties, and of results on the uniformity test, even for parts of the period, can also be found in Lidl and Niederreiter [193, Chap. 7]. A matrix-theoretic approach to elementary properties of
shift-register PRN was presented by Marsaglia and Tsay [206]. Further results
on the serial test, even for parts of the period and for arbitrary irreducible
characteristic polynomials over F_p, are proved in Niederreiter [246] for digital
multistep PRN and in Niederreiter [242] for GFSR PRN. Upper bounds for the
(star) discrepancy in terms of the figure of merit that are weaker than those in
Corollaries 9.6 and 9.15 where shown by Niederreiter [241], [242], and, in the special case where $p = 2$, for the GFSR method by Tezuka [345]. Theorem 9.9 was
first proved in Niederreiter [241]. A notion of "k-distribution" for shift-register
PRN was studied, e.g., by Fushimi and Tezuka [112], but this property is weaker
than the net property established in Theorems 9.5 and 9.14, since it amounts
to considering the distribution of the points x_n in elementary cubes rather than
in arbitrary elementary intervals, as in the case of nets. Historical remarks and
further references on shift-register PRN can be found in Niederreiter [257].

Pseudorandom Vector Generation

The task in *random vector generation* is to produce a sequence of vectors (or points) that simulates a sequence of independent and identically distributed random vector variables with a given multivariate distribution. Random vectors are becoming more important because of the trend toward parallelization in scientific computing. Typical applications of random vectors arise in parallelized probabilistic algorithms, in parallel Monte Carlo and simulation methods, and in multivariate statistics. If the generation proceeds by a deterministic algorithm, then we speak of *pseudorandom vectors* (abbreviated PRV). We discuss here only the case of *uniform pseudorandom vectors* where the target distribution is the uniform distribution on $\bar{I}^k$, $k \geq 2$. One possibility of generating k-dimensional uniform PRV is to derive them from uniform pseudorandom numbers $x_0, x_1, \ldots$ by formulas such as

$$\mathbf{u}_n = (x_{nk}, x_{nk+1}, \ldots, x_{nk+k-1}) \in \bar{I}^k \quad \text{for } n = 0, 1, \ldots .$$

However, it seems to be preferable to generate uniform PRV directly, and such methods form the subject of this chapter.

Section 10.1 is devoted to the matrix method, which is a multidimensional analogue of the multiplicative congruential method for generating uniform pseudorandom numbers (see §7.3). The matrix method inherits some of the drawbacks of the linear congruential method, such as the coarse lattice structure. In §10.2 we consider nonlinear methods for uniform pseudorandom vector generation. This subject is still in its infancy, and so our report on it will be rather brief.

10.1. The matrix method.

For given $k \geq 2$, the generation of k-dimensional uniform PRV by the *matrix method* proceeds as follows. We choose a large positive integer M, called the *modulus*, and a $k \times k$ matrix A with entries from Z_M. Then we generate a sequence $\mathbf{z}_0, \mathbf{z}_1, \ldots$ of row vectors in Z_M^k by starting from an initial vector $\mathbf{z}_0 \neq \mathbf{0}$ and using the recursion

$$(10.1) \qquad \mathbf{z}_{n+1} \equiv \mathbf{z}_n A \bmod M \quad \text{for } n = 0, 1, \ldots .$$

The sequence $\mathbf{z}_0, \mathbf{z}_1, \ldots$ is referred to as a *matrix generator* modulo M. From this sequence, we derive the uniform PRV

(10.2) $$\mathbf{u}_n = \frac{1}{M}\mathbf{z}_n \in I^k \quad \text{for } n = 0, 1, \ldots ,$$

which are called *uniform pseudorandom vectors generated by the matrix method*. We can guarantee that the sequences $\mathbf{z}_0, \mathbf{z}_1, \ldots$ and $\mathbf{u}_0, \mathbf{u}_1, \ldots$ are (purely) periodic if we assume that the matrix A is nonsingular modulo M, i.e., that $\gcd(\det(A), M) = 1$.

We first consider the case where $M = p$ is a prime modulus. Then we can view (10.1) as a vector recursion over the finite field F_p and A as a matrix over F_p. We assume that A is nonsingular, so that A belongs to the general linear group $GL(k, F_p)$. Note that then $\text{per}(\mathbf{u}_n) = \text{per}(\mathbf{z}_n) \leq p^k - 1$ since there are $p^k - 1$ nonzero vectors in F_p^k. Theorem 10.2, below, characterizes the cases in which the upper bound is attained.

LEMMA 10.1. *If the characteristic polynomial of A is irreducible over F_p, then* $\text{per}(\mathbf{u}_n)$ *is equal to the order of A in the group $GL(k, F_p)$ for every* $\mathbf{z}_0 \neq \mathbf{0}$ *in F_p^k.*

Proof. From (10.1) we obtain in F_p^k,

(10.3) $$\mathbf{z}_n = \mathbf{z}_0 A^n \quad \text{for } n = 0, 1, \ldots .$$

Thus, if m is the order of A in $GL(k, F_p)$, then $\mathbf{z}_{n+m} = \mathbf{z}_n$ for all $n \geq 0$, and so $\text{per}(\mathbf{z}_n)$ divides m. The characteristic polynomial $f(x) = x^k - \sum_{l=0}^{k-1} a_l x^l$ is also the minimal polynomial of A under our hypothesis; hence

$$A^k = \sum_{l=0}^{k-1} a_l A^l.$$

Premultiplying by $\mathbf{z}_n$ and using (10.3), we see that

$$\mathbf{z}_{n+k} = \sum_{l=0}^{k-1} a_l \mathbf{z}_{n+l} \quad \text{for } n = 0, 1, \ldots .$$

Since $\mathbf{z}_0 \neq \mathbf{0}$, there exists a j with $1 \leq j \leq k$ such that the jth component of $\mathbf{z}_0$ is $\neq 0$. If y_n is the jth component of $\mathbf{z}_n$, then

$$y_{n+k} = \sum_{l=0}^{k-1} a_l y_{n+l} \quad \text{for } n = 0, 1, \ldots .$$

Since $y_0 \neq 0$, we get $\text{per}(y_n) = \text{ord}(f)$ by [192, Thm. 8.28], where $\text{ord}(f)$ is the least positive integer h such that $f(x)$ divides $x^h - 1$, and, from the fact that f is the minimal polynomial of A, we deduce $\text{ord}(f) = m$. Now $\text{per}(\mathbf{z}_n)$ is also a period length of the sequence $y_0, y_1, \ldots$; thus $\text{per}(y_n) = m$ implies that m divides $\text{per}(\mathbf{z}_n)$. Consequently, $\text{per}(\mathbf{u}_n) = \text{per}(\mathbf{z}_n) = m$. $\square$

THEOREM 10.2. *For $A \in GL(k, F_p)$ the following properties are equivalent:*

(i) $\text{per}(\mathbf{u}_n) = p^k - 1$ *for every* $\mathbf{z}_0 \neq \mathbf{0}$ *in* Z_p^k;

(ii) A *has order* $p^k - 1$ *in* $GL(k, F_p)$;

(iii) *The characteristic polynomial of A is primitive over* F_p.

Proof. (i) $\Rightarrow$ (ii). If m is the order of A in $GL(k, F_p)$, then the argument following (10.3), which holds for any $A \in GL(k, F_p)$, shows that $\text{per}(\mathbf{u}_n)$ divides m, and so $m \geq p^k - 1$. We now prove $m \leq p^k - 1$ for any $A \in GL(k, F_p)$. If $g \in F_p[x]$ is the minimal polynomial of A, then m is equal to the order of $x + (g)$ in the group U of units of the residue class ring $F_p[x]/(g)$. Therefore $m \leq \text{card}(U) \leq p^{\deg(g)} - 1 \leq p^k - 1$.

(ii) $\Rightarrow$ (iii). If $m = p^k - 1$, then, from the last chain of inequalities, it follows that $\deg(g) = k$ and $m = \text{card}(U) = p^k - 1$, so that $F_p[x]/(g)$ is a field and $x + (g)$ generates U. Hence g, which is then also the characteristic polynomial of A, is primitive over F_p since it has $x + (g)$ as a root in $F_p[x]/(g)$.

(iii) $\Rightarrow$ (i). If the characteristic polynomial f of A is primitive over F_p, then it is irreducible over F_p and equal to g. The order of $x + (g)$ in U is then the same as the order of a root of f in $F_{p^k}^*$, which is $p^k - 1$. Thus $m = p^k - 1$ by the first part of the proof, and the rest follows from Lemma 10.1. $\square$

We henceforth assume that the characteristic polynomial of A is primitive over F_p, so that $\text{per}(\mathbf{u}_n) = \text{per}(\mathbf{z}_n) = p^k - 1 = T$ by Theorem 10.2. Then $\mathbf{z}_0, \mathbf{z}_1, \dots, \mathbf{z}_{T-1}$ run exactly through all nonzero vectors in F_p^k. For the PRV $\mathbf{u}_n$, this means that $\mathbf{u}_0, \mathbf{u}_1, \dots, \mathbf{u}_{T-1}$ run exactly through all points $p^{-1}\mathbf{a}$ with a nonzero $\mathbf{a} \in Z_p^k$, and so

$$D_T^*(\mathbf{u}_0, \dots, \mathbf{u}_{T-1}) = 1 - (1 - p^{-1})^k.$$

The number $M(k, p)$ of $k \times k$ matrices over F_p with a primitive characteristic polynomial over F_p is given by

(10.4) $$M(k, p) = \frac{\phi(p^k - 1)}{k} \prod_{j=1}^{k-1} (p^k - p^j),$$

a result derived by Niederreiter [254] from a formula of Reiner [292]. If f is a fixed primitive polynomial over F_p of degree k, then it follows from the theory of rational forms of matrices that a $k \times k$ matrix A over F_p has the characteristic polynomial f if and only if $A = SBS^{-1}$, where $S \in GL(k, F_p)$ and B is the companion matrix of f. Furthermore, if an $A \in GL(k, F_p)$ with a primitive characteristic polynomial over F_p has been found, then all such matrices (with repetitions) are obtained by forming $SA^h S^{-1}$ with $S \in GL(k, F_p)$ and an integer h satisfying $1 \leq h < p^k - 1$ and $\gcd(h, p^k - 1) = 1$. This provides a way of explicitly constructing matrices with primitive characteristic polynomial over F_p. A probabilistic algorithm for producing such matrices proceeds by randomly selecting a $k \times k$ matrix A over F_p and then testing whether A belongs to $GL(k, F_p)$ and has order $p^k - 1$ (compare with Theorem 10.2). This is done by checking whether $A^{p^k - 1} = E$ and $A^{(p^k - 1)/r} \neq E$ for every prime divisor r of $p^k - 1$, where $E \in GL(k, F_p)$ is the identity matrix.

The analysis of the structural and statistical properties of uniform PRV proceeds in analogy with that for uniform PRN. If the $\mathbf{u}_n$ are given by (10.2) with $M = p$, then, for a given integer $s \geq 2$, we consider the points

(10.5) $\mathbf{v}_n = (\mathbf{u}_n, \mathbf{u}_{n+1}, \ldots, \mathbf{u}_{n+s-1}) \in I^{ks}$ for $n = 0, 1, \ldots$.

Because of $\mathrm{per}(\mathbf{v}_n) = p^k - 1 = T$, it suffices to take $0 \leq n \leq T - 1$. The lattice structure of these points was determined by Afflerbach and Grothe [4]; compare with case (i) of Theorem 7.6 for the analogous result for linear congruential PRN. For the terminology used here, we refer to §5.3.

THEOREM 10.3. *If the characteristic polynomial of A is primitive over F_p, then for $s \geq 2$ we have*

$$\{\mathbf{0}, \mathbf{v}_0, \mathbf{v}_1, \ldots, \mathbf{v}_{T-1}\} = L \cap I^{ks},$$

where L is the ks-dimensional lattice with generator matrix

$$\begin{pmatrix} p^{-1}E & p^{-1}A & p^{-1}A^2 & \cdots & p^{-1}A^{s-1} \\ 0 & E & 0 & \cdots & 0 \\ 0 & 0 & E & \cdots & 0 \\ \vdots & \vdots & \vdots & & \vdots \\ 0 & 0 & 0 & \cdots & E \end{pmatrix}$$

and where E is the $k \times k$ identity matrix over $\mathbb{R}$.

Proof. Note that L contains $\mathbb{Z}^{ks}$ and is thus an integration lattice. For any $n \geq 0$, we obtain, using (10.5), (10.2), and (10.3),

$$\mathbf{v}_n \equiv \frac{1}{p}(\mathbf{z}_n, \mathbf{z}_{n+1}, \ldots, \mathbf{z}_{n+s-1}) \equiv \frac{1}{p}(\mathbf{z}_n, \mathbf{z}_n A, \mathbf{z}_n A^2, \ldots, \mathbf{z}_n A^{s-1})$$

$$\equiv \mathbf{z}_n (p^{-1}E \quad p^{-1}A \quad p^{-1}A^2 \quad \cdots \quad p^{-1}A^{s-1}) \bmod \mathbb{Z}^{ks},$$

and so

$$\{\mathbf{0}, \mathbf{v}_0, \mathbf{v}_1, \ldots, \mathbf{v}_{T-1}\} \subseteq L \cap I^{ks}.$$

The set on the left-hand side has p^k elements. Now $\det(L) = p^{-k}$; hence $\mathrm{card}(L \cap I^{ks}) = p^k$ by Theorem 5.30, and the desired result follows. $\square$

The fact that $\det(L) = p^{-k}$ is independent of s means that we again have a coarse lattice structure, as in the case of the linear congruential method. In analogy with the s-dimensional serial test for uniform PRN, we now consider the s-dimensional *serial test* for uniform PRV. In the present context, this means that we study the discrepancy $D_N^{(s)}$ of the point set consisting of $\mathbf{v}_0, \mathbf{v}_1, \ldots, \mathbf{v}_{N-1} \in I^{ks}$. We define

(10.6) $R^{(s)}(A, p) = \sum_{\mathbf{h}} r(\mathbf{h}, p)^{-1},$

where the sum is over all ks-dimensional column vectors $\mathbf{h} \in C_{ks}^*(p)$, which, when represented as a concatenation of the k-dimensional column vectors

$\mathbf{h}_0, \mathbf{h}_1, \dots, \mathbf{h}_{s-1}$, satisfy

(10.7)
$$\sum_{i=0}^{s-1} A^i \mathbf{h}_i \equiv \mathbf{0} \bmod p.$$

Furthermore, $r(\mathbf{h}, p)$ is defined as in the beginning of §3.2. The following is a slight variant of a result of Niederreiter [254] for the full period.

THEOREM 10.4. *If the characteristic polynomial of A is primitive over F_p, then for $s \geq 2$ we have*

$$D_T^{(s)} \leq \frac{1}{T} + \left(1 + \frac{1}{T}\right)\left(\frac{ks}{p} + R^{(s)}(A, p)\right).$$

Proof. If $P = \{\mathbf{0}, \mathbf{v}_0, \mathbf{v}_1, \dots, \mathbf{v}_{T-1}\}$, then by Theorems 3.10 and 10.3 and Lemma 5.21, we obtain

$$D_{T+1}(P) \leq \frac{ks}{p} + \sum_{\mathbf{h}} r(\mathbf{h}, p)^{-1},$$

where the sum is over all $\mathbf{h} \in C_{ks}^*(p) \cap L^\perp$ and where $L^\perp$ is the dual lattice of the lattice L in Theorem 10.3. If $\mathbf{h}$ is a concatenation of $\mathbf{h}_0, \mathbf{h}_1, \dots, \mathbf{h}_{s-1}$, then the form of L shows that $\mathbf{h} \in L^\perp$ if and only if (10.7) holds. Therefore

$$D_{T+1}(P) \leq \frac{ks}{p} + R^{(s)}(A, p).$$

It remains to observe that, as in the proof of Theorem 7.3, we obtain

$$T D_T^{(s)} \leq (T+1) D_{T+1}(P) + 1. \qquad \square$$

Note that $R^{(s)}(A, p)$ has some similarity with the quantity $R_1(L)$ defined in (5.43), which can, in turn, be bounded in terms of the quantity $R(L)$ introduced in Definition 5.24. Pursuing this analogy further, we define a *figure of merit* similar to that in Definition 5.31 by putting

$$\rho^{(s)}(A, p) = \min_{\mathbf{h}} r(2\mathbf{h}),$$

where the minimum is extended over all $\mathbf{h} \in C_{ks}^*(p)$ for which (10.7) holds. It is easily seen that we always have $2 \leq \rho^{(s)}(A, p) \leq 2p^k$. By arguments similar to those in the proof of Theorem 5.35, it is shown that

$$R^{(s)}(A, p) < \frac{(2\log 2p)^{ks} + 3(2\log 2p)^{ks-1}}{(\log 2)^{ks-1}\rho^{(s)}(A, p)};$$

compare with [254]. Together with Theorem 10.4, this implies that $\rho^{(s)}(A, p)$ should be large to make the upper bound for the discrepancy $D_T^{(s)}$ as small as possible. In [254] there is also a lower bound of the form

$$D_T^{(s)} \geq \frac{c(k, s)}{\rho^{(s)}(A, p)}$$

with a constant $c(k, s) > 0$ depending only on k and s. Furthermore, it is shown in [254] that, for every prime p and for every $k \geq 2$ and $s \geq 2$, there exists a $k \times k$ matrix A over F_p with a primitive characteristic polynomial over F_p such that

$$\rho^{(s)}(A, p) > \frac{c_1(k, s)p^k}{(\log p)^{ks-1} \log \log(p + 1)}$$

with a constant $c_1(k, s) > 0$ depending only on k and s.

We now study the average order of magnitude of $R^{(s)}(A, p)$ for fixed p, k, and s. We use the convention that an eigenvector of A corresponding to the eigenvalue α is a k-dimensional row vector $\mathbf{c} \neq \mathbf{0}$ with $\mathbf{c}A = \alpha\mathbf{c}$.

LEMMA 10.5. *Let A be a $k \times k$ matrix over F_p whose characteristic polynomial is irreducible over F_p. If $(\gamma_1, \ldots, \gamma_k) \in F_q^k$ is an eigenvector of A when A is considered as a matrix over F_q with $q = p^k$, then $\{\gamma_1, \ldots, \gamma_k\}$ is a basis of F_q over F_p.*

Proof. Let $\alpha \in F_q$ be the eigenvalue corresponding to the given eigenvector. Then α is a root of the characteristic polynomial of A; hence $\{1, \alpha, \ldots, \alpha^{k-1}\}$ is a basis of F_q over F_p. We have

$$(10.8) \qquad (\gamma_1, \ldots, \gamma_k)A^m = \alpha^m(\gamma_1, \ldots, \gamma_k) \qquad \text{for } m = 0, 1, \ldots.$$

Furthermore, there exists a j with $1 \leq j \leq k$ such that $\gamma_j \neq 0$. If $\beta \in F_q$ is arbitrary, then, for some $f \in F_p[x]$ with $\deg(f) < k$, we have $\beta\gamma_j^{-1} = f(\alpha)$. By forming a suitable linear combination of the identities in (10.8), we obtain

$$(\gamma_1, \ldots, \gamma_k)f(A) = f(\alpha)(\gamma_1, \ldots, \gamma_k).$$

Now we compare the jth components in this identity. Since $f(A)$ is a matrix over F_p, we obtain on the left-hand side a linear combination of $\gamma_1, \ldots, \gamma_k$ with coefficients from F_p, while, on the right-hand side, we obtain $f(\alpha)\gamma_j = \beta$. Thus we have shown that $\gamma_1, \ldots, \gamma_k$ span F_q over F_p. $\square$

THEOREM 10.6. *Let a prime p and integers $k \geq 2$ and $s \geq 2$ be given. Then the average value R of $R^{(s)}(A, p)$, taken over all $k \times k$ matrices A over F_p with a primitive characteristic polynomial over F_p, satisfies*

$$R < \frac{s-1}{\phi(p^k - 1)}\left(\frac{2}{\pi}\log p + \frac{7}{5}\right)^{ks}.$$

Proof. If Q is the indicated range of matrices A, then $\text{card}(Q) = M(k, p)$ in the notation of (10.4), and so

$$R = \frac{1}{M(k, p)} \sum_{A \in Q} R^{(s)}(A, p).$$

Inserting the definition of $R^{(s)}(A, p)$ from (10.6), interchanging the order of summation, and using the fact that every primitive polynomial over F_p is irreducible over F_p, we obtain

(10.9)
$$R \le \frac{1}{M(k,p)} \sum_{\mathbf{h} \in C_{ks}^*(p)} \frac{N(k,p,\mathbf{h})}{r(\mathbf{h},p)},$$

where $N(k,p,\mathbf{h})$ is the number of $k \times k$ matrices A over F_p with irreducible characteristic polynomial over F_p, which satisfy

(10.10)
$$\sum_{i=0}^{s-1} A^i \mathbf{h}_i = \mathbf{0} \in F_p^k.$$

Here we have interpreted the congruence (10.7) as an identity in the vector space F_p^k and we have represented $\mathbf{h} \in C_{ks}^*(p)$ as a concatenation of the column vectors $\mathbf{h}_0, \mathbf{h}_1, \dots, \mathbf{h}_{s-1} \in F_p^k$. It follows from Lemma 10.5 that every matrix counted by $N(k,p,\mathbf{h})$, when considered as a matrix over F_q with $q = p^k$, has an eigenvector $(1, \gamma_2, \dots, \gamma_k) \in F_q^k$ and $\{1, \gamma_2, \dots, \gamma_k\}$ is a basis of F_q over F_p. In addition to $\mathbf{h} \in C_{ks}^*(p)$, we now also fix a row vector $\mathbf{c} = (1, \gamma_2, \dots, \gamma_k) \in F_q^k$ such that $\{1, \gamma_2, \dots, \gamma_k\}$ is a basis of F_q over F_p, and we count the $k \times k$ matrices A over F_p with irreducible characteristic polynomial over F_p, which satisfy (10.10) and have $\mathbf{c}$ as an eigenvector. If A is such a matrix, then let $\alpha \in F_q$ be the eigenvalue corresponding to the eigenvector $\mathbf{c}$. Premultiplying (10.10) by $\mathbf{c}$, we derive

(10.11)
$$\sum_{i=0}^{s-1} \alpha^i \mathbf{c} \mathbf{h}_i = 0.$$

Now $\mathbf{h}_i \ne \mathbf{0}$ for some i with $0 \le i \le s-1$, and then the scalar $\mathbf{c}\mathbf{h}_i$ is $\ne 0$, since $\{1, \gamma_2, \dots, \gamma_k\}$ is a basis of F_q over F_p. Thus (10.11) is a nonzero polynomial equation for $\alpha \in F_q$ of degree $\le s-1$, and so (10.11) has at most $s-1$ solutions $\alpha \in F_q$. For each solution α the matrix A is uniquely determined from $\mathbf{c}A = \alpha\mathbf{c}$, since $\{1, \gamma_2, \dots, \gamma_k\}$ is a basis of F_q over F_p.

Let G be the Galois group of F_q over F_p. We let G act componentwise on the vector space F_q^k. Let $\sigma \in G$ and let $\mathbf{c} \in F_q^k$ be as above. If the $k \times k$ matrix A over F_p has the eigenvector $\sigma\mathbf{c}$ when considered as a matrix over F_q, then let $\beta \in F_q$ be the corresponding eigenvalue. Applying σ^{-1} to $(\sigma\mathbf{c})A = \beta(\sigma\mathbf{c})$, we get $\mathbf{c}A = (\sigma^{-1}\beta)\mathbf{c}$. Thus, if we assume in addition that A has an irreducible characteristic polynomial over F_p and satisfies (10.10), then A is already obtained in the counting procedure above by considering the eigenvector $\mathbf{c}$. Therefore all vectors in the orbit of $\mathbf{c}$ under G yield the same solutions A, and there are at most $s-1$ solutions A from each orbit.

The above argument shows that $N(k,p,\mathbf{h})$ is at most $s-1$ times the number of different orbits that are obtained from the action of G on the vectors $\mathbf{c}$. There are exactly

$$\prod_{j=1}^{k-1} (p^k - p^j)$$

choices for vectors $\mathbf{c} = (1, \gamma_2, \dots, \gamma_k)$ with the property that $\{1, \gamma_2, \dots, \gamma_k\}$ is a basis of F_q over F_p. We claim that each orbit contains exactly k distinct elements. Let σ_1 be the Frobenius automorphism (see [192, p. 75]) that generates the cyclic group G, and suppose that $\sigma_1^j \mathbf{c} = \sigma_1^l \mathbf{c}$ for some $0 \le l < j < k$. Then $\sigma_1^{j-l} \mathbf{c} = \mathbf{c}$; hence, if m is the least positive integer with $\sigma_1^m \mathbf{c} = \mathbf{c}$, then $m < k$ and m divides k. This shows that $1, \gamma_2, \dots, \gamma_k$ all lie in the proper subfield F_{p^m} of F_q, a contradiction to $\{1, \gamma_2, \dots, \gamma_k\}$ being a basis of F_q over F_p. Thus the orbit of $\mathbf{c}$ under G consists exactly of the distinct elements $\sigma_1^j \mathbf{c}$, $j = 0, 1, \dots, k-1$. It follows that the number of different orbits is exactly

$$\frac{1}{k} \prod_{j=1}^{k-1} (p^k - p^j),$$

and so we have

$$N(k, p, \mathbf{h}) \le \frac{s-1}{k} \prod_{j=1}^{k-1} (p^k - p^j).$$

Together with (10.4) and (10.9), this yields

$$R \le \frac{s-1}{\phi(p^k - 1)} \sum_{\mathbf{h} \in C_{ks}^*(p)} r(\mathbf{h}, p)^{-1},$$

and the desired bound on R is obtained from [224, Lemma 2.3]. $\square$

Theorem 10.6 was proved by Niederreiter [254] and shows, in particular, that for any given p, k, s, there are matrices A as in Theorem 10.6 for which

$$R^{(s)}(A, p) = O\big(T^{-1}(\log p)^{ks} \log\log T\big)$$

with an implied constant depending only on k and s. For such A, the quantity $R^{(s)}(A, p)$ is of a smaller order of magnitude than the term ks/p in the upper bound for $D_T^{(s)}$ in Theorem 10.4. Note that ks/p is essentially the discretization error, since it follows from Theorem 3.14 that

$$D_T^{(s)} \ge 1 - \left(1 - \frac{1}{p}\right)^{ks},$$

which is ks/p in first approximation. For these PRV, it thus seems to be reasonable to consider, instead of $D_T^{(s)}$, a discrete version of the discrepancy in which the discretization error does not play a role. This will be discussed further in §10.2.

We now consider the case where M is a prime power modulus, say $M = p^\alpha$ with a prime p and an integer $\alpha \ge 2$. We assume that A is nonsingular modulo M, i.e., that $\det(A) \not\equiv 0 \bmod p$. Then the sequences $\mathbf{z}_0, \mathbf{z}_1, \dots$ and $\mathbf{u}_0, \mathbf{u}_1, \dots$ generated by (10.1) and (10.2) are periodic. The following is an upper bound on the least period length of these sequences which also holds in the case where $\alpha = 1$ (compare with the remark prior to Lemma 10.1).

LEMMA 10.7. *If $M = p^\alpha$ with a prime p and an integer $\alpha \geq 1$ and if the $k \times k$ matrix A is nonsingular modulo M, then* $\mathrm{per}(\mathbf{u}_n) \leq (p^k - 1)p^{\alpha-1}$.

Proof. It suffices to show that there exists an integer m with $1 \leq m \leq (p^k - 1)p^{\alpha-1}$ such that $A^m \equiv E \bmod M$, where E is the $k \times k$ identity matrix, for then $\mathbf{z}_m \equiv \mathbf{z}_0 A^m \equiv \mathbf{z}_0 \bmod M$, and so $\mathrm{per}(\mathbf{u}_n) = \mathrm{per}(\mathbf{z}_n) \leq m \leq (p^k - 1)p^{\alpha-1}$. We proceed by induction on α. The case where $\alpha = 1$ was settled in the first part of the proof of Theorem 10.2. Under the induction hypothesis for some $\alpha \geq 1$, we have $A^m = E + p^\alpha B$ for some m with $1 \leq m \leq (p^k - 1)p^{\alpha-1}$ and some integer matrix B. Since E and B commute, we can apply the binomial theorem to obtain

$$A^{mp} = (E + p^\alpha B)^p = \sum_{r=0}^{p} \binom{p}{r} p^{\alpha r} B^r \equiv E \bmod p^{\alpha+1}.$$

Since $1 \leq mp \leq (p^k - 1)p^\alpha$, the induction is complete. $\square$

In the case where $\alpha = 1$, we have already seen that the upper bound $p^k - 1$ in Lemma 10.7 can be attained. For $\alpha \geq 2$, Eichenauer-Herrmann, Grothe, and Lehn [86] have given a construction of matrices A such that the bound for $\mathrm{per}(\mathbf{u}_n)$ in Lemma 10.7 is again attained. We mention only a simple special case of this construction. Start from a matrix $B \in GL(k, F_p)$ with a primitive characteristic polynomial over F_p and view B as an integer matrix. Then, by Theorem 10.2,

$$B^{p^k - 1} \equiv E + pC \bmod p^2$$

for some $k \times k$ integer matrix C. Now define the $k \times k$ matrix A with entries from Z_M with $M = p^\alpha$ by

$$A \equiv B + p(BC - B^2) \bmod M.$$

Then, for any initial vector $\mathbf{z}_0 \not\equiv \mathbf{0} \bmod p$, we have $\mathrm{per}(\mathbf{u}_n) = (p^k - 1)p^{\alpha-1}$. Further work must be done on the matrix method with composite moduli to assess structural and statistical properties.

10.2. Nonlinear methods.

We present some recent attempts at extending the nonlinear congruential methods for pseudorandom number generation in Chapter 8 to the case of pseudorandom vector generation.

The general *first-order nonlinear method* for the generation of k-dimensional uniform PRV proceeds as follows. Let p be a large prime and let F_q be the finite field with $q = p^k$ elements. We generate a sequence $\gamma_0, \gamma_1, \ldots \in F_q$ by selecting an initial value γ_0 and using the recursion

(10.12) $$\gamma_{n+1} = \psi(\gamma_n) \quad \text{for } n = 0, 1, \ldots,$$

where the map $\psi : F_q \to F_q$ is chosen in such a way that the sequence $\gamma_0, \gamma_1, \ldots$ is periodic with $\mathrm{per}(\gamma_n) = q$. Such maps ψ always exist; compare with the simple argument following (8.1). Now view F_q as a k-dimensional vector space over F_p and let $\{\beta_1, \ldots, \beta_k\}$ be a basis of F_q over F_p. If Tr denotes the trace from F_q to F_p, then we derive a sequence of uniform PRV by putting

$$(10.13) \qquad \mathbf{u}_n = \frac{1}{p}(\mathrm{Tr}(\beta_1\gamma_n), \ldots, \mathrm{Tr}(\beta_k\gamma_n)) \in I^k \qquad \text{for } n = 0, 1, \ldots .$$

This proposal is due to Niederreiter [263] .

THEOREM 10.8. *The sequence* $\mathbf{u}_0, \mathbf{u}_1, \ldots$ *defined by* (10.13) *is periodic with* $\mathrm{per}(\mathbf{u}_n) = p^k$. *Over the full period this sequence runs exactly through all the* p^k *points of the form* $p^{-1}\mathbf{a}$ *with* $\mathbf{a} \in Z_p^k$.

Proof. Since the sequence $\gamma_0, \gamma_1, \ldots$ is periodic with $\mathrm{per}(\gamma_n) = q = p^k$, it is clear that the sequence $\mathbf{u}_0, \mathbf{u}_1, \ldots$ is periodic with period length q. To prove that q is the least period length, we show that $\mathbf{u}_0, \mathbf{u}_1, \ldots, \mathbf{u}_{q-1}$ are distinct. Suppose we had $\mathbf{u}_m = \mathbf{u}_n$ for some m and n with $0 \le m < n \le q - 1$. Then $\mathrm{Tr}(\beta_j\gamma_m) = \mathrm{Tr}(\beta_j\gamma_n)$ for $1 \le j \le k$. From the F_p-linearity of the trace and from the fact that $\{\beta_1, \cdots, \beta_k\}$ is a basis of F_q over F_p, it follows then that $\mathrm{Tr}(\alpha(\gamma_m - \gamma_n)) = 0$ for all $\alpha \in F_q$. By the surjectivity of the trace, this implies $\gamma_m = \gamma_n$, which is impossible. The second part of the theorem is obtained by noting that every $\mathbf{u}_n$ is of the form $p^{-1}\mathbf{a}$ for some $\mathbf{a} \in Z_p^k$ and that $\mathbf{u}_0, \mathbf{u}_1, \ldots, \mathbf{u}_{q-1}$ are distinct, as we have just proved. □

A special first-order nonlinear method is the *inversive method* proposed in Niederreiter [258]. This is a natural extension of the inversive congruential method discussed in §8.2. We use the recursion (10.12) with a simple class of maps ψ. Let p and F_q be as above. For $\gamma \in F_q$ we define $\bar{\gamma} \in F_q$ by $\bar{\gamma} = \gamma^{-1}$ if $\gamma \ne 0$ and $\bar{\gamma} = 0$ if $\gamma = 0$. Then we choose parameters $\alpha, \beta \in F_q$ with $\alpha \ne 0$ and generate a sequence $\gamma_0, \gamma_1, \ldots \in F_q$ by selecting an initial value γ_0 and using the recursion

$$(10.14) \qquad\qquad \gamma_{n+1} = \alpha\bar{\gamma}_n + \beta \qquad \text{for } n = 0, 1, \ldots .$$

The uniform PRV $\mathbf{u}_0, \mathbf{u}_1, \ldots$ are then obtained by (10.13). As in Theorem 8.4, we have the following sufficient condition for $\mathrm{per}(\mathbf{u}_n) = p^k$.

THEOREM 10.9. *If* $\alpha, \beta \in F_q$ *are such that* $x^2 - \beta x - \alpha$ *is a primitive polynomial over* F_q, *then the sequence* $\mathbf{u}_0, \mathbf{u}_1, \ldots$ *defined by* (10.13) *and* (10.14) *is periodic with* $\mathrm{per}(\mathbf{u}_n) = p^k$. *Furthermore, over the full period, this sequence runs exactly through all the* p^k *points of the form* $p^{-1}\mathbf{a}$ *with* $\mathbf{a} \in Z_p^k$.

Proof. By Theorem 10.8 it suffices to show that the sequence $\gamma_0, \gamma_1, \ldots$ generated by (10.14) is periodic with $\mathrm{per}(\gamma_n) = q$. This is demonstrated by the same arguments as in the proof of Theorem 8.4; obviously, the fields F_p and F_{p^2} in that proof have to be changed into F_q and F_{q^2}, respectively. □

In §10.1 we briefly described the s-dimensional serial test for sequences of k-dimensional PRV. We now apply this test to a sequence $\mathbf{u}_0, \mathbf{u}_1, \ldots$ of PRV generated by the inversive method. For a given $s \ge 2$, we define the points

$$\mathbf{v}_n = (\mathbf{u}_n, \mathbf{u}_{n+1}, \ldots, \mathbf{u}_{n+s-1}) \in I^{ks} \qquad \text{for } n = 0, 1, \ldots .$$

The s-dimensional serial test amounts to considering the discrepancy $D_N^{(s)} = D_N(\mathbf{v}_0, \ldots, \mathbf{v}_{N-1})$. Note that by Theorem 3.14 we have

$$D_N^{(s)} \geq 1 - \left(1 - \frac{1}{p}\right)^{ks} \qquad \text{for all } N \geq 1.$$

This is a large discretization error, which, as we have already seen in §10.1, can dominate the other terms in upper bounds for $D_N^{(s)}$. Thus it seems more appropriate here to consider the *discrete discrepancy* $E_N^{(s)}$ of $\mathbf{v}_0, \ldots, \mathbf{v}_{N-1}$, which is defined by replacing the family $\mathcal{J}$ in Definition 2.2 by the family of all subintervals of I^{ks} of the form

$$\prod_{i=1}^{ks} \left[\frac{a_i}{p}, \frac{b_i}{p}\right)$$

with $a_i, b_i \in \mathbb{Z}$ for $1 \leq i \leq ks$. The discrete discrepancy satisfies a bound as in Theorem 3.10, but without the term corresponding to the discretization error.

If α and β are as in Theorem 10.9, then, for $E_N^{(s)}$ with $N = q$, i.e., for the full period, analogues of Theorems 8.7 and 8.8 can be established. The upper bound for the discrete discrepancy has the form $E_q^{(s)} = O(q^{-1/2}(\log p)^{ks})$ for $2 \leq s < p$, with an implied constant depending only on k and s. There are $\phi(q^2 - 1)/2$ parameter pairs (α, β) satisfying the condition in Theorem 10.9, and, for a positive proportion of these, we have $E_q^{(s)} \geq Cq^{-1/2}$ for all $s \geq 2$, where $C > 0$ is an absolute constant. The proofs require deep results from the theory of character sums over finite fields.

Notes.

Matrix generators have long been studied in the theory of linear modular systems (see [192, Chap. 9]). In the context of pseudorandom vector generation, the first detailed analysis was performed by Tahmi [339], who investigated periodicity properties for arbitrary moduli. Independently, the matrix method was proposed by Grothe [116], [117], who showed the equivalence between (i) and (iii) in Theorem 10.2. Another approach was pursued by Niederreiter [236] and Niki [279], but their method was later found to be equivalent to the matrix method (see [254]). The classical work of Franklin [109] can be viewed as an analysis of a stochastic model for the matrix method.

In the proofs of Lemma 10.1 and Theorem 10.2, we have noted that the order of A in $GL(k, F_p)$ is equal to $\mathrm{ord}(g)$, where g is the minimal polynomial of A. Detailed information on $\mathrm{ord}(g)$ is contained in [192, Chap. 3]. Further work on the lattice structure of PRV generated by the matrix method, including computational results for specific matrices A, is presented in Afflerbach and Grothe [4] and Grothe [118]. In particular, the latter dissertation contains tables of matrices A with primitive characteristic polynomial over F_p for some large primes such as $p = 2^{24} - 3$ and $p = 2^{31} - 1$. For the matrix method, bounds on $D_N^{(s)}$ for parts of the period have been given in Niederreiter [236] for $s = 1$ and in Niederreiter [254] for $s \geq 2$.

Theorems 10.8 and 10.9 have been shown in Niederreiter [263]. The sequences $\gamma_0, \gamma_1, \ldots \in F_q$ considered in a first-order nonlinear method are uniformly distributed in F_q; see, e.g., Niederreiter and Shiue [271], [272] for an investigation of this property in the context of recursions. Higher-order recursions in place of (10.12) could also be contemplated. The transition from a sequence $\gamma_0, \gamma_1, \ldots \in F_q$ generated by such a recursion to a sequence of uniform PRV would then again be achieved by (10.13).

Expository accounts of random and pseudorandom vector generation are given in the books of Dagpunar [50], Deák [53], and Devroye [62]. The survey article of L'Ecuyer [186] contains a discussion of the matrix method. The uses of pseudorandom vectors in parallel Monte Carlo calculations are explained, e.g., in Bhavsar and Isaac [28]. For a recent discussion of the problems of random number and vector generation for parallel processors, we refer to Eddy [75]. The interesting concept of a pseudorandom tree for parallel computations was introduced by Fredrickson et al. [110]; see also Anderson [7] and Halton [126].

Finite Fields and Linear Recurring Sequences

We collect some basic facts about finite fields and linear recurring sequences, which are used in various parts of these lecture notes. A suitable reference for this material is the book of Lidl and Niederreiter [192].

For any prime power q, all finite fields with q elements are isomorphic, and so we can speak of *the* finite field F_q with q elements (or of order q). If q is a power of the prime p, then F_q is a simple extension of its prime subfield F_p, and the latter field can be identified with the residue class field of $\mathbb{Z}$ modulo p. The field F_q with $q = p^m$, $m \geq 1$, is usually constructed as a factor ring $F_p[x]/(f)$, where f is an irreducible polynomial over F_p of degree m. The multiplicative group F_q^* of nonzero elements of F_q is cyclic.

If k is a positive integer, then every irreducible polynomial over F_q of degree k has a root in the extension field F_{q^k} of F_q. Conversely, every defining element of the extension F_{q^k} over F_q, i.e., every element of F_{q^k} that does not belong to any proper subfield F of F_{q^k} with $F \supseteq F_q$, is a root of some irreducible polynomial over F_q of degree k. This leads to the formula

$$I_q(k) = \frac{1}{k} \sum_{d|k} \mu\left(\frac{k}{d}\right) q^d$$

for the number $I_q(k)$ of monic irreducible polynomials over F_q of degree k, where μ is the Möbius function and the sum is over all positive divisors d of k. The following class of polynomials is of particular importance.

DEFINITION A.1. A monic polynomial over F_q of degree $k \geq 1$ is called a *primitive polynomial* over F_q if it has a root in F_{q^k} that generates the cyclic group $F_{q^k}^*$.

Since every generator of $F_{q^k}^*$ is a defining element of F_{q^k} over F_q, it follows that every primitive polynomial over F_q is irreducible over F_q. A useful map from F_{q^k} to F_q is the *trace*

$$\mathrm{Tr}(\alpha) = \sum_{j=0}^{k-1} \alpha^{q^j} \quad \text{for } \alpha \in F_{q^k}.$$

The trace is F_q-linear and surjective. The following notion is connected with the trace: For every ordered basis $\{\alpha_1, \ldots, \alpha_k\}$ of F_{q^k} over F_q, there is a uniquely determined *dual basis*, i.e., an ordered basis $\{\beta_1, \ldots, \beta_k\}$ of F_{q^k} over F_q such that, for $1 \leq i, j \leq k$, we have $\text{Tr}(\alpha_i \beta_j) = 0$ if $i \neq j$ and $\text{Tr}(\alpha_i \beta_j) = 1$ if $i = j$.

A sequence $y_0, y_1, \ldots$ of elements of F_q is called a (*kth-order*) *linear recurring sequence* if it satisfies a linear recursion

$$y_{n+k} = \sum_{l=0}^{k-1} a_l y_{n+l} \qquad \text{for } n = 0, 1, \ldots$$

with constant coefficients $a_0, \ldots, a_{k-1} \in F_q$. A kth-order linear recurring sequence $y_0, y_1, \ldots$ is uniquely determined by the recursion and by the initial values $y_0, \ldots, y_{k-1}$. A linear recurring sequence is always ultimately periodic, and it is (purely) periodic if $a_0 \neq 0$. The polynomial $f(x) = x^k - \sum_{l=0}^{k-1} a_l x^l \in F_q[x]$ is called the *characteristic polynomial* of the recursion and also a characteristic polynomial of the linear recurring sequence. The constant polynomial 1 is also viewed as a characteristic polynomial of the zero sequence.

THEOREM A.2. *If the kth-order linear recurring sequence $y_0, y_1, \ldots$ has an irreducible characteristic polynomial f over F_q and $\alpha \in F_{q^k}$ is a root of f, then there exists a uniquely determined $\theta \in F_{q^k}$ such that*

$$y_n = \text{Tr}(\theta \alpha^n) \qquad \text{for } n = 0, 1, \ldots.$$

If $y_0, \ldots, y_{k-1}$ are not all zero, then $\theta \neq 0$.

If $y_0, y_1, \ldots$ is a kth-order linear recurring sequence with a primitive characteristic polynomial over F_q and with initial values that are not all zero, then we speak of a *maximal period sequence*, and we have $\text{per}(y_n) = q^k - 1$.

Let $F_q((x^{-1}))$ be the field of formal Laurent series over F_q in the variable x^{-1} (compare with §4.4). Then, with an arbitrary sequence $y_0, y_1, \ldots$ of elements of F_q, we associate its generating function $\sum_{n=0}^{\infty} y_n x^{-n-1} \in F_q((x^{-1}))$. If $f \in F_q[x]$ is monic, then the sequence $y_0, y_1, \ldots$ is a linear recurring sequence with characteristic polynomial f if and only if

$$\sum_{n=0}^{\infty} y_n x^{-n-1} = \frac{g(x)}{f(x)}$$

with $g \in F_q[x]$ and $\deg(g) < \deg(f)$. This follows immediately by considering the coefficients in the Laurent series expansion of $f(x) \sum_{n=0}^{\infty} y_n x^{-n-1}$. The rational generating function of a linear recurring sequence has a uniquely determined reduced form h/m with a monic $m \in F_q[x]$ and with $h \in F_q[x]$, $\deg(h) < \deg(m)$, and $\gcd(h, m) = 1$. The polynomial m is called the *minimal polynomial* of the linear recurring sequence. It follows from this definition that the minimal polynomial of a linear recurring sequence divides any characteristic polynomial of the linear recurring sequence. For a linear recurring sequence that is not the zero sequence, the degree of its minimal polynomial can thus be interpreted as the least order of a linear recursion satisfied by the sequence.

Continued Fractions

Connections with continued fractions appear in several parts of these lecture notes. We provide a brief summary of the theory of continued fractions for real numbers and formal Laurent series. All the results on continued fraction expansions of real numbers that we need can be found in LeVeque [188, Chap. 9]. The theory of continued fractions for formal Laurent series is quite analogous (see, e.g., [192, pp. 235–237] and [250]), except for a result on best approximations, which we prove in Theorem B.1, below.

Every irrational number z has a uniquely determined infinite continued fraction expansion

$$z = a_0 + 1/(a_1 + 1/(a_2 + \cdots)) =: [a_0; a_1, a_2, \ldots],$$

where the *partial quotients* a_i, $i = 0, 1, \ldots$, are integers with $a_0 = \lfloor z \rfloor$ and $a_i \geq 1$ for $i \geq 1$. For $i \geq 0$, the *ith convergent* r_i to z is defined by

$$r_i = [a_0; a_1, \ldots, a_i].$$

The rationals r_i are also obtained by the following algorithm. Define

$$p_{-2} = 0, \quad p_{-1} = 1, \quad p_i = a_i p_{i-1} + p_{i-2} \quad \text{for } i \geq 0,$$
$$q_{-2} = 1, \quad q_{-1} = 0, \quad q_i = a_i q_{i-1} + q_{i-2} \quad \text{for } i \geq 0.$$

Then, for $i \geq 0$, we have $r_i = p_i/q_i$, and the fractions p_i/q_i are in reduced form, i.e., $\gcd(p_i, q_i) = 1$. Moreover, we have $1 = q_0 \leq q_1 < q_2 < \cdots$ and

$$\left| z - \frac{p_i}{q_i} \right| < \frac{1}{q_i q_{i+1}} \quad \text{for } i \geq 0.$$

The continued fraction expansion of a rational number is finite, but it is not unique since we have the identity $[a_0; a_1, \ldots, a_l] = [a_0; a_1, \ldots, a_{l-1}, a_l - 1, 1]$ if $a_l > 1$. However, the continued fraction expansion of a rational z becomes unique if we write it in the form

$$z = [a_0; a_1, \ldots, a_l] \quad \text{with } a_l = 1 \text{ and } l \geq 1.$$

The integers $a_0, \ldots, a_l$ satisfy $a_i \geq 1$ for $1 \leq i \leq l$ and are again called the *partial quotients*. For $0 \leq i \leq l$, the *ith convergent* to z is again defined as the rational number $[a_0; a_1, \ldots, a_i]$, which can be represented by the reduced fraction p_i/q_i, where p_i and q_i are obtained by the same recursions as in the case of irrational z. We have $1 = q_0 \leq q_1 < q_2 < \cdots < q_l$ and

$$\frac{1}{q_i(q_i + q_{i+1})} \leq \left| z - \frac{p_i}{q_i} \right| \leq \frac{1}{q_i q_{i+1}} \qquad \text{for } 0 \leq i \leq l-1.$$

Furthermore, p_i/q_i is a best approximation to z in the sense that, if h is any integer satisfying $1 \leq h < q_{i+1}$ for some i with $0 \leq i \leq l-1$, then

$$|hz - b| \geq |q_i z - p_i| \qquad \text{for all integers } b.$$

Let F be an arbitrary field and let $F((x^{-1}))$ be the field of formal Laurent series over F in the variable x^{-1}. Every $L \in F((x^{-1}))$ has a unique continued fraction expansion

$$L = [A_0; A_1, A_2, \ldots],$$

where the *partial quotients* A_i, $i = 0, 1, \ldots$, are polynomials over F and $\deg(A_i) \geq 1$ for $i \geq 1$. This expansion is finite if L represents a rational function over F and is infinite otherwise. If the continued fraction expansion of L is broken off after the term A_i, $i \geq 0$, we get a rational function, which is called the *ith convergent* to L. The polynomials P_i and Q_i over F are defined recursively by

$$P_{-2} = 0, \quad P_{-1} = 1, \quad P_i = A_i P_{i-1} + P_{i-2} \qquad \text{for } i \geq 0,$$
$$Q_{-2} = 1, \quad Q_{-1} = 0, \quad Q_i = A_i Q_{i-1} + Q_{i-2} \qquad \text{for } i \geq 0,$$

where these recursions can be used as long as A_i exists. For such i, we have $[A_0; A_1, \ldots, A_i] = P_i/Q_i$, $\gcd(P_i, Q_i) = 1$, and

$$\deg(Q_i) = \sum_{r=1}^{i} \deg(A_r) \qquad \text{if } i \geq 1.$$

For rational L, we now interpret $\deg(A_i) = \deg(Q_i) = \infty$ whenever A_i and Q_i do not exist.

We introduce the discrete exponential valuation ν on $F((x^{-1}))$, which extends the degree function on $F[x]$. For a nonzero $L \in F((x^{-1}))$, we put

$$\nu(L) = -w \qquad \text{if } L = \sum_{k=w}^{\infty} t_k x^{-k} \text{ and } t_w \neq 0,$$

where all $t_k \in F$, and we set $\nu(0) = -\infty$. Then we have

$$\nu\left(L - \frac{P_i}{Q_i} \right) = -\deg(Q_i) - \deg(Q_{i+1}) \qquad \text{for } i \geq 0.$$

The following strong result on best approximations holds in this setting.

THEOREM B.1. *Let $L \in F((x^{-1}))$ be given. If $h \in F[x]$ with $0 \leq \deg(h) < \deg(Q_{i+1})$ for some $i \geq 0$, then*

$$\nu\left(L - \frac{b}{h}\right) \geq \nu\left(L - \frac{P_i}{Q_i}\right) \quad \text{for all } b \in F[x].$$

Proof. Suppose that for some $b \in F[x]$ we have

$$\nu\left(L - \frac{b}{h}\right) < \nu\left(L - \frac{P_i}{Q_i}\right).$$

Then

$$\nu(hL - b) < \nu\left(L - \frac{P_i}{Q_i}\right) + \nu(h) = -\deg(Q_i) - \deg(Q_{i+1}) + \deg(h) < 0,$$

and so it follows from Lemma 3 in [250] that $h = \sum_{r=j}^{m} C_r Q_r$ with $C_r \in F[x]$ and $\deg(C_r) < \deg(A_{r+1})$ for $j \leq r \leq m$ and $C_j \neq 0$, and that

$$\nu(hL - b) = \deg(C_j) - \deg(Q_{j+1}) \geq -\deg(Q_{j+1}).$$

On the other hand, from the above, we get $\nu(hL - b) < -\deg(Q_i)$, and so we must have $j \geq i$. Since $\deg(h) < \deg(Q_{i+1})$, we cannot have $j \geq i+1$; thus $j = i$ and $h = C_i Q_i$. This implies

$$\deg(C_i) - \deg(Q_{i+1}) = \nu(hL - b) < -\deg(Q_i) - \deg(Q_{i+1}) + \deg(h)$$
$$= \deg(C_i) - \deg(Q_{i+1}),$$

which is a contradiction. $\square$

Bibliography

[1] V. G. ADLAKHA, *A Monte Carlo technique with quasirandom points for the stochastic shortest path problem*, Amer. J. Math. Management Sci., 7 (1987), pp. 325–358.

[2] L. AFFLERBACH, *The sub-lattice structure of linear congruential random number generators*, Manuscripta Math., 55 (1986), pp. 455–465.

[3] L. AFFLERBACH AND H. GROTHE, *Calculation of Minkowski-reduced lattice bases*, Computing, 35 (1985), pp. 269–276.

[4] ———, *The lattice structure of pseudo-random vectors generated by matrix generators*, J. Comp. Appl. Math., 23 (1988), pp. 127–131.

[5] L. AFFLERBACH AND R. WEILBÄCHER, *The exact determination of rectangle discrepancy for linear congruential pseudorandom numbers*, Math. Comp., 53 (1989), pp. 343–354.

[6] T. J. AIRD AND J. R. RICE, *Systematic search in high dimensional sets*, SIAM J. Numer. Anal., 14 (1977), pp. 296–312.

[7] S. L. ANDERSON, *Random number generators on vector supercomputers and other advanced architectures*, SIAM Rev., 32 (1990), pp. 221–251.

[8] D. A. ANDRÉ, G. L. MULLEN, AND H. NIEDERREITER, *Figures of merit for digital multistep pseudorandom numbers*, Math. Comp., 54 (1990), pp. 737–748.

[9] I. A. ANTONOV AND V. M. SALEEV, *An economic method of computing LP_τ-sequences*, Zh. Vychisl. Mat. i Mat. Fiz., 19 (1979), pp. 243–245. (In Russian.)

[10] I. I. ARTOBOLEVSKII, M. D. GENKIN, V. K. GRINKEVICH, I. M. SOBOL', AND R. B. STATNIKOV, *Optimization in the theory of machines by an LP-search*, Dokl. Akad. Nauk SSSR, 200 (1971), pp. 1287–1290. (In Russian.)

[11] I. I. ARTOBOLEVSKII, V. I. SERGEYEV, I. M. SOBOL', AND R. B. STATNIKOV, *On the computer aided formulation of mechanical optimum design problems*, Dokl. Akad. Nauk SSSR, 233 (1977), pp. 567–570. (In Russian.)

[12] H. BABOVSKY, F. GROPENGIESSER, H. NEUNZERT, J. STRUCKMEIER, AND B. WIESEN, *Application of well-distributed sequences to the numerical simulation of the Boltzmann equation*, J. Comp. Appl. Math., 31 (1990), pp. 15–22.

[13] N. S. BAKHVALOV, *Approximate computation of multiple integrals*, Vestnik Moskov. Univ. Ser. Mat. Mekh. Astr. Fiz. Khim., 4 (1959), pp. 3–18. (In Russian.)

[14] T. BANDYOPADHYAY AND P. K. SARKAR, *A quasi random search technique for functional fitting of detector responses*, Pramāna, 24 (1985), pp. 643–655.

[15] ———, *Implementation and comparative study of random sequences for nonlinear least square data fitting*, Pramāna, 28 (1987), pp. 97–107.

[16] W. BAYRHAMER, *Some remarks on quasi-random optimization*, in Nondifferentiable Optimization: Motivations and Applications, Sopron, 1984, Lecture Notes in Economics and Math. Systems, Vol. 255, Springer, Berlin, 1985, pp. 305–309.

[17] ———, *Quasi-zufällige Suchmethoden der globalen Optimierung*, dissertation, Univer-

sität Salzburg, Salzburg, Austria, 1986.

[18] J. BECK, *Irregularities of distribution and combinatorics*, in Surveys in Combinatorics 1985, Glasgow, 1985, London Math. Soc. Lecture Note Series, Vol. 103, Cambridge University Press, Cambridge, UK, 1985, pp. 25–46.

[19] ———, *A two-dimensional van Aardenne-Ehrenfest theorem in irregularities of distribution*, Compositio Math., 72 (1989), pp. 269–339.

[20] J. BECK AND W. W. L. CHEN, *Irregularities of Distribution*, Cambridge University Press, Cambridge, UK, 1987.

[21] R. BÉJIAN, *Sur certaines suites présentant une faible discrépance à l'origine*, C. R. Acad. Sci. Paris Sér. A, 286 (1978), pp. 135–138.

[22] ———, *Minoration de la discrépance d'une suite quelconque sur T*, Acta Arith., 41 (1982), pp. 185–202.

[23] R. BÉJIAN AND H. FAURE, *Discrépance de la suite de van der Corput*, C. R. Acad. Sci. Paris Sér. A, 285 (1977), pp. 313–316.

[24] V. BERGSTRÖM, *Einige Bemerkungen zur Theorie der diophantischen Approximationen*, Fysiogr. Sälsk. Lund. Förh., 6 (1936), no. 13, pp. 1–19.

[25] W. A. BEYER, *Lattice structure and reduced bases of random vectors generated by linear recurrences*, in Applications of Number Theory to Numerical Analysis, S. K. Zaremba, ed., Academic Press, New York, 1972, pp. 361–370.

[26] W. A. BEYER, R. B. ROOF, AND D. WILLIAMSON, *The lattice structure of multiplicative congruential pseudo-random vectors*, Math. Comp., 25 (1971), pp. 345–363.

[27] V. C. BHAVSAR, U. G. GUJAR, J. D. HORTON, AND L. A. LAMBROU, *Evaluation of the discrepancy of the linear congruential pseudo-random number sequence*, BIT, 30 (1990), pp. 258–267.

[28] V. C. BHAVSAR AND J. R. ISAAC, *Design and analysis of parallel Monte Carlo algorithms*, SIAM J. Sci. Statist. Comput., 8 (1987), pp. s73–s95.

[29] M. BLÜMLINGER AND R. F. TICHY, *Bemerkungen zu einigen Anwendungen gleichverteilter Folgen*, Sitzungsber. Österr. Akad. Wiss. Math.-Natur. Kl. II, 195 (1986), pp. 253–265.

[30] I. BOROSH AND H. NIEDERREITER, *Optimal multipliers for pseudo-random number generation by the linear congruential method*, BIT, 23 (1983), pp. 65–74.

[31] M. BOURDEAU AND A. PITRE, *Tables of good lattices in four and five dimensions*, Numer. Math., 47 (1985), pp. 39–43.

[32] E. BRAATEN AND G. WELLER, *An improved low-discrepancy sequence for multidimensional quasi-Monte Carlo integration*, J. Comp. Physics, 33 (1979), pp. 249–258.

[33] P. BRATLEY AND B. L. FOX, *Algorithm 659: Implementing Sobol's quasirandom sequence generator*, ACM Trans. Math. Software, 14 (1988), pp. 88–100.

[34] P. BRATLEY, B. L. FOX, AND L. E. SCHRAGE, *A Guide to Simulation*, 2nd ed., Springer, New York, 1987.

[35] M. CAR, *Sommes de carrés dans $F_q[X]$*, Dissertationes Math. (Rozprawy Mat.), 215, 1983.

[36] L. CARLITZ, *The arithmetic of polynomials in a Galois field*, Amer. J. Math., 54 (1932), pp. 39–50.

[37] ———, *The singular series for sums of squares of polynomials*, Duke Math. J., 14 (1947), pp. 1105–1120.

[38] J. W. S. CASSELS, *An Introduction to the Geometry of Numbers*, Springer, Berlin, 1971.

[39] G. J. CHAITIN, *On the length of programs for computing finite binary sequences*, J. Assoc. Comput. Mach., 13 (1966), pp. 547–569.

[40] ———, *Information, Randomness & Incompleteness. Papers on Algorithmic Information Theory*, World Scientific Publishers, Singapore, 1987.

[41] K. L. CHUNG, *An estimate concerning the Kolmogoroff limit distribution*, Trans. Amer. Math. Soc., 67 (1949), pp. 36–50.

[42] T. COCHRANE, *On a trigonometric inequality of Vinogradov*, J. Number Theory, 27 (1987), pp. 9–16.

[43] B. J. COLLINGS, *Compound random number generators*, J. Amer. Statist. Assoc., 82 (1987), pp. 525–527.

[44] R. R. COVEYOU AND R. D. MACPHERSON, *Fourier analysis of uniform random number generators*, J. Assoc. Comput. Mach., 14 (1967), pp. 100–119.

[45] R. CRANLEY AND T. N. L. PATTERSON, *Randomization of number theoretic methods for multiple integration*, SIAM J. Numer. Anal., 13 (1976), pp. 904–914.

[46] T. W. CUSICK, *Continuants with bounded digits*, Mathematika, 24 (1977), pp. 166–172.

[47] ——, *Continuants with bounded digits – II*, Mathematika, 25 (1978), pp. 107–109.

[48] ——, *Continuants with bounded digits – III*, Monatsh. Math., 99 (1985), pp. 105–109.

[49] ——, *Products of simultaneous approximations of rational numbers*, Arch. Math. (Basel), 53 (1989), pp. 154–158.

[50] J. DAGPUNAR, *Principles of Random Variate Generation*, Clarendon Press, Oxford, UK, 1988.

[51] P. J. DAVIS AND P. RABINOWITZ, *Methods of Numerical Integration*, 2nd ed., Academic Press, New York, 1984.

[52] I. DEÁK, *Multidimensional integration and stochastic programming*, in Numerical Techniques for Stochastic Optimization, Yu. Ermoliev and R. J.-B. Wets, eds., Springer, Berlin, 1988, pp. 187–200.

[53] ——, *Random Number Generators and Simulation*, Akadémiai Kiadó, Budapest, Hungary, 1989.

[54] L. DE CLERCK, *A proof of Niederreiter's conjecture concerning error bounds for quasi-Monte Carlo integration*, Adv. in Appl. Math., 2 (1981), pp. 1–6.

[55] ——, *De exacte berekening van de sterdiscrepantie van de rijen van Hammersley in 2 dimensies*, Ph.D. thesis, Katholieke Universiteit Leuven, Leuven, Belgium, 1984.

[56] ——, *A method for exact calculation of the stardiscrepancy of plane sets applied to the sequences of Hammersley*, Monatsh. Math., 101 (1986), pp. 261–278.

[57] P. DEHEUVELS, *Strong bounds for multidimensional spacings*, Z. Wahrsch. Verw. Geb., 64 (1983), pp. 411–424.

[58] A. DE MATTEIS AND S. PAGNUTTI, *Parallelization of random number generators and long-range correlations*, Numer. Math., 53 (1988), pp. 595–608.

[59] J. DÉNES AND A. D. KEEDWELL, *Latin Squares and Their Applications*, Academic Press, New York, 1974.

[60] V. DENZER AND A. ECKER, *Optimal multipliers for linear congruential pseudo-random number generators with prime moduli*, BIT, 28 (1988), pp. 803–808.

[61] L. P. DEVROYE, *Progressive global random search of continuous functions*, Math. Programming, 15 (1978), pp. 330–342.

[62] ——, *Non-Uniform Random Variate Generation*, Springer, New York, 1986.

[63] U. DIETER, *Pseudo-random numbers: The exact distribution of pairs*, Math. Comp., 25 (1971), pp. 855–883.

[64] ——, *How to calculate shortest vectors in a lattice*, Math. Comp., 29 (1975), pp. 827–833.

[65] ——, *Probleme bei der Erzeugung gleichverteilter Zufallszahlen*, in Zufallszahlen und Simulationen, L. Afflerbach and J. Lehn, eds., Teubner, Stuttgart, Germany, 1986, pp. 7–20.

[66] S. DISNEY, *Error bounds for rank 1 lattice quadrature rules modulo composites*, Monatsh. Math., 110 (1990), pp. 89–100.

[67] S. DISNEY AND I. H. SLOAN, *Error bounds for the method of good lattice points*, Math. Comp., 56 (1991), pp. 257–266.

[68] ——, *Lattice integration rules of maximal rank*, SIAM J. Numer. Anal., 29 (1992), pp. 566–577.

[69] M. DRMOTA, *Applications of uniformly distributed functions and sequences in statistic ergodic measuring techniques*, J. Comp. Appl. Math., 31 (1990), pp. 57–62.

[70] M. DRMOTA AND R. F. TICHY, *Deterministische Approximation stochastisch-ergodischer Signale*, Messen-Steuern-Regeln, 32 (1989), pp. 109–113.

[71] V. DROBOT, *On dispersion and Markov constants*, Acta Math. Hungar., 47 (1986),

pp. 89–93.

[72] Y. DUPAIN, *Discrépance de la suite* $(\{n\alpha\})$, $\alpha = (1 + \sqrt{5})/2$, Ann. Inst. Fourier, 29 (1979), no. 1, pp. 81–106.

[73] Y. DUPAIN AND V. T. SÓS, *On the discrepancy of* $(n\alpha)$ *sequences*, in Topics in Classical Number Theory, Budapest, 1981, Colloq. Math. Soc. János Bolyai, Vol. 34, North-Holland, Amsterdam, 1984, pp. 355–387.

[74] R. ECKHARDT, *Stan Ulam, John von Neumann, and the Monte Carlo method*, in Stanislaw Ulam 1909-1984, Los Alamos Sci. No. 15 Special Issue, Los Alamos National Laboratory, Los Alamos, NM, 1987, pp. 131–137.

[75] W. F. EDDY, *Random number generators for parallel processors*, J. Comp. Appl. Math., 31 (1990), pp. 63–71.

[76] J. EICHENAUER, H. GROTHE, AND J. LEHN, *Marsaglia's lattice test and non-linear congruential pseudo random number generators*, Metrika, 35 (1988), pp. 241–250.

[77] J. EICHENAUER, H. GROTHE, J. LEHN, AND A. TOPUZOĞLU, *A multiple recursive non-linear congruential pseudo random number generator*, Manuscripta Math., 59 (1987), pp. 331–346.

[78] J. EICHENAUER AND J. LEHN, *A non-linear congruential pseudo random number generator*, Statist. Papers, 27 (1986), pp. 315–326.

[79] ――――, *On the structure of quadratic congruential sequences*, Manuscripta Math., 58 (1987), pp. 129–140.

[80] J. EICHENAUER, J. LEHN, AND A. TOPUZOĞLU, *A nonlinear congruential pseudorandom number generator with power of two modulus*, Math. Comp., 51 (1988), pp. 757–759.

[81] J. EICHENAUER AND H. NIEDERREITER, *On Marsaglia's lattice test for pseudorandom numbers*, Manuscripta Math., 62 (1988), pp. 245–248.

[82] J. EICHENAUER-HERRMANN, *Inversive congruential pseudorandom numbers avoid the planes*, Math. Comp., 56 (1991), pp. 297–301.

[83] ――――, *On the discrepancy of inversive congruential pseudorandom numbers with prime power modulus*, Manuscripta Math., 71 (1991), pp. 153–161.

[84] J. EICHENAUER-HERRMANN AND H. GROTHE, *A remark on long-range correlations in multiplicative congruential pseudo random number generators*, Numer. Math., 56 (1989), pp. 609–611.

[85] ――――, *Upper bounds for the Beyer ratios of linear congruential generators*, J. Comp. Appl. Math., 31 (1990), pp. 73–80.

[86] J. EICHENAUER-HERRMANN, H. GROTHE, AND J. LEHN, *On the period length of pseudorandom vector sequences generated by matrix generators*, Math. Comp., 52 (1989), pp. 145–148.

[87] J. EICHENAUER-HERRMANN, H. GROTHE, H. NIEDERREITER, AND A. TOPUZOĞLU, *On the lattice structure of a nonlinear generator with modulus* 2^α, J. Comp. Appl. Math., 31 (1990), pp. 81–85.

[88] J. EICHENAUER-HERRMANN AND H. NIEDERREITER, *On the discrepancy of quadratic congruential pseudorandom numbers*, J. Comp. Appl. Math., 34 (1991), pp. 243–249.

[89] ――――, *Lower bounds for the discrepancy of inversive congruential pseudorandom numbers with power of two modulus*, Math. Comp., 58 (1992), pp. 775–779.

[90] J. EICHENAUER-HERRMANN AND A. TOPUZOĞLU, *On the period length of congruential pseudorandom number sequences generated by inversions*, J. Comp. Appl. Math., 31 (1990), pp. 87–96.

[91] S. M. ERMAKOV, *Note on pseudorandom sequences*, Zh. Vychisl. Mat. i Mat. Fiz., 12 (1972), pp. 1077–1082. (In Russian.)

[92] YU. G. EVTUSHENKO, *Numerical Optimization Techniques*, Springer, New York, 1985.

[93] H. FAURE, *Suites à faible discrépance dans* T^s, Publ. Dép. Math., Université de Limoges, Limoges, France, 1980.

[94] ――――, *Discrépances de suites associées à un système de numération (en dimension un)*, Bull. Soc. Math. France, 109 (1981), pp. 143–182.

[95] ――――, *Discrépance de suites associées à un système de numération (en dimension s)*,

Acta Arith., 41 (1982), pp. 337–351.

[96] ——, *Étude des restes pour les suites de van der Corput généralisées*, J. Number Theory, 16 (1983), pp. 376–394.

[97] ——, *Lemme de Bohl pour les suites de van der Corput généralisées*, J. Number Theory, 22 (1986), pp. 4–20.

[98] ——, *On the star-discrepancy of generalized Hammersley sequences in two dimensions*, Monatsh. Math., 101 (1986), pp. 291–300.

[99] ——, *Using permutations to reduce discrepancy*, J. Comp. Appl. Math., 31 (1990), pp. 97–103.

[100] ——, *Good permutations for extreme discrepancy*, J. Number Theory, to appear.

[101] R. P. FEDORENKO, *Minimization of nonsmooth functions*, Zh. Vychisl. Mat. i Mat. Fiz., 21 (1981), pp. 572–584. (In Russian.)

[102] L. FEJES TÓTH, *Lagerungen in der Ebene, auf der Kugel und im Raum*, 2. Aufl., Springer, Berlin, 1972.

[103] G. S. FISHMAN, *Multiplicative congruential random number generators with modulus 2^β: An exhaustive analysis for $\beta = 32$ and a partial analysis for $\beta = 48$*, Math. Comp., 54 (1990), pp. 331–344.

[104] G. S. FISHMAN AND L. R. MOORE III, *An exhaustive analysis of multiplicative congruential random number generators with modulus $2^{31} - 1$*, SIAM J. Sci. Statist. Comput., 7 (1986), pp. 24–45; Erratum, ibid., 7 (1986), p. 1058.

[105] P. FLAJOLET, P. KIRSCHENHOFER, AND R. F. TICHY, *Deviations from uniformity in random strings*, Probab. Theory Related Fields, 80 (1988), pp. 139–150.

[106] ——, *Discrepancy of sequences in discrete spaces*, in Irregularities of Partitions, G. Halász and V. T. Sós, eds., Springer, Berlin, 1989, pp. 61–70.

[107] B. L. FOX, *Algorithm 647: Implementation and relative efficiency of quasirandom sequence generators*, ACM Trans. Math. Software, 12 (1986), pp. 362–376.

[108] J. N. FRANKLIN, *Deterministic simulation of random processes*, Math. Comp., 17 (1963), pp. 28–59.

[109] ——, *Equidistribution of matrix-power residues modulo one*, Math. Comp., 18 (1964), pp. 560–568.

[110] P. FREDRICKSON, R. HIROMOTO, T. L. JORDAN, B. SMITH, AND T. WARNOCK, *Pseudo-random trees in Monte Carlo*, Parallel Comput., 1 (1984), pp. 175–180.

[111] K. K. FROLOV, *On the connection between quadrature formulas and sublattices of the lattice of integral vectors*, Dokl. Akad. Nauk SSSR, 232 (1977), pp. 40–43. (In Russian.)

[112] M. FUSHIMI AND S. TEZUKA, *The k-distribution of the generalized feedback shift register pseudorandom numbers*, Comm. ACM, 26 (1983), pp. 516–523.

[113] A. GENZ, *Testing multidimensional integration routines*, in Tools, Methods and Languages for Scientific and Engineering Computation, B. Ford, J. C. Rault, and F. Thomasset, eds., North-Holland, Amsterdam, 1984, pp. 81–94.

[114] M. GOLDSTERN, *Eine Klasse vollständig gleichverteilter Folgen*, in Zahlentheoretische Analysis II, E. Hlawka, ed., Lecture Notes in Math., Vol. 1262, Springer, Berlin, 1987, pp. 37–45.

[115] P. GRITZMANN, *Finite Packungen und Überdeckungen*, Habilitationsschrift, Universität-Gesamthochschule Siegen, Siegen, Germany, 1984.

[116] H. GROTHE, *Matrixgeneratoren zur Erzeugung gleichverteilter Zufallsvektoren*, in Zufallszahlen und Simulationen, L. Afflerbach and J. Lehn, eds., Teubner, Stuttgart, Germany, 1986, pp. 29–34.

[117] ——, *Matrix generators for pseudo-random vector generation*, Statist. Papers, 28 (1987), pp. 233–238.

[118] ——, *Matrixgeneratoren zur Erzeugung gleichverteilter Pseudozufallsvektoren*, Dissertation, Technische Hochschule Darmstadt, Darmstadt, Germany, 1988.

[119] A. GRUBE, *Mehrfach rekursiv-erzeugte Pseudo-Zufallszahlen*, Z. Angew. Math. Mech., 53 (1973), pp. T223–T225.

[120] B. GYIRES, *Doubly ordered linear rank statistics*, Acta Math. Acad. Sci. Hungar., 40 (1982), pp. 55–63.

[121] ———, *Linear rank statistics generated by uniformly distributed sequences*, in Nonparametric Statistical Inference, Budapest, 1980, Colloq. Math. Soc. János Bolyai, Vol. 32, North-Holland, Amsterdam, 1982, pp. 391–400.

[122] S. HABER, *On a sequence of points of interest for numerical quadrature*, J. Res. Nat. Bur. Standards Sect. B, 70 (1966), pp. 127–136.

[123] ———, *Parameters for integrating periodic functions of several variables*, Math. Comp., 41 (1983), pp. 115–129.

[124] M. HALL, *Combinatorial Theory*, 2nd ed., John Wiley, New York, 1986.

[125] J. H. HALTON, *On the efficiency of certain quasi-random sequences of points in evaluating multi-dimensional integrals*, Numer. Math., 2 (1960), pp. 84–90; Berichtigung, ibid., 2 (1960), p. 196.

[126] ———, *Pseudo-random trees: Multiple independent sequence generators for parallel and branching computations*, J. Comp. Physics, 84 (1989), pp. 1–56.

[127] J. H. HALTON AND G. B. SMITH, *Algorithm 247: Radical-inverse quasi-random point sequence* [G5], Comm. ACM, 7 (1964), pp. 701–702.

[128] J. H. HALTON AND S. K. ZAREMBA, *The extreme and L^2 discrepancies of some plane sets*, Monatsh. Math., 73 (1969), pp. 316–328.

[129] J. M. HAMMERSLEY, *Monte Carlo methods for solving multivariable problems*, Ann. New York Acad. Sci., 86 (1960), pp. 844–874.

[130] J. M. HAMMERSLEY AND D. C. HANDSCOMB, *Monte Carlo Methods*, Methuen, London, 1964.

[131] D. R. HAYES, *The expression of a polynomial as a sum of three irreducibles*, Acta Arith., 11 (1966), pp. 461–488.

[132] P. HELLEKALEK, *Regularities in the distribution of special sequences*, J. Number Theory, 18 (1984), pp. 41–55.

[133] D. HENSLEY, *The distribution of badly approximable rationals and continuants with bounded digits. II*, J. Number Theory, 34 (1990), pp. 293–334.

[134] E. HLAWKA, *Funktionen von beschränkter Variation in der Theorie der Gleichverteilung*, Ann. Mat. Pura Appl., 54 (1961), pp. 325–333.

[135] ———, *Zur angenäherten Berechnung mehrfacher Integrale*, Monatsh. Math., 66 (1962), pp. 140–151.

[136] ———, *Discrepancy and uniform distribution of sequences*, Compositio Math., 16 (1964), pp. 83–91.

[137] ———, *Discrepancy and Riemann integration*, in Studies in Pure Mathematics, L. Mirsky, ed., Academic Press, New York, 1971, pp. 121–129.

[138] ———, *Gleichverteilung auf Produkten von Sphären*, J. Reine Angew. Math., 330 (1982), pp. 1–43.

[139] ———, *Beiträge zur Theorie der Gleichverteilung und ihren Anwendungen I–V*, Sitzungsber. Österr. Akad. Wiss. Math.-Natur. Kl. II, 197 (1988), pp. 1–94, 95–120, 121–154, 209–259, 261–289.

[140] ———, *Näherungsformeln zur Berechnung von mehrfachen Integralen mit Anwendungen auf die Berechnung von Potentialen, Induktionskoeffizienten und Lösungen von Gleichungssystemen*, in Number-Theoretic Analysis, E. Hlawka and R. F. Tichy, eds., Lecture Notes in Math., Vol. 1452, Springer, Berlin, 1990, pp. 65–111.

[141] E. HLAWKA, F. FIRNEIS, AND P. ZINTERHOF, *Zahlentheoretische Methoden in der Numerischen Mathematik*, Oldenbourg, Vienna, 1981.

[142] J. HORBOWICZ, *Criteria for uniform distribution*, Indag. Math. (N.S.), 43 (1981), pp. 301–307.

[143] J. HORBOWICZ AND H. NIEDERREITER, *Weighted exponential sums and discrepancy*, Acta Math. Hungar., 54 (1989), pp. 89–97.

[144] L. K. HUA AND Y. WANG, *On uniform distribution and numerical analysis (Number-theoretic method) I–III*, Sci. Sinica, 16 (1973), pp. 483–505; 17 (1974), pp. 331–348; 18 (1975), pp. 184–198.

[145] ———, *Applications of Number Theory to Numerical Analysis*, Springer, Berlin, 1981.

[146] F. JAMES, *A review of pseudorandom number generators*, Computer Physics Comm.,

60 (1990), pp. 329–344.

[147] S. JOE, *The generation of lattice points for numerical multiple integration*, J. Comp. Appl. Math., 26 (1989), pp. 327–331.

[148] ——, *Randomization of lattice rules for numerical multiple integration*, J. Comp. Appl. Math., 31 (1990), pp. 299–304.

[149] D. KAHANER, *Sources of information on quadrature software*, in Sources and Development of Mathematical Software, W. R. Cowell, ed., Prentice-Hall, Englewood Cliffs, NJ, 1984, pp. 134–164.

[150] M. H. KALOS AND P. A. WHITLOCK, *Monte Carlo Methods, Vol. 1: Basics*, John Wiley, New York, 1986.

[151] B. K. KHASNABIS, T. BANDYOPADHYAY, P. K. SARKAR, AND G. MUTHUKRISHNAN, *Spectrum measurement of neutrons from 40 MeV alpha particle bombardment of tantalum*, Indian J. Physics, 61A (1987), pp. 93–100.

[152] J. KIEFER, *On large deviations of the empiric d.f. of vector chance variables and a law of the iterated logarithm*, Pacific J. Math., 11 (1961), pp. 649–660.

[153] P. KIRSCHENHOFER AND R. F. TICHY, *Some distribution properties of 0, 1-sequences*, Manuscripta Math., 54 (1985), pp. 205–219.

[154] D. E. KNUTH, *The Art of Computer Programming, Vol. 2: Seminumerical Algorithms*, 2nd ed., Addison-Wesley, Reading, MA, 1981.

[155] J. F. KOKSMA, *Een algemeene stelling uit de theorie der gelijkmatige verdeeling modulo 1*, Mathematica B (Zutphen), 11 (1942/1943), pp. 7–11.

[156] A. N. KOLMOGOROV, *Three approaches to the definition of the concept "quantity of information,"* Problemy Peredachi Informasii, 1 (1965), no. 1, pp. 3–11. (In Russian.)

[157] A. N. KOLMOGOROV AND V. A. USPENSKII, *Algorithms and randomness*, Teor. Veroyatnost. i Primenen., 32 (1987), pp. 425–455. (In Russian.)

[158] N. M. KOROBOV, *The approximate computation of multiple integrals*, Dokl. Akad. Nauk SSSR, 124 (1959), pp. 1207–1210. (In Russian.)

[159] ——, *Properties and calculation of optimal coefficients*, Dokl. Akad. Nauk SSSR, 132 (1960), pp. 1009–1012. (In Russian.)

[160] ——, *Number-Theoretic Methods in Approximate Analysis*, Fizmatgiz, Moscow, 1963. (In Russian.)

[161] ——, *On the computation of optimal coefficients*, Dokl. Akad. Nauk SSSR, 267 (1982), pp. 289–292. (In Russian.)

[162] E. KRANAKIS, *Primality and Cryptography*, John Wiley, Chichester, UK, 1986.

[163] L. KUIPERS AND H. NIEDERREITER, *Uniform Distribution of Sequences*, John Wiley, New York, 1974.

[164] M. LACZKOVICH, *Equidecomposability and discrepancy; A solution of Tarski's circle-squaring problem*, J. Reine Angew. Math., 404 (1990), pp. 77–117.

[165] J. P. LAMBERT, *Quasi-Monte Carlo, low-discrepancy sequences, and ergodic transformations*, J. Comp. Appl. Math., 12/13 (1985), pp. 419–423.

[166] ——, *Quasi-random sequences for optimization and numerical integration*, in Numerical Integration: Recent Developments, Software and Applications, P. Keast and G. Fairweather, eds., NATO Adv. Sci. Inst. Ser. C, Vol. 203, Reidel, Dordrecht, the Netherlands, 1987, pp. 193–203.

[167] ——, *A sequence well dispersed in the unit square*, Proc. Amer. Math. Soc., 103 (1988), pp. 383–388.

[168] ——, *Quasi-random sequences in numerical practice*, in Numerical Mathematics Singapore 1988, R. P. Agarwal, Y. M. Chow, and S. J. Wilson, eds., Internat. Series of Numer. Math., Vol. 86, Birkhäuser, Basel, 1988, pp. 273–284.

[169] B. LAPEYRE AND G. PAGÈS, *Familles de suites à discrépance faible obtenues par itération de transformations de [0, 1]*, C.R. Acad. Sci. Paris Sér. I Math., 308 (1989), pp. 507–509.

[170] B. LAPEYRE, G. PAGÈS, AND K. SAB, *Sequences with low discrepancy. Generalisation and application to Robbins-Monro algorithm*, Statistics, 21 (1990), pp. 251–272.

[171] G. LARCHER, *Optimale Koeffizienten bezüglich zusammengesetzter Zahlen*, Monatsh.

Math., 100 (1985), pp. 127–135.

[172] ——, *Über die isotrope Diskrepanz von Folgen*, Arch. Math. (Basel), 46 (1986), pp. 240–249.

[173] ——, *On the distribution of sequences connected with good lattice points*, Monatsh. Math., 101 (1986), pp. 135–150.

[174] ——, *The dispersion of a special sequence*, Arch. Math. (Basel), 47 (1986), pp. 347–352.

[175] ——, *A best lower bound for good lattice points*, Monatsh. Math., 104 (1987), pp. 45–51.

[176] ——, *On the distribution of s-dimensional Kronecker-sequences*, Acta Arith., 51 (1988), pp. 335–347.

[177] ——, *A new extremal property of the Fibonacci ratio*, Fibonacci Quart., 26 (1988), pp. 247–255.

[178] ——, *On the distribution of the multiples of an s-tuple of real numbers*, J. Number Theory, 31 (1989), pp. 367–372.

[179] G. LARCHER AND H. NIEDERREITER, *Optimal coefficients modulo prime powers in the three-dimensional case*, Ann. Mat. Pura Appl., 155 (1989), pp. 299–315.

[180] ——, *Kronecker-type sequences and nonarchimedean diophantine approximations*, in preparation.

[181] C. LÉCOT, *Low discrepancy sequences for solving the Boltzmann equation*, J. Comp. Appl. Math., 25 (1989), pp. 237–249.

[182] ——, *A direct simulation Monte Carlo scheme and uniformly distributed sequences for solving the Boltzmann equation*, Computing, 41 (1989), pp. 41–57.

[183] ——, *An algorithm for generating low discrepancy sequences on vector computers*, Parallel Comput., 11 (1989), pp. 113–116.

[184] ——, *A quasi-Monte Carlo method for the Boltzmann equation*, Math. Comp., 56 (1991), pp. 621–644.

[185] P. L'ECUYER, *Efficient and portable combined random number generators*, Comm. ACM, 31 (1988), pp. 742–749,774.

[186] ——, *Random numbers for simulation*, Comm. ACM, 33 (1990), no. 10, pp. 85–97.

[187] D. H. LEHMER, *Mathematical methods in large-scale computing units*, in Proc. 2nd Sympos. on Large-Scale Digital Calculating Machinery, Cambridge, MA, 1949, Harvard University Press, Cambridge, MA, 1951, pp. 141–146.

[188] W. J. LEVEQUE, *Fundamentals of Number Theory*, Addison-Wesley, Reading, MA, 1977.

[189] M. B. LEVIN, *On the choice of parameters in generators of pseudorandom numbers*, Dokl. Akad. Nauk SSSR, 307 (1989), pp. 529–534. (In Russian.)

[190] T. G. LEWIS AND W. H. PAYNE, *Generalized feedback shift register pseudorandom number algorithm*, J. Assoc. Comput. Mach., 20 (1973), pp. 456–468.

[191] P. LIARDET, *Regularities of distribution*, Compositio Math., 61 (1987), pp. 267–293.

[192] R. LIDL AND H. NIEDERREITER, *Finite Fields*, Addison-Wesley, Reading, MA, 1983.

[193] ——, *Introduction to Finite Fields and Their Applications*, Cambridge University Press, Cambridge, UK, 1986.

[194] J. LINHART, *Approximation of a ball by zonotopes using uniform distribution on the sphere*, Arch. Math. (Basel), 53 (1989), pp. 82–86.

[195] A. LUBOTZKY, R. PHILLIPS, AND P. SARNAK, *Hecke operators and distributing points on the sphere. I*, Comm. Pure Appl. Math., Suppl., 39 (1986), S149–S186.

[196] ——, *Hecke operators and distributing points on S^2. II*, Comm. Pure Appl. Math., 40 (1987), pp. 401–420.

[197] J. N. LYNESS, *Some comments on quadrature rule construction criteria*, in Numerical Integration III, H. Braß and G. Hämmerlin, eds., Internat. Series of Numer. Math., Vol. 85, Birkhäuser, Basel, 1988, pp. 117–129.

[198] ——, *An introduction to lattice rules and their generator matrices*, IMA J. Numer. Anal., 9 (1989), pp. 405–419.

[199] J. N. LYNESS AND I. H. SLOAN, *Some properties of rank-2 lattice rules*, Math. Comp.,

53 (1989), pp. 627–637.

[200] J. N. LYNESS AND T. SØREVIK, *The number of lattice rules*, BIT, 29 (1989), pp. 527–534.

[201] J. N. LYNESS, T. SØREVIK, AND P. KEAST, *Notes on integration and integer sublattices*, Math. Comp., 56 (1991), pp. 243–255.

[202] M. D. MACLAREN AND G. MARSAGLIA, *Uniform random number generators*, J. Assoc. Comput. Mach., 12 (1965), pp. 83–89.

[203] D. MAISONNEUVE, *Recherche et utilisation des "bons treillis." Programmation et résultats numériques*, in Applications of Number Theory to Numerical Analysis, S. K. Zaremba, ed., Academic Press, New York, 1972, pp. 121–201.

[204] G. MARSAGLIA, *Random numbers fall mainly in the planes*, Proc. Nat. Acad. Sci. U.S.A., 61 (1968), pp. 25–28.

[205] ———, *The structure of linear congruential sequences*, in Applications of Number Theory to Numerical Analysis, S. K. Zaremba, ed., Academic Press, New York, 1972, pp. 249–285.

[206] G. MARSAGLIA AND L.-H. TSAY, *Matrices and the structure of random number sequences*, Linear Algebra Appl., 67 (1985), pp. 147–156.

[207] P. MARTIN-LÖF, *The definition of random sequences*, Inform. Control, 9 (1966), pp. 602–619.

[208] J. MATYAS, *Random optimization*, Automat. Remote Control, 26 (1965), pp. 244–251.

[209] H. G. MEIJER, *The discrepancy of a g-adic sequence*, Indag. Math., 30 (1968), pp. 54–66.

[210] N. METROPOLIS, *The beginning of the Monte Carlo method*, in Stanislaw Ulam 1909–1984, Los Alamos Sci. No. 15 Special Issue, Los Alamos National Laboratory, Los Alamos, NM, 1987, pp. 125–130.

[211] N. METROPOLIS AND S. M. ULAM, *The Monte Carlo method*, J. Amer. Statist. Assoc., 44 (1949), pp. 335–341.

[212] R. A. MITCHELL, *Error estimates arising from certain pseudorandom sequences in a quasi-random search method*, Math. Comp., 55 (1990), pp. 289–297.

[213] B. J. T. MORGAN, *Elements of Simulation*, Chapman and Hall, London, 1984.

[214] S. MOTTA, G. RUSSO, H. MOOCK, AND J. WICK, *A number-theoretical convergence proof of a point approximation of a space homogeneous transport equation*, Matematiche (Catania), 41 (1986), pp. 161–178.

[215] G. L. MULLEN AND H. NIEDERREITER, *Optimal characteristic polynomials for digital multistep pseudorandom numbers*, Computing, 39 (1987), pp. 155–163.

[216] M. NEWMAN, *Integral Matrices*, Academic Press, New York, 1972.

[217] H. NIEDERREITER, *Discrepancy and convex programming*, Ann. Mat. Pura Appl., 93 (1972), pp. 89–97.

[218] ———, *Methods for estimating discrepancy*, in Applications of Number Theory to Numerical Analysis, S. K. Zaremba, ed., Academic Press, New York, 1972, pp. 203–236.

[219] ———, *Application of diophantine approximations to numerical integration*, in Diophantine Approximation and Its Applications, C. F. Osgood, ed., Academic Press, New York, 1973, pp. 129–199.

[220] ———, *Metric theorems on the distribution of sequences*, in Proc. Sympos. Pure Math., Vol. 24, American Mathematical Society, Providence, RI, 1973, pp. 195–212.

[221] ———, *On the distribution of pseudo-random numbers generated by the linear congruential method. II*, Math. Comp., 28 (1974), pp. 1117–1132.

[222] ———, *On the distribution of pseudo-random numbers generated by the linear congruential method. III*, Math. Comp., 30 (1976), pp. 571–597.

[223] ———, *Statistical independence of linear congruential pseudo-random numbers*, Bull. Amer. Math. Soc., 82 (1976), pp. 927–929.

[224] ———, *Pseudo-random numbers and optimal coefficients*, Adv. in Math., 26 (1977), pp. 99–181.

[225] ———, *Quasi-Monte Carlo methods and pseudo-random numbers*, Bull. Amer. Math. Soc., 84 (1978), pp. 957–1041.

[226] ——, *Existence of good lattice points in the sense of Hlawka*, Monatsh. Math., 86 (1978), pp. 203–219.

[227] ——, *Statistical tests for Tausworthe pseudo-random numbers*, in Probability and Statistical Inference, W. Grossmann, G. C. Pflug, and W. Wertz, eds., Reidel, Dordrecht, the Netherlands, 1982, pp. 265–274.

[228] ——, *A quasi-Monte Carlo method for the approximate computation of the extreme values of a function*, in Studies in Pure Mathematics (To the Memory of Paul Turán), Birkhäuser, Basel, 1983, pp. 523–529. (Submitted in 1977.)

[229] ——, *Applications des corps finis aux nombres pseudo-aléatoires*, Sém. Théo. Nombres Bordeaux 1982–1983, Exp. 38, Univ. de Bordeaux I, Talence, France, 1983.

[230] ——, *On a measure of denseness for sequences*, in Topics in Classical Number Theory, Budapest, 1981, Colloq. Math. Soc. János Bolyai, Vol. 34, North–Holland, Amsterdam, 1984, pp. 1163–1208.

[231] ——, *Optimal multipliers for linear congruential pseudo-random numbers: The decimal case*, in Statistics and Probability, J. Mogyoródi, I. Vincze, and W. Wertz, eds., Reidel, Dordrecht, the Netherlands, 1984, pp. 255–269.

[232] ——, *The performance of k-step pseudorandom number generators under the uniformity test*, SIAM J. Sci. Statist. Comput., 5 (1984), pp. 798–810.

[233] ——, *Number-theoretic problems in pseudorandom number generation*, in Proc. Sympos. on Applications of Number Theory to Numerical Analysis, Kyoto, 1984, Lecture Notes No. 537, Research Inst. of Math. Sciences, Kyoto University, Kyoto, Japan, 1984, pp. 18–28.

[234] ——, *The serial test for pseudo-random numbers generated by the linear congruential method*, Numer. Math., 46 (1985), pp. 51–68.

[235] ——, *Quasi-Monte Carlo methods for global optimization*, in Proc. Fourth Pannonian Sympos. on Math. Statistics, Bad Tatzmannsdorf, 1983, Reidel, Dordrecht, the Netherlands, 1986, pp. 251–267.

[236] ——, *A pseudorandom vector generator based on finite field arithmetic*, Math. Japon., 31 (1986), pp. 759–774.

[237] ——, *Multidimensional numerical integration using pseudorandom numbers*, Stochastic Programming 84, Part I, A. Prékopa and R. J.-B. Wets, eds., Math. Programming Study, Vol. 27, North–Holland, Amsterdam, 1986, pp. 17–38.

[238] ——, *Dyadic fractions with small partial quotients*, Monatsh. Math., 101 (1986), pp. 309–315.

[239] ——, *Low-discrepancy point sets*, Monatsh. Math., 102 (1986), pp. 155–167.

[240] ——, *Good lattice points for quasirandom search methods*, in System Modelling and Optimization, A. Prékopa, J. Szelezsán, and B. Strazicky, eds., Lecture Notes in Control and Inform. Sci., Vol. 84, Springer, Berlin, 1986, pp. 647–654.

[241] ——, *Pseudozufallszahlen und die Theorie der Gleichverteilung*, Sitzungsber. Österr. Akad. Wiss. Math.-Natur. Kl. II, 195 (1986), pp. 109–138.

[242] ——, *A statistical analysis of generalized feedback shift register pseudorandom number generators*, SIAM J. Sci. Statist. Comput., 8 (1987), pp. 1035–1051.

[243] ——, *Rational functions with partial quotients of small degree in their continued fraction expansion*, Monatsh. Math., 103 (1987), pp. 269–288.

[244] ——, *Point sets and sequences with small discrepancy*, Monatsh. Math., 104 (1987), pp. 273–337.

[245] ——, *Continued fractions with small partial quotients*, in Proc. 1986 Nagasaki Sympos. on Number Theory, Y. Morita, ed., Tōhoku University, Sendai, Japan, 1987, pp. 1–11.

[246] ——, *The serial test for digital k-step pseudorandom numbers*, Math. J. Okayama Univ., 30 (1988), pp. 93–119.

[247] ——, *Low-discrepancy and low-dispersion sequences*, J. Number Theory, 30 (1988), pp. 51–70.

[248] ——, *Remarks on nonlinear congruential pseudorandom numbers*, Metrika, 35 (1988), pp. 321–328.

[249] ——, *Statistical independence of nonlinear congruential pseudorandom numbers*, Monatsh. Math., 106 (1988), pp. 149–159.

[250] ——, *Sequences with almost perfect linear complexity profile*, in Advances in Cryptology — EUROCRYPT '87, D. Chaum and W. L. Price, eds., Lecture Notes in Computer Science, Vol. 304, Springer, Berlin, 1988, pp. 37–51.

[251] ——, *Quasi-Monte Carlo methods for multidimensional numerical integration*, in Numerical Integration III, H. Braß and G. Hämmerlin, eds., Internat. Series of Numer. Math., Vol. 85, Birkhäuser, Basel, 1988, pp. 157–171.

[252] ——, *The serial test for congruential pseudorandom numbers generated by inversions*, Math. Comp., 52 (1989), pp. 135–144.

[253] ——, *Pseudorandom numbers generated from shift register sequences*, in Number-Theoretic Analysis, E. Hlawka and R. F. Tichy, eds., Lecture Notes in Math., Vol. 1452, Springer, Berlin, 1990, pp. 165–177.

[254] ——, *Statistical independence properties of pseudorandom vectors produced by matrix generators*, J. Comp. Appl. Math., 31 (1990), pp. 139–151.

[255] ——, *Lower bounds for the discrepancy of inversive congruential pseudorandom numbers*, Math. Comp., 55 (1990), pp. 277–287.

[256] ——, *The distribution of values of Kloosterman sums*, Arch. Math. (Basel), 56 (1991), pp. 270–277.

[257] ——, *Recent trends in random number and random vector generation*, Ann. Oper. Res., 31 (1991), pp. 323–345.

[258] ——, *Finite fields and their applications*, in Contributions to General Algebra 7, Vienna, 1990, Teubner, Stuttgart, Germany, 1991, pp. 251–264.

[259] ——, *The existence of efficient lattice rules for multidimensional numerical integration*, Math. Comp., 58 (1992), pp. 305–314, S7–S16.

[260] ——, *A combinatorial problem for vector spaces over finite fields*, Discrete Math., 96 (1991), pp. 221–228.

[261] ——, *Low-discrepancy point sets obtained by digital constructions over finite fields*, Czechoslovak Math. J., 42 (1992), pp. 143–166.

[262] ——, *Lattice rules for multiple integration*, in Proc. Workshop on Stochastic Optimization, Neubiberg, 1990, Springer Lecture Notes, to appear.

[263] ——, *Nonlinear methods for pseudorandom number and vector generation*, in Simulation and Optimization, G. Pflug and U. Dieter, eds., Lecture Notes in Economics and Math. Systems, Vol. 374, Springer, Berlin, 1992, pp. 145–153.

[264] ——, *Improved error bounds for lattice rules*, submitted for publication.

[265] H. NIEDERREITER AND J. HORBOWICZ, *Optimal bounds for exponential sums in terms of discrepancy*, Colloq. Math., 55 (1988), pp. 355–366.

[266] H. NIEDERREITER AND K. MCCURLEY, *Optimization of functions by quasi-random search methods*, Computing, 22 (1979), pp. 119–123.

[267] H. NIEDERREITER AND P. PEART, *A comparative study of quasi-Monte Carlo methods for optimization of functions of several variables*, Caribbean J. Math., 1 (1982), pp. 27–44.

[268] ——, *Quasi-Monte Carlo optimization in general domains*, Caribbean J. Math., 4 (1985), pp. 67–85.

[269] ——, *Localization of search in quasi-Monte Carlo methods for global optimization*, SIAM J. Sci. Statist. Comput., 7 (1986), pp. 660–664.

[270] H. NIEDERREITER AND C. P. SCHNORR, *Local randomness in polynomial random number and random function generators*, SIAM J. Comput., to appear.

[271] H. NIEDERREITER AND J.-S. SHIUE, *Equidistribution of linear recurring sequences in finite fields*, Indag. Math., 80 (1977), pp. 397–405.

[272] ——, *Equidistribution of linear recurring sequences in finite fields, II*, Acta Arith., 38 (1980), pp. 197–207.

[273] H. NIEDERREITER AND I. H. SLOAN, *Lattice rules for multiple integration and discrepancy*, Math. Comp., 54 (1990), pp. 303–312.

[274] H. NIEDERREITER AND R. F. TICHY, *Beiträge zur Diskrepanz bezüglich gewichteter*

Mittel, Manuscripta Math., 42 (1983), pp. 85–99.

[275] ——, *Solution of a problem of Knuth on complete uniform distribution of sequences,* Mathematika, 32 (1985), pp. 26–32.

[276] ——, *Metric theorems on uniform distribution and approximation theory,* in Journées Arithmétiques de Besançon, Besançon, 1985, Astérisque, Vols. 147-148, Soc. Math. France, Paris, 1987, pp. 319–323.

[277] H. NIEDERREITER, R. F. TICHY, AND G. TURNWALD, *An inequality for differences of distribution functions,* Arch. Math. (Basel), 54 (1990), pp. 166–172.

[278] H. NIEDERREITER AND J. M. WILLS, *Diskrepanz und Distanz von Maßen bezüglich konvexer und Jordanscher Mengen,* Math. Z., 144 (1975), pp. 125–134; Berichtigung, ibid., 148 (1976), p. 99.

[279] N. NIKI, *Finite field arithmetics and multidimensional uniform pseudorandom numbers,* Proc. Inst. Statist. Math., 32 (1984), pp. 231–239. (In Japanese.)

[280] P. PEART, *The dispersion of the Hammersley sequence in the unit square,* Monatsh. Math., 94 (1982), pp. 249–261.

[281] O. E. PERCUS AND J. K. PERCUS, *Long range correlations in linear congruential generators,* J. Comp. Physics, 77 (1988), pp. 267–269.

[282] J. PINTÉR, *On the convergence and computational efficiency of random search optimization,* Meth. Oper. Res., 33 (1979), pp. 347–362.

[283] P. D. PROINOV, *Note on the convergence of the general quadrature process with positive weights,* in Constructive Function Theory '77, Blagoevgrad, 1977, Bulgar. Acad. Sci., Sofia, 1980, pp. 121–125. (In Russian.)

[284] ——, *Upper bound for the error of a general quadrature process with positive weights,* C.R. Acad. Bulgare Sci., 35 (1982), pp. 605–608. (In Russian.)

[285] ——, *Generalization of two results of the theory of uniform distribution,* Proc. Amer. Math. Soc., 95 (1985), pp. 527–532.

[286] ——, *Numerical integration and approximation of differentiable functions,* C.R. Acad. Bulgare Sci., 38 (1985), pp. 187–190.

[287] ——, *Numerical integration and approximation of differentiable functions,* II, J. Approx. Theory, 50 (1987), pp. 373–393.

[288] ——, *Discrepancy and integration of continuous functions,* J. Approx. Theory, 52 (1988), pp. 121–131.

[289] ——, *Integration of smooth functions and φ-discrepancy,* J. Approx. Theory, 52 (1988), pp. 284–292.

[290] P. D. PROINOV AND G. KH. KIROV, *A quadrature formula for approximate integration of functions of class $C^r[0,1]$,* C.R. Acad. Bulgare Sci., 36 (1983), pp. 1027–1030. (In Russian.)

[291] L. RAMSHAW, *On the discrepancy of the sequence formed by the multiples of an irrational number,* J. Number Theory, 13 (1981), pp. 138–175.

[292] I. REINER, *On the number of matrices with given characteristic polynomial,* Illinois J. Math., 5 (1961), pp. 324–329.

[293] R. D. RICHTMYER, *The evaluation of definite integrals, and a quasi-Monte-Carlo method based on the properties of algebraic numbers,* Report LA-1342, Los Alamos Scientific Laboratory, Los Alamos, NM, 1951.

[294] B. D. RIPLEY, *The lattice structure of pseudo-random number generators,* Proc. Roy. Soc. London Ser. A, 389 (1983), pp. 197–204.

[295] ——, *Stochastic Simulation,* John Wiley, New York, 1987.

[296] K. F. ROTH, *On irregularities of distribution,* Mathematika, 1 (1954), pp. 73–79.

[297] R. Y. RUBINSTEIN, *Simulation and the Monte Carlo Method,* John Wiley, New York, 1981.

[298] ——, *Monte Carlo Optimization, Simulation and Sensitivity of Queuing Networks,* John Wiley, New York, 1986.

[299] H. J. RYSER, *Combinatorial Mathematics,* Mathematical Association of America, Washington, DC, 1963.

[300] J. W. SANDER, *On a conjecture of Zaremba,* Monatsh. Math., 104 (1987), pp. 133–137.

[301] P. K. SARKAR AND M. A. PRASAD, *A comparative study of pseudo and quasi random sequences for the solution of integral equations*, J. Comp. Physics, 68 (1987), pp. 66–88.

[302] W. M. SCHMIDT, *Metrical theorems on fractional parts of sequences*, Trans. Amer. Math. Soc., 110 (1964), pp. 493–518.

[303] ———, *Irregularities of distribution. VII*, Acta Arith., 21 (1972), pp. 45–50.

[304] C. P. SCHNORR, *Zufälligkeit und Wahrscheinlichkeit*, Lecture Notes in Math., Vol. 218, Springer, Berlin, 1971.

[305] J. SCHOISSENGEIER, *On the discrepancy of* $(n\alpha)$, Acta Arith., 44 (1984), pp. 241–279.

[306] ———, *Über die Diskrepanz der Folgen* $(n\alpha)$, in Zahlentheoretische Analysis, E. Hlawka, ed., Lecture Notes in Math., Vol. 1114, Springer, Berlin, 1985, pp. 148–153.

[307] ———, *On the discrepancy of* $(n\alpha)$, *II*, J. Number Theory, 24 (1986), pp. 54–64.

[308] I. F. SHARYGIN, *A lower estimate for the error of quadrature formulas for certain classes of functions*, Zh. Vychisl. Mat. i Mat. Fiz., 3 (1963), pp. 370–376. (In Russian.)

[309] J. E. H. SHAW, *A quasirandom approach to integration in Bayesian statistics*, Ann. Statist., 16 (1988), pp. 895–914.

[310] S. Z. SHI, *Optimal uniform distributions generated by M-sequences*, Acta Math. Sinica, 22 (1979), pp. 123–128. (In Chinese.)

[311] ———, *Estimate of error for quadrature of a multidimensional continuous function*, Math. Numer. Sinica, 3 (1981), pp. 360–364. (In Chinese.)

[312] I. E. SHPARLINSKII, *The distribution of the fractional parts of recurrent sequences*, Zh. Vychisl. Mat. i Mat. Fiz., 21 (1981), pp. 1588–1591. (In Russian.)

[313] ———, *A sequence of pseudorandom numbers*, Avtomat. i Telemekh., 7 (1988), pp. 185–188. (In Russian.)

[314] I. H. SLOAN, *Lattice methods for multiple integration*, J. Comp. Appl. Math., 12/13 (1985), pp. 131–143.

[315] I. H. SLOAN AND P. KACHOYAN, *Lattices for multiple integration*, in Math. Programming and Numerical Analysis Workshop, Canberra, 1983, Proc. Centre Math. Analysis Austral. Nat. Univ., Vol. 6, Australian National University, Canberra, Australia, 1984, pp. 147–165.

[316] ———, *Lattice methods for multiple integration: Theory, error analysis and examples*, SIAM J. Numer. Anal., 24 (1987), pp. 116–128.

[317] I. H. SLOAN AND J. N. LYNESS, *The representation of lattice quadrature rules as multiple sums*, Math. Comp., 52 (1989), pp. 81–94.

[318] ———, *Lattice rules: Projection regularity and unique representations*, Math. Comp., 54 (1990), pp. 649–660.

[319] I. H. SLOAN AND T. R. OSBORN, *Multiple integration over bounded and unbounded regions*, J. Comp. Appl. Math., 17 (1987), pp. 181–196.

[320] I. H. SLOAN AND L. WALSH, *Lattice rules — classification and searches*, in Numerical Integration III, H. Braß and G. Hämmerlin, eds., Internat. Series of Numer. Math., Vol. 85, Birkhäuser, Basel, 1988, pp. 251–260.

[321] ———, *A computer search of rank-2 lattice rules for multidimensional quadrature*, Math. Comp., 54 (1990), pp. 281–302.

[322] I. M. SOBOL', *An accurate error estimate for multidimensional quadrature formulae for the functions of the class* S_p, Dokl. Akad. Nauk SSSR, 132 (1960), pp. 1041–1044. (In Russian.)

[323] ———, *The distribution of points in a cube and the approximate evaluation of integrals*, Zh. Vychisl. Mat. i Mat. Fiz., 7 (1967), pp. 784–802. (In Russian.)

[324] ———, *Multidimensional Quadrature Formulas and Haar Functions*, Izdat. "Nauka," Moscow, 1969. (In Russian.)

[325] ———, *On the systematic search in a hypercube*, SIAM J. Numer. Anal., 16 (1979), pp. 790–793; Erratum, ibid., 16 (1979), p. 1080.

[326] ———, *On an estimate of the accuracy of a simple multidimensional search*, Dokl. Akad. Nauk SSSR, 266 (1982), pp. 569–572. (In Russian.)

[327] ———, *On functions satisfying a Lipschitz condition in multidimensional problems of computational mathematics*, Dokl. Akad. Nauk SSSR, 293 (1987), pp. 1314–1319. (In

Russian.)

[328] ——, *On the search for extreme values of functions of several variables satisfying a general Lipschitz condition*, Zh. Vychisl. Mat. i Mat. Fiz., 28 (1988), pp. 483–491. (In Russian.)

[329] I. M. SOBOL' AND R. B. STATNIKOV, *LP-search and problems of optimal design*, in Problems of Random Search, Vol. 1, Izdat. "Zinatne," Riga, 1972, pp. 117–135. (In Russian.)

[330] F. J. SOLIS AND R. J.-B. WETS, *Minimization by random search techniques*, Math. Oper. Res., 6 (1981), pp. 19–30.

[331] V. T. SÓS, *On strong irregularities of the distribution of* {nα} *sequences*, in Studies in Pure Mathematics (To the Memory of Paul Turán), Birkhäuser, Basel, 1983, pp. 685–700.

[332] ——, *Irregularities of partitions: Ramsey theory, uniform distribution*, in Surveys in Combinatorics, E. K. Lloyd, ed., London Math. Soc. Lecture Note Series, Vol. 82, Cambridge University Press, Cambridge, UK, 1983, pp. 201–246.

[333] S. SRINIVASAN, *On two-dimensional Hammersley's sequences*, J. Number Theory, 10 (1978), pp. 421–429.

[334] H. STEGBUCHNER, *Numerische Quadratur glatter Funktionen mit Gleichverteilungs-methoden*, Rend. Mat. (7), 2 (1982), pp. 593–599.

[335] S. A. STEPANOV, *On estimating rational trigonometric sums with prime denominator*, Trudy Mat. Inst. Steklov., 112 (1971), pp. 346–371. (In Russian.)

[336] M. SUGIHARA, *Method of good matrices for multi-dimensional numerical integrations — An extension of the method of good lattice points*, J. Comp. Appl. Math., 17 (1987), pp. 197–213.

[337] A. G. SUKHAREV, *Optimal strategies of the search for an extremum*, Zh. Vychisl. Mat. i Mat. Fiz., 11 (1971), pp. 910–924. (In Russian.)

[338] ——, *Best sequential search strategies for finding an extremum*, Zh. Vychisl. Mat. i Mat. Fiz., 12 (1972), pp. 35–50. (In Russian.)

[339] E. A. D. E. TAHMI, *Contribution aux générateurs de vecteurs pseudo-aléatoires*, Thèse, Univ. Sci. Techn. H. Boumedienne, Algiers, 1982.

[340] R. J. TASCHNER, *Eine zahlentheoretische Methode zur Bestimmung von Näherungslö-sungen einer Anfangswertaufgabe*, Sitzungsber. Österr. Akad. Wiss. Math.-Natur. Kl. II, 189 (1980), pp. 277–284.

[341] ——, *Eine zahlentheoretische Methode zur Bestimmung von Näherungslösungen nichtlinearer Gleichungssysteme*, Sitzungsber. Österr. Akad. Wiss. Math.-Natur. Kl. II, 189 (1980), pp. 285–289.

[342] R. C. TAUSWORTHE, *Random numbers generated by linear recurrence modulo two*, Math. Comp., 19 (1965), pp. 201–209.

[343] V. N. TEMLYAKOV, *On reconstruction of multivariate periodic functions based on their values at the knots of number-theoretical nets*, Anal. Math., 12 (1986), pp. 287–305. (In Russian.)

[344] ——, *Error estimates for quadrature formulas for classes of functions with a bounded mixed derivative*, Mat. Zametki, 46 (1989), pp. 128–134. (In Russian.)

[345] S. TEZUKA, *On the discrepancy of GFSR pseudorandom numbers*, J. Assoc. Comput. Mach., 34 (1987), pp. 939–949.

[346] ——, *On optimal GFSR pseudorandom number generators*, Math. Comp., 50 (1988), pp. 531–533.

[347] A. THOMAS, *Discrépance en dimension un*, Ann. Fac. Sci. Toulouse Math. (5), 10 (1989), pp. 369–399.

[348] R. F. TICHY, *Zur Diskrepanz bezüglich gewichteter Mittel*, Manuscripta Math., 37 (1982), pp. 393–413.

[349] ——, *Über eine zahlentheoretische Methode zur numerischen Integration und zur Be-handlung von Integralgleichungen*, Sitzungsber. Österr. Akad. Wiss. Math.-Natur. Kl. II, 193 (1984), pp. 329–358.

[350] ——, *Ein metrischer Satz über vollständig gleichverteilte Folgen*, Acta Arith., 48

(1987), pp. 197–207.

[351] ——, *Random points in the cube and on the sphere with applications to numerical analysis*, J. Comp. Appl. Math., 31 (1990), pp. 191–197.

[352] A. TÖRN AND A. ŽILINSKAS, *Global Optimization*, Lecture Notes in Computer Science, Vol. 350, Springer, Berlin, 1989.

[353] G. A. TOTKOV, *On the convergence of multidimensional quadrature formulae*, C.R. Acad. Bulgare Sci., 37 (1984), pp. 1171–1174. (In Russian.)

[354] N. TRENDAFILOV, *Uniformly distributed sequences and vector-valued integration*, C.R. Acad. Bulgare Sci., 40 (1987), no. 10, pp. 23–25.

[355] V. A. USPENSKII, A. L. SEMENOV, AND A. KH. SHEN', *Can an individual sequence of zeros and ones be random?*, Uspekhi Mat. Nauk, 45 (1990), no. 1, pp. 105–162. (In Russian.)

[356] J. G. VAN DER CORPUT, *Verteilungsfunktionen* I, II, Nederl. Akad. Wetensch. Proc. Ser. B, 38 (1935), pp. 813–821, 1058–1066.

[357] A. WEIL, *On some exponential sums*, Proc. Nat. Acad. Sci. U.S.A., 34 (1948), pp. 204–207.

[358] B. A. WICHMANN AND I. D. HILL, *An efficient and portable pseudo-random number generator*, Appl. Statist., 31 (1982), pp. 188–190; Corrections, ibid., 33 (1984), p. 123.

[359] ——, *Building a random-number generator*, Byte, 12 (1987), no. 3, pp. 127–128.

[360] S. WOLFRAM, *Random sequence generation by cellular automata*, Adv. Appl. Math., 7 (1986), pp. 123–169.

[361] S. K. ZAREMBA, *Good lattice points, discrepancy, and numerical integration*, Ann. Mat. Pura Appl., 73 (1966), pp. 293–317.

[362] ——, *Good lattice points in the sense of Hlawka and Monte Carlo integration*, Monatsh. Math., 72 (1968), pp. 264–269.

[363] ——, *Some applications of multidimensional integration by parts*, Ann. Polon. Math., 21 (1968), pp. 85–96.

[364] ——, *La discrépance isotrope et l'intégration numérique*, Ann. Mat. Pura Appl., 87 (1970), pp. 125–136.

[365] ——, *La méthode des "bons treillis" pour le calcul des intégrales multiples*, in Applications of Number Theory to Numerical Analysis, S. K. Zaremba, ed., Academic Press, New York, 1972, pp. 39–119.

[366] ——, *Good lattice points modulo composite numbers*, Monatsh. Math., 78 (1974), pp. 446–460.

[367] ——, *Computing the isotropic discrepancy of point sets in two dimensions*, Discrete Math., 11 (1975), pp. 79–92.

[368] A. A. ZHIGLJAVSKY, *Theory of Global Random Search*, Kluwer Academic Publishers, Dordrecht, the Netherlands, 1991.

[369] P. ZINTERHOF, *Über einige Abschätzungen bei der Approximation von Funktionen mit Gleichverteilungsmethoden*, Sitzungsber. Österr. Akad. Wiss. Math.-Natur. Kl. II, 185 (1976), pp. 121–132.

[370] ——, *Gratis lattice points for multidimensional integration*, Computing, 38 (1987), pp. 347–353.

[371] P. ZINTERHOF AND H. STEGBUCHNER, *Trigonometrische Approximation mit Gleichverteilungsmethoden*, Studia Sci. Math. Hungar., 13 (1978), pp. 273–289.

Index

adaptive methods, 152
antithetic variates, 8, 107

basis test, 173
bounded metric space, 148

Cartesian product
    of integration rule, 1
    of trapezoidal rule, 2
central limit theorem, 5
characteristic polynomial, 218
completely uniformly distributed, 162
composition method, 165
congruential generator, 177
convergent, 219, 220
copy rule, 144
crude search, 150
curse of dimensionality, 2

determinant of lattice, 131
diaphony, 22
digital multistep method, 192
digital multistep pseudorandom numbers, 192
discrepancy, 13, 21
    discrete, 215
    extreme, 14
    isotropic, 17, 21
    star, 14
discrete discrepancy, 215
discretization error, 42

dispersion, 148
dual basis, 218
dual lattice, 126

elementary interval, 48
extreme discrepancy, 14

Fibonacci numbers, 122
figure of merit, 108, 133, 171, 193, 200, 209
first-order congruential method, 177
first-order nonlinear method, 213
formal Laurent series, 88, 98
fractional part, 26, 28
frequency test, 166, 168

gap test, 166
generalized feedback shift-register (GFSR) method, 198
generalized feedback shift-register (GFSR) pseudorandom numbers, 199
generalized Halton sequence, 44
generalized Hammersley point set, 44
generalized van der Corput sequence, 25
generator matrix, 131
good lattice point, 109, 158
grid, 173

Halton sequence, 29, 44, 45, 157, 159